MAKING THE EMPIRE WORK

D1291007

CULTURE, LABOR, HISTORY SERIES
General Editors: Daniel E. Bender and Kimberley L. Phillips

*The Forests Gave Way before Them: The Impact of African Workers on the
Anglo-American World, 1650–1850*
Frederick C. Knight

*Unknown Class: Undercover Investigations of American Work and Poverty
from the Progressive Era to the Present*
Mark Pittenger

Steel Barrio: The Great Mexican Migration to South Chicago, 1915–1940
Michael D. Innis-Jiménez

*Fueling the Gilded Age: Railroads, Miners, and Disorder in Pennsylvania
Coal Country*
Andrew B. Arnold

*A Great Conspiracy against Our Race: Italian Immigrant Newspapers and
the Construction of Whiteness in the Early 20th Century*
Peter G. Vellon

*Reframing Randolph: Labor, Black Freedom, and the Legacies of
A. Philip Randolph*
Edited by Andrew E. Kersten and Clarence Lang

The New Deportations Delirium: Interdisciplinary Responses
Edited by Daniel Bender and Jana K. Lipman

*Whose Harlem Is This, Anyway? Community Politics and Grassroots
Activism during the New Negro Era*
Shannon King

*Health in the City: Race, Poverty and the Negotiation of Women's Health in
New York City, 1915–1930*
Tanya Hart

Making the Empire Work: Labor and United States Imperialism
Edited by Daniel E. Bender and Jana K. Lipman

Making the Empire Work

Labor and United States Imperialism

Edited by Daniel E. Bender and Jana K. Lipman

NEW YORK UNIVERSITY PRESS

New York and London

NEW YORK UNIVERSITY PRESS
New York and London
www.nyupress.org

© 2015 by New York University
All rights reserved

References to Internet websites (URLs) were accurate at the time of writing. Neither the author nor New York University Press is responsible for URLs that may have expired or changed since the manuscript was prepared.

ISBN: 978-1-4798-7125-4 (hardback)
ISBN: 978-1-4798-5622-0 (paperback)

For Library of Congress Cataloging-in-Publication data, please contact the Library of Congress.

New York University Press books are printed on acid-free paper, and their binding materials are chosen for strength and durability. We strive to use environmentally responsible suppliers and materials to the greatest extent possible in publishing our books.

Manufactured in the United States of America

10 9 8 7 6 5 4 3 2 1

Also available as an ebook

CONTENTS

ACKNOWLEDGMENTS

This collection is a collaboration of scholars across fields and even disciplines. We are grateful, above all, to our authors for their excitement in reading each others' work when we gathered in Toronto in late summer 2012 for the workshop that eventually produced this book. Will Riddell's skillful planning helped make that workshop a success. He contributed as well to the final editing and we hope, in return, that our essays have advanced his own scholarship. We thank Karina Cespedes, Nan Enstad, John Hogue, Paul Kramer, and Kimberley Phillips, who added to our conversations at different stages in the project.

This collection benefited from the financial support of the Canada Research Chair program, which underwrote our workshop. We are grateful, as well, to Tulane University and the University of Toronto Scarborough for their administrative support.

Daniel E. Bender, Toronto, July 2014

Jana K. Lipman, New Orleans, July 2014

Introduction

Through the Looking Glass: U.S. Empire through the Lens of Labor History

DANIEL E. BENDER AND JANA K. LIPMAN

If one were to hold up a mirror to the U.S. empire, what would one see? Historians have focused on charging armies, busy bureaucrats, emerging local elites, and anti-empire skeptics at home. To be sure, the empire had its key dates and government and military infrastructure. Historians have often cited the War of 1898, the bureaucratic organization of the U.S. Department of Insular Affairs, the imposition of colonial governors in Puerto Rico and the Philippines, and the technological spectacle of U.S. military bases. Yet alongside these potent political markers, one would see the hundreds of thousands of men and women who worked for, created, and at times, challenged the U.S. empire. Looking closer at the inner workings of empire, there were millions mobilized to build roads and bases, extract natural resources, provide care and comfort, and maintain order.

Empire has a labor history, and it is just beginning to be written. From Hawai'i to Panama, the daily gyrations of empire had direct consequences on working people. Historians have recorded the contrasts between the metropolitan immigrant worker, the faraway plantation laborer, and the domestic guest worker. All were joined by flows of goods and commodities, yet still separated by notions of ineffable distance. Their stories raise questions about the relationships between worker and employer, solidarity and dissent, distance and proximity, and production and consumption.

In this volume, we gaze through the looking glass at the working people and labor systems that made the U.S. empire. For U.S. historians, an emphasis on empire and labor forces an engagement with a global economy that intimately connects the tropics with industrial production. For labor historians, it complicates the standard understanding of the motor behind the domestic economy, which generally traces a progression from an agricultural to an industrial to a service economy. An imperial framework demonstrates that the economy relied on all three types of labor. Simultaneously, looking for the workers who harvested the sugar, cleaned the hotel rooms, provided sexual services, and in some cases migrated to the United States allows diplomatic historians to envision new maps of U.S. empire. This laboring perspective challenges how these stories of empire intersected with "grand narratives" and diplomatic affairs at the national and international levels. In short, missile defense, Cold War showdowns, development politics, military combat, touristic performances, and banana economics have something in common—they all have labor histories.

To plot the borders of the U.S. empire on a map solely dotted with flags would be to minimize it; instead we see the U.S. empire as a project of labor mobilization, coercive management, working-class politics, and a multifaceted military workforce. Labor mobilization created a range of new relationships, including and beyond the relation of employer and worker. Individuals often spent the majority of their daily life in work settings, and the contours of imperial work sites often filtered into racial tensions among migrant groups and native populations, intimate relations of sex and service, and the domestic dynamics of the home. Together we challenge historians to consider the labor that formed, worked, and rendered the U.S. empire visible. The U.S. empire grew, less because flags were raised, than because millions made it so.

Defining Empire, Defining Labor

This volume places workers at the center of the story of the U.S. empire. Their origins and locales are expansive and diverse: some were U.S. citizens who served in the U.S. military or traveled abroad in managerial positions. In Guam, the Philippines, Puerto Rico, the Marshall Islands, and Hawai'i, workers labored in U.S. territories under a wide range of euphemistic legal categories, but ultimately all negotiated their positions as colonial workers in the shadow of the flag. Others were local men and women who labored within U.S. labor systems in plantation agriculture and the service industry in Central America, the Caribbean, and even West Africa. Far from passive or voiceless but equally far from radical anti-imperialists, most men and women confronted the U.S. empire in their daily work lives and through relationships with their employers. The making of the U.S. empire mobilized millions of workers in small and massive workplaces—few of which have received significant attention from U.S. labor or diplomatic historians.[1]

Debating whether or not the United States is an empire, and if so, what kind of empire it is, has been a kind of Sisyphean exercise within U.S. historiography. Since William Appleman Williams's seminal insistence on the United States as an imperial polity, scholars have analyzed how anti-colonialism and the denial of empire have enabled the U.S. empire to grow under the mantle of benevolence and liberalism. By the turn of the twenty-first century, most historians recognized that American modernity and empire go together. As Alfred McCoy, Francisco Scarano, and Courtney Johnson wrote, "putting empire back into American history has been the single greatest achievement" in the field of "U.S. foreign relations" over the last three decades.[2] It is part of our goal in this volume to recognize that not only did nations and empires grow together, but that they were built by working men and women in a vast range of geographies. The study of work places empire at the heart of American modernity.

Since 2001 and the U.S. wars in Iraq and Afghanistan, empire has become a more accepted word and analytic in both academic and popular discourse; however, it often remains a sweeping explanatory device, rather than a subject of close investigation. In the aftermath of September 11, conservative and progressive pundits alike recognized and even embraced the United States as an empire. Empire is now widely used as a metaphor or a blanket explanation to describe more than a century's worth of U.S. actions. For those on the right, there has been a new acceptance of the term "empire," and rather than critique imperial excesses, these commentators and public intellectuals have called on the United States to embrace its power in order to be a *better* imperial power. For those on the left, "empire" has become a form of critique, associating recent U.S. unilateralism and military adventures with a long, tainted history of other—that is, non-U.S.—empires. Think of Gary Trudeau's representation of George W. Bush in a tattered Roman legionnaire's hat.

The message is clear: here we have a president, exceptional to the central flows of U.S. history and a vainglorious buffoon driven to disastrous adventure. The comic pages aside, in popular and even academic discourse, the U.S. empire is often presented as something that begins abruptly in 1898 and drifts out of focus, and then returns in a kind of parody of the past after 2001. In almost all of these renditions, the workers who fight the wars, pick the bananas, wash the laundry, toil in the oil fields, and serve the cocktails are invisible. Equally obscured is the longer history of settler colonialism and the military, agricultural, and even industrial labor it demanded.

In fact, much of the best scholarship written on the U.S. empire does not come from U.S. historians, but rather from Latin Americanists. Because of the power of the United Fruit Company (UFC) and other U.S. corporations, particularly in Central America and the Caribbean, Latin American historians have long been at the forefront of recognizing the interplay of U.S. military, corporate, and colonial expansion. In addition, far more than U.S. historians, Latin Americanists have prioritized labor and working people as key agents and subjects of analysis, as they narrate the "encounters" and "contacts" between U.S. and Latin American men and women. As Gilbert Joseph deftly noted in *Close Encounters of Empire*, the etymology of "encounter" epitomizes the paradox of being simultaneously "in" and "against" within the same relationship.[3]

As this volume builds on earlier scholarship, we define empire by its geographic boundaries *and* by its labor systems. The United States participated in and, in turn, shaped a global imperial system. Historians have often distinguished between "formal" and "informal" empire—but that artificial binary obscures the nature of working-class experience as well as the braided deployment of state, military, and corporate power and sovereignty. In this iteration, "formal" empire designates direct political and military control as, for example, in the cases of Puerto Rico, the Philippines, Cuba, Hawai'i, and Guam, while "informal" empire is meant to connote private, corporate, and cultural power as it operated in Nicaragua or Liberia.[4] However, for workers this distinction between "formal" and "informal" empire did not always reflect the threat of state violence or the potential for worker control. For example, banana workers in Colombia still confronted the full brunt of state violence despite the informal status of the United Fruit Company's authority, and these categories collapsed even further for Korean sex workers who faced invasive physical and bodily regulations in close proximity to U.S. military bases, despite their country's formal sovereignty.

Therefore, instead of positing an "informal" or "soft" empire, we argue that the United States engaged with imperial systems and economies throughout the world, and that its models were often at the forefront of imperial adaptation to changing global economies and local resistance movements. As such, we are investigating the creation and management of labor systems. Analyzing the mobilization of workers encourages historians to think about an imperial system. The U.S. imperial system included formal colonies, corporate capitalism, military bases, and interactions across empires. These vast systems mobilized workers through colonial networks, created mass migrations, and often disenfranchised and removed local, indigenous populations. Throughout this volume, we focus on the specific working relationships between workers, their employers, and the labor systems they traversed. The routes followed by labor migrants represent a kind of imperial geography, tracing boundaries of an empire of mobility, just as much as an empire of colonies.

Our contributors demonstrate how the U.S. competed with, and sometimes cooperated with, British, Japanese, and German imperial polities. Instead of charting a multicolored map of competing empires, this framework redefines empire through the lives of the men and women who labored within it, across it, and against it. We are not arguing that the U.S. empire was everywhere and nowhere at the same time. The U.S. empire was not all-powerful or monolithic. In some regions, U.S. imperial labor practices were deep and systematic, while in other places, U.S. imperial control was more improvisational. In the face of these distinctions, we argue that the U.S. empire harvested the raw materials of the tropics in specific workplaces, mobilized military force in an archipelago of bases, and constructed tropical paradises in precise Caribbean and Pacific settings, all of which contributed to U.S. empire-making.

An emphasis on work and workers also fundamentally reorients the standard historiographies and chronologies of both diplomatic and labor history. More than fifty years ago, in *The Tragedy of American Diplomacy*, William Appleman Williams argued that the U.S. economic imperative for expansion drove U.S. foreign relations in what he dubbed the "Open Door Policy" or "non-colonial imperial expansion."[5] While Williams carried the analysis of the "Open Door" through the early twentieth century, World War I, World War II, and into the Cold War era, most scholars cite his work as the watershed text whereby a leading U.S. scholar called the United States out as an imperial player.[6] In particular, his interpretation of the War of 1898 still holds sway, and he went on to influence a generation of scholars, including Walter LaFeber. While Williams's book predated the escalation of U.S. military force in Vietnam, his economic critique became more popular and generative in the years during and after the U.S. war in Vietnam. Yet despite Williams, and later LaFeber's, emphasis on economics, their focus remained on Washington, D.C., and when they thought about production, it was through U.S. trade policy and not labor or working-class experiences.

With the fall of the Berlin Wall and the "end of the Cold War," Amy Kaplan's groundbreaking 1993 essay in *Cultures of United States Imperialism* relaunched academic inquiry into the contours and consequences of the U.S. empire.[7] She argued that the treatment of the U.S. empire as an aberration or exceptional moment could be explained by the blindness to empire in the study of American culture, and likewise, the ignorance of culture in the study of empire. Kaplan's essay has been taken to heart by many scholars, especially for understanding how race and gender making were critically shaped by the imperial project. Yet in one of the relatively overlooked arguments in her essay, Kaplan links the expansion of the U.S. empire less to its territorial coherence, than to the way dominion birthed visions of how land could be used and peoples mobilized to work it.

Kaplan's work, now several decades old, launched numerous academic ventures, rich in their archival findings and all speaking to what has become virtually a truism: the United States had an empire, stretching back beyond 1898, and that empire produced a sea change in American consumer, cultural, and representational practice.[8] Yet despite our debt to Kaplan and this prolific literature, we continue to note the absence of work and working people in a cultural history of empire that has above all concerned itself with U.S. middle-class and elite consumption and representational practice. This volume redirects the focus of scholars of U.S. empire onto the men and women who worked in and built the U.S. empire. While recognizing the key place of the study of cultural production and consumerism, we call for greater investigation of the laboring practices that produced coffee, bananas, or the lei. For example, along with recognizing the racial and gender norms that military and pleasure tourists found in buying lei in Hawai'i, Vernadette Vicuña Gonzalez investigates the time, skill, labor, value, and economy that created and defined the lei buying and selling experience.

The absence of workers in the history of U.S. empire also creates its own discourse of denial and romantic imperial imagination. As Kevin Coleman argues, the power of photography and the archive can serve to preserve *or* erase worker activism. In this vein, we must also consider the subtle and overt violence that removed working people from the gaze of metropolitan audiences and turned the tropics into paradise, disguising industrial landscapes with palm trees.

As Kaplan and others introduced a new imperial American history, labor historians also looked beyond borders. Rather than empire, many labor historians have been working with a transnationalist analytic. The concept of transnationalism has served to internationalize and reframe U.S. history, but it is not synonymous with empire. Coined by Randolph Bourne during World War I, "transnationalism" was his answer to the growing xenophobia and anti-immigrant legislation promoted during the era.[9] Using the term more capaciously, Thomas Bender in the 1990s pressed U.S. scholars to think "transnationally."[10] Immigration specialists subsequently seized on transnationalism as a way to understand migrant communities who bridged two nation-states, thus forming diasporic communities in the United States, while maintaining emotional and economic relationships in their home country.[11] The "transnational turn" and its emphasis on the movement of non-state actors across borders challenged U.S. historians to conceptualize the United States as something more than a hermetic entity. For diplomatic history, transnationalism decentered its traditional interest in state actors and high politics and reoriented who "counted" in diplomatic history.

There are multiple traditions and definitions of transnationalism, many augmented and well developed by historians of labor movements, the circulation and migration of workers, and, most recently, capitalism. For labor history, transnationalism seems, at once, an obvious and valuable new analytical tool. If Thomas Bender's frame focused on both state and elite actors, in the hands of labor historians, transnationalism has reinvigorated the tried and true bottom-up approach to political history and embraced the movement of workers as central to its analysis. Building on labor history's long affinity with histories of migration, Leon Fink's *Maya of Morgantown*, for example, offers a compelling example of the value and possibilities of transnational history, highlighting the multiple ways workers crossed borders and created transnational communities, and sometimes, labor movements.[12]

While some of the essays in this volume also document transnational populations, empire provides an alternate analytic, which identifies a distinct, and massive, cohort of workers. It also identifies the forces that accelerated labor migrations and catalyzed new types of work and workplaces. For example, the Filipino "American nationals" who traveled to California in the 1920s and the Jamaican guest workers who toiled in Florida's citrus industry in the 1950s were both part of transnational communities and participants in migratory networks defined by empire. Yet these were not the only workers of empire. This volume includes Marshallese workers who never left the Pacific islands, El Salvadoran coffee workers who labored and starved in the fields, and Filipino Scouts who protested their wages within the vicinity of Manila, all men and women who would not be visible through a lens of transnationalism and the United States.[13] There is common ground, not yet realized, between labor and diplomatic histories. A labor history of U.S. empire links the study of transnational populations to the imperial structures that disciplined labor, structured new conditions of work, and linked cultural formations, notably of race, to the experience of work.

Beyond the transnational turn, historians have advanced the concept of borderlands. These are also distinct spaces populated by peoples caught in the middle of racial and national categories. The expanding interest of labor historians beyond older industrial belts helps recast borderlands as occupied spaces in which blurred racial and national identities can produce intensely industrialized zones. The auto industry that spreads from Michigan into Ontario or the *maquiladora* economies that link, for example, El Paso and Ciudad Juárez belie longer histories that entwine work, labor wars, and cross-border migration.[14] Linda Gordon's recent recovery of the concept of "internal colonialism" builds upon an older Marxist explanation for unequal rights and development within domestic populations that served to create a reserve army of labor. She expands on this notion to examine Mexican Americans whose transnational lives, often within borderlands spaces, were profoundly shaped by U.S. economic domination within Mexico.[15]

Our authors in their analysis of imperial and colonial labor within and at U.S. national borders accept Gordon's "invitation to comparison with external colonialism." In the process, they describe the emergence of an imperial labor system that structured, above all, borders between race and between types of work. This, in turn, could reinforce national borders and centers immigration firmly within an imperial analytic. Mae Ngai, in distinguishing between "internal" and "imported" colonialism, notes that imperial and colonial relations, whether in Mexico or the Philippines (and beyond), marked the experience of nonwhite migrants as they entered the domestic United States. In this way, the politics of immigration restriction were intimately intertwined with imperial relationships and histories, and the two often came to a head in matters of labor control and labor recruitment. Kornel Chang's recent work on the Pacific Northwest, for example, aptly maps the routes of white working-class activists working and organizing along an imperial circuit that included Great Britain, South Africa, Canada, Australia, New Zealand, and the United States, demonstrating how imperial practices in Transvaal or Brisbane generated an anti-Asian, white supremacist solidarity in the Pacific Northwest. He argues that "in the Pacific Northwest the nexus of white supremacy and Asiatic exclusion was born out of U.S. and British imperialism and the large-scale project to demarcate the boundaries of a 'White Pacific.'"[16] In this way, an imperial analytic can explain both the crossing of borders and the creation of new migratory circuits alongside the politics of exclusion.

As we demarcate the spatial formations of empire and insist upon the routes of labor migrations as key to the geographies of empire, so, too, do we intervene chronologically. This volume takes the era and empire that emerged in the aftermath of emancipation in the United States as its subject of inquiry, thereby challenging flawed notions that empire "begins" abruptly and accidently in 1898. It was in the post-emancipation moment when fierce debates over free and unfree labor, the value and restriction of migratory labor, and the territorial acquisition of noncontinental territories took hold. This is not to deny the imperial history of white settlement throughout the West, the complex role of American Indians as they fought to maintain their sovereignty, or U.S. aspirations in Central America and Mexico before the Civil War. Richard Drinnon, Anders Stephanson, and Bruce Cummings have all documented the history of white settlement and Indian warfare that set the stage for the U.S. continental conquest that defined early American history.[17] In fact, we would encourage more scholarship on American Indian labor history that integrates American Indians' economic roles, as both agents and resisters of U.S. empire, and the military labor used to control and limit their sovereignty.

Chronologically, we begin this volume, however, following the seismic shift of the emancipation of slave labor and the resulting need for U.S. capital and political interests to reimagine and mobilize workers who vacillated between "free" and "unfree" existences. Binaries of freedom and slavery, in the long age of the U.S. empire, became, to paraphrase Rebecca Scott, "degrees of unfreedom" characterized by migrant labor, military discipline, and everyday violence.[18]

Notably, not a single essay takes the War of 1898 as its central node of analysis. A post-emancipation chronology releases us from a fixation on the War of 1898, and rather allows us to foreground the modern practice of labor mobilization and empire building. As we expand upon a historiography indebted to Williams and later Kaplan, we insist upon uncovering the slow dance of U.S. empire and emphasize not its definition, but its making. This process was central to the creation of the modern U.S. empire. Julie Greene's and Andrew Zimmerman's essays both foreground the importance of African American labor and the control of that work for U.S. and German conceptions of empire in the late nineteenth century. Andrew T. Urban examines free white labor in settler California and the gendered fear of Chinese migrant domestic servants in the post-emancipation era. In turn, other essays concentrate on the volatile period at the end of World War I, which was marked by rising anti-colonial movements and a crackdown on labor radicalism. Augustine Sedgewick's essay interrogates the liberal regime of free trade, and then the volume moves forward well into the Cold War era, when the dual projects of militarism and the colonial nostalgia of tourism in the Pacific and the Caribbean emerged.

This turns our attention to the definition of "labor." In contrast to "empire," which historians have struggled to define, "labor" appears self-evident. The breadth of labor examined by the authors in this volume reveals multiple kinds of work needed to "make" an empire. Work was necessary at all levels: the physical labor of plantation agriculture, the military labor of control, and the affective work of personal care or sexual labor. Empire, as well, demanded intellectual labor—the hard ethnographic or anthropological work of classifying and documenting new populations incorporated into the imperium.

Perhaps the most obvious cohort of workers who built the U.S. empire are those who labored in agriculture, producing and harvesting sugar, bananas, coffee, strawberries, and citrus fruits whether in Honduras or California. At the very least, they are generally legible to historians as "workers." However, because many of these men and women labored outside the United States and beyond the purview of organized labor or national labor relations law, U.S. labor historians have not often investigated the networks between tropical and metropolitan workplaces and communities.

The recognition of an imperial system brings new kinds of work, workers, and workplaces into the context that we use to understand American labor relations. No one would question whether factory workers are workers, but labor historians have only just begun to incorporate military personnel into a broader narrative of working-class history. Some of the scholars most attuned to military history as labor history are feminist and women's historians. Cynthia Enloe inspired a generation of scholars to consider the gendered elements of U.S. military empire, and how the "work" of the military ranged from the "work of killing" to the mundane tasks of doing the laundry.[19] More recently, new works by Kimberley Phillips, Beth Bailey, Catherine Lutz, and Jennifer Middlestadt have begun to consider the culture and economics of U.S. military work; however, given the scope of the military, the officers, enlisted men and women, families, civilian workers, giant defense corporations, increasingly subcontracted private employees, and bars and commercial establishments that rely on off-duty consumption, the possibilities for scholarly engagement remain extensive.[20]

Placing empire at the heart of labor history challenges our definitions of labor, while expanding our view of labor relations. U.S. labor historians have long documented the struggle to defend and expand workers' rights through government protections and the centrality of the New Deal in U.S. labor relations. Historians have linked the exclusion of domestic servants and agricultural labor from the National Labor Relations Act, Social Security, and unemployment insurance to the liberal preoccupation with factory labor and to the legacy of racism within the New Deal.[21] The imperial frame offers a new perspective that highlights the entwining of empire into domestic labor relations and suggests the need for new interpretations of labor law that consider how labor activists and government officials distinguished metropolitan industrial workers from "colonial" agricultural workers, domestic servants, sex workers, and the military.

The imperial labor and national labor relations systems divided workers, domestic and imperial, into separate spheres. Closer examination elucidates how labor mobilization and migratory routes connected these workers. It also draws attention away from industrialized and unionized workers, and toward the migratory workers, the vast majority men and women of color, who circulated through the nodes of U.S. imperial workplaces. Thus, an imperial analytic unsettles many of the foundations of U.S. labor history. It decenters industrial work as the paradigmatic twentieth-century working experience. It elevates the importance of agricultural work within and outside of the continental United States. It also argues for the centrality of military work in working-class history. Finally, it privileges the millions of working people of color who circulated within and through sites of U.S. empire over the white working-class factory worker as the central story of U.S. labor history. In this process, hundreds of thousands, if not millions, more workers who labored on plantations, in the military, and below the decks belong under U.S. labor history's purview.

The invisibility and legibility of work and workers is more than a historiographic oversight; it is the result of a historical process. As Kevin Coleman and Moon-Ho Jung argue in this volume, state surveillance systems and U.S. corporations had clear objectives in sanitizing their archives. The military, as well, so often used in U.S. history for the disciplining of American workers, had a stake in structuring its archival memory to erase the realities of its labor history. Could military structure, discipline, and martial control survive if military work had been recognized as a category of largely unfree labor?

As we probe the visibility and invisibility of workers within the archive, we ask how "looking for the workers" can reorient our understandings of empire. To date, there are few accounts of the men and women who labored in the tourist industries that remapped the geographies of empire in the Caribbean and the Pacific. Perhaps one of the most productive strategies will involve juxtaposition. Vernadette Vicuña Gonzalez's *Securing Paradise: Tourism and Militarism in Hawai'i and the Philippines* juxtaposes military practices of occupation, defeat, and victory with the contemporary tourist economies of the Philippines and Hawai'i.[22] We would encourage scholars to investigate not just the consumption of tourist fantasies, but the labor that produced them. These stories might suggest new studies of the transition in the West Indies from British decolonization to U.S. vacation lands. Or a history of the Hilton hotels in Puerto Rico could illuminate commonalities with the experience of Puerto Rican women who worked in the tourist industry on the island and those who worked as nannies and domestic servants in New York City.

In particular, Ann Laura Stoler's work on archival practices and elisions has created new openings for scholarship on empire and domestic intimacies. One of Stoler's most significant contributions has been to return to imperial archives and recognize an abundant preoccupation with the intimate, including wet nurses, nannies, and sexual partners. She demonstrated that bureaucratic agencies cared about who was taking care of the children and who was in the family in order to establish order and control. Stoler's landmark essay "The Tense and Tender Ties of Empire," followed by her edited collection, *Haunted by Empire*, challenged U.S. scholars to take up the tools and methodologies of postcolonial scholars and apply these questions to U.S. history.[23] Stoler's scholarship continues to influence the field, this volume included. However, given the general absence of anything treated as "labor" in her volume on the U.S. empire, Stoler's earlier works on labor and working people are just as prescient and deserve to be reconsidered.[24] In these texts, she reads both across and against the grain to unpack the complicated contours of working men and women's lives in Dutch Indonesia, whether their workplace was the rubber fields or the home. In this context, we turn to Stoler as we reread the archives, not only to see the intimacies and violence of empire, but also to consider how the archive could reveal the nature of work, or simultaneously, obscure imperial labor from the eyes of metropolitan publics.

Labor became most visible when workers resisted. This resistance could be passive or militant, collective or individual, covert or revolutionary. It was in these moments, as well, that the U.S. empire became legible and workers revealed the disguised strands of empire's power.

Solidarities and Resistance: A Strike against Empire?

Solidarity is perhaps one of the most evoked, but least analyzed concepts in U.S. labor history. Solidarity has always been a central assumption—rarely a topic of analysis. It is not a stretch to claim that labor historians, ourselves included, support labor rights, worker activism, and union organizing drives, and we hope that our scholarly work illuminates the potential for solidarities to thrive across space and constructed difference.[25] In turn, much of labor historians' ongoing research investigates the conditions under which workers' mobilizations are successful and the moments when their solidarity unravels. Topics that have traditionally informed labor history include union struggles in a single factory or industry, the politics of organizing men and women across workplaces, the power of solidarity within communities, and the complex dynamics of cross-class and cross-racial alliances. However, the concept of solidarity is itself simultaneously a powerful ideal and a slippery category, and one that has not always generated the scholarship that it deserves.[26]

Together with the authors in this volume, we argue that the intersection of labor and empire allows historians to complicate the analysis of solidarity and to investigate how workers adapted and accommodated to, negotiated with, resisted, and struggled to achieve economic stability and political rights within different forms of imperial rule. It is also through these studies that we see how unstable the categories of solidarity and complicity can be. For many workers, the jobs generated by U.S. imperial projects brought them steady cash and newfound class status, even as, for others, they set up patterns of dependency and decline. And for many, imperial labor created an ambivalence whereby their economic well-being and their nationalist and political impulses were set if not in opposition, then, at the very least, in an uneasy balance. Although our refusal to place solidarity in a binary with complicity might result in fewer accounts of anti-colonial "heroes" and more sympathetic accounts of those whose work maintained the quotidian stability of empire, workers' stories allow scholars to uncover how workers navigated between and within imperial systems and migratory routes.[27] This close attention to workers' actions and intellects could reveal solidarities and imaginations across oceans and continents. As examples from sugar plantations to military barracks suggest workers often engaged in actions that simultaneously buttressed *and* destabilized imperial networks.

U.S. men in the military, from the post–Civil War struggles with trans-Mississippi Indian populations to present-day Iraq, could embrace the U.S. imperial project; they could also bristle against its dictates. Some have recognized how the military's own discipline mirrored the colonial discipline imposed on the Philippines or the Panama Canal. When did workers in the U.S. metropole embrace the privileges of empire and in what circumstances did they develop solidarities across oceans and continents? U.S. labor history has begun to recognize the importance of empire, particularly in its creation of a white working-class nationalism.[28] Yet what roles did race and class place in mobilizing, or disrupting, solidarities? If working people did stand united against companies or colonial regimes, even under overwhelming conditions of repression, they could also turn on other workers and claim what Julie Greene calls the "wages of empire."

Greene draws on W.E.B. Du Bois's classic works and emphasizes the specific military labors of African American and white American men. Unlike other authors in this collection who focus on workers in colonial or liminal spaces, Greene emphasizes the role of U.S. workers in order to connect the military in the continental United States with labor in explicitly colonial spaces. Her essay ties the histories of imperialism and capitalism to both nineteenth-century Indian warfare and overseas expansion. For some men, their purpose lay in the promotion of white supremacy. Yet, Greene notes, working people of color could realize new and profoundly radical solidarities whether it was in Cuba or the Philippines. Or, they too could cling to the privileges of empire, claiming more rights as U.S. citizens than local workers. Solidarity could clearly cut both ways.

While the labor history of solidarity in colonial settings engages with familiar themes of unions, strikes, and organizing, it also highlights the local and international politics workers needed to navigate the violence constitutive of U.S. empire. The repressive responses to three strikes, in Hawai'i, the Philippines, and Colombia, in the years immediately following World War I, demonstrate how the working-class articulation of solidarity revealed the shadowy, if complex, nature of imperial power. Moon-Ho Jung, Christopher Capozzola, and Kevin Coleman all investigate the micro-politics of labor organizing and resistance in the early 1920s. While the U.S. empire often relied on its own invisibility and "informality" to shield it from critique, strikes and labor strife worked to make imperial labor visible. In these local struggles, the U.S. empire was never overthrown, but its pretense of liberalism, free trade, benevolence, and good neighborliness was unmasked. In this moment of labor radicalism immediately after World War I, Jung emphasizes the state surveillance and oppression that met the merest hint of a "colored international" that might have existed in spirit among workers of color. Even the whisper of a transnational solidarity of the proletariat of color could catalyze the state into a frenzy of violence and repression.

Working for the U.S. military or a UFC plantation could provide men and women with a modicum of economic stability, but it could also become a fulcrum for anti-colonial protest. As such, working-class solidarities could stabilize *and* challenge U.S. imperial power. Capozzola turns our attention to colonial subjects who worked for the U.S. military. He dissects the refusal of 380 Filipino Scouts to report to duty. In this act of organized resistance for better wages and greater respect, the defiant Scouts threw the logic of colonial loyalty into disarray. Capozzola's questions again recast the politics of solidarity. The Scouts acted collectively, but was their action a strike or a mutiny, an act of colonial defiance or an ultimate act of faith in the republican ideals of the modern state?

Coleman uses visual evidence to analyze the union activism and the responding violence in the United Fruit Company. His analysis of photographs in the UFC archives reveals a campaign of violence and terror against banana workers. It also demonstrates how the nature of the archive, the corporate empire's way of remembering and representing, systematically removed, or cleansed, both workers and labor violence from the record. In addition, the politics of solidarity are also thrown into relief, as Coleman argues that the very soldiers who were ordered to put down the banana workers' strike were often seen as suspect, since many had themselves been banana workers in the past.

In these chapters that narrate moments of resistance, solidarity, and even intimacy, violence is never far from the surface. These chapters also offer a portrait of the U.S. empire from the Pacific to South America in which solidarities took multiple forms. If we reshape solidarity, not simply as working people standing together, but as affective ties that were often fleeting, contingent, and contradictory, we can begin to consider how workers looked at others, often across vast imperial space, and saw what they had in common. Such recognition also reshapes the contours of how we examine intimacy in empires. Like solidarity, intimacy could cut both ways; it could signal deep knowledge and shared experience, which could lead to romantic and affective relationships, or it could signal the violence and unequal power dynamic in imperial relationships.

From the Barracks to the Resort: Intimacies in Colonial Spaces

If solidarities could potentially create political ties within workplaces and across continents, intimacies often defined the nature of men and women's worksites. New scholarship on intimacy and empire, influenced above all by Stoler's work, but now involving increasing numbers of scholars, has focused especially on empire's obsession with domestic spaces and sexual relations. Stoler herself notes the need for greater investigation into the intimacies of workplaces, including prisons and army barracks.[29] Workplaces outside the home and the bedroom, ranging from the union hall to the ship galley to the cocktail bar, could also be intimate spaces. Intimacy also produced its industries, most obviously in sex work, and in tourist work, as well.[30]

Seungsook Moon, like Greene, examines military labor, but focuses in particular on how the U.S. military was dependent on sexual labor in both East Asia and Western Europe. She maps the contours of the postwar U.S. military empire onto older legacies of empire and sexual labor in Japan and Korea. Women could develop deeply personal relationships with individual U.S. military personnel, complicating their identification with either their home country or the United States. Moon argues that the women and men who perform in clubs, sleep with servicemen for money, and pour the drinks must be seen as workers whose relationship to the U.S. military complicates singular analyses of intimacy and anti-militarism. In turn, Gonzalez provides an intimate portrait of the

Native Hawaiian labor that generates the cultural and physical production of lei. While her subject is far from the bedroom, she describes the intensely personal relationship of individual women lei makers to their products and how they depended on the close, intimate contact with arriving tourists as they "sold aloha."

Migration and Mobilizing Labor for the Empire

This volume argues that U.S. immigration history needs to wrestle with histories of U.S. empire, and in the process, help integrate the histories of empire, labor, migration, indigeneity, and foreign relations. As the U.S. empire was part of an interlocking global imperial system, working people navigated between competing empires as they looked for work *and* as empires sought to recruit cheap and vulnerable laborers.[31] How does privileging the labor history of empire transform the narrative of U.S. immigration history? Empire mobilized workers from a distance but could also incorporate native or indigenous groups into the imperial laboring system. Equally, from the American West to the Central American banana fields, indigenous groups were disenfranchised and removed from the land. How have native groups been cast by employers and anthropologists, often working in alliance, as incapable of withstanding the demands of plantation or wage work?

U.S. labor history has developed alongside immigration history to explain the peopling of American industry. We argue that this relationship should now be reconceptualized given the findings of imperial history. Recent accounts have shifted away from a paradigm of migrant aspiration toward an examination of global labor mobilizations. As Marilyn Lake and Henry Reynolds have argued, the migration of Chinese workers to the goldfields of California, Australia, and South Africa was part of a shared racialized system of labor recruitment, immigrant restriction, deportation, and racial segregation.[32]

The massive mobilizations of labor for the U.S. empire ran parallel to the exclusion of Asian migrants and, in different forms, Southern and Eastern Europeans and Mexicans. Asian exclusion has generally been understood as the racist, nationalist response advanced partly by a local labor movement. However, the long march toward exclusion and restriction occurred alongside the institutionalization of a transient labor force and guest worker systems. These transient workers were (and are) almost always workers of color.

Immigration, exclusion, restriction, and guest work together mobilized labor and helped create a multitiered system of labor relations, as the experience of California demonstrates so dramatically. Both Andrew T. Urban and Dorothy Fujita-Rony identify California as a key location for debates over empire, migration, and Asian exclusion. In the tradition of Carey McWilliams, who argued for the centrality of California in U.S. politics, California's militarized landscape, settler colonial politics, and colonial labor force became bellwethers of U.S. imperial politics.[33] Urban examines white male workers' opposition to Chinese domestic servants in San Francisco and northern California. In dialogue with scholars who study Canada, Australia, and South Africa, Urban challenges U.S. historians to consider settler colonialism as a central thread that complicates U.S. narratives of "immigration." In this case, white male settlers favored white female domestic servants over Chinese men, not just as a personal preference, but as a matter of political and economic control over domestic workspaces. In the intimacy of domestic work, settlers articulated their campaign in the vocabulary of empire and settlement. In the same region, Fujita-Rony traces the routes that led Filipina/o workers to California in the 1920s and 1930s. Like many historians, she notes that Filipina/os came to the United States both because of the U.S. colonial presence in the Philippines and because the restriction on other Asian populations created a demand for this cohort of "American nationals."[34] Filipina/o workers "made" California a colonial space complete with militarized surveillance and plantation agriculture.[35] She examines how working people traveled to the United States, and in this case, how one man returned to the Philippines in a coffin, traversing urban and rural spaces, and dislodging the commonsense distinction that locates agricultural work in the colonies and industrial work in the metropole.

Working men and women often navigated multiple empires in their search for employment. Vicente Rafael, in his examination of the colonial histories of the Philippines, introduces the notion of "double colonization." A formal colony of Spain, then of the United States, the Philippines—and, as this book demonstrates, its mobile working peoples—were also linked into what Rafael calls "the expansive geography of a world capitalist system."[36] Colonial subjects already, Filipina/

os encountered new regimes during their migrant experience. Applied broadly, the notion of double colonization captures the lived reality of mobilized imperial workers. Rafael's notion of double colonization speaks most obviously to the transfer of flags—when the Spanish flag lowered over Manila, the U.S. flag was raised. His formulation, though, is also useful in understanding the working-class experience of empire. Working men and women's experiences highlight just how interconnected imperial systems could be, and how nimbly they could complement and strengthen each other.

Expanding on the concept of double colonialism in the context of worker mobilization and migration, Cindy Hahamovitch documents the ways the U.S. adapted to and took advantage of older systems of imperial labor mobilization. She concentrates on the twentieth-century guestworker program for Jamaican men who, until 1962, were still subjects of the British Empire and often sought amelioration from British consular officials.[37] It was not simply that the United States recruited its workers from other empires, but that the faltering, even extinct, labor systems of those empires provided mobile peoples and, as Hahamovitch notes, models of discipline.

Collectively, these chapters offer a new paradigm for reimagining the migration history in the United States. While not all immigrants to the United States were part of a U.S. imperial framework, long histories of migration provide key chronologies and geographies of the U.S. empire. This includes recognizing the power of settler colonialism in U.S. history even as late as the 1890s *and* the role of imperial circuits that drove men and women to the United States. These essays specifically focus on the movement of working people *to* the United States. Alongside these migrations to the United States, the United States also exported its labor systems abroad, creating new working-class cohorts of Ewe, El Salvadoran, and Marshalese workers who might have never left their local communities, and yet found themselves dependent on and disciplined by U.S. labor systems.

Imperial Labor and Control in the Tropics

By the dawn of the 20th century, it was a common domestic logic that the tropics were rich in resources, but ill suited for labor. This was an understanding of the tropics expressed by social scientists like Ellsworth Huntington, who, in multiple volumes stretching over decades, gave voice to the idea that the tropics were too hot and too abundant to force its natives to labor and reap the riches from the land. In contrast, according to Huntington, the temperate zone was unforgiving and trained its inhabitants to labor. The northern industrial factory had its opposite in the southern jungle.[38] Huntington was not alone in his contrasts of tropical and temperate. Corporations from Firestone in Liberia to the United Fruit Company in Central America echoed his logic as they sought to mobilize workers.

In the long history of the U.S. empire, the tropics emerge in imperial discourse as a space for development, a plantation for raw materials, and a paradise for the privileges and powers of empire. All three of these visions intertwined to create the cultural imaginary of U.S. empire. How do the tropics come to be understood as a site for massive resource extraction and luxurious tourism? And how did the cultural imagining of the tropics, and the work necessary for the tropics to be profitable, define U.S. imperial labor practices?

For this, we might turn to historian David Arnold who, in his analysis of British India, argues that empires produce specific understandings of the tropics that link evocations of luxuriant nature with the possibility of production, fostered, naturally, by the British Empire. Economic longings rested in representations of imperial space as abundant beyond the recognition of indigenous peoples. As Arnold as well as Felicia Martins and Felix Driver have noted, the tropics, in the imperial imagination, appeared as spaces both for self-realization by explorers, entrepreneurs, and the military, and for capitalist fantasies of development.[39] The discourse of what Arnold terms "tropicality" was enabled by racialized representations of native peoples as lulled into laziness by the abundance of the land. However, Arnold approaches but stops short of engaging with labor history, resting his analysis instead on the examination of the imperial traveler, rather than the imperial entrepreneur or the imperial worker, as the key figure in the articulation of tropicality.

If local workers were "savage" or "lazy" or incompatible with the work needed to produce imperial profit, then who would imperial actors find to do the work? In brief, they would often find other mobile or more vulnerable populations. The histories of empire are replete with population removals.[40] If we understand population removal as a form of imperial enclosure in which land use is radically altered and developed, often for resource extraction, we must examine the forms in which local communities are evaluated—and, most frequently, rejected—as suitable laboring groups. In turn, the U.S. military and corporations imported new working populations and developed new forms of labor discipline and management.

Andrew Zimmerman challenges us to think about the U.S. empire not simply for the lands used for the production of goods, but for the export of U.S. racialized labor systems. Zimmerman argues that German colonial officials were desperate to reduce the autonomy of local villagers in the early twentieth century. To create a dependent colonial workforce, they relied on brute force and violence, but also more interestingly the technical expertise of the Tuskegee Institute and the post-emancipation, racial share-cropping system in the U.S. South. Zimmerman's chapter raises questions about the travels of working-class African Americans and their own vacillations between solidarity and empire making and the politics of unfree labor in the post-emancipation era. Zimmerman is not arguing that somehow a German colony had become a part of a formal U.S. empire, but rather that U.S. racialized labor systems were more than effective in making empires work.

Empire produced its share of boosters, triumphant in their stories of turning tropics to profit, and the German case in Togo is one of the more curious ones. At the same time, such ambitions left behind legions of frustrated employers, unable to wrest wage labor from indigenous populations. Sometimes, their frustration generated anthropological, racialized evaluations that cast local populations as incapable of the labor needed for imperial modernity. Jason Colby and Augustine Sedgewick turn our attention to Central America, the region with one of the best documented histories of U.S. empire and work. First, Colby argues how Progressive ideology defined U.S. imperial ideology. Notably, his reading of tropicality diverges from that of Arnold and commentators on the British Empire, who are more inclined to place geography and anthropology at the center of their narratives. Colby, instead, emphasizes the UFC managers' definitions of and imaginations about British West Indian workers in Central America. In turn, Sedgewick examines the management practices of an El Salvador coffee plantation. He highlights not only the struggle of imperial management to wrest labor from those they denigrated as lazy, but also how the nature of consumption blinded metropolitan audiences to the realities of tropical labor. The myths of the idyllic tropics could persist alongside the extraordinary violence of tropical management.

Finally, Lauren Hirshberg returns us to the U.S. military empire and the Cold War era. She focuses on Kwajalein, which is so distant from U.S. shores that its very invisibility served to increase, rather than limit, U.S. power. Outside the public eye, the U.S. government has used Kwajalein as a testing site for intercontinental ballistic missiles, and this highly sophisticated defense apparatus exists alongside, and at the expense, of the local Marshallese population. To accomplish the requisite technological feats, the U.S. government transported knowledge workers from the continental United States to the middle of the Pacific, and in turn, mobilized local Marshallese workers. Many Marshallese men and women were evicted from the island of Kwajalein itself, and instead live on the nearby, overcrowded and resource-depleted island of Ebeye. In her close analysis of the interdependence of knowledge, military, and local service labor, Hirshberg shows how tropical spaces like Kwajalein, as distant and unusual as they might seem, are in fact not exceptional or anomalous atolls, but rather mirrors of U.S. politics and empire.

Conclusion: The Empire's Work

The United States, as an imperial polity, has, at different moments, endorsed and rejected the colonial project. Working people challenged, adapted to, and placed expansive demands on an empire, whose existence the state itself often denied. The corporate and state responses that working people provoked revealed the gap between the rhetoric of civilization, peace, stability, and the "denial of empire" and the lived practice of management, resource exploitation, and military exigency. When historians place labor and working people at the center, empire appears as a pivotal dynamic of U.S. history, rather than as a brief chronological blip or a moment of European envy. Empire, like the global economy itself, had its metamorphoses, its crisis, and its rebirths, as it passed from the eras of slave emancipation, Indian removal, and continental expansion to the colonial empire to the New Deal empires of free trade to the postwar and contemporary military empires.

The imperial system also had its continuities. Empire, in 1898 or 1998, produced its intimacies, engendered its solidarities, and mobilized workers for the hard labor of resource extraction, tourist work, domestic service, sex work, and the military. The military base, like the tourist resort, demanded domestic work, service labor, and the sex trade. The sugar plantation, like the factory or agribusiness conglomerate, needed malleable workers and looked widely for them, often into the heart of other empires, thereby stitching together imperiums into a global system of shared management, corporate fantasies, and racialized class formation. When labor history is in dialogue with U.S. diplomatic history, the precise boundaries that divide colony from protectorate or one empire from another merge into entwined systems of labor, management, and worker mobilization.

Empires have their fluttering flags and their unique governance— sometimes openly colonial and at other times not. Distinctions between metropolitan and imperial space also dissolve as national labor relations compete with guest work. For the coffee bean picker, the sex worker, the infantry private, the domestic servant, and the other millions who made the U.S. empire work, maps matter much less than the intimacies, violence, discipline, and solidarities that characterized their encounters with empire. With this in mind, perhaps we might rely on the experiences of working men and women as we recognize that the United States, too, had its empire.

NOTES

1. For select works that place labor at the center of their analyses of U.S. empire, see Jason Colby, *The Business of Empire: United Fruit, Race and U.S. Expansion in Central America* (Ithaca, NY: Cornell University Press, 2011); Julie Greene, *The Canal Builders: Making America's Empire at the Panama Canal* (New York: Penguin, 2009); Jana K. Lipman, *Guantánamo: A Working-Class History between Empire and Revolution* (Berkeley: University of California, 2009); Harvey Neptune, *Caliban and the Yankees: Trinidad and the United States Occupation* (Chapel Hill: University of North Carolina Press, 2007).

2. Alfred McCoy, Francisco A. Scarano, and Courtney Johnson, "On the Topic of Cancer: Transitions and Transformations in the U.S. Imperial State," in *Colonial Crucible: Empire in the Making of the Modern American State*, ed. Alfred W. McCoy and Francisco A. Scarano (Madison: University of Wisconsin Press, 2009), p. 11. For a sampling of other recent historiographical essays on the prominence of empire in U.S. historiography, see Matthew Frye Jacobson, "Where We Stand: U.S.

Empire at the Street Level and in the Archive," *American Quarterly* 65.2 (June 2013): 265–90; Paul Kramer, "Power and Connection: Imperial Histories of the U.S. in the World," *American Historical Review* (December 2011); Bruce M. Knauft, "Provincializing America: Imperialism, Capitalism, and Counterhegemony in the Twenty-First Century," *Current Anthropology* 48.6 (December 2007): 781–805; Amy Kaplan, "Violent Belongings and the Question of Empire Today," 2003 American Studies Association Presidential Address, *American Quarterly* 56.1 (2004): 1–18. For a dissenting voice, see Jeremi Suri, "The Limits of American Empire: Democracy and Militarism in the Twentieth and Twenty-First Centuries," in *Colonial Crucible*, ed. McCoy and Scarano, pp. 523–31.

3. Gilbert Joseph, "Close Encounters: Towards a New Cultural History of U.S.–Latin American Relations," in *Close Encounters of Empire: Writing the Cultural History of U.S.–Latin American Relations*, ed. Gilbert Joseph, Catherine LeGrande, and Ricardo Salvatore (Durham, NC: Duke University Press, 1998), p. 8. Also see LeGrande, "Living in Macondo: Economy and Culture in a United Fruit Company Banana Enclave in Colombia" in *Close Encounters of Empire*; John Soluri, *Banana Cultures: Agriculture, Consumption, and Environmental Change in Honduras and the United States* (Austin: University of Texas Press, 2006); Miguel Tinker Salas, *The Enduring Legacy: Oil, Culture, and Society in Venezuela* (Durham, NC: Duke University Press, 2009); Greg Grandin, *Fordlandia: The Rise and Fall of Henry Ford's Forgotten Jungle City* (New York: Picador, 2010). While less developed, there is also a valuable literature on U.S. empire and corporate power outside of Latin America; see Robert Vitalis, *America's Kingdom: Mythmaking on the Saudi Oil Frontier* (Stanford, CA: Stanford University Press, 2007); Nan Enstad, "To Know Tobacco: Southern Identity in China in the Jim Crow Era," *Southern Cultures* (Winter 2007): 6–23.

4. For example, Alfred McCoy and Francisco Scarano emphasize the formal empire under direct U.S. control, while Ricardo Salvatore analyzes the "informal empire" in South and Central America. McCoy and Scarano, *Colonial Crucible*; Ricardo D. Salvatore, "The Enterprise of Knowledge: Representational Machines of Informal Empire," in *Close Encounters of Empire*, ed. Joseph et al., pp. 69–104.

5. William Appleman Williams, *The Tragedy of American Diplomacy* (New York: W.W. Norton and Co., 1972 [1959]), p. 50. For recent commentary on the book's continued influence, see "Fifty Years of William Appleman William's *Tragedy of American Diplomacy*: An Anniversary, a Discussion, and a Celebration," *Passports* (September 2009). Williams also inspired what became known as the "Wisconsin School," with Walter LaFeber becoming the leading scholar arguing for economic imperatives as central to U.S. foreign relations. See Walter LaFeber, *The New Empire: An Interpretation of American Expansion, 1860–1898* (Ithaca, NY: Cornell University Press, 1963, 1998).

6. The historiography of the War of 1898 is quite extensive and well known. For example, George Kennan, Samuel Bemis, and Ernest May all wrote about the Spanish-American War in the mid-century, which solidified an interpretation of

U.S. empire as anomalous, an aberration, and/or benevolent. For example, Ernest May ended *Imperial Democracy* with the classic formulation that through the Spanish-American War "the United States had greatness thrust upon it." The analyses by these authors, particularly Kennan and May, are more complex and nuanced than generally recognized in recent scholarship, with key insights into European imperial politics; however, collectively they generated a scholarly understanding of the United States' empire as both benevolent and accidental. George F. Kennan, "The War with Spain," in Kennan, *American Diplomacy, 1900–1950 (Chicago: University of Chicago Press, 1951)*; Ernest May, *Imperial Democracy: The Emergence of America as a Great Power* (Chicago: Imprint Publications, 1961, 1991); and Samuel Bemis, "American Foreign Policy and the Blessings of Liberty," 1961 American Historical Association Presidential Address, http://www.historians.org/info/aha_history/sfbemis.htm. For more recent reiterations of the United States as an "empire of invitation" or as less than a "real" empire, see Geir Lundestad, "Empire by Invitation in the American Century," *Diplomatic History* 23.2 (December 2002); John Lewis Gaddis, *We Now Know: Rethinking Cold War History* (New York: Oxford University Press, 1998), pp. 284–85; Suri, "The Limits of American Empire."

 Since the 1998 centennial of the War of 1898, there has been a substantial revisionist trend in the historiography, reemphasizing the war's intentional and imperial motivations and consequences. See, in particular, Louis Perez, *The War of 1898: The United States and Cuba in History and Historiography* (Chapel Hill: University of North Carolina Press, 1998); Kristin Hoganson, *Fighting for American Manhood: How Gender Politics Provoked the Spanish American and Philippine American Wars* (New Haven, CT: Yale University Press, 2000); Christina Duffy Burnett, *Foreign in a Domestic Sense: Puerto Rico, American Expansion, and the Constitution* (Durham, NC: Duke University Press, 2001); Paul Kramer, *The Blood of Government* (Chapel Hill: University of North Carolina Press, 2006); Mariola Espinosa, *Epidemic Invasions: Yellow Fever and the Limits of Cuban Independence, 1878–1930* (Chicago: Chicago University Press, 2009).

7. Amy Kaplan, "'Left Alone with America': The Absence of Empire in the Study of American Culture," in *Cultures of United States Imperialism*, ed. Amy Kaplan and Donald E. Pease (Durham, NC: Duke University Press, 1993), pp. 3–21.

8. For some key works that explore cultural elements of the U.S. empire, see Laura Wexler, *Tender Violence: Domestic Visions in an Age of U.S. Imperialism* (Chapel Hill: University of North Carolina Press, 2000); Melani McAllister, *Epic Encounters: Culture, Media, and U.S. Interests in the United States since 1945* (Berkeley: University of California Press, 2001); Mary Renda, *Taking Haiti: Military Occupation and the Cultures of U.S. Imperialism* (Chapel Hill: University of North Carolina Press, 2001); Amy Kaplan, *The Anarchy of Empire in the Making of U.S. Culture* (Cambridge, MA: Harvard University Press, 2005); Christina Klein, *Cold War Orientalism: Asia in the Middlebrow Imagination, 1945–61* (Berkeley: University of California Press, 2005); Kristin Hoganson, *Consumers' Imperium: The*

Global Production of American Domesticity, 1865–1920 (Chapel Hill: University of North Carolina Press, 2007); Julian Go, *American Empire and the Politics of Meaning: Elite Political Cultures in the Philippines and Puerto Rico during U.S. Colonialism* (Durham, NC: Duke University Press, 2008); Keith Camacho, *Cultures of Commemoration: The Politics of War, Memory, and History in the Mariana Islands* (Honolulu: University of Hawai'i Press, 2011); Adria Imada, *Aloha America: Hula Circuits through the U.S. Empire* (Durham, NC: Duke University Press, 2012).

9. Randolph Bourne, "Trans-national America," *Atlantic Monthly* 118 (July 1916): 86–97; Gary Gerstle, *American Crucible: Race and Nation in the Twentieth Century* (Princeton, NJ: Princeton University Press, 2002).

10. Thomas Bender, "The La Pietra Report: A Report to the Profession," *Organization of American Historians* (September 2000), http://www.oah.org/about/reports/reports-statements/the-lapietra-report-a-report-to-the-profession; Thomas Bender, ed., *Rethinking American History in a Global Age* (Berkeley: University of California Press, 2002). Additionally, a set of influential articles on this topic appeared in the *Journal of American History*: David Thelen, "The Nation and Beyond: Transnational Perspectives on U.S. History"; Ian Tyrell, "Making States/Making Nations: American Historians in the Context of Empire"; Marcel van der Linden, "Transnationalizing American Labor History"; Donna Gabaccia, "Is Everywhere Nowhere? Nomads, Nations, and the Immigrant Paradigm in American History"; Robin Kelley, "'But a Local Phase of a World Problem': Black History's Global Vision, 1883–1950," all in *Journal of American History* 86.3 (December 1999).

11. Linda Basch, Nina Glick Schiller, and Cristina Szanton Blanc, *Nations Unbound: Transnational Projects, Postcolonial Predicaments, and De-territorialized Nation States* (New York: Routledge, 1993); Peggy Levitt, *Transnational Villagers* (Berkeley: University of California, 2001): Rhacel Salazar Parreñas, *Servants of Globalization: Women, Migration, and Domestic Work* (Stanford, CA: Stanford University Press, 2001).

12. Leon Fink, *The Maya of Morgantown: Work and Community in the Nuevo New South* (Chapel Hill: University of North Carolina Press, 2007); Leon Fink, ed., *Workers across the Americas: The Transnational Turn in Labor History* (New York: Oxford University Press, 2011).

13. Robert Gregg, "Making the World Safe for American History," in *After the Imperial Turn: Thinking with and through the Nation*, ed. Antoinette Burton (Durham, NC: Duke University Press, 2003), pp. 170–85.

14. Adele Perry, *On the Edge of Empire: Gender, Race, and the Making of British Columbia* (Toronto: Toronto University Press, 2001); Alicia Schmidt-Camacho, *Migrant Imaginaries: Latino Cultural Politics in the U.S.-Mexican Borderlands* (New York: New York University Press, 2008); Holly Karibo, "Detroit's Border Brothel: Sex Tourism in Windsor, Ontario, 1945–1960," *American Review of Canadian Studies* 40.3 (2010): 362–78; Katherine Benton-Cohen, *Borderline Americans: Racial Division and Labor War in the Arizona Borderlands* (Cambridge, MA:

Harvard University Press, 2011); Rachel St. John, *Line in the Sand: A History of the Western U.S.-Mexico Border* (Princeton, NJ: Princeton University Press, 2011).

15. Linda Gordon, "Internal Colonialism and Gender," in *Haunted by Empire: Geographies of Intimacy in North American History*, ed. Ann Laura Stoler (Durham, NC: Duke University Press, 2006), p. 437; Linda Gordon, *The Great Arizona Orphan Abduction* (Cambridge, MA: Harvard University Press, 1999).

16. Mae Ngai, *Impossible Subjects: Illegal Aliens and the Making of Modern America* (Princeton, NJ: Princeton University Press, 2005); Kornel Chang, "Circulating Race and Empire: Transnational Labor Activism and the Politics of Anti-Asian Agitation in the Anglo-American Pacific World, 1880–1910," *Journal of American History* 96.3 (2009); Kornel Chang, *Pacific Connections: The Making of the U.S.-Canadian Borderland* (Berkeley: University of California Press, 2012).

For other works on Asian migration, racial formation, and labor regimes, see Evelyn Hu-DeHart, "Chinese Coolie Labour in Cuba in the Nineteenth Century: Free Labour or Neo-Slavery?" *Slavery and Abolition* 14.1 (1993): 67–83; Moon-Kie Jung, "Different Racisms and the Differences They Make: Race and 'Asian Workers' of Prewar Hawai'i," *Critical Sociology* 28.1–2 (2002): 77–100; Vijay Prashad, *Everybody Was Kung Fu Fighting: Afro-Asian Connections and the Myth of Cultural Purity* (Boston: Beacon, 2001); Matthew Pratt Guterl, "After Slavery: Asian Labor, the American South, and the Age of Emancipation," *Journal of World History* 14 (2003): 209–41; Helen Jun, "Black Orientalism: Nineteenth-Century Narratives of Race and US Citizenship," *American Quarterly* 58.4 (2006): 1047–66; Moon-Ho Jung, *Coolies and Cane: Race, Labor, and Sugar Production in the Age of Emancipation* (Baltimore: Johns Hopkins University Press, 2006); Moon-Kie Jung, *Reworking Race: The Making of Hawaii's Interracial Labor Movement* (New York: Columbia University Press, 2006).

17. Works that argue for the continuity of U.S. empire since colonial times include Anders Stephanson, *Manifest Destiny: American Expansion and the Empire of Right* (New York: Hill and Wang, 1996); Michael Hunt, *Ideology and U.S. Foreign Policy* (New Haven, CT: Yale University Press, 1987); Richard H. Immerman, *Empire for Liberty: A History of American Imperialism from Benjamin Franklin to Paul Wolfowitz* (Princeton, NJ: Princeton University Press, 2010); Bruce Cummings, *Dominion from Sea to Sea: Pacific Ascendancy and American Power* (New Haven, CT: Yale University Press, 2009).

For works specifically on American Indians and empire, see Richard White, *The Middle Ground: Indians, Empires, and Republics in the Great Lakes Region, 1650–1815* (Cambridge, UK: Cambridge University Press, 1991); Richard Drinnon, *Facing West: The Metaphysics of Indian-Hating and Empire-Building* (Norman: University of Oklahoma Press, 1997). For newer works, see Jeffrey Ostler, *The Plains Sioux and US Colonialism from Lewis and Clark to Wounded Knee* (Cambridge, UK: Cambridge University Press, 2004); Paige Raibmon, *Authentic Indians: Episodes of Encounter from the Late-Nineteenth-Century Northwest Coast* (Durham, NC: Duke University Press, 2005); Brian DeLay, *War of a Thousand Deserts: Indian Raids and the U.S.-Mexican War* (New Haven, CT: Yale University Press, 2009); Pekka Hämäläinen, *The Comanche Empire* (New Haven, CT: Yale University Press, 2009).

18. Rebecca Scott, *Degrees of Freedom: Louisiana and Cuba after Slavery* (Cambridge, MA: Harvard University Press, 2008).

19. Cynthia Enloe, *Bananas, Beaches, and Bases: Making Feminist Sense of International Politics* (Berkeley: University of California Press, 2000 [1989]); Cynthia Enloe, *Maneuvers: The International Politics of Militarizing Women's Lives* (Berkeley: University of California Press, 2000). For works that emphasize the military role in women's lives, particularly the politics and economy of sex work and U.S. bases, see Saundra Pollack Sturdevant and Brenda Stoltzfus, *Let the Good Times Roll: Prostitution and the U.S. Military in Asia* (New York: Free Press, 1993); Katherine H. S. Moon, *Sex among Allies: Military Prostitution in U.S.-Korean Relations* (New York: Columbia University Press, 1997); Ji-Yeon Yuh, *Beyond the Shadow of Camptown: Korean Military Brides in America* (New York: NYU Press, 2004); Jin-Kyung Lee, *Service Economies, Sex Work, and Migrant Labor in South Korea* (Minneapolis: University of Minnesota Press, 2010); Maria Hohn and Seungsook Moon, eds., *Over There: Living with the U.S. Military Empire from World War II to the Present* (Durham, NC: Duke University Press, 2010); Kimberley L. Phillips, *War: What Is It Good For? Black Freedom Struggles and the U.S. Military from World War II to Iraq* (Chapel Hill: University of North Carolina Press, 2012)

20. There are numerous excellent books on African Americans and Mexican Americans in the Vietnam War, but few of these books examine the military as "work." For key exceptions, see Christian Appy, *Working-Class War: American Combat Soldiers in Vietnam* (Chapel Hill: University of North Carolina Press, 1993); Catherine Lutz, *Homefront: A Military City and the American Twentieth Century* (Boston: Beacon Press, 2002); Beth Bailey, *America's Army: Making the All-Volunteer Force* (New York: Oxford University Press, 2009); Phillips, *War: What Is It Good For?*; Peter Way, "'black service . . . white money': The Peculiar Institution of Military Labor in the British Army during the Seven Years' War," in *Workers across the Americas*, ed. Leon Fink (New York: Oxford University Press, 2011), pp. 57–80. In 2011, the *International Labor and Working-Class History* journal (ILWCH) published a special series on labor and military history. See in particular, Jennifer Mittlestadt, "'The Army Is a Service and Not a Job': Unionization, Employment, and the Meaning of Service in the Late-Twentieth-Century United States"; Elizabeth Shesko, "Constructing Roads, Washing Feet, and Cutting Cane for the *Patria*: Building Bolivia with Military Labor, 1900–1975"; Michelle Moyd, "Making the Household, Making the State: Colonial Military Communities and Labor in German East Africa"; Priscilla Murolo, "Wars of Civilization: The U.S. Army Contemplates Wounded Knee, the Pullman Strike, and the Philippine Insurrection," all in *ILWCH* 80.1 (2011).

21. Joshua Freeman, *American Empire, 1945–2000: The Rise of a Global Power, the Democratic Revolution at Home* (New York: Penguin, 2013).

22. Vernadette Vicuña Gonzalez, *Securing Paradise: Tourism and Militarism in Hawai'i and the Philippines* (Durham, NC: Duke University Press, 2013).

23. Ann Laura Stoler, *Race and the Education of Desire: Foucault's* History of Sexuality *and the Colonial Order of Things* (Durham, NC: Duke University Press, 1995); Ann Laura Stoler, *Carnal Knowledge and Imperial Power: Race and the Intimate in Colonial Rule* (Berkeley: University of California Press, 2002); Ann Laura Stoler, "Tense and Tender Ties: The Politics of Comparison in North American History and (Post) Colonial Studies," *Journal of American History* 88.3 (2001): 829–65; Ann Laura Stoler, ed., *Haunted by Empire: Geographies of Intimacy in North American History* (Durham, N.C.: Duke University Press, 2006).

24. Ann Laura Stoler, *Capitalism and Confrontation in Sumatra's Plantation Belt, 1870–1979* (Ann Arbor: University of Michigan Press, 1995); Stoler, *Carnal Knowledge*, pp. 162–203.

25. For a critique of what he terms the "Solidarity Left," see Steve Striffler, "Solidarity, the Labor Movement, and the Challenge of Building a Left in the United States," *Dialectical Anthropology* 35 (2011): 233–38.

26. In the contemporary moment, much of the work on international labor solidarity has focused on globalization and the challenge of transnational labor organizing in response to multinational corporations. See Jefferson Cowie, *Capital Moves: RCA's Seventy-Year Quest for Cheap Labor* (New York: New Press, 1999), pp. 180–209; Michael P. Hanagan, "Labor Internationalism: An Introduction," *Social Science History* 27.4 (2003): 485–99; Andrew Herod, "Geographies of Labor Internationalism," *Social Science History* 27.4 (2003): 501–23; Aviva Chomsky, *Linked Labor Histories: New England, Colombia, and the Making of a Global Working-Class* (Durham, NC: Duke University Press, 2008).

27. Frederick Cooper, in a broad critique of postcolonial studies and its lack of attention to the quotidian experience and struggles of ordinary people, has identified a tendency toward "story plucking." That is, he criticizes postcolonial scholars for finding in specific examples of romantic and revolutionary anti-colonialism an "essence of being colonized independent of what anybody did in a colony." Simply "naming the colonial" reveals little about how ordinary people challenged, adapted to, and transformed imperial power and the particular vocabulary they employed. See Frederick Cooper, *Colonialism in Question: Theory, Knowledge, History* (Berkeley: University of California Press, 2005).

28. Marilyn Lake and Henry Reynolds, *Drawing the Global Color Line: White Men's Countries and the International Challenge of Racial Equality* (Cambridge, UK: Cambridge University Press, 2008); Chang, *Pacific Connections*; David Roediger and Elizabeth Esch, *The Production of Difference: Race and the Management of Labor in U.S. History* (New York: Oxford University Press, 2012); Adam Ewing, "Caribbean Labor Politics in the Age of Garvey," *Race and Class* (July 2013): 23–45; Adam Ewing, *The Age of Garvey: How a Jamaican Activist Created a Mass Movement and Changed Global Black Politics* (Princeton, NJ: Princeton University Press, 2014).

29. Stoler, *Haunted by Empire*.
30. For recent works on tourism, see F. Robert Hunter, "Tourism and Empire: The Thomas Cook & Son Enterprise on the Nile, 1868–1914," *Middle Eastern Studies* 40.5 (September 2004): 28–54; Dennis Merrill, *Negotiating Paradise: U.S. Tourism and Empire in Twentieth-Century Latin America* (Chapel Hill: University of North Carolina Press, 2009); Christine Skwiot, *The Purpose of Paradise: U.S. Tourism and Empire in Cuba and Hawai'i* (Philadelphia: University of Pennsylvania Press, 2010); Dina Berger and Andrew Grant Wood, eds., *Holiday in Mexico: Critical Reflections on Tourism and Tourist Encounters* (Durham, NC: Duke University Press 2010); James W. Martin, "Mapping an Empire: Tourist Cartographies of the Caribbean in the Early Twentieth Century," *Popular Visual Culture* 9.1 (February 2011): 1–14. On domestic service, see Julia Martinez and Claire Lowrie, "Everyday American Imperialism: The Politics of Chinese Domestic Servants in the Philippines," *Pacific Historical Review* 81.4 (2012): 511–36.
31. For works that link imperial and immigration histories, see Donna Gabaccia, *Foreign Relations: American Immigration in Global Perspective* (Princeton, NJ: Princeton University Press, 2012); Desmond King, *Making Americans: The Origins of the Diverse Democracy* (Cambridge, MA: Harvard University Press, 2002); Matthew Frye Jacobson, *Barbarian Virtues: The United States Encounters Foreign People at Home and Abroad, 1876–1917* (New York: Hill and Wang, 2001); Gilbert G. Gonzalez, *Culture of Empire: American Writers, Mexico and Mexican Immigrants, 1880–1930* (Austin: University of Texas Press, 2004).
32. Lake and Reynolds, *Drawing the Global Color Line*; Cindy Hahamovitch, *Jamaican Guest Workers in America and the Global History of Deportable Labor* (Princeton, NJ: Princeton University Press, 2011); David G. Gutiérrez and Pierrette Hondagneu-Sotelo, eds., *Nation and Migration: Past and Future, American Quarterly* (special issue) 60.3 (September 2008); Paul R. Spickard, *Almost All Aliens: Immigration, Race, and Colonialism in American History and Identity* (New York: Routledge, 2007); Ngai, *Impossible Subjects*; Cindy Hahamovitch, *Fruits of Their Labor* (Chapel Hill: University of North Carolina, 1997).
33. Carey McWilliams, *Factories in the Field* (Berkeley: University of California Press, 2000); Michael Denning, *The Cultural Front* (London: Verso, 1997), pp. 260–69.
34. Rick Baldoz, *The Third Asiatic Invasion: Empire and Migration in Filipino America, 1898–1946* (New York: NYU Press, 2011); Catherine Ceniza Choy, *Empire of Care: Nursing and Migration in Filipino American History* (Durham, NY: Duke University Press, 2003); Dorothy Fujita-Rony, *American Workers, Colonial Power: Philippine Seattle and the Transpacific West, 1919–1941* (Berkeley: University of California Press, 2002); Parreñas, *Servants of Globalization*.
35. McWilliams, *Factories in the Field*.
36. Vicente Rafael, *White Love and Other Events in Filipino History* (Durham, NC: Duke University Press, 2000), p. 5.
37. Andrea Queeley, "Somos Negros Finos: Anglophone Caribbean Cultural Citizenship in Revolutionary Cuba," in *Global Circuits of Blackness: Race,*

Citizenship, and Modern Subjectivities, ed. Percy C. Hintzen, Jean Muteba Rahier, and Felipe Smith (Champaign: University of Illinois Press, 2010); David Vine, *Island of Shame: The Secret History of the U.S. Military Base on Diego Garcia* (Princeton, NJ: Princeton University Press, 2009); Jorge Giovannetti, "The Elusive Organization of 'Identity': Race, Religion, and Empire among Caribbean Migrants in Cuba," *Small Axe* 19 (February 2006): 1–27.

38. Ellsworth Huntington, *The Character of Races* (New York: Charles Scribner's Sons, 1924); Ellsworth Huntington, *Civilization and Climate* (New Haven, CT: Yale University Press, 1924 [1915]). See, also, Gary Okihiro, *Pineapple Culture: A History of the Tropical and Temperate Zones* (Berkeley: University of California Press, 2010); Daniel E. Bender, *American Abyss: Savagery and Civilization in the Age of Industry* (Ithaca, NY: Cornell University Press, 2009), 40–68.

39. David Arnold, *The Tropics and the Traveling Gaze: India, Landscape, and Science, 1800–1856* (Seattle: University of Washington Press, 2006); David Arnold, "'Illusory Riches': Representations of the Tropical World, 1840–1950," *Singapore Journal of Tropical Geography* 21 (March 2000): 6–18; Felix Driver, "Imagining the Tropics: Views and Visions of the Tropical World," *Singapore Journal of Tropical Geography* 25 (March 2004): 1–17; Felix Driver and Luciana Martins, *Tropical Visions in an Age of Empire* (Chicago: University of Chicago Press, 2005). For related works, see Nancy Leys Stepan, *Picturing Tropical Nature* (Ithaca, NY: Cornell University Press, 2001); Krista Thompson, *An Eye for the Tropics: Tourism, Photography, and Framing the Caribbean Picturesque* (Durham, NC: Duke University Press, 2006); James W. Martin, "Becoming Banana Cowboys: White-Collar Masculinity, the United Fruit Company, and Tropical Empire in Early-Twentieth-Century Latin America," *Gender & History* 25.2 (August 2013): 317–38; Greg Bankoff, "First Impressions: Diarists, Scientists, Imperialists, and the Management of the Environment in the American Pacific, 1899–1902," *Journal of Pacific History* 44.3 (December 2009): 261–80; Paul Sutter, "Nature's Agents or Agents of Empire? Entomological Workers and Environmental Change during the Construction of the Panama Canal," *Isis* 98.4 (December 2007): 724–54; Karen Morin, "Embodying Tropicalities," *Singapore Journal of Tropical Geography* 25.1 (March 2004): 23–25; Greg Bankoff, "In the Eye of the Storm: The Social Construction of the Forces of Nature and the Climactic and Seismic Construction of God in the Philippines," *Journal of Southeast Asian Studies* 35.1 (February 2004): 91–111; Natalie Ring, "Inventing the Tropical South: Race, Region, and the Colonial Model," *Mississippi Quarterly* 56.4 (October 2003).

40. Jodi A. Byrd, *The Transit of Empire: Indigenous Critiques of Colonialism* (Minneapolis: University of Minnesota Press, 2011). Also see, Vine, *Island of Shame*; J. Kehaulani Kauanui, *Hawaiian Blood: Colonialism and the Politics of Sovereignty and Indigeneity* (Durham, NC: Duke University Press, 2008); Noenoe Silva, *Aloha Betrayed* (Durham, NC: Duke University Press, 2004); Huanani Kay Trask, *From a Native Daughter: Colonialism and Sovereignty in Hawai'i* (Honolulu: University of Hawai'i Press, 1999).

PART I

Solidarities and Resistance

1

The Wages of Empire

Capitalism, Expansionism, and Working-Class Formation

JULIE GREENE

In 1963, Edward Thompson focused our attention on the ways the working class made itself, framing class formation as an active and dynamic process; in 1973, Herbert Gutman demonstrated that the U.S. working class in effect made *and* remade itself as waves of immigrants, possessing a variety of cultural traditions and workplace strategies, entered the country between 1815 and 1919.[1] Then, in 1990, David Roediger broadened our understanding by exploring how the crucible of whiteness made class formation possible. Building upon the writings of W.E.B. Du Bois, Roediger coined the phrase "wages of whiteness" to denote the psychological and emotional benefits some workers received from their whiteness, which compensated for the class oppression they experienced.[2]

This essay builds upon the insights of those and other scholars, asking how thinking more globally—and looking in particular at U.S. expansionism in the decades after the Civil War—might illuminate working-class history. To do so, we return as Roediger did to W.E.B. Du Bois. Du Bois's masterful *Black Reconstruction in America, 1860–1880* explored white racial identity, yet at its heart the book is concerned with global historical currents and particularly with the workings of imperialism. The end of the U.S. Civil War initiated a new engine of economic, political, and military expansionism. The result, as Du Bois saw it, was an emergent global slavery in which workers, especially those who were nonwhite, were enmeshed in serving the U.S. empire. Du Bois proclaimed: "Out of the exploitation of the dark proletariat comes the Surplus Value filched from human beasts which, in cultural lands, the Machine and harnessed Power veil and conceal." The burst of imperialism that characterized the late nineteenth and early twentieth centuries, built as it was upon an aggressively expansionist industrial capitalism, had combined the problems of labor and race into one. Building upon Du Bois's insights regarding imperialism, we might employ the concept of the "wages of empire" to reassess labor and working-class history in the decades from 1865 to 1920, thereby shifting our understanding of class formation to consider flows and dynamics that stretch beyond the territorial limits of the United States.[3] My contention is that the U.S. imperial project always and everywhere involved the recruitment, managing, and disciplining of labor, and that historians of both U.S. labor and its empire might fruitfully focus more attention on those connections.

Imperial processes created new systems of mobility and ideology, they ingeniously organized labor in order to extract value and profit efficiently, and they generated hierarchies of difference as a way of organizing labor. In all their manifestations, imperial processes placed the control and regulation of labor at the very heart of the enterprise. Thus empire constituted a force that articulated and shaped class experience and formation as much as did, say, race or gender. To paraphrase Stuart Hall, empire served as a modality through which class was lived, experienced, organized, and struggled through. These processes shaped metropolitan workers as well as working men and women on the various sites of empire.[4] Furthermore, while it is undeniable that imperial processes profoundly shaped racial identities, generating new racial hierarchies and racializations, their complex impact should not be reduced purely to race. New kinds of circulation and exchange, new patterns of demographic mobility, new notions of a people's relationship to the world, new strategies of occupation and conquest, and more, changed the worlds of working men and women. A key effect of this hypermobile circulatory system was to make the very composition of the working classes much more fluid and quick to change, and to make racial and gender relations themselves more fluid and changeable. Speedy and continuous transformation is itself central to the period and to workers' experiences during it. Furthermore, to speak of empire's impact as consisting only in generating a racial consciousness that united white workers is to render invisible the many workers of color who toiled for U.S. empire.

Globalizing our understanding of U.S. labor and working-class history requires attention to the varied sites of empire and the gradated forms of sovereignty that emerged as the power of the U.S. spread halfway around the world, and most of the essays in this volume focus on those topics. It also necessitates exploration of empire's impact on metropolitan workers and the society and politics of the metropole, and this essay focuses on that. It addresses four problems involved in the history of U.S. labor and empire: conceptualizing the links between expansionist capitalism and imperialism; continuities and ruptures in our periodization of U.S. empire; the role of white and African American U.S. soldiers who labored to build the infrastructure of capitalism, accumulate territory and resources, and occupy, colonialize, and kill; and finally, the impact of empire on metropolitan politics and notions of national identity.

Linkages of Imperialism and Capitalism

The United States in the late nineteenth and early twentieth centuries was a powerhouse of two processes tightly connected by a rapidly transforming capitalist economy: expansionism and industrialization. Its success in both endeavors was spectacular. United States capitalism was extremely innovative, relying heavily on technological advances, new labor management strategies and forms of discipline and, hugely important, its invention of the modern corporation. The U.S. was especially skilled, as Perry Anderson has written, at "disembedding the market as far as possible from ties of custom, tradition, or solidarity, whose very abstraction from them later proved . . . exportable and reproducible across the world, in a way that no other competitor could quite match."[5] The corporation as a legal personality emerged and blossomed earlier and more fully in the U.S. than anywhere else, and this occurred amid a concentration of capital unlike anything the world had seen. New technologies and new forms of labor discipline made capital accumulation highly efficient and this was in turn supported by rapid expansionism across the continent and then, increasingly, outward to international markets. In 1901, the British journalist Frederick Mackenzie wrote in *The American Invaders* that U.S. corporations now dominated in almost every new industry created within the previous 15 years. Thus well before the War of 1898 allowed the U.S.—having acquired an empire that stretched halfway around the world—to achieve new status as one of the "Great Powers," U.S. corporations had been aggressively expanding internationally.[6]

This great strength of corporate, industrial capitalism gave U.S. empire building after 1898 a special flavor. An imperial ideology developed that cloaked the aggressive expansionism of the U.S. government and corporations in notions of technological and industrial know-how. With its victory over Spain, the U.S. thus benefitted from its economic power and domination of global markets to forge a complex and varied empire that continued to rely upon economic strategies and agroindustrial strength while adding formal colonialism, unincorporated territories, protectorates, repeated military interventions and occupations, and a strenuous insistence on "Open Door" market relations (though we note that the Open Door shut firmly when it came to many countries' desire to enter U.S. markets). This required transforming, recalibrating, and rearticulating the role of the federal government and its laws in order to protect the property rights of U.S. corporations overseas and ensure efficient capital accumulation. United States rule became especially creative at gradated forms of sovereignty and disfranchisement in diverse sites like Samoa, Guam, Hawai'i, Cuba, and Puerto Rico. Meanwhile, even as corporations continued to plumb the largest domestic market in the world, they pushed into Mexico, Central America, the Caribbean, and Asia.[7]

In short, U.S. imperialism and capitalism were profoundly intertwined, mutually supportive, and to some degree mutually constitutive. One could go back to Rosa Luxemburg or Vladimir Ilyich Lenin to track the evolving debates about the links between empire and capitalism. It is an old and continuing saw in Marxist theories of capitalism.[8] However, earlier ideas about imperialism as the final stage of capitalism, or not, have been superseded by a focus on the ways the two make one another possible. Fernando Coronil articulates it this way: "Just as imperialism makes evident the political dimension of capitalism, capitalism makes visible the economic dimension of imperialism, revealing 'states' and 'markets' as dual facets of a unitary process."[9] Nonetheless, because states and corporations do not possess identical interests, the goals of the U.S. government often diverged from those of U.S. corporations. This requires nimble disentangling of the diverse strategies and tactics deployed by state and corporate actors. As bureaucrats and politicians like William Howard Taft or Charles Magoon circulated through their new empire, from the Philippines to Cuba to Panama, they worked not only to support the activities of U.S. corporations but also to generate and stabilize new forms of government and degrees of sovereignty that would benefit the American state.

Our understanding of U.S. empire at the turn of the twentieth century, in short, builds upon the work done over the last several decades by economic, labor, and business historians on the key dynamics and character of U.S. capitalism. Recent suggestions by journalists and some historians that the study of capitalism is a new phenomenon ignore the fact that generations of scholars have toiled to illuminate precisely these matters.[10] Not the least of those scholars was Du Bois, for whom the interwoven character of imperialism and capitalism stood as a defining hallmark of the decades that followed the Civil War. The end of Reconstruction generated a new era in which labor exploitation and racism combined in the interest of capital and empire. Taking Du Bois's observations to heart, we need not focus on defining what is or is not the American "empire," but rather see U.S. economic, cultural, military, and colonial forms of domination as reciprocal. Much of the power of the U.S., indeed, came from the multifaceted character of its expansionist project. Ann Laura Stoler has argued for perceiving imperial processes as "macropolities whose technologies of rule thrive on the production of exceptions and their uneven and changing proliferation. Critical features of imperial formations include harboring and building on territorial ambiguity, redefining legal categories of belonging and quasi-membership, and shifting the geographic and demographic zones of *partially* suspended rights."[11] Focusing on the interconnections between empire building and capitalism clarifies the central role played by working people in the dreams of both state and corporate actors. The working man or woman was the instrument that made capital accumulation possible; recruiting, managing, and disciplining their bodies was the necessary goal of expansionists, regardless of whether this involved indigenous or imported labor. In this sense, the Slavic immigrants employed in factories, or the Chinese immigrants living in snow caves as they struggled to lay tracks across the Sierra Nevada, are just as relevant to our story as the labor of Jamaicans or Italians building the Panama

Canal, or Filipinos building the infrastructure required by U.S. military officials on their islands. The railroads built by Chinese and Irish workers, for example, were needed not only to expand the marketing and distribution of domestic commodities. That infrastructure was itself central to the project of United States transcontinental expansionism.[12]

Continuities and Ruptures from Indian Wars to Overseas Expansion

Interrogating the role of expansionism in the remaking of the working class requires rethinking the relationship between the Indian wars of the postbellum period and the overseas expansionism of 1898 and beyond. This is crucial given the intertwined and reciprocal character of imperialism and capitalism. The notion that the War of 1898 marked a complete rupture with previous U.S. history has been surprisingly persistent, and corresponds to the old idea that expansionism across the North American continent was somehow foreordained, "Manifest Destiny." This in turn relies upon archaic notions that Native American peoples do not deserve the status of foreign nations and so conquest of their territory somehow does not constitute imperialism. Walter Williams noted this as long ago as 1980 in "United States Indian Policy and the Debate over Philippine Annexation," in which he pointed out also that imperialists like Theodore Roosevelt never failed to recognize the continuities between conquest of Native Americans in the nineteenth century and Filipinos in the early twentieth. Indeed, Roosevelt's rhetorical campaign explicitly conflated the two, referring to the latter as "Apaches" or "Sioux." Despite Williams's influential article, and more recent, promising work by scholars like Brian DeLay and Pekka Hämäläinen, fully integrating continental expansionism and wars against indigenous peoples into our understanding of U.S. empire building remains a challenge. The final stages of those wars intersected with and shaped U.S. imperial ambitions across the Caribbean and Pacific Ocean. The physical and rhetorical labors involved in warfare against Plains Indians from 1866 to 1890—building and staffing of army forts, military campaigns, pacification, creation of reservations—established a foundation that would make possible the rapid growth of overseas expansionism across the late nineteenth and early twentieth centuries.

Many of the personnel involved were the same, and lessons learned in conquest of Native lands shaped later imperial battles. There are famous cases like John J. Pershing, whose career took him from campaigns against Apache and Sioux Indians to the Filipino insurrection, and onward to Mexico and World War I; and military doctors like William Gorgas, who cut his teeth at Indian forts in the 1880s before going on to battle yellow fever in Cuba and Panama in the early twentieth century. But there remains a history to be written of soldiers and nurses, as well, whose work building the infrastructure of Indian conquest evolved into the labor involved in new forms of domination over Filipinos, Cubans, Puerto Ricans, and others. Furthermore, how did relations between the U.S. government and Native Americans *after* the end of military warfare shape U.S. treatment of other subject peoples on sites of empire like the Philippines or Cuba?[13]

Labor historian Priscilla Murolo has recently explored connections between imperial and domestic military actions, focusing on the Seventh Cavalry, with its history stretching from the infamous Battle of Little Bighorn to the massacre at Wounded Knee, the Pullman strike, and onward to the U.S.-Filipino war of 1899 to 1903. Much like Walter Williams 30 years earlier, Murolo found remarkable continuities in strategy and discourse across the decades: "Applying the same negative stereotypes to one and all who resisted the Army's agenda, military men consistently paired condemnations of enemies with venerations of soldiers." She suggests that there existed similar "mechanisms of state control of workers and colonial subjects."[14] Richard Slotkin likewise traced notions of savagery as they were deployed against Indians, strikers, and Filipinos, and argued that military strategies of guerilla warfare from the Missouri campaigns of the Civil War to the Indian Wars and onward to war in the Philippines all demonstrated continuities of military policy.[15]

These are suggestive arguments, yet in important ways sociohistorical changes differentiated imperial adventures of the early twentieth century from those of the late nineteenth. Transformations of class, racial, and gender ideologies changed the ways subject groups were conceptualized and managed in the early twentieth century. Indeed, the continuous use of certain language—e.g., referring to female strikers or Filipinas as "squaws"—likely indicated a need to mask dramatically changed circumstances rather than serving as evidence that

nothing had changed. By the early twentieth century, corporate capitalism had expanded and consolidated its control both within and beyond
the territorial boundaries of the United States. After 1900, Progressivism
inspired efforts to ameliorate the harshest effects of economic, political,
and military expansionism. As a result of these transformations, imperial actors sought to employ modern notions of urban development and
modernism in the sites of empire. Such impulses were paired with new
anxieties that U.S. imperialism and the cruel tactics it involved, rather
than elevating "savages" in the Philippines to a higher stage of civilization, were in fact reducing U.S. soldiers to a state of savagery.

Reconceptualizing Military History

The U.S. military served as a linchpin in the complex interconnections
between capitalism and imperialism.[16] The labor history of military
service and the vicissitudes of capitalism intersected in numerous ways
during the late nineteenth and early twentieth centuries. The relatively
small army, hovering at around 25,000 men from the end of the Civil War
until the War of 1898, has often been discounted as a significant social
organization in the Gilded Age and its importance to working-class history has gone largely unnoticed. Yet the army's role, in helping build the
infrastructure required for capitalist and imperial expansion and in carrying out the conquest of Native Americans in the wars of 1867 to 1890, was
indispensable for nineteenth-century capital accumulation, territorial
expansion, and articulations of national identity. Peter Way has written
that eighteenth-century soldiers of the British empire were both "instruments and objects of imperial authority." The same was true of nineteenth
and early-twentieth-century soldiers. These workers of empire were
regimented and regulated, exposed to harsh and sometimes cruel punishments as well as intense regimes of discipline. Although soldiers signed
up for service, so the labor was contractual and hence "free," once in the
military they faced a regime of harsh discipline, limits on their freedom,
and severe punishment for a wide range of behaviors. Thus military labor
was, as Peter Way describes it, "a peculiar institution straddling the axis
of free and unfree." The army relied upon notions of valor, patriotism,
and manliness as well as its labyrinthine disciplinary policies to compel
soldiers to complete the onerous tasks required of them.[17]

Common labor dominated the everyday lives of soldiers as they worked toward the goals of expansionist capitalism: constructing and maintaining forts, roads, and bridges, chopping wood, cutting hay, gardening, laying telegraph wire, surveying land, and fighting drought or blizzards. A judge in 1884 undoubtedly captured the impression shared by many soldiers when he referred to military service as "the drudgery of a common laborer." When enlisted men's wives followed them to their posts, they typically found work as laundresses or domestic servants.[18] Soldiers not engaged in mundane labor required for reproducing the conditions of capital accumulation worked at the labor of pacification and domination, suppressing uprisings, disciplining others' labor, depriving certain groups of their land or possessions, ending empires or dreams of independence, propping up friendly regimes, and, when necessary, engaging in the labor of killing.

Working-class men in need of jobs dominated the enlisted ranks of the army during the late nineteenth and early twentieth centuries. Immigrants (most from Germany and Ireland) constituted one-third to one-half of all recruits until the 1890s, when Congress passed a law making it more difficult for immigrants to enlist. They then dropped to only one-quarter of the enlisted. Their prevalent occupational background seems to have varied depending upon the economic context. In prosperous times, recruits were more often unskilled laborers; during a depression such as that of 1893 to 1897, army officers noted that they were recruiting more respectable "mechanics, mill men, and laboring men generally." Farmers made up a very small segment of the army. White enlisted men were most often from northern cities; very few came from the South or West. On the other hand, many African Americans serving in the six segregated regiments created after the Civil War came from Southern states, although the share of recruits from border states and the North came to dominate over time.[19]

Workers in these decades made strategic use of military service. Some enlisted in order to secure free transportation to the West, and then quickly deserted. Others served only until they could find better paying work. Army officers struggled to cope with extremely high desertion rates as a result—between 1867 and 1891, an astonishing 88,475 men deserted the army. At its worst, in 1871–72, about one-third of the army deserted each year. There were many causes of desertion: the harsh labor conditions, low pay (starting at $13 per month for most of this period), and scarce and unappetizing food. But officers noted that desertion rates were highest in areas where better-paying jobs were available. Desertion also increased the moment economic depressions lifted. In some regions desertions increased at harvest time. And, reflecting the much more limited economic opportunities as well as the racism and racial violence African Americans across the United States endured, their desertion rates were extremely low during the Gilded Age. In short, military service was a way for working-class men—white or black, native-born or immigrant—to hedge their bets and improve their economic and social circumstances, sometimes relying on service only for very short periods.[20]

Beginning with the insurrection of 1877, the army was employed in suppressing urban protests and strikes. In the 1890s, with the Indian wars drawn to a close, this became especially important and, indeed, many thought the army would now and forever be focused on quelling domestic disturbances. Suppression of the Pullman boycott, the strike at Coeur d'Alene, and a coal miners' strike in Indian Territory all saw the army playing a central role. Under the command of generals like Nelson Miles, the army bluntly and blatantly enforced the demands of capital. This led to condemnation by labor activists as well as politicians and other civilians. During the Pullman boycott, General Miles so exaggerated the amount of disorder—he claimed that anarchism and social revolution were overtaking Chicago—that military leaders found him difficult to control. In the years after Pullman, calls were made to expand both the army and National Guard to better prepare for civil disorder. Yet the close alliance between capital and the army that existed during the 1890s, and the ways army leaders had stoked the flames of crisis, disturbed many. By the early twentieth century, the army continued to be used in civil disputes, but the government took pains to ensure its role was less prejudicial.[21]

Thoughts that the future of the U.S. military lay entirely in suppressing urban insurrections were clearly extinguished as the War of 1898 made overseas expansionism and empire building into a major expression of U.S. global power. On the eve of war with Spain, the U.S. military was smaller than Mexico's. But it grew rapidly to a force of 61,000 enlisted men and 200,000 volunteers.[22] After the short war that allowed the U.S. to take control over what remained of the Spanish Empire, those numbers declined, but when war erupted in the Philippines in early 1899, the army expanded again. From then until the eve of World War I, its size would stand somewhere between 54,000 and 100,000. The most common occupations of those enlisting in the early twentieth century were laborer and farmer; the military remained the choice of men facing financial troubles and relatively few social or economic choices. In these decades service was predominantly overseas, spread across the vast new territories and expansionist commitments of the United States: from Cuba and Puerto Rico to the Panama Canal Zone, from Alaska and Hawai'i to China and the Philippines. The army played a hugely important role in several of these sites, helping the U.S. suppress indigenous insurrection and establish colonial government in the Philippines; occupying Cuba and Haiti; managing and disciplining laborers in Puerto Rico, Hawai'i, and the Philippines; and suppressing civil disorder and protecting the tens of thousands of employees from nations around the world in the Canal Zone.

Soldiers and sailors worked not only to expand the power of the U.S., but also served as the nation's representatives and as mediators between the U.S. empire and people in the sites of conquest. Mary Renda has brought to life the complex role played by military personnel in her examination of Marines who carried out the occupation of Haiti between 1915 and 1934. She portrays the white working-class communities from which recruits were drawn—dockworkers, construction workers, migrant workers—all of them shaped not only by the economic needs and vulnerabilities of working families, but also by images and fantasies of masculinity played out on a global scale. In Haiti, Marines established and represented the power of the United States in diverse ways, disarming Port-au-Prince at the beginning of occupation, putting down rebellions of Cacos, overseeing the vast labor projects involving local labor, or conducting armed patrols to enforce curfews. In dozens of sites, Marines, soldiers, and sailors played similar roles: subduing rebellions, guarding and protecting elections, breaking up strikes, maintaining order on plantations or railroad or canal construction projects. Military personnel occupied a challenging position: they were representatives of the U.S. military and its imperial ideology, harshly disciplined by military superiors and sometimes resentful of that fact. One soldier wrote home from the Philippines about having been sent to the guard house for speaking disrespectfully to a sergeant: "I had not quite got used to being spoken to like a dog by the high and mighty beings called non-commissioned officers."[23] Yet simultaneously soldiers felt superior to those they dominated in the Philippines, Panama, or Cuba, and relied on racial and imperial ideologies to enforce order, often through violent means.[24]

As black and white workingmen entered the U.S. army for service in the wars in Cuba and the Philippines, they were required to navigate through confusing changes in military goals and strategy as well as rapidly transforming power and race relations. When the U.S. imperial project shifted from one designed to liberate the Cubans and Filipinos from Spanish tyranny to one focused on occupying and dominating those islands for the good of U.S. power, world civilization, and general "uplift," the soldiers who labored in the service of the U.S. military found their perspectives shifting as well. Consider the case of a young California blacksmith who volunteered in 1898 in his enthusiasm to curb the power of the corrupt Spanish empire. James Dabney moved from his family's California farm to San Francisco in the 1890s to learn blacksmithing. In early 1898, he joined the 1st California Volunteer Regiment and by June of that year his ship had arrived in the Philippines. At first Dabney was exhilarated by his role as liberator. He wrote to his parents, "The natives like the American boys fine they want to be free they have been murdered and starved to death the same way as the Cubans." For the next several weeks, his letters detailed efforts to capture and imprison Spaniards, often working at the task alongside Filipinos. But by mid-August, the military goals had shifted. They had captured 7,000 "native" prisoners "who have been fighting to capture [M]anila for three years so they thought they could come into the city and do as they pleased but we think differently." In the months to come his references to Filipinos became far more brutal. Dabney explained they were hunting Filipinos as if they were wild animals: "it seems cruel to chase them up and shoot them down like deer but it is their own fault. . . . [w]e don't expect to stand this very long if they don't lay down their arms and surrender pretty soon we will kill and drive them off the earth."[25]

The changing nature of war that had shaped Dabney's perspective was captured best by an old friend. Uncle Riley read all your letters, she related, and "he says it is something terrible for you boys to now have to fight those natives when you enlisted to fight the Spanish. Well it is terrible. I don't think it is right."[26] Dabney's family no longer saved any letters after he departed the Philippines for home. His story reminds us that military service involved more than building roads and fortifications; the hard labor of conquest and killing, and the ways those experiences shaped class and racial formation, were central to the "unfree labor" of military service.

In the late 1960s, the U.S. Army Heritage and Education Center in Carlisle, Pennsylvania, began surveying veterans of the War of 1898 and the U.S.-Philippines war to learn about their experiences. Thousands responded to the survey and, as well, many families sent letters or diaries that capture the world of military service as U.S. empire blossomed. For many working-class men, the military served as a route to at least limited social and economic mobility as well as much needed masculine mentorship. Alabaman David Kennybrook, the son of Scottish immigrants, exemplifies this. Kennybrook grew up in the household of an often unemployed Birmingham steelworker. His daughter described his youth in a long letter sent to the Institute: "my father grew up poorly clothed, poorly housed, poorly fed, and totally uneducated." He enlisted as a 17-year-old during the patriotic surge following the *Maine's* explosion. He served in the Philippines and in China, hoping to make a career of military service, but eventually fell ill and mustered out after some seven years. Kennybrook entered the military completely illiterate but with an ear for language and mimicry. His facility with Filipino dialects led to work as an interpreter, and his illiteracy perhaps explains why he was chosen to work as a courier; unable to read the messages, he worked for a year transmitting notes back and forth between General Elwell Stephen Otis and Civil Governor William Howard Taft. Kennybrook wrote of the usual soldier's complaints of contaminated food, hard tack, harsh discipline, obsolete equipment, and crippling homesickness among his peers.[27]

Kennybrook's daughter summed up her father's service: "Dad went into the army an illiterate boy of 17 years and came out of the army with proof of his manhood, with a broader vision of the world and of life, and with an amazing power of speech . . . he bears to this day the stamp of the courtly manner, the attitudes, and the sophisticated vocabulary of those men with whom he was associated in such a special way under such specifically trying condition. He often says he was educated in the army and might not ever have been educated otherwise." The army may have educated Kennybrook, but it did not teach him to read; in 1969, as he told his stories to the Carlisle Military History Institute, he remained illiterate. Yet after he completed his military service he found work as a legal investigator for railroads and coal companies, and spent the rest of his working life in that occupation.[28]

Many other soldiers focused their tales on the labor of encampment and warfare. Thomas Speer, a farm boy from Connecticut, joined the 11th Cavalry. Stationed in Virginia before heading to the Philippines, he described the work involved: "they slammed us into shape," he said, as he and his fellow recruits trained to ride and work with horses, scrubbed down horse stalls, cleaned and exercised the horses, and rode to parade drill. After all that, soldiers traveled to the Philippines lacking in sufficient horses and learned to fight like infantry. Speer described the nature of warfare as endless small skirmishes. U.S. soldiers would approach a village and begin firing, trying to isolate the enemy-occupied buildings. When they determined where return shots originated from, a few soldiers would torch the huts and then fire upon those who fled the flames. As the smoke cleared, troops examined the dead bodies and many soldiers' letters report trauma and a hardening of emotions particularly upon seeing women and children among the deceased. General Adna Chaffee reflected this in reports to the secretary of war, coldly stating that soldiers had to "withstand the demoralizing influence of prolonged mental strain" as a result of warfare. "Only the officers and men who actually participated in the work of hunting for the enemy in the pathless wilderness of the island can form an appreciative idea of the hardship which the terrain and climate exacted."[29] As in all warfare, central to the labor of killing was a process of distancing soldiers from the humanity of those they battled, and in the Philippines this was aided, at least for white soldiers, by exoticizing and racializing the enemy. If Dabney, above, referred to killing Filipinos as similar to shooting deer, many other white soldiers used racial epithets to separate themselves from their enemies.[30]

The centrality of race in the conquests of U.S. empire placed the thousands of African American soldiers in a complex position. African

American regiments served in the Southwest and Great Plains during the Indian Wars, intervened in the Johnson County War of 1892 which pitted small Wyoming farmers against wealthy ranchers, fought in Cuba during the War of 1898, helped colonize the Philippines when insurrection exploded in 1899, and served in Mexico in 1916. Wondering why they should enlist to support a nation that oppressed them, yet thinking they might win more respect through such service, African American troops embodied the contradictions of race, class, and empire.[31]

Before 1898, before Cuba and the Philippines, African American soldiers were much less likely to desert than were whites. Despite the racism and exploitation they faced in the military, as well as the drudgery and hardship, service there proved far superior to civilian life and its dangers in Jim Crow America. This was true even though, in the West, they confronted opposition and sometimes violence from the white citizens they were protecting—or from white soldiers. Black soldiers also were more likely to reenlist and build a lengthy career out of military service.

With the outbreak of war in 1898, racial hostilities heightened as many black regulars and volunteers were stationed in the South and began to rebel against Jim Crow. In Tampa, African American soldiers pistol whipped the owner of a Tampa drug store who refused to serve them. One group of black volunteers, upon being given white officers when they had been promised black ones, mutinied, refusing to obey any orders. Camped at Macon, Georgia, another group of black soldiers took their guns and an ax and cut down a tree from which lynch victims had hung; then they went about town destroying signs that read "No Niggers or Dogs Allowed." Black soldiers refused to ride in Jim Crow trolley cars, demanding the right to ride in the "white" car, and in several cases conductors responded by shooting them.[32]

When black soldiers headed off to fight Filipinos demanding independence, the contradictions of their role heightened. As the 25th Infantry, an African American regiment, marched into Manila from their ship, white spectators yelled, "What are you coons doing here?" The soldiers shouted back, "We've come to take up the White Man's Burden." Their sense of military duty made many focus on obedience. Yet superiors worried, with good reason, that African American soldiers' sympathy for Filipinos struggling against racial subordination might limit their ability to fight. Black soldiers were certainly alert to the ways the U.S. military officials imposed racial laws and ideologies as part of their effort to dominate Filipinos, whom many felt had a just grievance against the United States. Signs left mysteriously around their camps, urging them not to fight against freedom for Filipinos when they themselves faced lynching and disfranchisement at home, found a sympathetic audience. As a result, while desertion by blacks was almost unheard of during the Indian wars, now it soared. A census taken after the official end of the U.S.-Philippines war found 500 African Americans living in the Philippines, most of them military deserters; others have estimated the number who settled in the Philippines after the war to be 1,200 or more. And to the anger and frustration of military officials, some of those deserters joined with the insurgents to fight against U.S. soldiers. By the end of the war, African Americans' hopes that service would earn them full citizenship were crushed, yet their expectations and transformed perspectives on their nation and their roles as citizens fueled resistance during and after their military service.[33]

In short, the problem of how military service shaped class and racial or ethnic identities is central to understanding the linkages between empire, class, and race at the turn of the twentieth century. Military service could provide a path to class mobility, it could shape accommodation, or it could fuel resistance and protest. Lessons learned through military service shaped understandings of racial hierarchy and more generally of the nation-state, the citizen's role, and the role of the U.S. in the wider world. Military service exemplifies the ways in which empire cloaked the class experience—so much so that the labor it involved has historically been neglected or ignored altogether.

Reassessing the Impact of Empire and Expansionism

U.S. expansionism also influenced understandings *and* expectations of the nation and state, of racial and class hierarchies, and of citizenship itself. Given the expansionist character of the U.S., present from even before the birth of the nation-state, notions of what constitutes "domestic" vs. "foreign" affairs have themselves been historically constructed. With ever-changing territorial boundaries and processes of U.S. global power, defining what constitutes "home" and "abroad" was a fluid historical process filled with significance and causal force. Turning land seized from Native Americans in the Great Plains into a suitable home for white settlers, or constructing the Panama Canal Zone into a "civilized" territory of the U.S. and thereby fit for white skilled workers and their families—these are examples of central dynamics in the expansionist logic of the United States. Such transformed sites also became laboratories for testing what a nation-state could and should do to provide for, manage, and/or discipline its citizens and imperial subjects. Because an ability to hide the imperial character of its international activities is a basic characteristic—indeed, a talent—of the U.S. empire, it has historically been easy to assume that few "domestic" affairs were shaped by that empire. But close examination demonstrates that the empire influenced social, political, and cultural relationships in the U.S. in myriad ways.

After 1900, reformers and interested citizens watched events in Cuba, Puerto Rico, Hawai'i, the Panama Canal Zone, and the Philippines for lessons about what strong state intervention could accomplish. In all these sites, U.S. government officials, given the realities of colonialism and military occupation, possessed far more freedom to enact what they considered ideal policies than was feasible in the United States. The new political culture around Progressivism, with its interest in proactive government and the application of ideas from the social sciences, also shaped U.S. policies around the world. The Panama Canal Zone, where the U.S. government possessed complete control, provides an example. After the U.S. acquired the Canal Zone in 1904 to begin construction of the canal, its first responsibility was to create the infrastructure needed for the mixture of white and African American U.S. citizens, Europeans, and Afro-Caribbeans who would provide the needed labor. The Isthmian Canal Commission built everything needed, from hotels, dormitories, cafeterias, and single-family homes to commissaries, hospitals, fire stations, and post offices. In devising their policies, officials balanced the classic tensions of progressive political culture—between democracy and social control—but with a greater emphasis on the latter. And reformers also sought lessons in events in the Canal Zone about how domestic U.S. policies might be improved. The socialist writer Arthur Bullard was one of many who traveled to the Isthmus of Panama, where he interviewed workers and government officials. He declared that "[t]he more one stays here, the more one realizes that the Isthmian Canal Commission has gone further towards Socialism than any other branch of our government—further probably than any government has ever gone."[34] The government ran everything and with the elimination of the profit incentive, the machine shops hummed along more efficiently, workers were less exploited, and everyone was treated fairly. It was not quite socialism, since the workers did not run the government and there was no democracy. But it provided a powerful example of what collective activity and the elimination of the profit incentive could achieve.

Bullard was not the only one inspired by the government's example in the Canal Zone. Journalists, travel writers, labor activists, reformers, and politicians all found lessons in the successes of the canal project. Miners in Butte, Idaho, for example, who demanded government ownership of the mines pointed to the conditions found in the Canal Zone. In 1908, the editors of *Machinists' Monthly Journal* proclaimed the work of Uncle Sam in the Zone would "hasten the day of universal brotherhood."[35] Even William Gorgas, the renowned medical officer who defeated yellow fever in Cuba and the Isthmus of Panama, got involved. Sounding much like Henry George, Gorgas attributed his triumphs in public health in part to the absence of idle land and the result this had on the ability to pay decent wages and create comfortable living conditions. He called for the U.S. to tax uncultivated land and argued that the result would not only increase wages, but also lower death rates and improve public health and worker efficiency.[36] Remarkably few observers focused on the negative aspects of U.S. policies: the racialized management of labor that relied on a Jim Crow segregation system, the authoritarianism, the extensive use of police and labor spies, the deportation of anyone deemed "unproductive," and the sentencing of idle workers to prison sentences involving hard labor. Indeed, the Zone became a perfect example of Du Bois's argument that imperialism and inhumanity toward some ran alongside progressive advancement for others. White U.S. citizens lived in a virtual utopia in the Canal Zone while people of color and white foreigners were relegated to various liminal positions within the complex racial hierarchy. White U.S. workers not only accepted the segregation policies that shaped life and work in the Zone; they also emerged as key enforcers of it, informing on mixed-race men who sought entry to the clubhouses reserved for whites only.[37]

African Americans in the Canal Zone, a couple hundred in number, felt trapped in an unjust racial system. They were treated better than the tens of thousands of Afro-Caribbeans, yet denied most comforts provided to white U.S. citizens and excluded from white clubhouses and cafeterias. In response, African Americans launched protests on the grounds of their rights as U.S. citizens. In 1909, for example, six blacksmiths working in the town of Empire—the industrial hub of the Canal Zone—protested their bad treatment: "Why should not we American Negroes who assisted in fighting so bravely for the independence of our country not parcipitate [sic] in all the rights and privilidges [sic], which is by far more than what the Panamanian negroes can say."[38] In this case, U.S. imperialism generated notions among African Americans of the benefits their citizenship should provide; at the same time, like white U.S. workers, these blacksmiths assumed that they were entitled to more rights than Afro-Panamanians. Here was the logic of empire that Du Bois had identified, albeit with racial dimensions more complex than he had suggested.

Conclusion

"The race problem," Du Bois wrote, "is the other side of the labor problem." In an era of aggressively expansionist capitalism and imperialism, those who labored in the service of empire hoped to earn a range of benefits. Du Bois argued that white workers' agitation for greater rights and an expansive whites-only democracy meant that they saw their interests and those of the bourgeoisie as identical, and that the classes conspired together to oppress a global, racialized working class. Many white working men and women participated in or supported imperial adventures that exploited and colonized people of color. Yet the analysis here suggests that class and race interacted in a complex and highly contingent way, and that the imperial processes of the U.S. exerted a much broader impact on the workers of empire. Empire could generate wages and benefits for African American as well as white soldiers. The connections between imperialist adventure and evolving notions of citizenship, social hierarchy, and nationalism differed depending on the individuals and historical periods in question, yet for all those connections were complex and requiring of careful interrogation.

In the end, the key point is that race and class formation occurred upon the stage of global capitalism and imperialism.[39] White and African American working people's attitudes toward the state, toward social relations at home, and indeed toward their own identities were formed via the rapidly changing lens of global power and conquest. Empire, in other words, served as a key modality through which class was experienced. In addition, the dynamics of imperial processes changed rapidly—and changed the character of the U.S. empire's working classes rapidly—and their impact was multilayered and uneven. The impact, benefits, and costs of empire, in short, came in many different forms. If they constituted sometimes a psychological wage, we might remember that they came in a wide range of currencies—and sometimes they failed to arrive at all. A broad definition of the international working classes generated by U.S. empire helps us globalize the insights of Thompson, Gutman, and Roediger. The working classes indeed made and remade themselves, but immigration into the metropole formed just one part of a much larger process. As the U.S. empire expanded, as the number of soldiers moving globally to support that empire increased, and as labor systems and strategies of discipline were transformed, the ways of being and thinking and living as working men and women changed as well.

NOTES

1. I am grateful to members of the Race, History, and the State reading group at the National Humanities Center, especially Cindy Hahamovitch, Abigail Manzella, Evelyn Brooks Higginbotham, Luis Cárcamo-Huechante, and Tim Marr, for their suggestions and feedback; and to Jim Maffie for, as always, the dialogue that helped me refine my ideas. My greatest debt is to Daniel Bender and Jana Lipman, for their inspiring leadership on this project and for their insights and editorial help on this article.

2. E. P. Thompson, *The Making of the English Working Class* (New York: Vintage, 1966; orig. 1963); Herbert G. Gutman, "Work, Culture, and Society in Industrializing America, 1815–1919," *American Historical Review* 78 (3), June 1973, 531–88; David Roediger, *The Wages of Whiteness: Race and the Making of the American Working Class* (London: Verso Press, new edition, 2007; orig. 1991).

3. W.E.B. Du Bois, *Black Reconstruction in America, 1860–1880* (New York: Macmillan, 1992; orig. 1935), 15–17; W.E.B. Du Bois, "The African Roots of War," *Atlantic Monthly*, 115 (5), May 1915, 707–14; W.E.B. Du Bois, "The Negro Mind Reaches Out," in *The New Negro, An Interpretation* (New York: Albert and Charles Boni, 1925), 385. I am indebted to Moon-Ho Jung for his advice on Du Bois; see his "*Black Reconstruction* and Empire," *South Atlantic Quarterly* 112 (3), Summer 2013.

4. Stuart Hall, "Race, Articulation and Societies Structured in Dominance," in *Sociological Theories: Race and Colonialism*, ed. UNESCO (Paris: UNESCO, 1980), 341.

5. Perry Anderson is quoted in Leo Panitch and Sam Gindin, *The Making of Global Capitalism: The Political Economy of American Empire* (London: Verso, 2012), 25.

6. Frederick Arthur Mackenzie, *The American Invaders* (London: Grant Richards, 1902); see also Emily Rosenberg, *Financial Missionaries to the World: The Politics and Culture of Dollar Diplomacy, 1900–1930* (Durham, NC: Duke University Press, 2003).

7. On gradated sovereignty, see Ann Laura Stoler, "On Degrees of Imperial Sovereignty," *Public Culture* 18 (1), 2006, 125–46.

8. See, e.g., Rosa Luxemburg, *The Accumulation of Capital* (London: Routledge and Kegan Paul, 1951; orig. 1913); Vladimir Lenin, *Imperialism, the Highest Stage of Capitalism*, accessed September 5, 2013, at http://www.marxists.org/archive/lenin/works/1916/imp-hsc.

9. Fernando Coronil, "After Empire: Reflections on Imperialism from the Americas," in *Imperial Formations*, ed. Ann Laura Stoler, Carole McGranahan, and Peter C. Perdue (Santa Fe: School for Advanced Research Press, 2007), 259.

10. Given the central influence exerted by Marxist thought on the discipline of history over the course of the twentieth century, the notion that the study of capitalism is new seems misguided at best. For foundational books of labor and working-class history concerned with capitalism, although the list is vast, one might see David Montgomery, *The Fall of the House of Labor: The Workplace, the State, and American Labor Activism, 1865–1925* (New York: Cambridge University Press, 1989); Harry Braverman, *Labor and Monopoly Capital: The Degradation of Work in the Twentieth Century* (New York: Monthly Review Press, 1998; orig. 1974); Maurice Dobb, *Studies in the Development of Capitalism* (Whitefish, MT: Kessinger Publishing, 2010; orig. 1947). For an example of claims that the history of capitalism is a new field, see Sven Beckert, "History of American Capitalism," in *American History Now*, ed. Eric Foner and Lisa McGirr (Philadelphia: Temple University Press, 2011), 314–35.

11. Ann Laura Stoler, "On Degrees of Imperial Sovereignty," 127–28.

12. Paul Kramer, "Power and Connection: Imperial Histories of the United States in the World," *American Historical Review* 116 (5), December 2011, 1348–91.

13. Walter L. Williams, "United States Indian Policy and the Debate over Philippine Annexation: Implications for the Origins of American Imperialism," *Journal of American History* 66 (4), March 1980, 810–31. See also Brian DeLay, *War of a Thousand Deserts: Indian Raids and the U.S.-Mexican War* (New Haven, CT: Yale University Press, 2009); Pekka Hämäläinen, *The Comanche Empire* (New Haven, CT: Yale University Press, 2008); Frank Vandiver, *Black Jack: The Life and Times of John J. Pershing* (College Station: Texas A&M Press, 1977); Marie Gorgas and Burton J. Hendrick, *William Crawford Gorgas: His Life and Work* (New York: Doubleday, 1924).

14. Priscilla Murolo, "Wars of Civilization: The US Army Contemplates Wounded Knee, the Pullman Strike, and the Philippine Insurrection," *International Labor and Working-Class History* 80, Fall 2011, 77–102, 83.

15. Richard Slotkin, *Gunfighter Nation: The Myth of the Frontier in Twentieth-Century America* (Norman: Oklahoma University Press, 1998), 88–121.

16. On military service as labor, see Peter Beattie, *The Tribute of Blood: Army, Honor, Race, and Nation in Brazil, 1864–1945* (Durham, NC: Duke University Press, 2001); *International Labor and Working-Class History* 80, Fall 2011, a special issue devoted to military labor.

17. Peter Way, "'Black Service ... White Money': The Peculiar Institution of Military Labor in the British Army during the Seven Years' War," in *Workers across the Americas: The Transnational Turn in Labor History*, ed. Leon Fink, with Eileen Boris, John French, Julie Greene, Joan Sangster, and Shelton Stromquist, associate editors (New York: Oxford University Press, 2011), 57–80. The quotes are on pages 74 and 58. During the copyediting, I encountered A. Hope McGrath's work on soldiering and U.S. empire, and I will be eager to read her dissertation, currently in progress at the University of Pennsylvania: "'An Army of Working-Men': Military Labor and the Construction of American Empire, 1865–1915."

18. Edward M. Coffman, *The Old Army: A Portrait of the American Army in Peacetime, 1784–1898* (New York: Oxford University Press, 1988), 373. See also Michael L. Tate, *The American Army in Transition, 1865–1898* (Westport, CT: Greenwood Press, 2007), 49–51.

19. Coffman, *The Old Army*, 329, 331–32; also Kevin Adams, *Class and Race in the Frontier Army: Military Life in the West, 1870–1890* (Norman: University of Oklahoma Press, 2009).

20. Coffman, *The Old Army*, 339–73. See also Frederick S. Harrod, *Manning the New Navy: The Development of a Modern Naval Enlisted Force, 1899–1940* (Westport, CT: Greenwood Press, 1978); Adams, *Class and Race in the Frontier Army*.

21. Jerry Cooper, *The Army and Civil Disorder: Federal Military Intervention in Labor Disputes, 1877–1900* (Westport, CT: Greenwood Press, 1980), especially the Conclusion; Murolo, "Wars of Civilization"; Clayton D. Laurie, "The United States Army and the Return to Normalcy in Labor Dispute Interventions: The Case of the West Virginia Coal Mine Wars, 1920–1921," *West Virginia History* 50, 1991, 1–24.

22. Mexico's army had 10,000 more men than its U.S. counterpart in 1898. See Edward M. Coffman, *The Regulars: The American Army, 1898–1941* (Cambridge, MA: Belknap Press, 2004), 4.

23. Edward F. Dunbar to Edgar, July 26, 1898, Spanish American War Veterans Survey Collection, Box 1, Folder 30, U.S. Army Heritage and Education Center, Carlisle, Pennsylvania.

24. Mary Renda, *Taking Haiti: Military Occupation and the Culture of U.S. Imperialism* (Chapel Hill: University of North Carolina Press, 2001), especially 66–71. For more on this theme, see Julie Greene, *The Canal Builders: Making America's Empire at the Panama Canal* (New York: Penguin Press, 2009).

25. James Dabney to his parents, July 10, Aug. 14, 1898, and Feb. 14, 1899, Dabney Family Papers, Bancroft Library, University of California at Berkeley. On soldiers in the U.S.-Philippines war, see also James Grant Crawford, "The Warriors of Civilization: Soldiers, American Culture, and the Conquest of the Philippines," Ph.D. dissertation, University of North Carolina, 2002.

26. Lola McGrew to James Dabney, April 21, 1899, Dabney Family Papers.

27. David Kennybrook, Company K, 23rd Regiment, Box 58, Folder 16, Spanish American War Veterans Survey Collection, U.S. Army Heritage and Education Center.

28. *Ibid.*

29. Thomas Speer, Spanish American War Veterans Survey Collection, Box 43, Folder 41, U.S. Army Heritage and Education Center; for General Chaffee's comment, see John Albright, "A Vignette of Imperialism: The 11th Cavalry in the Philippines, 1901–1904," also within the Speer Folder.

30. For an example of racial language, see the letters of Edward F. Dunbar, Spanish American War Veterans Survey Collection, Box 1, Folder 30, U.S. Army Heritage and Education Center.

31. The most illuminating work on African American soldiers in the U.S.-Philippines war is Cynthia L Marasigan, "'Between the Devil and the Deep Sea': Ambivalence, Violence, and African-American Soldiers in the Philippine-American War and Its Aftermath," Ph.D. dissertation, University of Michigan, 2010. On African American military service in the late nineteenth and early twentieth centuries, see also William A. Dobak and Thomas D. Phillips, *The Black Regulars, 1866–1898* (Norman: University of Oklahoma Press, 2001); Quintard Taylor, *In Search of the Racial Frontier: African Americans in the American West, 1528–1990* (New York: W. W. Norton & Company, 1998); Charles L. Kenner, *Buffalo Soldiers and Officers of the Ninth Cavalry, 1867–1898: Black and White Together* (Norman: University of Oklahoma Press, 1999); John M. Carroll, ed., *The Black Military Experience in the American West* (New York: Liverlight, 1971); Willard B. Gatewood, Jr., *Black Americans and the White Man's Burden, 1898–1903* (Champaign: University of Illinois Press, 1975); Elizabeth D. Leonard, *Men of Color to Arms! Black Soldiers, Indian Wars, and the Quest for Equality* (W. W. Norton & Company, 2010).

32. Dobak and Phillips, *The Black Regulars, 1866–1898*, especially 242; George W. Prioleau, Ninth Cavalry, to Editor, *Christian Recorder*, October 1, 1898, in Willard B. Gatewood, Jr., *"Smoked Yankees" and the Struggle for Empire: Letters from Negro Soldiers, 1898–1902* (Fayetteville: University of Arkansas Press, 1987), 24, 74–76. See also Willard B. Gatewood, Jr., "Negro Troops in Florida, 1898," *Florida Historical Quarterly*, 49 (1), July 1970, 1–15; and Amy Kaplan, "Black and Blue on San Juan Hill," in *Cultures of United States Imperialism*, ed. Amy Kaplan and Donald E. Pease (Durham, NC: Duke University Press, 1993), 219–36.

33. Gatewood, *"Smoked Yankees"*; Marasigan, "'Between the Devil and the Deep Sea,'" 47; Oscar V. Campomanes, "Figures of the Unassimilable: American Empire,

Filipino American Postcoloniality, and the U.S.-Philippine War of 1898–1910s," Ph.D. dissertation, Brown University, 2011.

34. Arthur Bullard, *Panama: The Canal, the Country, and the People* (New York: Macmillan, 1911), 562. See also Albert Edwards, "Testing Socialism in the Canal Zone," in *The Amana Society: A Study in Co-operation, from the Viewpoint of a Socialist* (Girard, KS: A.W. Ricker, n.d.), 55–83.

35. Joint Strike Bulletin, July 9, 1917, issued by the Metal Miners Union and the Electrical Workers' Union in Butte, Butte-Silver Bow Public Archives, Labor History Collection, Butte, Montana; *Machinists' Monthly Journal*, Oct. 1908, 20 (10), 872.

36. Henry George, *Progress and Poverty: An Inquiry into the Cause of Industrial Depressions, and of Increase of Want with Increase of Wealth: the Remedy* (New York: Appleton, 1882); on Gorgas and the single tax see "Tax Idle Land to Aid Health, Plan of Gorgas," *Chicago Daily Tribune*, Sep. 7, 1915, 7.

37. For more on this see Greene, *The Canal Builders*. On racialized labor management, see also David R. Roediger and Elizabeth C. Esch,, *The Production of Difference: Race and the Management of Labor in U.S. History* (New York: Oxford University Press, 2012).

38. Charlie Walker, John Hicks, Charlie Woodard, A. Benson, Tom. Onsley, Sandy Odom, Blacksmiths of the Mechanical Department of Empire, to George Goethals, Jan. 13, 1909, ICC Records 2-C-55, U.S. National Archives, RG 85, U.S. National Archives and Record Administration, College Park, Maryland.

39. See Linda Colley, *Captives: Britain, Empire, and the World, 1600–1850* (New York: Anchor Books, 2004), ch. 10, 334–35.

2

Revolutionary Currents

Interracial Solidarities, Imperial Japan, and the U.S. Empire

MOON-HO JUNG

Infused by a wave of migrations and radical politics, Harlem was abuzz at the end of World War I. And no one demanded to be heard more than Hubert Harrison, the self-described "radical internationalist" whose West Indian roots had led him to see beyond Harlem, beyond the United States. "We must organize, plan and act, and the time for the action is now," he argued in 1921. "A call should be issued for a congress of the darker races, which should be frankly anti-imperialistic and should serve as an international center of cooperation from which strength may be drawn for the several sections of the world of color." His call for "a colored international" beckoned "representatives and spokesmen of the oppressed peoples of India, Egypt, China, West and South Africa, and the West Indies, Hawaii, the Philippines, Afghanistan, Algeria, and Morocco." Building on V. I. Lenin's theorization of imperialism as "the monopoly stage of capitalism" by placing race at the heart of his analysis, Harrison argued that "capitalist imperialism" was the common enemy, "which mercilessly exploits the darker races for its own financial pur-poses . . . [and] which we must combine to fight with arms as varied as those by which it is fighting to destroy our manhood, independence and self-respect." He was calling for a revolutionary politics across racial and national borders, a kind of global and interracial solidarity that exceeded and challenged the nation-state form. The U.S. state, in turn, kept a close eye on Harrison's activities.[1]

On the other side of the world, a wave of migrations and radical politics likewise pulsated across the islands of Hawai'i. In very concrete terms, Japanese and Filipino workers were forging a local "colored in-ternational" against "capitalist imperialism" and initiated a massive labor strike in 1920 that reverberated across the Pacific. Lieutenant Colonel George M. Brooke of the Military Intelligence Division (MID) grew alarmed. When a Japanese worker agreed to return to work on Aiea plantation, Brooke reported to his superiors in Washington, D.C., his compatriots seized and carried him to a labor rally in Honolulu. "He was taken to the platform and compelled to sit there for fifteen minutes facing the audience, from which came fierce cries of 'Kill him,'" he stated. To Brooke, such confrontations illustrated the racial solidarity of Japanese workers, not their political differences. "This may be a case of labor against capital, but it sounds more like a declaration of final racial allegiance," the MID agent surmised. "It is a reflection of Pan Asianism." For many workers, however, the labor strike represented a local expression of a wider struggle against capital and empire. "The strikers, therefore," a Japanese-language newspaper argued during the strike, "should be very careful in their conduct in making the present strike a lawful one to win the victory of industrial democracy over capitalistic imperialism and not only the laborers themselves but all the others may share the fortune and happiness of the victory."[2]

As radical appeals for interracial movements against white supremacy and colonialism echoed around the world, from Harlem to Hawai'i and beyond, the U.S. state reacted vigilantly and violently. More than the personal inclinations of individual agents like Brooke, such responses were endemic to the modern nation-state. The formation of the modern rational state in the sixteenth and seventeenth centuries, Michel Foucault observed, correlated with "the elimination of the imperial theme." It was not that empires disappeared, far from it, but that a "new historical perception" emerged, "no longer focused on the end of time and the unification of all particular sovereignties in the empire of the last days." The new perception fixated instead on "an indefinite time" of inter-state struggles for survival. The "raison d'État" now rested on a "military-diplomatic technology" (the development of the state's forces through international alliances and armed apparatuses) and the "police" ("the set of means for bringing about the internal growth of the state's forces"). The new matrix of state power, driven to increase wealth and population (workers, armies), Foucault argued, evolved into "political economy," wherein the "population" was no longer "the simple sum of subjects who inhabit a territory" but "a variable dependent on a number of factors, and these are by no means all natural." But those factors could be "rationally analyzed" to appear natural, ripe for "concerted interventions" legally and culturally.[3] That is, the emergence of the modern nation-state proved integral to rationalizing, advancing, and eliding empire, processes that interracial labor movements in Hawai'i and elsewhere exposed and challenged.

Perceived and framed persistently by officials of the U.S. state as a racial and international conflict between the United States and Japan, the 1920 labor strike and its aftershocks, on one level, elided the circuits of empire that had shaped U.S. claims to sovereignty over and its exercise of state interventions in Hawai'i. Scarcely twenty years after the U.S. state claimed Hawai'i—along with the Philippines, Guam, and Puerto Rico—the imperial theme disappeared. The labor strike, on another level, revealed and represented a series of what Foucault called "counter-conducts," acts that redistributed, reversed, nullified, and partially or totally discredited U.S. domination. Through incipient, if fleeting, interracial solidarities, plantation workers engaged in "counter-conducts" that drove the U.S. state to fortify its armed and policing apparatuses.[4] And the dialectics of radical organizing and state reaction pivoted around race and empire, the sources behind labor migrations and movements and the emergent raison d'état. Those widespread and intense struggles, in turn, justified and produced a U.S. national security state spanning the Pacific that sanctified and naturalized the nation-state form and, in turn, monitored and criminalized radical movements and interracial solidarities. If the 1920 labor strike in Hawai'i bore a momentary testament to "a colored international" that Harrison and others called for, its brutal repression marked a new phase of the U.S. empire, where "domestic" and "foreign" politics converged in a seemingly endless racial and international confrontation with imperial Japan.

Striking Hawai'i

The 1920 labor strike in Hawai'i was decades in the making. Galvanized by commercial treaties between Hawai'i and the United States beginning in 1876, the sugar industry grew exponentially in the last quarter of the nineteenth century to dominate Hawaii's physical and social landscape. That phenomenal growth—from 12,540 tons in 1875 to 289,544 tons in 1900—rested fundamentally on the backbreaking labor of workers under penal contract, beginning with Native Hawaiian and Chinese workers and increasingly dependent on recruits from Japan. By 1902, Japanese workers made up 73.5 percent of the plantation labor force. It was a system of migrant labor pervasive in sugar-exporting colonies around the world in the nineteenth century, predicated on lip service to freedom and formal rights and daily realities of superexploitation. The accelerated and expanded flow of sugar to the U.S. market also rendered the Kingdom of Hawai'i essentially a colony of the United States, all except in name. The U.S. annexation of Hawai'i in 1898, following a coup d'état by the *haole* elite five years earlier, removed all legal vestiges of nominal independence, formalizing U.S. claims to sovereignty over the islands, the same year the United States laid similar claims over the Philippines, Guam, and Puerto Rico.[5] America's colonial archipelago stretched around the world, a world produced and inhabited by workers.

The passage of the Organic Act in 1900, which prohibited penal labor contracts in Hawai'i, generated a new wave of labor struggles among sugar plantation workers, as the frequency and size of labor strikes increased dramatically. When Motoyuki Negoro, an attorney based in Honolulu, suggested the need for greater organization and immediate action in 1908, the Japanese community came together to form the Higher Wages Association (HWA). When sugar planters rebuffed HWA's appeals for wage increases—to be on par with Portuguese and Puerto Rican workers—and better working conditions, seven thousand Japanese workers staged an islandwide strike on O'ahu beginning in May 1909. Hawaii's sugar planters, unified under the Hawaiian Sugar Planters' Association (HSPA), retaliated vigorously and viciously, vowing never to concede to workers' demands. They evicted striking workers and their families, hired Native Hawaiian, Chinese, Korean, and Portuguese strikebreakers, established an espionage network to monitor the HWA, and conspired with the police to arrest and imprison labor leaders. "I took the position in making these arrests," explained the high sheriff of the territory, "that the Higher Wages Association, together with its organ, the Nippu Jiji [a Japanese-language newspaper], was a criminal organization, organized in the first instance with the deliberate plan to violate the law in carrying out the purposes of that organization." The violent campaign of repression brought the strike to an end by August 1909.[6]

Partly in response to the massive strike, sugar planters turned to the Philippines to recruit new workers. After years of lobbying U.S. officials in the Philippines, the HSPA had secured permission from the Philippine Commission in 1906 to transport Filipino workers under three-year contracts, with fixed wages, an arrangement that did not take root fully until the 1909 strike. The number of Filipino recruits skyrocketed afterward, rising rapidly from a mere 0.3 percent of Hawaii's plantation labor force that year to 19.3 percent five years later. Upon hearing of the possible legal prohibition of Filipino emigration to Hawaiʻi by the Philippine legislature in 1914, William Matson of the Matson Navigation Company, which was owned and controlled principally by Hawaii's big sugar firms, pleaded for a reconsideration. "[I]f the Japanese see no new element ready to replace them," he explained, "their tendency to be overbearing will undoubtedly assert itself on all occasions, with the danger of strikes and other disturbances." It was "a matter of concern to the National Government . . . ," he warned ominously, "particularly from the standpoint of the Military authorities." Filipino migration continued. In contrast, the number of Japanese workers declined precipitously, as fresh memories of the strike and its brutal repression drove them off the plantations. By 1919, Japanese workers continued to form the majority of the sugar plantation labor force (54.7 percent), but the shift to Filipino workers (22.9 percent) was decisively underway.[7]

The stage was set for a bigger standoff between planters and workers. In response to the 1909 strike, planters had instituted in 1911 a bonus pay system attached to the sugar market—the higher the price of sugar, the higher workers' bonus payments. During World War I, as sugar prices soared, bonus payments made up an increasing percentage of workers' annual earnings, rising from 5 percent in 1914 to 20 percent a year later. In 1917, as sugar prices continued to rise, Hawaii's sugar planters decided to reverse course, arbitrarily lowering the bonus rate and, to discourage labor mobility, withholding half of all bonus payments until the end of the year (under the former policy, four-fifths of bonus payments had been withheld every six months). Workers, in the meantime, received no increase in their basic wage rates despite ever higher costs of living, trends that persisted after the war's conclusion. "Our object in dis[cu]ssing the labor question is to improve the position of the Oriental Laborer in his relation to the labor situation," stated a fiery editorial in *Hawaii Hochi*.

"THE JAPANESE LABORERS MUST BE PAID THE SAME WAGES AS THE PORTUGUESE AND HAWAIIANS in order that they may escape severe and unbearable hardships and what we say is not at all dangerous."[8]

Japanese workers organized, fired by their distressed circumstances and stirrings on both sides of the Pacific. As in Hawai'i, food prices in Japan rose exponentially during World War I, a situation created and exacerbated by the Japanese government's stockpiling of rice for the military. In the summer of 1918, a wave of "rice riots" engulfed Japan, as millions of ordinary women and men stormed into the streets to protest high food prices and government policies. Protests rocked the U.S. mainland a year later, as more than four million workers waged strikes from coast to coast, often coming to violent blows with state militias and federal troops. On plantations across Hawai'i, Japanese workers eagerly discussed these movements afoot in their ancestral homeland and in the U.S. metropole and took stock of their own predicament. They congregated in countless meetings facilitated through the Young Men's Buddhist Association (YMBA), a socio-religious organization intimately rooted in plantation communities. Through the fall of 1919, workers organized local plantation unions across the islands of Hawai'i, making demands for higher wages and better working conditions, including the reformation or the elimination of the unpredictable bonus system. On December 1, 1919, the local unions converged in Honolulu to ally themselves into the Federation of Japanese Labor (FJL).[9]

Filipino workers organized a parallel and at times convergent movement. The main force behind the formation of the Filipino Labor Union (FLU) in August 1919 was Pablo Manlapit, who had arrived in Hawai'i in 1910 as a plantation worker under contract. Born to a working-class family in southern Luzon, Manlapit worked a series of jobs as a teenager in the U.S.-occupied Philippines, until he was fired for trying to organize a labor union. In 1913, he spearheaded a labor strike on his plantation on the island of Hawai'i, for which the HSPA promptly blacklisted him. Three years later, he joined an interracial longshoremen's strike and received a beating for urging Filipinos to stop working as strikebreakers. While studying to become an attorney in his spare time in 1919, Manlapit conversed with plantation workers on their plight and emerged as the president of FLU by the summer's end. And he readily recognized the need to cooperate with the local Japanese labor movement. "Japanese and Filipino laborers should get together and work [for] their mutual benefit as the interests of both parties are practically the same," he stated before Japanese workers in October 1919. Two months later, FJL and FLU put forward to the HSPA common demands for wage raises, eight-hour work days, and regular bonus payments (75 percent paid monthly).[10]

The planters' reply precipitated the strike. Without officially recognizing the workers' demands, the HSPA immediately announced a policy on bonus payments in line with the workers' call and established a new office to inquire into living conditions on the plantations. The HSPA flatly rejected all other demands, uniting and dividing workers in the process. Both unions had already resolved to strike if their demands were not met, but they disagreed on how and when to move forward. The FLU wanted to strike immediately, perhaps as early as December 20, 1919. Heeding lessons from 1909, the FJL attempted to petition the HSPA once more and to bide time until the late spring or early summer, when the harvest would be in full swing and their strike fund would be in better shape. The FJL was able to convince Manlapit and the FLU to postpone their strike deadline to January 19, 1920. When Manlapit tried to delay the strike again on January 17, upon another request by the FJL, he discovered that he lacked the resources to reach the rank and file in time. On January 20, 1920, 2,600 Filipino workers and several hundred other workers walked off their jobs. With many Japanese workers refusing to cross the picket lines, out of sympathy and fear, and the HSPA repudiating any move toward concession or conciliation, the FJL voted to strike beginning on February 1. Involving upward of 8,300 workers (77 percent of the plantation labor force on the island of O'ahu), the strained and fragile alliance of Filipino and Japanese workers brought sugar production to a halt.[11]

U.S. authorities took notice right away, interpreting the strike as a racial and radical movement against U.S. interests across the Pacific. "Manla Pit [sic] principal Filipino agitation," George M. Brooke of the MID telegrammed his superiors after the Filipino workers initiated the strike. "It is expected that the Japanese will strike. By an intense campaign of agitation, the entire Japanese language press is encouraging the Filipinos and urging the Japanese to strike. . . . Shimpo urges a red flag parade of the Japanese in Honolulu. This agitation has the appearance of centralized propaganda. A general unrest, financial losses and anti-American feeling are the results." He became more alarmed two days later, after learning that Filipino veterans of the U.S. military had developed plans to organize fellow Filipino workers into "military camps" and that some Chinese workers had also gone on strike. "Strongly suspect that the Japanese government is behind this movement, which is wide and concerted," Brooke surmised. "It expresses pan-American-Asianisum [sic]." He requested "more white troops here" right away to preserve "safety." On the eve of Japanese workers joining the strike, Brooke grew more certain of its racial bases. "It is not too much to say that the study of this situation leads to the presumption that the Japanese Government is behind this movement . . . in order to weld together and to whip into line the oriental population of this territory in the furtherance of its Pan Asian policies," he concluded. "We have, in other words, a powerful, potential and masked enemy in our midst."[12]

Brooke's hyperbolic rhetoric duplicated and reinforced planter propaganda. "Is control of the industrialism of Hawaii to remain in the hands of Anglo-Saxons or is it to pass into those of alien Japanese Agitators?" asked the pro-planter *Honolulu Star-Bulletin*. The strike was nothing but "a dark conspiracy to Japanize this American territory," a threat the planters would fight "to the end, no matter what the cost, the delay, or the inconvenience might be." The stakes were too high for anything less, according to the newspaper. "A compromise of any nature or any degree with the alien agitators would be a victory for them and an indirect but nonetheless deadly invasion of American sovereignty in Hawaii," it proclaimed. The contention that the strike represented alien agitators' growing influence over Hawai'i quickly became the standard refrain of the strike's opponents. "Being steadfastly and unalternably [sic] opposed to any alien or nationalistic domination of the sugar industry within this American territory," the HSPA's president argued, "we are resolved never to permit it under any guise or form." At the first territorywide convention of the American Legion, which met coincidently in February 1920, its members adopted "100% Americanism" as their top mission, to promote it and to root out "disloyalty, alien propaganda and activities, lawlessness." "A clear understanding of these things is the sovereign antidote for anti-American propaganda of all sorts, for Bolshevism and all the rest," the leader of Hawaii's American Legion proclaimed.[13]

Anticipating such reactions, which echoed planters' responses to striking Japanese workers in 1909, the FJL took great pains to deflect them from the outset. "We consider it a great privilege and pride to live under the Stars and Stripes," delegates to the FJL's inaugural meeting declared in December 1919, "which stands for freedom and justice, as a factor of this great industry and as a part of the labor of Hawaii." When a strike appeared imminent, the FJL stressed to its members the need for patience and peace. "*And In Particular*, if a strike of Japanese labor shall be called, our countrymen and countrywomen are requested and cautioned to quit their places in a quiet and peaceable manner, delivering tools to the plantations, and doing no damage to property," the FJL secretary cautioned, "and, MOST PARTICULARLY, to refrain from disputes with, or assaults upon either the remaining laborers, or the officers of the plantations, or any strike-breakers who may be engaged to take your places." Embracing and appealing to U.S. nationalism—ironically, earnestly, or wearily—formed a critical aspect of plantation workers' repertoire of "counter-conducts." "We want peace and order; we love labor and production," the FJL insisted in its final report on the strike. "But when we think of the group of capitalists who show no sympathy whatever toward the struggling laborers, turn deaf ears to their cries and reject their just and reasonable demands under the pretense that they are formulated by 'agitators,' we cannot remain silent. We must act. And so we went on strike . . . honorably and bravely, as laborers living under the great flag of freedom and justice."[14]

Facing an onslaught of planter propaganda, the FJL issued a statement to the public in February 1920 to explain at length the material conditions prevailing on the plantations. "We admit that laborers are furnished free houses," the FJL noted. "But what kind of houses are they? Many of them are such that they do not permit of sitting space when two beds are put in. How about the kitchen? There are stoves made of empty kerosene tins in them. And how about the toilet? They are hardly endurable." The strike was strictly about improving workers' laboring and living conditions, nothing else. "The present movement in favor of higher wages for labor, is an economic movement, pure and simple," Japanese workers declared in refutation of the planters' and English-language dailies' charges. "It is entirely dissociated from any considerations of local or foreign politics, as well as from questions of the advantage or disadvantage to other groups of nationals resident in Hawaii, as such. . . . The suggestion, frequently put forward in print, that 'the Filipinos are simply being used as a cat's paw by the Japanese' . . . has no more foundation in reality than any other untruth." Although the FJL would "receive with gratitude every act of assistance, whether material or otherwise," it had no interest in the "racial composition of our associates" or the Japanese government. "The Federation has no official connection (not even a backstairs connection) with the Japanese Government or any of its officials, whether resident in Japan or in Hawaii," the FJL stressed.[15]

As a settlement appeared nowhere in sight, a committee of prominent whites and elite Japanese headed by Reverend Albert W. Palmer proposed a plan for the "common good." The Palmer Plan sought to remove the source behind "the widespread suspicion that the causes of the strike are not only economic but racial and nationalistic." Purportedly to restore "the spirit of aloha and good will between races," the plan called on the FJL to "recognize the unwisdom and peril of any such organization along racial lines and that it therefore call off the present strike, abandon the field of plantation labor and thus leave that field clear for an organization of the employees within the sugar industry itself and so arranged as to be inter-racial in scope." The committee asked the HSPA, in turn, to establish through an election "an employees' committee" on each plantation "to confer with the plantation manager in securing the utmost cooperation between the management and the men." The FJL appealed to Acting Governor Curtis P. Iaukea to highlight the plan's absurdity. The Palmer Plan "proposes, in short, that we shall dissolve our organization, efface ourselves as a compact of laborers–throw up our hands, shout 'Kamarad'—and return to our work as before the strike, leaving the equities to be adjusted or not adjusted—by a series of fantastic committees . . . that will be (to a great extent) under the control of the plantation managers, and that will have no 'teeth,'" the FJL argued. "Workmen's sovi[e]ts, in short, but destitute of any of the powers of the soviet, as we have come to understand it."[16]

If the strike placed Japanese "agitation" and "invasion" in the spotlight, even in denial, that racial framing hinged on acknowledging, indeed exalting, the U.S. empire. Any talk of "Anglo-Saxon" dominance and "100% Americanism" could not but point to an imperial past and present in Hawai'i. In a sermon on "The Strike Situation" to promote his plan, Palmer began by acknowledging the centennial of Christian missions in Hawai'i. "A hundred years ago a band of brave and devoted missionaries came to build a Kingdom of God in these islands, to bring justice, peace and brotherhood to savage tribes," he said. If those white Christians successfully fought off "tyranny, slavery and despotism," their descendants faced new forms of savagery in their midst. To his credit, Palmer attempted to provide some credence to workers' complaints— "there must have been, on some plantations at least, real grievances or the agitators could not have gotten a hearing"—but he discredited the labor movement wholesale by replicating the planters' racial charge that it had the appearance of "a nationalistic Japanese movement, using the Filipinos as tools, but aiming at Japanese control of the sugar industry and the islands." The strike's continuance would have dire consequences, according to Palmer, with the hastening of "moral degradation," the slowing down of "Americanization," and "the deepening and embittering of race antagonisms." "Organization will be driven into secrecy and a fertile ground will have been prepared for Bolshevist and other destructive and revolutionary social teachings," he preached.[17]

Belatedly and begrudgingly accepted by the FJL in principle and categorically rejected by the HSPA, which refused to engage the FJL, the Palmer Plan fell by the wayside. The debates around the strike and the Palmer Plan, however, heightened the contradictions of race and nationalism, so much so that they compelled critiques of the U.S. empire. A longtime diplomat for the Kingdom of Hawai'i before the *haole* coup d'état, Acting Governor Iaukea was accustomed to the sugar planters' duplicity and hypocrisy. Taking the helm of the territory during the *haole* governor's absence, Iaukea sought to work toward a compromise and commended the Palmer Plan as a step in the right direction. Unlike Palmer, Iaukea offered a sharp rebuke of the HSPA in the process. "I wish we had more such men [like Palmer] in this country," Iaukea stated, "for there would be no reason then for all this hullabaloo about 100 percent Americanism." Demanding concrete evidence of a Japanese conspiracy if there was one, he expressed his "mistrust" of the planters. "For quite a while there has been such pressure brought to bear upon me to petition the United States government to use its military forces against the strikers," he explained. "It is a matter of history that armed forces of the United States were used to overawe the Hawaiians at the time of the overthrow of the monarchy, and there seems to be a desire to repeat this measure of intimidation."[18]

Likening Japanese and Filipino plantation workers to Native Hawaiians—all subject to *haole* domination and potentially U.S. military intervention—recalled a history of race and empire that the HSPA, the American Legion, and Palmer embraced but tried to erase. It was much easier to hide behind the cloak of "Americanism." But Iaukea and others forcibly removed that cloak—the emperor's new clothes, so to speak—to generate sympathy, however limited, for the striking workers. He could not understand the planters' motives to call for "any military display . . . that might seriously endanger the relations of the United States and Japan," Iaukea stated. "Perhaps the kindliest construction would be to consider that, like the rest of capital, they are the first to resent government control of their property and the first to ask that government for aid when they think they are threatened." Snubbed by the planters, Palmer attempted to disentangle race and "Americanism," an impossible task, particularly for this reverend. "Let us have faith, courage, grit, determination and make Hawaii 100 per cent American. . . . . The Oriental who gives to Red Cross and Liberty loans and is capable of organizing a labor union (typically an Anglo-Saxon organization) is already far more Americanized" than otherwise, he pleaded. "Democracy in the public schools, the playground, the Boy Scouts, the church, and the utter denial of democracy in industry promotes Bolshevism and anarchy, not Americanism." Another Native Hawaiian politician had cut to the chase earlier, reminding those in Hawai'i of a self-evident truth. "The fact is that Haoles draw the color line more than any other people," he said.[19]

The struggles of Filipino workers likewise brought to the fore a history of the U.S. empire, even as they made claims on U.S. nationalism for their own ends. Beginning in mid-February, the HSPA began evicting striking workers and their families from their plantation homes, resulting in the displacement of 12,020 persons, including 4,127 children. The FJL responded by setting up makeshift homes to minimize Japanese and Filipino workers' hardship, particularly amid an influenza epidemic then spreading across Hawai'i. When three hundred Filipinos relocated to an old sake brewery, the Honolulu Board of Health ordered them removed for violating the city's sanitary code, a turn of events that shocked local residents. "Filipino people who are under protection of the Stars and Stripes are being threatened with 'actual killing' by the white Americans," a local Japanese newspaper reported. The degree to which living under the flag afforded Filipino workers protection was questionable at best, but Filipino claims to America served as a bitter reminder that chickens had come home to roost. When Manlapit, the FLU president, announced an end to the Filipino laborers' strike on February 9, 1920, it did not mark his finest hour. But it was a moment of racial incongruities. Perhaps bribed by the HSPA, a charge he denied, Manlapit decried the Japanese as "an unscrupulous alien race" plotting to take over Hawai'i. "As Americans we cannot be parties to any such a program and it becomes our duty as citizens of the United States to help the people of Hawaii to break the strangle hold which the Japanese community is trying to obtain upon it," he stated.[20]

The Filipino rank and file remained on strike, forcing Manlapit to retract his call, but the HSPA's entrenched position and policies—no concession or recognition, mass eviction and espionage, and legal and criminal harassment—had their grinding effect. In early April 1920, approximately three thousand Japanese and Filipino workers, families, and supporters paraded in Honolulu in support of the strike. They carried U.S. flags, portraits of President Abraham Lincoln, and banners with slogans that aimed to minimize their radicalism and maximize their "Americanism." "We Want to Live Like Americans," "We Pledge to God That We Are Not Radicals," "God Has Created Us Equal," "We Believe in Lincoln's Ideas," they proclaimed. The pro-planter *Honolulu Star-Bulletin* essentially vowed racial revenge, stating, "Americans do not take kindly to the spectacle of several thousand alien Asiatics parading through the streets with banners flaunting their hatred of Americanism and American institutions and insulting the memory of the greatest American president since Washington." The parade turned out to be the strike's last gasp. With new recruits from the Philippines and nonstriking and returning workers, sugar production resumed almost full force by the end of April. On July 1, 1920, the FJL, renamed the Hawaii Laborers' Association, formally announced the strike's end, praising workers for their resolve and admitting, perhaps unwittingly, the power of the U.S. empire. "You have faithfully stood to the last this long strike, as inhabitants under the rule of the United States, respecting and obeying its laws, as members of this association, and as laborers, preserving your honor and dignity," the statement read.[21] The empire had won.

Seeing Race like a State

The racial idea that Filipino workers represented mere "catspaws" to Japanese "agitators" proved central to the HSPA campaign to delegitimize the strike's demands and to malign the Japanese as the greatest threat to U.S. national security. Indeed, the HSPA, the English-language press, and U.S. military intelligence voiced little to no concern over Filipino workers during the 1920 strike, dismissing them generally as gullible dupes ensnared in a wider Japanese conspiracy. Particularly given that Filipino workers walked off their jobs first, pressing Japanese workers to do likewise, such racial depictions seemed conspicuously at odds with what was happening on the ground. Admittedly somewhat far afield, in his study of catastrophic state projects of the twentieth century, James C. Scott contrasts central elements of the modern state—"the administrative ordering of nature and society," the "high-modernist ideology" of unwavering faith in scientific and technical progress—and local knowledge, or "mētis." The fundamental cause behind social engineering fiascos, he argues, was "the *imperialism* of high-modernist, planned social order." There was nothing faulty about bureaucratic planning or high-modernist ideology per se, according to Scott, but disaster struck with the emergence of "an imperial or hegemonic planning mentality that excludes the necessary role of local knowledge and know-how."[22] The racialization of Filipino and Japanese workers in Hawai'i, in a sense, excluded or dismissed local radicalizing contexts and conditions, placing larger imperial circuits of knowledge front and center as the U.S. state devised military and political plans in the first decades of the twentieth century. Seeing race like a state would lead to fiascos suffered by local peoples of the U.S. empire.

The racial formation of the Japanese as "alien agitators" seeking to undermine U.S. sovereignty took root years earlier, not in Hawai'i but in the Philippines. In the wake of Japan's victory in the Russo-Japanese War (1904–1905), historian Reynaldo C. Ileto reminds us, nationalist activists across colonized Asia looked to Japan as a source of inspiration. In the Philippines, where the United States had recently claimed military victory and continued to encounter insurgencies, the specter of Japanese intervention against the United States sparked hopes for a new stage of the Philippine Revolution. Casting the United States as the "Russia of the

Orient," nationalist newspapers in the Philippines spread visions of U.S. military defeat, with reports of Filipinos "saying in all the meetings of workmen that the United States would not conquer Japan." Artemio Ricarte, a general who had fought against Spain and then the United States, embodied the spirit of the renewed independence movement. Captured and exiled in Guam during the U.S.-Philippine War, Ricarte was imprisoned by U.S. authorities for sedition in 1904. Upon his release in 1910, he refused to salute the Stars and Stripes, a crime for which he was deported to Hong Kong, where he proceeded to organize the Consejo Revolucionario de Filipinas, which demanded the "immediate and complete independence and the equalization of wealth." He relocated to Japan in 1915. Reports and rumors of Ricarte returning to the Philippines, with the support of Japan, circulated widely among Filipino working peoples.[23]

Within that historical and geopolitical context, the modern U.S. security apparatus—which, Alfred W. McCoy argues, had germinated and proliferated in the Philippines during and after the U.S.-Philippine War—began gathering intelligence reports for a potential war with Japan soon after the Russo-Japanese War. In perhaps one of the earliest global surveys of U.S. national security interests, Lieutenant Colonel T. W. Jones of the Military Information Division (the precursor to the Military Intelligence Division) submitted to the War Department's chief of staff in 1907 a confidential report on the "Activities of Japanese and Japanese Officials in Relation to the United States and Her Possessions." Although Japanese workers formed the majority of the plantation labor force and were initiating labor struggles that would lead to the 1909 strike, Jones surprisingly paid scant attention to Hawai'i (three pages in a fifty-seven-page report). Toward the end of 1906, he noted, there were rumors of Japanese organizing militarily on the islands, with some residents brazenly engaging in drill exercises. "Upon investigation, it was found that drilling was going on in the Nuwana Avenue School," Jones reported. "Very careful investigation of this story revealed the fact that about twenty-five or thirty Chinese had been drilling there, getting ready for the celebration of the Chinese New Year." That was the extent of his coverage of Hawai'i, except to draw racial concerns over the utter lack of democracy. "This condition may result in danger in the future," he concluded, "as there is probability of friction under such conditions, and especially with a population like the Japanese."[24]

With the Spanish-American War and the U.S.-Philippine War—and the related revolutionary movements in the Philippines and Cuba preceding them—fresh in everyone's memory, the former Spanish colonies and their potential for insurrection against the United States constituted the foremost security matter for Jones. Japanese presence in Cuba, for example, elicited greater alarm than in Hawai'i. "A report from Cuba seens [sic] to indicate that Japanese agents are not only gathering military information there but that they may also be engaged in fomenting insurrection," Jones stated. "Taken in connection with the work of a similar nature which they have been carrying on in the Philippines for several years past, this matter should be carefully investigated." It was indeed Japanese maneuvers in the Philippines that preoccupied Jones and occupied more than half of his report. He began by noting a racial difference between the Japanese and Filipinos, a difference critical to gathering intelligence. "In making this investigation, we must bear in mind that we are dealing with the most secretive nation on earth," he observed. "The fact that there is any evidence at all is due to the fact that the Filipinos always treasure up all sorts of written matter. Just why they do this is hard to tell, but such is the fact."[25]

The ties between Japan and the Philippines dated back to the Philippine Revolution against Spain, Jones argued, when exiled revolutionaries sought refuge and support in Japan beginning in 1896. The Japanese government demonstrated every inclination to support Filipino revolutionaries against Spain, according to Jones, but, once the United States entered the picture, its position turned restrained and clandestine. Gearing up for war with Russia, he surmised, Japan could not risk becoming embroiled in a conflict with the United States, but its officials maintained close communications with Filipino revolutionaries in Manila and Hong Kong. Japan's designs in the Philippines became evident in December 1899, according to Jones, by which time the United States had annexed the Philippines and was engaged in a protracted war to sustain its claim over the archipelago. "Briefly stated, it is this: As is well known to all who have taken the trouble to look into the matter, Japan has, for many years, desired to unite the people of Asia, with herself as the dominant and controlling power," Jones argued. "She believes that she has a Heaven-sent mission to control the affairs of the Extreme Orient and all her efforts have been directed to this end for a long time back." It was in Japan's interest, therefore, to assist Filipino revolutionaries, for "a Philippines governed and controlled by Filipinos, especially when that control was acknowledgedly acquired with the aid of Japan, would be much easier to dominate than a Philippines governed by an European nation or by the United States."[26]

Through diplomatic channels and at times military personnel, Jones concluded, Japan actively aided and abetted the Filipino insurgency against the United States. Over the course of the U.S.-Philippine War, "there were frequent rumors current among the Filipinos to effect that Japan was about to intervene in their behalf: that a Japanese army was about to land in the Philippines, etc. etc." Discounted at the time as a stratagem to encourage Filipino forces, Jones now believed that there was substance to those widespread rumors. "Nor have these rumors ceased with the suppression of the insurrection," he added, "but have been more or less constant up to the present time." For the moment, however, Jones felt that Japanese agents in the Philippines were not laying the groundwork for a full-scale military invasion. Instead, their aim was "to incite the Filipinos to frequent uprisings and disturbances in the hope of creating such a disgust in America that our government would be willing to get rid of the Islands at any price, and as near as I can see, our government is not well equipped for stopping or preventing this kind of work on the part of the Japanese." Jones concluded his report by noting anti-American sentiments among ordinary Japanese, whose "national and racial pride" had been offended by anti-Japanese racism in the United States, and Japan's escalating investment in the military. "*Why* she is doing this is by no means clear," he admitted. "Is she preparing to establish a Monroe Doctrine for the Orient with herself as the dominant power?"[27]

Whether or not Jones could verify his claims, growing numbers of U.S. military intelligence officers and informants *and* Filipinos resisting the U.S. empire had come to believe that Japan would side imminently with the Philippines against the United States. Beginning in late 1909, as during the Philippine Revolution thirteen years earlier, popular *espiritistas* (spirit mediums) began prophesying across the Philippines that war would commence between the United States and Japan in 1910 and that, if Filipinos sided with Japan, the islands would finally win national independence. The coincident appearance of Halley's Comet in the middle of 1910 intensified the anticipatory atmosphere. While peasants in Luzon mobilized in rebellion, nationalist politicians in Manila were reportedly "visiting houses, streets and districts, preaching that the hour [was] approaching for the independence of the Filipino people, and that the only thing lacking [was] an effort on the part of the people in response to the call for everyone to sign a message addressed to the American government and people." In April 1910, a Filipino informant in Manila told MID officers that "the Filipino Japophiles have propagated the belief that America fears Japan." At a recent meeting of the Sociedad Patria, he claimed to have heard members preparing to go to war. "Gentlemen, it is necessary for us Filipinos to unite in order to shake off the yoke of the Americans, following the example that we previously followed with the Spaniards," they had said, according to the informant. "The times and circumstances oblige us to take up arms to throw off this yoke which is crushing us."[28]

By late spring and summer of 1910, U.S. intelligence authorities were on edge, having gathered countless confidential reports on secret meetings and surreptitious conversations to suggest a general rebellion in the works. They monitored Japanese residents in the Philippines, suspecting them all to be alien agitators in a widespread conspiracy against the United States. In May 1910, for instance, Filipino informant "Twenty-one" reported his recent conversation with his Japanese physician, Dr. Hayakawa. "Do not believe the papers and the good policy of the Americans," Hayakawa reportedly told the informant. "We do not talk much but we do much. You know how all the whites are to talk and paint their things. If you hear and believe them, you become stupid and cowardly. . . . What you must do is not to be afraid of death, because of those who die in war there are neither large nor small. They are all equal and one who dies in war becomes a saint." After discussing the likelihood of arms shipments from Japan, the physician vowed undying Japanese support for Filipinos. "We are all soldiers, even the women. We all die," he reportedly said. "If the Americans declare liberty now there will be war just the same, for we shall take Hawaii and they will pay us. Only here there will be no more war, brother. Because when all we of Asia are one, we will make the whites look foolish here. We all have orders to wait for the ultimatum."[29]

Regardless of the reliability of such confidential reports from informants, who might have stated what they figured U.S. intelligence officers expected to hear, rumors of an impending war between the United States and Japan undeniably affected the political mood in the Philippines. More and more Filipinos, including elite politicians and mainstream newspapers, spoke brazenly of national independence. When the U.S. secretary of war visited the city of Lucena in August 1910, he was welcomed with a banner on the provincial building that read "The Filipinos desire immediate Independence." When the secretary proceeded to deliver a speech on various improvements made by the U.S. government—such as that the "Americans will not consent that the banner hoisted here be hauled down through offensive means"—he reportedly "made the people indignant, arousing heated comments." In the wake of the official visit, *El Mercantil* issued a candid editorial. "The Filipino people do not ask the Americans to lend them their capital, nor to give them their lights, nor to exploit their wealth, nor to govern them with justice, nor to administer their affairs economically," the newspaper stated, "the only thing asked is that they go; a conclusive formula, the Basis and compendium of all their desires." The Philippine independence movement—and the U.S. state's surveillance of it—expanded apace. Informant "Eleven" of Manila grew worried. "I believe that in order to be better informed it is necessary for me to join them," he confided to his intelligence contact, "but I fear that the authorities may take me for one of them, and therefore I consult you about it."[30]

By the time military and naval intelligence officers instituted a significant network of surveillance in Hawai'i during World War I, the racial narrative of the Japanese as agitators engaged in a global conspiracy to undermine U.S. sovereignty had become commonsense knowledge within the U.S. state. Beginning in 1918, the Japanese in Hawai'i, a population that had prompted no alarm in 1907, comprised the focal point of military intelligence reports. In a war between the United States and Japan, Major H. C. Merriam reported to the head of the MID in Washington, D.C., "[p]ractically all the Japanese would side with Japan." The Japanese government, Japanese language schools, and Buddhist priests—all later represented as instigating the 1920 strike—were in a common mission, he claimed, to make all Japanese in Hawai'i loyal

Japanese subjects, ready to wage war with the United States. The Office of Naval Intelligence (ONI) reinforced the MID findings, noting that a Japanese informant in Hawai'i had exposed the real object of Buddhist priests. "Buddhist priests in Hawaii, while ostensibly loyal to the United States," the informant stated, "are in reality doing everything in their power to undermine any American intelligence entertained by the Japanese in Hawaii."[31] No matter what the local Japanese said or how they acted, their racial role within the U.S. empire was predetermined or overdetermined: they posed the greatest threat to U.S. national interests across the Pacific.

Three months after the conclusion of the 1920 labor strike, MID officer George M. Brooke decided to write a comprehensive report on the "Japanese situation," reflecting on the local labor movement and on the state of world affairs more generally. "All signs point to the approach of a new crisis in the relations of Japan and the United States," he began ominously. For Brooke, Japanese influence extended well beyond the Japanese community in Hawai'i. "Japan knows that . . . with the aid of hosts of aliens, of radicals, of pacifists and of renegades of every sort and description now rampant in the United States, as well as fermenting under cover," he proclaimed, "that she may be able to aid in tying up the United States with strikes, and that she may be able to make the aliens, the radicals and the discontented working classes buck war, even when war is necessary to preserve the vigor of our nationality." Fomenting unrest in the United States, Japan was simultaneously fostering "her Pan-Asian propaganda throughout the Orient" and leading to "the development in Asia of new conception of nationalism" and "a distinct lowering of the prestige of the white race." "Japan openly aspires to a dominant place in the Pacific," he concluded. "She aspires to leadership of the colored peoples. She classes herself as colored when appealing to colored races, but resents racial discrimination against herself, as a question of color."[32]

Brooke distinctly saw the recent labor strike in Hawai'i as a phase of a worldwide problem, a racial problem. In Hawai'i, he thought some Chinese, Koreans, Filipinos, and Native Hawaiians would serve as "admirable material for Japanese spies," but warned of their limited, racial value. "It is very probable that these races would be not only of very little assistance to the United States," he cautioned, "but instead a practical impediment, excepting perhaps for the Hawaiians who are very easy-going people." The stage was nearly set for Japan to execute its global designs, Brooke concluded. "Based on Asia she holds an island line from Korea to the mouth of the Amur," he wrote. "She is firmly based in Formosa close to the Philippines. She has by her propaganda in the Philippines rendered possible insurrections on a small scale. . . . She is undoubtedly plotting with the Germans in Mexico. . . . She controls the lanes of the Pacific from Hawaii to the Orient. . . . She has extended her espionage net from Puget Sound to Panama." Brooke's apocalyptic vision went on and on, so much so that his superiors noted that the report was "a peculiar paper for an official document. . . . It reads more like a piece of propaganda."[33] His report, however, was merely an uninhibited version of intelligence reports emanating from the Philippines, Hawai'i, and elsewhere. Concentrating on the "Japanese problem" not only enabled the great expansion of the U.S. national security state but also served to elide the ultimate source behind local labor and political struggles in the Philippines and in Hawai'i: the U.S. empire.

A Colored International

If the racialization of the Japanese as subversive agitators flowed smoothly from the U.S.-occupied Philippines to U.S.-occupied Hawai'i, the revolutionary currents encircling the United States and the world secured its reification and proliferation. Given new life by wartime laws on sedition, the Bureau of Investigation (BoI)—the forerunner to the Federal Bureau of Investigation and the civilian counterpart to the MID and ONI—instructed its agents across the United States to monitor Japanese subjects after World War I. Beginning in April 1921, the BoI agent in Springfield, Massachusetts, filed reports on the suspicious movements of M. Danchi Takeuchi, a "Hawaiian-Jap student at Y.M.C.A. College," who accompanied another "Jap" and a Filipino college student to visit a local "negro leader" affiliated with Marcus Garvey's Universal Negro Improvement Association (UNIA). "My people are of mixed races. . . . Eighty per cent are of dark skin," the Filipino student reportedly stated. "We are for complete independence." The mixing of races and politics unnerved the agent. "Many negroes attended picnic of Russian Club (Communists)," he noted to his superiors. "They sang the Internationale as lustily as did the Ruskys." The agent tracked Takeuchi's movements

closely—noting his meetings with UNIA officials and "locally fraternizing with Russian and Italian radicals"—and inspected his mail from
all over the world. Takeuchi, he learned, was soon planning a trip to
Puerto Rico. His destination, another unruly site of the U.S. empire, further convinced the agent that Takeuchi was working for the Japanese
government.[34]

BoI reports on Takeuchi were symptomatic of a U.S. state braced
for a wave of radical politics, specifically around race, labor, and empire, a politics its agents deemed seditious and, as such, pro-Japanese.
Reports on "Radical Activities" and "Japanese Activities"—major areas
monitored by BoI agents, along with "Negro Activities"—converged
and overlapped so much that they often came to represent the one
and the same, presumably spearheaded by the Japanese government.
In late summer 1919, for instance, a BoI report on the "Communist
Convention and Communist Labor Party Convention" stressed the
links between radical labor organizers and Japanese agents. Bill Haywood, a prominent radical labor organizer, met with a Japanese activist, it stated, "from whom it was learned that the 'Japanese People' are
having some 'Missionary Work' done in America, with permission of
the Japanese Government, and that the Japanese Agents are making
their headquarters at 1947 Broadway, N.Y., Room 62, which is also used
by Sen Katayama as the publishing office of the 'Heimin.'" From the
perspective of BoI agents, what marked Katayama and others as likely
"Japanese Agents" were their radical politics, racial backgrounds, and
interracial "missionary work," a combination and a conflation that
simplified and magnified the role of the Japanese state. In and beyond
Hawai'i, the specter of a Japanese-led insurgency rationalized and expanded the U.S. national security state.[35]

The notion that Katayama was working in alliance with the Japanese
state most likely would have made the renowned Japanese radical laugh.
Katayama had founded the *Heimin* largely to criticize the Japanese state
on behalf of "the interest of workers and socialists in America and also
in Japan." And he never wavered in that position. "We expect to get the
Heimin out oftener, since it is the only publication of its kind in America
or in fact anywhere where one can speak out freely and preach the International Socialism and can criticize and attack injustices and oppression
of the Japanese government that are constantly and increasingly heaped

upon the workers of Japan," Katayama explained in April 1918. "Against these awful wrongs our workers at home cannot raise a voice of protest. The Heimin will speak for the oppressed in Japan and raise a voice of protest against the injustice done by the bourgeoisie government and capitalists." The columns of Katayama's New York–based newspaper articulated worldly visions unequivocally opposed to the Japanese empire. Beseeching the Japanese in the United States not to be seduced by Japanese nationalism, the *Heimin* published reports on crimes committed by the Japanese colonial regime. Katayama's newspaper counseled, "Don't be consoled cheaply at a citation that England has her Ireland, Egypt and India and America her Negroes and practice of lynching and also her Mexico!"[36]

Rather than representing the Japanese state, Katayama's newspaper intimated an incipient and informal materialization of what Hubert Harrison was calling forth around the same time—"a colored international," in ways seen and unseen by the U.S. national security state. From Massachusetts to California to Hawai'i, intelligence agents witnessed during and following World War I interracial interactions that exceeded the bounds of race and nation-states. In July 1921, a black informant keeping tabs on Harrison and other Harlem radicals interviewed Sumio Uesugi, a Japanese Christian who had been speaking at Garvey's UNIA meetings. "He told me that the white people were hypocrites who called themselves Christians, but always turn him down on account of his color," the informant reported. Enthralled by Garvey's message and organization, Uesugi, a Harlem resident, planned to publicize "the great strength which lies in Garvey's movement" in Japan. The informant made it clear that Uesugi's racial and radical politics emanated from his daily encounters with white supremacy and his recent opportunities "to mix with the negroes," but he simultaneously insinuated that Uesugi was an agent of the Japanese government.[37] Like striking Japanese workers in Hawai'i, Uesugi's activities were monitored and interpreted within a widespread racial narrative that naturalized the U.S. empire and its ever growing security state. The U.S. state had developed a vital investment in locating and suppressing anyone who might associate with its racial and international enemy, Japan. In doing so, it rendered "a colored international" visible, but only in its unrelenting drive to make interracial solidarities disappear from the realm of political possibilities.

NOTES

1. Jeffrey B. Perry, *Hubert Harrison: The Voice of Harlem Radicalism, 1883–1918* (New York: Columbia University Press, 2009), 4, 231; Jeffrey B. Perry, ed., *A Hubert Harrison Reader* (Middletown, CT: Wesleyan University Press, 2001), 226; V. I. Lenin, *Imperialism: The Highest Stage of Capitalism* (New York: International Publishers, 1939), 88; Mark Ellis, *Race, War, and Surveillance: African Americans and the United States Government during World War I* (Bloomington: Indiana University Press, 2001), 121–25; Theodore Kornweibel, Jr., *"Seeing Red": Federal Campaigns against Black Militancy, 1919–1925* (Bloomington: Indiana University Press, 1998), 140–43.

2. George M. Brooke, "Situation Survey for period ending January 31, 1920," "Situation Survey for week ending 31 January 1920," and "Situation Survey for week ending 6 March 1920," Military Intelligence Division Correspondence, 1917–1941 (MID), Record Group (RG) 165, National Archives, Washington, D.C. (NA).

3. Michel Foucault, *Security, Territory, Population: Lectures at the Collège de France, 1977–78*, ed. Michel Senellart (New York: Palgrave Macmillan, 2007), 365–66.

4. Foucault, *Security, Territory, Population*, 204, 355–57.

5. Gary Y. Okihiro, *Cane Fires: The Anti-Japanese Movement in Hawaii, 1865–1945* (Philadelphia: Temple University Press, 1991), 7–18, 59; Moon-Kie Jung, *Reworking Race: The Making of Hawaii's Interracial Labor Movement* (New York: Columbia University Press, 2006), 11–21.

6. Okihiro, *Cane Fires*, 41–57 (sheriff quote, 53); Jung, *Reworking Race*, 21–33.

7. Wm. Haywood to Secretary of War, June 19, 1901; Philippine Commission, Executive Session, Minutes of Proceedings, July 23, 1906; Wm. Matson to W. I. Brobeck, September 16, 1914; Records of the Bureau of Insular Affairs, General Records, 1898–1945 (BIA), File 3037; RG 350, NA; Okihiro, *Cane Fires*, 55, 59; Jung, *Reworking Race*, 34, 42–44.

8. Okihiro, *Cane Fires*, 65; Jung, *Reworking Race*, 33; Edward D. Beechert, *Working in Hawaii: A Labor History* (Honolulu: University of Hawai'i Press, 1985), 196–97; translated copy of *Hawaii Hochi* in George M. Brooke, "Oriental labor question in Hawaii," August 29, 1919, MID, RG 165, NA.

9. Michael Lewis, *Rioters and Citizens: Mass Protest in Imperial Japan* (Berkeley: University of California Press, 1990); Masayo Umezawa Duus, *The Japanese Conspiracy: The Oahu Sugar Strike of 1920* (Berkeley: University of California Press, 1999), 45–47; Beechert, *Working in Hawaii*, 197–99.

10. Melinda Tria Kerkvliet, *Unbending Cane: Pablo Manlapit, A Filipino Labor Leader in Hawai'i* (Honolulu: Office of Multicultural Student Services, University of Hawai'i at Mānoa, 2002), 5–21; Beechert, *Working in Hawaii*, 158, 197–201; Jung, *Reworking Race*, 34–35.

11. Beechert, *Working in Hawaii*, 201–3; Okihiro, *Cane Fires*, 69–71.

12. Brooke to Milstaff, January 22 and 24, 1920; George M. Brooke, "Situation Survey for week ending 31 January 1920"; MID, RG 165, NA.

13. "What the Japanese Agitators Want," *Honolulu Star-Bulletin*, February 13, 1920, appended to George M. Brooke, "Situation Survey for week ending 6 March 1920"; John Waterhouse, President of HSPA, to Messrs. Albert W. Palmer et al., February 27, 1920, and "Opening Address by Department Commander Leonard Withington before the Convention of American Legion Department of Hawaii at Honolulu," February 23, 1920, both appended to George M. Brooke, "Situation Survey for period ending 29 February 1920," MID, RG 165, NA.

14. Okihiro, *Cane Fires*, 69, 71; I. Goto, Secretary, "Instructions to Members of Federation of Japanese Labor in Hawaii," January 17, 1920, appended to George M. Brooke, "Situation Survey for period ending 31 January 1920," MID, RG 165, NA.

15. "The Voice of Labor in Hawaii," appended to George M. Brooke, "Situation Survey for period ending 29 February 1920," MID, RG 165, NA.

16. Albert W. Palmer et al. to the Hawaiian Sugar Planters' Association, February 27, 1920 (the wrong date is listed on the MID copy; it should be dated February 14, 1920); Federation of Japanese Labor in Hawaii to Curtis P. Iaukea, Acting Governor of Hawaii, February 25, 1920; both appended to George M. Brooke, "Situation Survey for period ending 29 February 1920," MID, RG 165, NA.

17. "Sermon Delivered February 22, 1920," appended to George M. Brooke, "Situation Survey for period ending 29 February 1920," MID, RG 165, NA.

18. Okihiro, *Cane Fires*, 73; Duus, *The Japanese Conspiracy*, 73–75; John Waterhouse, President of HSPA, to Messrs. Albert W. Palmer et al., February 27, 1920, and "Iaukea Calls on Planters to Back Conspiracy Claim," both appended to George M. Brooke, "Situation Survey for period ending 29 February 1920," MID, RG 165, NA.

19. "Iaukea Calls on Planters to Back Conspiracy Claim"; "Mr. Palmer's Reply"; "Opinion of Jonah Kumalae, City and County Supervisor, of Japanese Language Schools, As Expressed in an Interview for the Nippu Jiji, January 8th"; all appended to George M. Brooke, "Situation Survey for period ending 29 February 1920," MID, RG 165, NA.

20. Beechert, *Working in Hawaii*, 203–4; "Filipinos Threatened with Death by Board of Health, Is Charged by Japanese Paper" and "Pablo Manlapit to-day Signed the Following Statement," February 9, 1920, appended to George M. Brooke, "Situation Survey for period ending 29 February 1920," MID, RG 165, NA.

21. Okihiro, *Cane Fires*, 73–76 (quotes from 74 and 76); Jung, *Reworking Race*, 37–38.

22. Jung, *Reworking Race*, 87–90; James C. Scott, *Seeing like a State: How Certain Schemes to Improve the Human Condition Have Failed* (New Haven, CT: Yale University Press, 1998), 4–6.

23. Reynaldo C. Ileto, *Filipinos and Their Revolution: Event, Discourse, and Historiography* (Manila: Ateneo de Manila University Press, 1998), 151–61. I thank Vince Rafael for pointing out Ricarte's significance.

24. Alfred W. McCoy, *Policing America's Empire: The United States, the Philippines, and the Rise of the Surveillance State* (Madison: University of Wisconsin Press, 2009); T. W. Jones, "A Report Compiled from Reports and Other Data Showing

the Activities of Japanese and Japanese Officials in Relation to the United States and Her Possessions," November 6, 1907, xxxix-xlii MID, RG 165, NA.

25. T. W. Jones, "A Report Compiled from Reports and Other Data Showing the Activities of Japanese and Japanese Officials in Relation to the United States and Her Possessions," November 6, 1907, l, ii, MID, RG 165, NA.

26. T. W. Jones, "A Report Compiled from Reports and Other Data Showing the Activities of Japanese and Japanese Officials in Relation to the United States and Her Possessions," November 6, 1907, x, MID, RG 165, NA.

27. T. W. Jones, "A Report Compiled from Reports and Other Data Showing the Activities of Japanese and Japanese Officials in Relation to the United States and Her Possessions," November 6, 1907, xxxii, xxxiii, xxxvi, lii, lvi-lvii, MID, RG 165, NA.

28. Ileto, *Filipinos and Their Revolution*, 151–52; Copy with Confidential Report (translation), Manila, April 10, 1910, appended to Lea Febiger to Adjutant General of the Army, June 14, 1910, MID, RG 165, NA.

29. Twenty-one, Confidential Report (translation), May 11, 1910, appended to Lea Febiger to Adjutant General of the Army, June 14, 1910, MID, RG 165, NA.

30. "The Voyage of the Secretary of War," *El Ideal*, August 16, 1910 (translated copy), and "Last Lines," *El Mercantil*, August 20, 1910, appended to "Confidential Report," August 6, 1910; Eleven, Confidential Report (translation), Manila, October 4, 1910, appended to Wm. P. Duvall to Adjutant General of the Army, November 11, 1910; MID, RG 165, NA.

31. Quoted in Okihiro, *Cane Fires*, 103–5.

32. George M. Brooke, "Estimate of the Japanese Situation as It Affects the Territory of Hawaii, from the Military Point of View," October 11, 1920, MID, RG 165, NA.

33. George M. Brooke, "Estimate of the Japanese Situation as It Affects the Territory of Hawaii, from the Military Point of View," October 11, 1920, MID, RG 165, NA.

34. Kornweibel, *"Seeing Red,"* 4–7; Adrian L. Potter, Weekly Confidential Report, April 5–11, 1921, April 12–18, 1921, May 10–16, 1921, May 17–23, 1921, May 24–30, 1921, Bureau Section (BS) File 202600–22; Adrian L. Potter, Weekly Confidential Report, June 7–13, 1921, June 14–20, 1921, September 6–12, 1921, September 13–19, 1921, September 20–26, 1921, BS File 202600–1804; Investigative Case Files of the Bureau of Investigation, 1908–1922, Records of the Federal Bureau of Investigation, RG 65, NA.

35. "Communist Convention and Communist Labor Party Convention," Chicago, August 28 to September 5, 1919, Old German (OG) File 229372, RG 65, NA.

36. *The Heimin*, no. 3 (July 1916), no. 15 (April 1918), no. 21 (July 1919), Yuji Ichioka Papers, Department of Special Collections, Charles E. Young Research Library, University of California, Los Angeles.

37. P-138, "In re: Negro Activities," July 30, 1921, BS File 202600–667, RG 65, NA.

3

The Secret Soldiers' Union

Labor and Soldier Politics in the Philippine Scout Mutiny of 1924

CHRISTOPHER CAPOZZOLA

On the morning of July 6, 1924, a group of 380 soldiers at Fort McKinley, a U.S. Army installation just outside Manila, refused to turn out for duty. They were proud members of a newly formed organization they called the Secret Soldiers' Union. All of them were Philippine Scouts, Filipinos who had enlisted in Uncle Sam's army to fight on behalf of the United States and in defense of its ongoing colonial rule of the Philippines. That morning, in what they called a "strike," the men of the Secret Soldiers' Union protested disparities in wages between white and Filipino soldiers, and the indignity of a raid on their barracks the night before by military police. But the commanders of the Philippine Scouts—American officers on Pacific assignment—saw things differently. The Scouts' actions, in their view, were not a collective protest over wages and work conditions but a mass mutiny. The officers quickly convened a court martial. The events of the summer of 1924—while almost completely forgotten in U.S. history—represent one of the largest mutinies in the history of the U.S. armed forces as well as a moment of crisis in U.S. imperial rule.

Restoring the Philippine Scout Mutiny of 1924 to history sheds light on the complex history of collective labor action in the U.S. empire, not least because it is unclear what name to give to the events that took place at Fort McKinley that summer. In fact, it may be useful to think of the Scout action three ways: as a mutiny by colonial soldiers in a world of empires and imperial armies; as a strike by workers in postwar Manila; and as a form of soldier politics embedded in U.S. political culture. Taken together, the three perspectives demonstrate the dependence of the interwar U.S. military on Filipino labor, and the centrality of labor politics to the ongoing contest over the terms of colonial rule.[1]

A munity is generally thought of as a distinctly military phenomenon, an act of resistance by soldiers or sailors to military discipline and a limited expression of their agency within rigidly hierarchical institutions. Military officers and governments have long understood, though, that mutinies could have political consequences far beyond the barrack or the berth, particularly in colonial contexts. When British officials crushed the 1857 rebellion of Indian soldiers or when French and British officers prosecuted dissent at the western front during World War I, they implicitly acknowledged the political content of mutinies by colonial troops. In 1924, in a world organized by competing empires that were challenged by increasingly international anticolonial movements, U.S. military officials at Fort McKinley could hardly have been expected not to link the Scouts' dissent to the colonial question.[2]

Given that the Scouts had organized themselves into something they called a "union," and referred to their action as a "strike," it is equally important to understand the week's events on those terms. Mutinies are also strikes—collective actions aimed at contesting the terms of labor power and its control—in which the army is best understood as an employer like any other. A glimpse at labor organizing and unrest in postwar Manila suggests that Scouts' actions at Fort McKinley were part of a broader movement of labor militancy across the metropolitan region of Manila and indeed throughout the United States' Pacific empire in the years after World War I. The Scouts' dissent was both cause and consequence of overlapping social networks among Filipino workers, who moved between on-base and off-base labor markets during the 1920s.[3]

Nor can the mutiny be dismissed as *merely* a strike, or, as its only serious historian concluded, a "largely economic" demand for wages lodged by men who "were not nascent nationalists." Scouts' actions were also of a piece with agitation over the terms of military service and citizenship by soldiers and veterans of the U.S. armed forces during and after World War I. Veterans—some four million strong—constituted a powerful and highly visible political constituency in the continental United States in the years after the November 1918 Armistice. Ex-soldiers regularly featured in the pages of newspapers and the frames of newsreels, whether organizing in formal groups such as the American Legion, articulating and defending their interests at the voting booth as candidates chased the so-called "soldier vote," or making economic claims on the state such as those that culminated in the mass movement of the 1932 Bonus Army.[4]

How, then, do the mutinous Philippine Scouts fit into these histories? They do and they don't, and therein lies a key to the contradictions between America's republican and imperial political cultures in the early twentieth century. In the metropole, military service functioned (albeit imperfectly) as a platform for claims making by many who had been previously excluded from full political belonging. During World War I, immigrants (including Mexican and Asian migrants), African Americans, and Native Americans all framed their demands for equality on the foundation of their own wartime service and the formal citizenship that accompanied it. The Philippine National Guard—a militia unit proposed during the war to create a similar path to citizenship through military service for Filipinos—never got off the ground, but it raised expectations and may have politicized some of the men who became the core members of the Secret Soldiers' Union. At a time when the civic claims that a soldier could make were very much up for grabs—both in the Philippines and in the metropolitan United States—the Scouts at Fort McKinley had reason to believe that their uniforms gave them political opportunities.[5]

They would learn, the hard way, that none of these three paths would improve their situations as soldiers, workers, or colonial subjects. The new colonial administration installed after the election of President Warren G. Harding was intent on reining in Filipinos' claims to national self-determination; fears of global communist revolution generated suppression of labor radicalism; and eight years before Douglas MacArthur dispersed the veteran marchers of the Bonus Army, he supervised the court martial that convicted nearly half the men who had disobeyed orders at Fort McKinley in July 1924.

The refusal of several hundred men to stand in straight lines on an open field on a hill outside Manila did not succeed in raising wages, liberating the Philippines, or making Philippine Scouts into citizen-soldiers. The Philippine Scout Mutiny exposed the contradictions between America's republican and imperial practices that the Philippine Scouts both embodied and had been recruited to suppress. Whereas during World War I, soldiers in the U.S. armed forces had sometimes successfully used the republican language of martial citizenship to renegotiate the terms of military labor, that rhetoric did not transfer to imperial contexts where military labor mattered to the maintenance and defense of empire itself. The Secret Soldiers' Union was dismissed as a mere strike and punished as a dangerous mutiny. In a polity that valued citizen-soldiers above others, the Scouts were never recognized as soldiers even when they were punished like soldiers.

***

The Philippine Scouts were an institutional irony masquerading as a program of uplift. In the immediate aftermath of the Spanish-American War, as the United States sought to suppress Filipino nationalist movements, military officials recruited into their ranks several thousand Filipino soldiers, many of them veterans of Spain's colonial army in its Philippine colony. Formally incorporated as a part of the U.S. Army in 1901, the Scouts gradually turned from a temporary counterinsurgency force to a permanent feature of colonial rule. By the early 1920s, the Philippine Scouts made up the preponderance of the colony's armed forces; about 10,000 Scouts and an additional 5,000 Constabularies (police officers serving in paramilitary roles) served under 2,500 white American officers, with about 5,000 U.S. Army soldiers in a separate American garrison. The Scouts trained for combat and Army strategy imagined them as the first line of defense against foreign invasion or—encapsulated in War Plan Brown, a top-secret plan for the defense of the territory in case of a mass uprising—domestic insurrection. Filipino soldiers thus labored to protect the largest U.S. imperial possession from threats posed by other Filipinos. At least in theory, by the 1920s Scouts were rarely called on for combat duty, and spent most of their time drilling and guarding the Army's military installations in the Philippines. Some, particularly in Manila, had so little to do that they even found time to take on second jobs or enroll in night classes at schools and universities.[6]

Their work was boring and routine, and like most military labor, strictly disciplined and rigidly hierarchical. By the 1920s, the Scouts were a remarkably experienced and well-trained force. Recruiting officers could afford to be choosy among the applicants presented to them, and they had time to develop talented soldiers, since Scout reenlistment rates hovered around 80 percent in the early 1920s. The Scouts had even become a family affair. "[A]pplicants for enlistment were frequently disregarded," recalled one officer, "and, instead, brothers, cousins and nephews—even sons—of the men already in the ranks appeared to take the examinations for enlistment." U.S. enlisted men posted to the Philippines were rarely married, but Scouts could marry and stay in uniform, and many did, bringing their families to live in unofficial Scout *barrios* that adjoined military bases.[7]

Scouts could be found throughout the islands, but most served in or near Manila at one of the military installations established by the U.S. Army and Navy after the end of the Philippine-American War. Some were stationed on Corregidor Island in Manila Bay, or at Sangley Point, a Navy base along the bay's edge in the town of Cavite. A few guarded Fort Santiago, an old Spanish post in the city's downtown near the colonial government buildings. The largest number could be found at Fort McKinley, five miles east of the city but closely connected to its political and economic life.

They were not well paid. Compared to American soldiers', Scouts' wages were low. While a U.S. Army private earned $21 a month, privates in the Philippine Scouts took home $8 a month in 1921, a figure almost unchanged since the first Scouts had joined up 20 years earlier in the midst of the Philippine-American War. That salary showed little sign of increase in the years after the war; the return to normalcy in the 1920s and a retreat from international commitments meant smaller budgets for the Army, making it more appealing than ever that Filipino soldiers cost less than Americans.[8]

Scouts supplemented their incomes by putting their families to work. Delbert Ausmus, an American officer posted near Manila, later recalled that "the women would do laundry for the officers' families and also some of the younger sons would work as house boys for the officers or run the shoe-and-belt shining stands for the enlisted men," although a guide written by an officer's wife described Corregidor's housekeepers as only "sometimes good." But by the 1920s, even a whole family's labor wasn't enough to make ends meet. The cost of living had risen dramatically in the wartime Philippines, as it had around the world, and by the summer of 1924, Scouts and their families were feeling the pinch.[9]

The stagnation in military wages meant that by 1924, Scouts on average were earning less than skilled Manila workers. On the other hand, benefits for soldiers and their dependents were far better, their employment was far more secure, and if they had incorporated relatives into the military labor system, overall family security was greater as well. And, of course, most Scouts—especially older ones who had enlisted two decades earlier during the Philippine-American War—did not grow up in Manila and could rarely read or write. Compared to the men they had grown up with in the countryside, Scouts' wages would have seemed remarkably high. But compared to how they had lived before the war, Scouts felt downward pressure, and seeing other workers in Manila winning higher pay through collective labor actions, they would have imagined their wages were ripe for renegotiation.[10]

Political developments in the Philippines during World War I may have also given Scouts the idea that colonial soldiering didn't have to be a dead-end job rewarded with second-class wages. The rhetoric of homefront mobilization that emerged from Washington linked wartime colonial loyalty in the Philippines to President Woodrow Wilson's public commitment to Philippine independence that followed the 1916 Jones Act. A proposed military force—the Philippine National Guard—promised to allow Filipinos to demonstrate their fitness for martial citizenship while forming the nucleus of an independent Philippine Army. The Army stonewalled the Guard, and Republican victories in 1920 stifled independence claims, but the idea that military service justified political claims did not disappear. Indeed it may have migrated into the ranks of the Scouts, as younger men who had attempted to enlist in the wartime Guard appear to have joined the Scouts in the years after the war.[11]

Sitting in the governor-general's office in Manila was the biggest supporter of the colonial undertaking and—ironically—the heartiest proponent of martial citizenship. Leonard Wood, a military officer who had built his career in the colonial Philippines and who later, as spokesman for the "preparedness" movement, organized volunteer military camps at Plattsburgh, New York, to train young men as officers for an expanding U.S. Army, had been governor-general of the Philippines since 1921. Wood brought to his office at the Malacanang Palace a military approach to colonial rule and a deliberate effort to roll back the moves toward self-governance that the Wilson administration had initiated in the previous decade. Wood surrounded himself with military advisers in a so-called "khaki cabinet" and continued to orate on the military obligations of citizenship, but never with Filipino soldiers in mind. He clearly had no intention of expanding the Philippine Scouts or using them in anything other than support roles, and few in the Army disagreed. By 1924, then, Filipino soldiers and colonial administrators held diametrically opposed views of what military service meant, creating conditions favorable for a conflagration. Labor unrest in Manila would provide the spark.[12]

***

Filipino workers spoke louder, more collectively, and in new organizations in the years following World War I. In 1924, the colony's 145 officially registered labor organizations counted over 90,000 members, who articulated specific demands about wages and work conditions and general critiques of U.S. power, imagining as they did so a shared community of labor across the Philippines and even beyond its shores. In Manila, the most visible organization was the Legionarios del Trabajo, founded in 1919 during a strike against the Manila Electric Company, and then reformulated in June 1923 as a fraternal society modeled on the Philippine Masons but with far lower membership dues so that it could attract working-class men to its ranks. Like most other workers' fraternal societies, the Legionarios existed primarily to pool funds and smooth economic hardships for its members, although they occasionally took on a public voice in labor disputes. A more radical alternative existed in the Partido Obrero de Filipinas, inspired by global movements toward communism, which in 1924 convened a congress of the National Confederation of Tenants and Farm Laborers. Spiritually oriented movements, often millenarian in nature, supplemented labor unions and labor-oriented fraternal organizations. By the 1920s, the Philippine countryside was rocked by the protests, sometimes violent, of the messianic Colorum movement and other peasant groups. Increasingly, the colonial administration came to fear that labor agitation was not a response to bread-and-butter issues but reflected a globally coordinated resistance to colonialism itself. Governor Wood bore much of the responsibility for this view. His intransigence on the independence question displaced every other subject from the political agenda, all but guaranteeing that any labor agitation was sure to be understood as anticolonial sedition. Nationalist leaders, in turn, sought to put the independence question on the agenda of other groups in civil society, including labor unions and fraternal societies. Military officers' conviction that *Independistas* were attempting to infiltrate and politicize the Scouts was partly colonial paranoia. It also happened to be true.[13]

Filipino labor organizations faced considerable opposition from employers and the colonial state. The Philippine Constabulary, the Scouts' counterpart organization, frequently policed labor conflict, broke strikes, and—through its secret-service wing—infiltrated labor organizations. Repression reflected a global fear of anticolonial movements common to all the Western empires, carried out through antilabor subversion methods developed during World War I. Both in the continental United States and its empire, organized labor had expanded its ranks during the war. Increased membership and the hard times generated by the rising cost of living made 1919 a year of marked labor unrest in the metropolitan United States. Most notable was the Boston Police Strike of September 1919, where the walkout of more than 1,000 uniformed officers led to violent reprisals and mass firings of the striking policemen, catapulted Massachusetts Governor Calvin Coolidge into the national political spotlight, and cast doubts on the reliability of working-class state security personnel both at home and abroad.[14]

By the summer of 1924, the Scouts at Fort McKinley were ripe for organization and collective action and the colonial state was on the lookout for it. Critiques of the wage differential between Filipino and American soldiers emerged soon after the war. As early as April 1921, Master Sergeant Bruno V. Madrid submitted an essay to the *Army and Navy Journal* (portions of which were published anonymously that July) noting that "the American people have shown the Filipinos their kindness . . . and made the Philippines a progressive country in all respects—except pay." In a demand for equality, Madrid noted that

> an American and a Scout soldier both fulfill the same Army regulations and orders . . . they are equally affected by the present high cost of living; they contribute the same life in fostering and preserving the Constitution—therefore it is an injustice to the Philippine Scout soldiers and repugnant to democratic government not to give them the pay, rights and privileges they deserve.[15]

Two years later, in May 1923, Madrid asked to form an association of enlisted men at Fort McKinley. Commanding officers denied the request, but by August 1923, the Soldiers' Mutual Aid Association, structured as a fraternal society, was in existence at Fort McKinley.[16]

As labor organizing continued throughout Manila—much of it among Scouts' relatives who worked in the civilian sector but lived with them in off-base *barrios*—it was only a matter of time before the two overlapping worlds of labor action became one. On July 1, 1924, as more than 700 civilian Filipino workers at the Cavite Navy Yard just outside Manila walked off the job to protest the introduction of a reduced wage scale, the Legionarios del Trabajo quietly began to organize the Philippine Scouts at nearby Fort McKinley and in the nearby *barrio* of Scout families.[17]

The Scouts were motivated not only by a wish for greater pay, but from a sense of unfair treatment by the Army. News had reached the soldiers at Fort McKinley that the U.S. Congress had voted to raise their pay, and indeed in April 1924, Congress had passed an omnibus military bill that raised the Scouts' rations and subsistence allowances, and awarded all Scouts pensions of three-quarters of their salary after 30 years of service. President Coolidge vetoed the military spending bill on May 3. On May 15, he also vetoed the Adjusted Compensation Act, which granted World War veterans bonus payments; Congress passed the Bonus Bill in an override that made headlines for weeks, but Coolidge's military spending veto stayed. Precisely what news reached the Scouts in Manila is unclear, but by the summer of 1924, they believed that Congress had awarded them a pay raise and that their commanding officers were deliberately withholding it from them.[18]

In response, a group of Scouts began to organize at Fort McKinley. They were mostly young, nearly all of them privates, and loosely affiliated with the Legionarios del Trabajo. They swore an oath of loyalty, and planned a demonstration for July 4, 1924, intending to gather on a hill near Fort McKinley and march five miles to downtown Manila, where they would present their demands to the commander of the Army's Philippine Department, and then to Malacanang to make their case before Governor Wood. In the "Declaration of Independence" of the Secret Soldiers' Union, the document's authors exhorted fellow soldiers: "Remember comrades that this Union is a Union that is bound together to render the burning necessity of our families and parents together with ourselves as a commendable cause."[19]

Deciding they were not sufficiently organized, the Scouts initially postponed the march to August 2, but by now there was no turning back. In the early hours of Sunday, July 6, 1924, Filipino secret informants notified Scout officers of the soldiers' plan "to step out for their rights." Thereafter Fort McKinley's Provost Guard raided a meeting in the 57th Infantry's hospital laundry, detained 26 Scout privates, and placed eight of them under arrest. During the late-night raid, military police seized papers demonstrating the existence of the Secret Soldiers' Union, which they feared was a sign of far greater unrest to come. A statement from Army headquarters in Manila suggested the society "was prompted by bolshevistic emissaries" who wanted to take "advantage of any fancied discontent among the troops."[20]

The discontent that followed the raid was more tangible than fanciful. When reveille came a few hours after the arrests on the morning of July 6, at least 380 Scouts of the 57th Infantry Regiment refused to drill. "The military authorities believed the infantrymen construe their action . . . as a peaceable strike for the purpose of obtaining increased pay and allowances," one U.S. newspaper noted. Elsewhere, the press carried reports of the increasing momentum among striking workers at the Cavite Navy Yard and the intervention of colonial officials to negotiate a settlement to the strike there, a victory for labor that may well have emboldened the Scouts at Fort McKinley. By Monday, July 7, warned that their refusal would be treated not as a strike but as a mutiny, most of the Scouts turned out in formation, but 104 refused, and the next day 202 soldiers from both the 57th Infantry Regiment and 12th Medical Regiment resisted as well.[21]

Despite the impressive resolve of the men at Fort McKinley, the Scouts were not unified in their action; age, class, and ideology divided them from the outset. Almost none of the non-commissioned officers stepped out. These were older men with years of military service under their belts, many having joined as far back as 1901 in the middle of the Philippine-American War. They were firmly incorporated in the ideological mission of U.S. colonialism, and a collective action meant more to lose, especially if they had succeeded in embedding their entire families into the Scouts' labor system. By contrast, recently enlisted privates made up the rank and file of the strike. Some of them were better educated: ringleaders such as Tomas Riveral and Alejandro Evardone were described in military documents as "studiente types." While Scouts in other areas—including Fort Stotsenburg and Fort Mills on Corregidor—remained on the job, those in Manila had more political initiative. Many had settled for the Scouts only after the Philippine National Guard experiment failed, and would have been more inclined than the older sergeants to link their military service to political claims.[22]

Colonial military officers exploited these divisions to discredit and undermine the munity, insisting that loyal service by noncoms showed that the Secret Soldiers' Union had no authority to speak for all Scouts. Filipino Scout leaders attempted to exert control over the strikers, both on their own initiative and at the behest of the American commanding officers. Major Vicente P. Lim of the 45th Infantry, one of the few Filipino graduates of West Point and the highest-ranking Filipino Scout, boasted that "we have had no mutineers in our regiment," and assigned the men of the 45th to patrol Fort McKinley in the days after the strike.[23]

In the midst of mutiny, Scout officers threatened investigations "with a view to weeding out malcontents," but initially decided they could not arrest large numbers of Scouts for fear that "sterner measures would precipitate a rebellion of all the native troops." Then on Tuesday, July 8, U.S. Navy authorities announced that they had foiled a plot among strikers to blow up the arsenal at nearby Cavite, and rumors of a mutiny at Camp Stotsenburg, 100 miles north of the city, also circulated. By now, panic was spreading through Manila's small American community. "Discharging these men and allowing them to return home," one Manila American told news correspondent Walter Wilgus, "is similar to turning smallpox into a hospital full of patients. Each man is carrying the germs of insurrection to his home province." Wilgus expressed his belief that the mutiny might require the "disbandment of the scouts, and the strengthening of the American forces," while the *Manila Daily Bulletin* warned of "Bolshevist agitators—real Russian Reds" and editorialized that the Scouts were "striking at the very root of efficient military organization."[24]

Army officers were divided about the mutiny's import. Back in Washington, Brigadier General LeRoy Eltinge spoke for many when he remarked that "I feel that the dependability of these two regiments is nil." Others worried that discharging the men would present more threat to labor control than imprisoning them, especially because it would prove disruptive to their families who lived on or near the base. Major General George W. Read, the commanding officer of the Army's Department of the Philippines, admitted that the cause was simple. "It is clear that the grievance these men allege as a basis for their mutinous action is discrimination against the Philippine Scouts soldier in pay, allowances, and benefits," he explained to the War Department in Washington.[25]

Governor Wood, who was away from Manila during the initial phase of the strike, later tried to blame "the spirit of insubordination" on "the public utterances of certain prominent political leaders condemning all who cooperated with and supported the Governor General." But Wood's post hoc announcement was nothing more than an obvious attack on his political enemies; even at the time many U.S. officials doubted the Army's insistence that there was a Bolshevik plot, arguing that the Legionarios del Trabajo were not a communist group and concurring with reports that "the disaffected scouts are more ignorant than disloyal." But with other sources noting that "many of the scouts have records of from 10 to 15 years in the United States army, in which time they have been drilled in the various military laws . . . and taught utmost loyalty," dismissing the mutiny as mere ignorance conceded that the Philippine Scouts were not, as an institution, the school for civilization and uplift that colonial rhetoric insisted.[26]

On Wednesday, July 9, military officers announced plans to discharge 190 of the men for insubordination and refusal to drill. They wanted to believe that the rest of the Scouts were merely ignorant, but evidence of continued resistance made that difficult. When initial interrogations convinced Army officers that the Scouts' "insubordination was much more active than at first supposed," and that the striking Scouts displayed "an attitude of disrespect and defiance," the Army cracked down. Major General Read, who had sought and obtained the support of Governor Wood, initiated a mass court martial, convened collectively "to save labor and expense." Beginning on July 29, three proceedings went forward: one for 17 alleged ringleaders, another for 209 men charged with "joining a mutiny," and a third court of inquiry for 298 who refused to obey orders.[27]

***

Presiding over the trials, convened at the Fort McKinley YMCA to accommodate the crowds of onlookers, was Brigadier General Douglas MacArthur, head of the Philippine Division's 23rd Brigade. In 1903, not long after his father, Arthur MacArthur, had left the Philippines, the young West Point grad spent an unremarkable tour of duty in the colony, working on fortification projects on Corregidor Island. During World War I, MacArthur had compiled a distinguished record as a field commander in Europe, and his postwar assignment to a minor post in the Philippines surprised many.[28]

Operating under strict rules of military justice, the Scouts' court martial addressed only the factual question of whether the soldiers had failed to turn out for drill on the mornings of July 7 and July 8, a violation of the 66th Article of War. Major Vicente Lim, who had boasted of the loyalty of his men during the mutiny, now found himself heading up the Scouts' defense team. Lim quickly concluded that his only hope was to play into Army officers' racist condescension toward the "ignorant" and "disaffected" Scouts, and convince the court that language difficulties had prevented the Scouts from understanding the consequences of their actions "as explained in the various dialects by the noncommissioned officers."[29]

Lim's argument failed: nearly all the men brought up on mutiny charges were found guilty, discharged, and sentenced to five years of hard labor. Tomas Riveral, identified during the course of the trial as the strike's leader, drew a sentence of 20 years. Except for strike leaders such as Riveral, Scouts were put to work in convict detachments on Corregidor Island; most were released about two years later. In 1928, four years after the strike, the Army finally raised the pay of a private in the Philippine Scouts—from $8 a month to $9.[30]

Thus ended the most dramatic episode of military unrest in the Philippines since the Philippine-American War, and with it the Scouts' hope that military service would give weight to political claims by Filipino soldiers. By any definition—as a mutinous attempt to overthrow colonial rule, as a collective effort to transform the terms of labor, as a political movement to make claims to republican citizenship—the Scouts' action can only be called a failure. Despite the fact that labor agitation in Manila's civilian workplaces continued through the 1920s and 1930s, the Secret Soldiers' Union was never heard from again, and the Philippine

Scout Mutiny faded quickly from view. The soldiers' action—seditious rebellion, grasping strike, bold assertion of citizenship, some combination of all three—was relegated to a footnote in an appendix of the War Department's annual report, while the Bureau of Insular Affairs blandly noted that "[t]he calendar year of 1924 in the Philippine Islands has been one of orderly progress." Years later, in his memoirs, Douglas MacArthur did not mention the mutiny at all.[31]

The War Department commissioned an internal study, fearful that the mutiny would jeopardize the fragile system of colonial governance adopted in the islands. In particular, officials worried because War Plan Brown, the top-secret plan for the defense of the territory in case of a mass uprising, depended on the loyal service of Philippine Scouts, which could no longer be taken for granted. "Our Brown Plan is now more or less shot," admitted one officer. The study, which recommended increases in Scout pay and changes in officer selection and supervision, languished in a file cabinet (as did War Plan Brown). But working in the service of U.S. empire and reaping second-class benefits in return, the Philippine Scouts themselves labored on.[32]

NOTES

1. There is a fourth way to think of the Scouts: as conscientious objectors, a term that colonial newspapers sometimes used to describe them in press coverage of the events. It is telling, though, that neither the soldiers nor their officers ever used the term. See, for instance, "Scout Objectors on Trial Today," *Manila Daily Bulletin*, July 29, 1924, p. 2.

2. Richard S. Fogarty, *Race and War in France: Colonial Subjects in the French Army, 1914–1918* (Baltimore: Johns Hopkins University Press, 2008); Joshua B. Freeman, "Militarism, Empire, and Labor Relations: The Case of Brice P. Disque," *International Labor and Working-Class History* 80 (Fall 2011): 103–120; James Hevia, *The Imperial Security State: British Colonial Knowledge and Empire-Building in Asia* (New York: Cambridge University Press, 2012); Thomas R. Metcalf, *The Aftermath of Revolt: India, 1857–1870* (Princeton, N.J.: Princeton University Press, 1964); Leonard V. Smith, *Between Mutiny and Obedience: The Case of the French Fifth Infantry Division during World War I* (Princeton, N.J.: Princeton University Press, 1994).

3. Jane Hathaway, ed., *Rebellion, Repression, Reinvention: Mutiny in Comparative Perspective* (Westport, Conn.: Praeger, 2000), esp. xi–xii. See also Leonard F. Guttridge, *Mutiny: A History of Naval Insurrection* (Annapolis, Md.: Naval Institute Press, 1992); Eric Leed, *No Man's Land: Combat and Identity in World War I* (New York: Cambridge University Press, 1979); Peter Linebaugh and

Marcus Rediker, *The Many-Headed Hydra: Sailors, Slaves, Commoners, and the Hidden History of the Revolutionary Atlantic* (Boston: Beacon Press, 2000); Elihu Rose, "The Anatomy of Mutiny," *Armed Forces and Society* 8 (Summer 1982): 562–574.

4. Richard Meixsel, "The Philippine Scout Mutiny of 1924," *South East Asia Research* 10 (November 2002): 358. "American political and social history and state development," writes Suzanne Mettler, "cannot be understood apart from the role, place, and significance of veterans and the policies created for them." Mettler, "Foreword," in *Veterans' Policies, Veterans' Politics: New Perspectives on Veterans in the United States*, ed. Stephen R. Ortiz (Gainesville: University Press of Florida, 2012), xi. See Roger Daniels, *The Bonus March: An Episode of the Great Depression* (Westport, Conn.: Greenwood Press, 1971); Jennifer D. Keene, *Doughboys, the Great War, and the Remaking of America* (Baltimore: Johns Hopkins University Press, 2001); Stephen R. Ortiz, *Beyond the Bonus March and the GI Bill: How Veteran Politics Shaped the New Deal Era* (New York: New York University Press, 2010).

5. Christopher Capozzola, *Uncle Sam Wants You: World War I and the Making of the Modern American Citizen* (New York: Oxford University Press, 2008); Nancy Gentile Ford, *Americans All!: Foreign-Born Soldiers in World War I* (College Station: Texas A&M University Press, 2001); Benjamin Heber Johnson, *Revolution in Texas: How a Forgotten Rebellion and Its Bloody Repression Turned Mexicans into Americans* (New Haven, Conn.: Yale University Press, 2003); Susan Applegate Krouse, *North American Indians in the Great War* (Lincoln: University of Nebraska Press, 2007); José A. Ramirez, *To the Line of Fire! Mexican Texans and World War I* (College Station: Texas A&M University Press, 2009); Lucy E. Salyer, "Baptism by Fire: Race, Military Service, and U.S. Citizenship Policy, 1918–1935," *Journal of American History* 91 (December 2004): 847–876; Christopher M. Sterba, *Good Americans: Italian and Jewish Immigrants during the First World War* (New York: Oxford University Press, 2003); Chad L. Williams, *Torchbearers of Democracy: African American Soldiers in the World War I Era* (Chapel Hill: University of North Carolina Press, 2010). See also Gregory Mann, *Native Sons: West African Veterans and France in the Twentieth Century* (Durham, N.C.: Duke University Press, 2006).

6. For more on the U.S. Army in the Pacific after World War I, see Edward M. Coffman, *The Regulars: The American Army, 1898–1941* (Cambridge: Harvard University Press, 2004), 324–371; Brian McAllister Linn, *Guardians of Empire: The U.S. Army and the Pacific, 1902–1940* (Chapel Hill: University of North Carolina Press, 1997), esp. 51–77 and 185–202. Meixsel, "Philippine Scout Mutiny," 344, explains that American officers who had seen the Philippines as a hardship post in the 1900s and 1910s now came to view it as a two-year "vacation with pay," although American enlisted men were markedly less enthusiastic. See D. Clayton James, *The Years of MacArthur* (Boston: Houghton Mifflin, 1970), vol. 1, 299–300.

7. Quote from Meixsel, "Philippine Scout Mutiny," 338. See also W. M. Belote, "The Rock in the 'Tween War Years," *Bulletin of the American Historical Collection* 19 (January–March 1991): 32–37; John Gordon IV, "Among the Best: The Philippine Scouts," *Military Review* 67 (September 1987): 70; Ralph Hirsch, "Our Filipino Regiment—The Twenty-Fourth Field Artillery (Philippine Scouts)," *Field Artillery Journal* 14 (July–August 1924): 354–357; Charles M. Hubbard and Collis H. Davis, Jr., *Corregidor in Peace and War* (Columbia: University of Missouri Press, 2006), 79; Linn, *Guardians of Empire*, 253–254; Meixsel, "Philippine Scout Mutiny," 339–340, 342, 346, 357.

8. "Pay of Enlisted Philippine Scouts," *Army and Navy Journal* 58 (December 18, 1920): 444. Scouts had several opportunities to supplement their own pay, through specialist ratings, long-term service bonuses, and food and housing allowances.

9. Delbert Ausmus Oral History, typescript (1965), 1106–1107, Papers of Delbert Ausmus, Young Research Library, UCLA, Los Angeles, Cal.; Belote, "Rock in the 'Tween War Years," 34; Meixsel, "Philippine Scout Mutiny," 348.

10. For more on wage rates on and off the base, see Meixsel, "Philippine Scout Mutiny," 356 n. 55; "Scout Soldiers' Income Greater than Teachers," *Manila Daily Bulletin*, July 12, 1924, p. 1.

11. Christopher Capozzola, "Minutemen for the World: Empire, Citizenship, and the National Guard, 1903–1924," in *Colonial Crucible: Empire in the Making of the Modern American State*, ed. Alfred W. McCoy and Francisco Scarano (Madison: University of Wisconsin Press, 2009), 421–430; Ricardo Trota Jose, "The Philippine National Guard in World War I," *Philippine Studies* 36 (Third Quarter 1988): 275–299; Headquarters, Philippine Department, Office Assistant Chief of Staff for Military Intelligence, "Mutiny of July 7–8, 1924 in Philippine Division, Fort William McKinley, P.I.," October 1, 1924, Military Intelligence Division Correspondence, 1917–1941, Box 3591, Record Group 165, National Archives and Records Administration, College Park, Md.

12. Jack McCallum, *Leonard Wood: Rough Rider, Surgeon, Architect of American Imperialism* (New York: New York University Press, 2006); Michael Onorato, "Leonard Wood and His Khaki Cabinet in the Philippines, 1921–1927," in *A Brief Review of American Interest in Philippine Development and Other Essays* (Berkeley, CA.: McCutchan Pub. Co., 1967), 123–124.

13. John J. Carroll, "Philippine Labor Unions," *Philippine Studies* 9 (April 1961): 227–228; Yoshihiro Chiba, "Cigar-Makers in American Colonial Manila: Survival during Structural Depression in the 1920s," *Journal of Southeast Asian Studies* 36 (October 2005): 394; Renato Constantino, with the collaboration of Letizia R. Constantino, *The Philippines: A Past Revisited* (Quezon City: Tala Pub., 1975), 357, 365; Dante G. Guevarra, *History of the Philippine Labor Movement* (Manila: Polytechnic University of the Philippines Institute of Labor and Industrial Relations, 1991), 37–48; "Island Labor to Form Own Party," *Manila Daily Bulletin*, July 8, 1924, p. 1; Melinda Tria Kerkvliet, *Manila Workers' Unions,*

1900–1950 (Quezon City: New Day Pub. Co., 1992), esp. 122–132; Carol Morris Petillo, *Douglas MacArthur: The Philippine Years* (Bloomington: Indiana University Press, 1981), 134; David R. Sturtevant, *Popular Uprisings in the Philippines, 1840–1940* (Ithaca, N.Y.: Cornell University Press, 1976), 213; David Wurfel, "Trade Union Development and Labor Relations Policy in the Philippines," *Industrial and Labor Relations Review* 12 (July 1959): 584. Organized labor in the United States rarely offered support or solidarity to Philippine workers in this period; some groups, such as the American Federation of Labor, were actively hostile to them. See Paul A. Kramer, *The Blood of Government: Race, Empire, the United States, and the Philippines* (Chapel Hill: University of North Carolina Press, 2006), 347–432.

14. Moon-Ho Jung, "Revolutionary Currents: Interracial Solidarities, Imperial Japan, and the U.S. Empire" (this volume); Alfred W. McCoy, *Policing America's Empire: The United States, the Philippines, and the Rise of the Surveillance State* (Madison: University of Wisconsin Press, 2009), 293–346; Francis Russell, *A City in Terror: 1919: The Boston Police Strike* (New York: Viking, 1975).

15. "Philippine Scouts Enlisted Personnel," *Army and Navy Journal* 58 (July 16, 1921): 1219.

16. Ibid; Meixsel, "Philippine Scout Mutiny," 348–349. In late 1923, a similar, if less dramatic, protest broke out among the Philippine Constabulary. See "Filipino Uprising against Americans Is Feared in Manila," *New York Times*, October 15, 1923, pp. 1, 3.

17. "Move Made to Settle Strike at Navy Yard," *Manila Daily Bulletin*, July 3, 1924, p. 1; "Navy Yard Strike Settlement Off," *Manila Daily Bulletin*, July 7, 1924, p. 1; "U.S. Navy Finds Plot to Blow Up Cavite Arsenal," *Chicago Tribune*, July 10, 1924, p. 14.

18. Donald R. McCoy, *Calvin Coolidge: The Quiet President* (New York: Macmillan, 1967), 232–234; "Senate Passes Measure Amending Military Law," *Washington Post*, April 22, 1924, p. 4. The men may also have been angered by the end of a pay supplement for skilled marksmen. While the cut applied to all Army soldiers in the belt-tightening 1920s, it fell harder on the Scouts, many of whom had served 20 years or more and racked up remarkable riflery skills. "300 Troopers Face Dismissal," *Manila Daily Bulletin*, July 8, 1924, p. 3.

19. "Unruly Soldiers to 'Get Air' within Few Days," *Manila Daily Bulletin*, July 11, 1924, p. 1.

20. Army statement quoted in "Arrest Ringleaders of Philippine Mutiny," *Atlanta Constitution*, July 9, 1924, p. 8; "Eight Filipino Soldiers Held," *Boston Globe*, July 7, 1924, p. 7; Linn, *Guardians of Empire*, 148–149; Meixsel, "Philippine Scout Mutiny," 333, 349; "Philippine Mutiny Confined to 200 Men," *New York Times*, July 11, 1924, p. 13; "300 Troopers Face Dismissal," *Manila Daily Bulletin*, July 8, 1924, pp. 1, 3. On secret informants, see "17 Scouts on Trial for Alleged Mutiny," *New York Times*, August 28, 1924, p. 2.

21. Quote from "Eight Filipino Soldiers Held," *Boston Globe*, July 7, 1924, p. 7. See also "Cavite Hit Hard by Yard Strike," *Manila Daily Bulletin*, July 8, 1924, p. 1;

"Eight Filipino Soldiers Held," *Boston Globe*, July 7, 1924, p. 7; Meixsel, "Philippine Scout Mutiny," 350; "Pay Strike Reported by Philippine Scouts," *New York Times*, July 7, 1924, p. 16; "Philippine Scouts End Strike Plan," *Boston Globe*, July 9, 1924, p. 8.

22. "Mutiny of July 7–8, 1924," NARA; J. P. Robinson, "Regimental Notes," *Field Artillery Journal* 16 (January–February 1926): 89–91.

23. "Major Lim New Athletic Head," *Manila Daily Bulletin*, July 21, 1924, p. 11; "90 Insubordinate Troopers Being Discharged Today," *Manila Daily Bulletin*, July 9, 1924, p. 1.

24. Quotes from "Will Discharge 190 Filipino Scouts," *Boston Globe*, July 10, 1924, p. 10; Walter Wilgus, "U.S. Navy Finds Plot to Blow Up Cavite Arsenal," *Chicago Tribune*, July 10, 1924, p. 14; "Where Obedience Is Essential" (editorial), *Manila Daily Bulletin*, July 8, 1924, p. 8. See also "Strikers Can't See Compromise," *Manila Daily Bulletin*, July 10, 1924, p. 1; "300 Troopers Face Dismissal," *Manila Daily Bulletin*, July 8, 1924, p. 1; "210 'Heroic' Soldier Strikers Waiting Discharge at McKinley, Present Hard Economic Puzzles," *Manila Daily Bulletin*, July 10, 1924, p. 8.

25. LeRoy Eltinge to Assistant Chief of Staff, August 12, 1924, in Military Intelligence Division Correspondence, 1917–1941, Box 3591, RG 165, NARA; George W. Read, quoted in James, *Years of MacArthur*, vol. 1, p. 303; "210 'Heroic' Soldier Strikers, Waiting Discharge at McKinley, Present Hard Economic Puzzles," *Manila Daily Bulletin*, July 10, 1924, pp. 1, 8.

26. Quotes from *Annual Report of the Governor General of the Philippine Islands for the Fiscal Year 1924* (Washington, D.C.: Government Printing Office, 1925), 3; "Native Noncooperation Failure, Wood Reports," *Washington Post*, September 25, 1924, p. 4; "90 Insubordinate Troopers Being Discharged Today," *Manila Daily Bulletin*, July 9, 1924, p. 2. See also "Governor Leaving for South Friday," *Manila Daily Bulletin*, July 3, 1924, p. 3.

27. Army statement, quoted in "Scouts Facing Court-Martial," *Los Angeles Times*, July 13, 1924, p. 8. See also "Mutiny Charge for 3 Groups," *Boston Globe*, July 23, 1924, p. 12; "More Than 500 Scouts Face Courts in Manila," *New York Times*, July 24, 1924, p. 1; "Philippine Mutineers Face Court Friday," *Washington Post*, July 20, 1924, p. 3; "Unruly Scouts Must Go," *New York Times*, July 10, 1924, p. 12.

28. "Begin Court-Martial of Philippine Scouts," *Washington Post*, August 1, 1924, p. 8; "Manila Lawyers to Aid Defense of 224 Scouts," *Manila Daily Bulletin*, July 23, 1924, p. 1; "Scout Trials on Next Week," *Manila Daily Bulletin*, July 16, 1924, p. 1. For more on MacArthur during this period, see Hubbard and Davis, *Corregidor*, 46; James, *Years of MacArthur*, vol. 1, esp. 300–303; William Manchester, *American Caesar: Douglas MacArthur, 1880–1964* (Boston: Little Brown, 1978), 116–135; Petillo, *Douglas MacArthur: The Philippine Years*, 125–154; Michael Schaller, *Douglas MacArthur: The Far Eastern General* (New York: Oxford University Press, 1989), 7–14.

29. "Tower of Babel Plea Is Used in Scouts' Defense," *Manila Daily Bulletin*, July 31, 1924, pp. 1, 2. On the Scouts' language skills, see Meixsel, "Philippine Scout Mutiny," 345.

30. Meixsel, "Philippine Scout Mutiny," 351–352, 356; "No Defense Offered by Alleged Mutineers," *Washington Post*, August 8, 1924, p. 3; "One Man Halts Troop Disorder," *Los Angeles Times*, August 3, 1924, p. 5; "203 Filipino Scouts Given Prison Terms for Mutiny," *Chicago Tribune*, August 21, 1924, p. 1.

31. Meixsel, "Philippine Scout Mutiny," 354; United States Bureau of Insular Affairs, *Annual Report of the Chief of the Bureau of Insular Affairs, 1925* (Washington, D.C.: Government Printing Office, 1925), 2. The War Department made no mention of the mutiny in its annual report, although statistical tables reveal the strikingly high number of discharges from the Scouts in late 1924. See United States Department of War, *Report of the Secretary of War to the President, 1925* (Washington, D.C.: Government Printing Office, 1925), 124ff.

32. Walter E. Prosser to Jarvis J. Bain, September 24, 1924, in Military Intelligence Division Correspondence, 1917–1941, Box 3591, RG 165, NARA.

4

The Photos That We Don't Get to See

Sovereignties, Archives, and the 1928 Massacre of Banana Workers in Colombia

KEVIN COLEMAN

A studio portrait that accompanied a United Fruit Company memo dated March 8, 1929.

Sometime between August and November 1928, five men posed for a picture in Magdalena, Colombia. About six months later, a United Fruit Company (UFC) supervisor sent that same photograph, along with a memo describing each of the subjects it depicted, to managers in the company's other divisions, including the one in Bocas del Toro, Panama, where the photo and memo were discovered by an anthropologist some fifty years later. Despite its apparent ordinariness, this photograph, in two slightly different iterations, has been reproduced countless times, appearing in YouTube videos, Wikipedia, and Google Images as well as in scholarly books and articles.

From the studio format and the suits and ties, the five men evidently sought out a photographer who could make a group portrait for them. Once a local artisan-entrepreneur made their likeness, they may have each kept a copy as a memento of the bond they were forging in a shared struggle. Against a backdrop of infinite black space, these workers came together in their best—and, perhaps, borrowed—clothes. They do not appear to be downtrodden. Instead, they represent themselves as serious and dignified. But the conventions of bourgeois portraiture are not enough to contain a few aberrant details, recorded in a light-sensitive emulsion that froze a fraction of a second in 1928. Those details disrupt the serene image of accomplished men.

In the center, wearing a white linen suit, sits Raúl Eduardo Mahecha. He fixes his gaze off to one side of the camera and has a fountain pen in his breast pocket. His companion with the number "2" written onto his image is Nicanor Serrano, a banana worker near Ciénaga, who furrows his brow and slightly tilts his head, yielding a countenance that bespeaks worry. At the time that the United Fruit Company manager affixed this photo to a memorandum that he sent to others within the company's internal network, Bernardino Guerrero, the young man labeled number "1," was serving a prison sentence of fourteen years. But here, prior to being locked up, he looks into the lens of the camera with patient, gentle eyes. Meanwhile, the manager reported that number "5," Erasmo Coronel, "was killed in the fighting at Sevilla." With skin darker than that of his companions, Pedro M. del Río, labeled number "3," calmly looks straight into the camera. Faintly visible on the surface that bears the image of man number "3," the photographer impressed the name of his studio. At every turn, this photo reminds the viewing subject of the temporality of the photographic space. Erasmo Coronel had, at the moment this picture was taken, looked at a photographer who took his picture. The photographer, in turn, saw a live human being. But those who received the company memo with this photograph attached saw the image of a man who was no more.

This image is worth examining because we have it (that is rare) and we know something about how the United Fruit Company used it. Although the company made extensive use of photography, we have few pictures of actual workers—most are of cars, bananas, buildings, and the construction of irrigation works. Furthermore, we should analyze it because it can stand for other images that we would like to see and that would enhance our understanding of the company's labor relations in Latin America. But nearly all of those images have been kept secret, hidden from generations of laborers, researchers, and the general public. With this solitary image that was liberated from an archive of capital, we can begin to imagine the other images like it that exist, or once existed, but that we will not be allowed to see. Such images invite us to reconsider the struggle of these workers while also revealing the violence exercised by the Colombian government and the United Fruit Company. This photo invites us to look at those that the company did not want to see and to listen to those whose voice it considered noise and not speech. From the stray fragments that have leaked out of an archive that refuses to let us in, we can begin to retrace the images that we cannot see and the futures that capital and the state violently cut short.

This photograph of friendship, a moment of male bonding between co-workers who later got caught in the snare of a violent and distinctively American form of imperialism, also helps us explain two important processes. First, the photo reveals how five working people sculpted themselves for a camera, projecting themselves to unknown viewers as respectable people at home with the comforts that the formal studio setting staged for early-twentieth-century cosmopolitan imaginaries. Second, the photo, with the numbers inscribed upon it, exposes one way that imperial sovereignty was challenged and reasserted. The workers went into the studio as self-conscious strike leaders, seeking to fashion a way of producing bananas that was consistent with Colombian labor laws. In that regard, this is a photograph of Colombian self-forging in an imperial contact zone. But the numbers written on that image are those of an identifying, selecting, and disciplinary gaze that sought to eliminate those workers and the local sovereignty that they nurtured. Thus this single photo tells a larger story about how working people contested neocolonialism, forcing the United Fruit Company and the Latin American state in which it was operating to decide whether or not to uphold the laws of Colombia or to use violence to restore the imperial relations that obtained in the banana zone. By focusing on how the striking workers put the question of local and national sovereignty into play, I show how merely insisting that the laws on the books should be enforced was interpreted as a revolutionary, anti-imperialist act that challenged the spatial and legal exceptions that the company had carved out in the tropics of Latin America and the Caribbean.

M E M O R A N D U M

March 8, 1929

The attached photograph shows five of the principal leaders in the recent disturbances in the Colombian Division. Their names are as follows:

No. 1. Bernadino Guerrero
No. 2. Nicanor Serrano
No. 3. P. M. del Rio
No. 4. Raúl Eduardo Mahecha
No. 5. Erasmo Coronel

No. 1 was secretary to Mahecha, the leader, and is now serving a term of fourteen years, seven months in the federal penitentiary in Tunja. No. 5 was killed in the fighting at Sevilla. Nos. 2 and 3 were simple laborers and were practically only figureheads in the organization.

No. 4, Mahecha, was the brains of the entire outfit and is one of the most dangerous communistic leaders in this country. He fomented the oil field strike in 1924 and last year was the leader of a bad strike in the coffee region in the interior. He came to Ciénaga about August of 1928 and immediately started fomenting the movement which culminated in the disturbance of December 6th. He is an ex-army captain, has a remarkable personality and an undoubted genius for organization. At the time the strikers were fired on in Ciénaga he fled and it is known that he was wounded in one leg. Since then he has disappeared completely and it is now reported in the press that he has escaped to Costa Rica.

Att.-photograph

"Memorandum, Colombian Division." United Fruit Company, March 8, 1929.

The Archive

During the early 1980s, anthropologist Philippe Bourgois was conducting fieldwork on the United Fruit Company's plantations in Costa Rica and Panama. One day, an aging warehouse foreman pointed him to an attic full of papers that the company probably thought had been destroyed. Bourgois managed to salvage nearly two thousand pages from the tens of thousands of documents that filled "four to five dozen unnumbered, mildewed, and rodent-eaten cardboard boxes."[1] About twenty-five years later, as I was conducting research in a banana-company town in Honduras, I was reading Bourgois's work and saw the picture of the Colombian labor leaders.

The United Fruit Company did not intend for images like the one from the historic strike in Colombia to be seen by those outside its own management team and the security forces upon which it relied. Consequently, historians have few such images to interpret and to draw upon as evidence that would allow photographs to fulfill their nineteenth-century mimetic function of providing immediate indices of particular moments. Photos like the one of the five Colombian labor leaders fit within a panoptic drive that Michel Foucault argued, in his early work, was emblematic of modernity and which now plays out in police and military surveillance programs. For these reasons and more, historians have an obligation to attend to the photographic traces left by imperial power in its encounter with workers. But with so few images available, how might we go about interpreting the images that have managed to break loose from a visual archive of power?

Photo theorist Ariella Azoulay gives us tools for considering images like the one of the Ciénaga strike leaders. First, in positing what she calls "the civil contract of photography," she argues that nobody owns photographs. Private individuals and organizations can temporarily care for photos. But, ultimately, photographs belong to everyone who engages with them, to every citizen in "the citizenry of photography." The citizenry of photography is not governed by a sovereign or limited by territoriality but is, instead, made up of anyone who addresses others through images or who takes the position of a photo's addressee. Second, as spectators, we have a duty to interpret these images.[2] Third, we must exercise what she calls "civil imagination" to think about the photographs not taken and about the photographs not seen.[3] Reading the image of the labor leaders in the Ciénaga strike in combination with the internal memorandum that it accompanied, we can infer that there were other, similar images. In fact, from just the papers that Bourgois recovered, we have several examples of the kinds of images that the company used to surveil its workforce. [4]

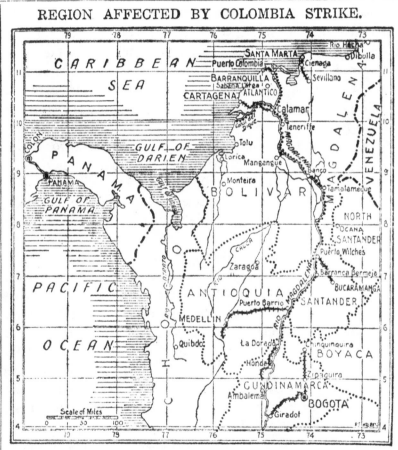

REGION AFFECTED BY COLOMBIA STRIKE.

Map Shows the Magdalena Department, Where the Uprising of 12,000 Laborers Endangers the Lives and Property of Americans.

New York Times, December 6, 1928.

Inscriptions

Born in 1884, Raúl Eduardo Mahecha joined the military of Colombia's conservative government and rose to the rank of captain. When Theodore Roosevelt shaved off part of Colombia to secure U.S. interests in building an interoceanic canal, Mahecha found himself in the newly created nation-state of Panama. In 1917, he settled in Medellín, where he founded two newspapers, *El Baluarte* and *El Luchador*, both of which sought to orient workers and to provide a space for them to voice their complaints.

Mahecha then became active in the three most important strikes in Colombia in the 1920s. In October 1924, nearly all of the workers of the U.S.-owned Tropical Oil Company went on strike. Within a couple of weeks, the government arrested Mahecha, who was serving as the vice president of the first Colombian socialist congress and had been helping to organize support for the strike through the publication of a leaflet demanding an increase in wages. Then, in early January 1927, Tropical Oil's workers put forward a list of demands that were similar to the ones that they had unsuccessfully made a couple years earlier: a salary increase of 25 percent, an eight-hour day, and screens on the windows of company housing. But the company was unwilling to negotiate. Meanwhile, the police shot two workers dead. The government declared a state of siege, arresting and deporting Mahecha and the other labor leaders.[5]

In February 1928, Mahecha and two other representatives of the Partido Socialista Revolucionario (PSR), Ignacio Torres Giraldo and María Cano, went on a lecture tour of the banana zone. Torres Giraldo described the fever of support that Mahecha inspired as "*mahechismo*." He described Mahecha as "bordering on forty" and as having "some vulgar manners that pleased the common people." Torres Giraldo also noted that Mahecha's speeches betrayed "a near total absence of knowledge of the Soviet revolution, but drew from his rich arsenal of memories of popular struggles in Colombia."[6]

While Mahecha is the outstanding figure in the photograph, the workers struck less because of him and more out of frustration with the contract system, the long hours, and the daily abuses to which they and their families were subjected by company employees and large growers.[7] One worker, Aristides López Rojano, remembers: "We worked from six in the morning until eleven and then from one in the afternoon until six. . . . The contractor paid the salary and reserved up to thirty percent for himself." In each of the strikes that led up to the big one in 1928, the banana workers insisted that the subcontract system be eliminated and that they be granted direct contracts with the company. Regarding the indignities that manual laborers suffered, José Maldonado, who worked for a Colombian grower who sold bananas to the UFC, reported that he used to work day and night to earn one and a half or two *pesos* a day. But he earned that wage only when he brought his children with him to help harvest the bananas and his wife to wash clothes or to make food for the workers. Maldonado complained that often the workers' wives or daughters were taken by the grower as his own private courtesans, indicating that the banana workers and their families remembered suffering intimate forms of violence that derived, in large part, from their structural position vis-à-vis the large growers.[8]

On the evening of October 6, 1928, the workers' delegates gathered to discuss their grievances and demands. Erasmo Coronel (the one wearing the bow tie in the group portrait) spoke in favor of a strike.[9] At around five in the morning, the workers agreed on their list of nine demands, summarized here by historian Marcelo Bucheli:

1. Collective insurance (which they defended using Law 37 [1921] and Law 32 [1922]).
2. Indemnification for work-related accidents (according to Law 57 [1915]).
3. Hygienic dwelling places and one day of rest every week (Law 46 [1918], Law 15 [1925], and Law 76 [1926]).
4. A 50% increase for lower-paid workers.
5. Discontinuance of the company's commissaries.
6. Elimination of the use of credit slips in place of money.
7. Weekly, rather than biweekly, payments.
8. Replacement of subcontractors with direct contracts with the company.
9. Establishment of hospitals in sufficient number and the proper sanitation of camps.[10]

These were not the demands of communist dupes. The workers' long-standing concern about the lack of formal contracts, along with the moderate demand that the company recognize them as its employees, indicate that the strike was, as Bucheli argues, a worker-initiated effort to modernize existing labor relations. In other words, the workers did not have to appeal to a communist or "subversive" imaginary. Rather, from the legal framework of 1920s Colombia, they took an already existing inscription of equality and demanded that it be implemented and enforced.

In repeatedly citing the Colombian constitution, the workers were demanding that the company comply with the laws already on the books, thus drawing attention to the nucleus of sovereign power in Colombia: the United Fruit Company. So despite the fact that the banana zone was not a bounded enclave, the UFC succeeded in placing itself outside the juridical order, choosing which laws it had to obey and which it could disregard. In the face of a massive strike, the company would soon reassert itself as the very definer of that order, summoning the repressive power of the Colombian state to do its bidding against a group of Colombian citizens in its indirect employ.

***

On the morning of October 7, the plantation workers appointed their negotiators: Erasmo Coronel, Nicanor Serrano, and Pedro M. del Río. The three men then traveled to Santa Marta to present the workers' demands to the company. The United Fruit Company's general manager, Thomas Bradshaw, declined to meet with them. Meanwhile, using a printing press that they brought with them to Ciénaga, Mahecha and Bernardino Guerrero publicized the workers' activities by printing fliers and the *Vanguardia* newspaper. On October 28, the delegation of workers tried again to meet with the company's management. But Bradshaw refused to negotiate, citing a 1925 decree from the Colombian government that stated that contract workers were not employees because there was no "juridical link" between the workers and the company. Then, the Colombian Congress passed a law sponsored by the Ministries of War, Interior, and the Treasury to curtail strikes, restrict freedom of assembly, and to allow censorship of the press. The "Law for Social Defense" (Law 69, October 30, 1928) allowed for strict surveillance and narrowed the parameters of what could count as legitimate public discourse.[11] This law created an official frame for political surveillance, an activity that, for the UFC, was ongoing in the banana plantations.[12]

On November 6, the executive committee of the Unión Sindical de Trabajadores de Magdalena issued the company an ultimatum: negotiate or the workers strike. Even the governor of Magdalena sought, to no avail, to persuade the company to negotiate with the workers. On November 11, the negotiating committee and representatives of sixty-three banana farms convened in Ciénaga. The workers declared a general strike, effective the next day.[13]

The workers argued that the UFC "was not obeying even one of the labor laws of Colombia, and had declared itself to be in open rebellion." Furthermore, "the workers of the Banana Zone comply with all of the laws of the country and, today, in declaring a strike, they obey the law to vindicate their rights, violated daily by the powerful Fruit Company, who looks at the worker with indifference as he wears himself out with ulcers, malaria, tuberculosis and other diseases, without even a humane sentiment that would move the company to comply with the labor legislation."[14] In other words, the workers were protesting the fact the Boston-based company had created an extrajudicial space in which it could exploit them. Within a few days of this declaration, thousands were withholding their labor.

The shopkeepers, for their part, resented the monopoly that the UFC enjoyed through its company stores. United Fruit paid its workers partly in vouchers valid only in its commissaries. The company also prohibited the entry of outside merchants into its plantation work camps. The merchants helped to formulate the list of nine demands and the fact that the workers included a call to eliminate the company stores helped them to secure the support of local storeowners. As Salvador Bornacelli recalled, "It was the merchants who practically sustained the strike. They gave us money, paper, medicines, and foodstuffs."[15]

⁂

On the first day of the strike, the commander of the Colombian armed forces appointed General Carlos Cortés Vargas as the military chief of the Plaza of Santa Marta and the banana zone. By the second day, Cortés Vargas was in Ciénaga with a battalion and relying upon, in his words, "the secret agents that we had throughout the Zone." Those "secret agents" were likely the United Fruit Company's paid informants. From the start, the military used the UFC's trains to transport soldiers throughout the zone. When the Colombian government's own labor inspector judged that the strike was legal, Cortés Vargas immediately had him jailed.[16]

The United Fruit Company and the Colombian military coordinated their response to the strike. The merchants in the banana zone noted that soldiers who only earned about 120 *pesos* monthly were suddenly arriving in their shops with 500-*peso* bills, which only the UFC distributed, evidently to break any real or potential solidarity between the soldiers and the striking workers.[17] Employees of the company rode the trains, indicating who should be arrested.[18] In the memories of workers, the bond between the company and the military was even more intimate, as Adán Ortiz noted: "For many nights in a row, Cortés Vargas had been meeting with the manager. There was an extravagance of liquor, food, and orgies with Colombian women and foreigners and even they got drunk with the soldiers. Everybody knew it, especially those in Ciénaga."[19]

But sovereignty in the banana zone remained contested, both by the workers and by the local officials who did not take kindly to the commands of newly arrived General Cortés Vargas. Santander Alemán, a foreman in the UFC's railroad division, recalled that he and about eight hundred other workers were traveling from one banana camp to another when the soldiers stopped them and asked who was in charge. The workers replied that they were all in charge (*"todos éramos jefes"*).[20] The soldiers then arrested and turned over 413 prisoners to Governor José María Núñez Roca. On November 13, the governor wrote to Cortés Vargas, informing him that the next day he would be receiving Erasmo Coronel, Pedro M. del Río, and Nicanor Serrano to settle the strike. But since Cortés Vargas had arrested Serrano, the governor unilaterally decided to release him so that he could serve as a representative of the workers' executive committee. After a few more days in the Santa Marta jail, the governor of Magdalena released the rest of the men that Cortés Vargas had sent.

The mayor of Ciénaga, a traditional Liberal Party stronghold, was even more outspoken in his solidarity with the striking workers and in his opposition to the militarization of the banana zone. On Saturday, December 1, an express boat arrived in Ciénaga with two hundred soldiers who immediately occupied the offices of the municipal government, converting them into barracks. The mayor of Ciénaga, Victor Manuel Fuentes Jiménez, complained in at least two newspapers, *La Prensa* of Barranquilla and *El Diario* of Córdoba, that the municipal buildings were property of the municipality and that "the federal government had not contributed one cent toward their construction."[21] He stated that he had not been consulted about this unlawful occupation and, under no circumstances, would he have permitted it.

With tens of thousands of workers defiantly withholding their labor and with local political leaders publicly criticizing the heavy-handed military tactics, Cortés Vargas had reason to worry about his tenuous hold on the region. He could not even trust his own troops. On December 4, 1928, *La Prensa* reported that a contingent of three hundred soldiers had just arrived in Santa Marta; the regiment was "made up exclusively of *antioqueños*, requested by the Commander of the zone, who feels that the soldiers from the coast do not provide any security at all, given that many of them are linked to the strikers. Almost all of them are former banana workers."[22] The general and military commander of the banana zone saw that the successful use of brute force was intimately bound to questions of loyalty. He worried that his underlings who had once worked for the UFC would side with the strikers and disobey the orders of their superiors. Command could be undone, Cortés Vargas worried, by affective ties and a sense that one was not fighting on the side of justice. Put differently, Cortés Vargas feared class solidarity.

Tensions escalated when the United Fruit Company paid strikebreakers to begin cutting fruit on December 4. The strikers sought to thwart the attempt by the company and the government to circumvent the strike. At eleven in the morning, the UFC train left the Ciénaga station carrying the regiment of *antioqueños* who were sent to accompany the strikebreakers as they worked in the plantations near Sevilla. From here, the stories diverge. Salvador Bornacelli recalls that the workers "explained the reasons for the strike and the soldiers comprehended those reasons and accompanied some of the guys up to the union house where the workers served them food." But Cortés Vargas claims that his soldiers had been assaulted by the workers and that his first concern was "to rescue the soldiers and their weaponry: the rifles and the cartridges of 250 rounds that each soldier carried."[23] Cortés Vargas returned with his men and took "hundreds" of the strikers as prisoners. With the strike in its fifth week, the banana zone militarized, and having lost the support of the local shop owners, whose revenues had dried up, the workers were increasingly frustrated. To block the trains loaded with fruit (and soldiers) from continuing to the port, women and children sat on the tracks.

On December 5, the workers received news that the governor of Magdalena had summoned them to Ciénaga to settle the strike. They began to gather by the thousands. Then, at just before midnight, Cortés Vargas received a telegram with Decree Number 1, the government's official declaration of a state of siege (*estado de sitio*) in the banana zone. Not content with an abstract document granting him emergency powers, Cortés Vargas set out the specifics in a separate decree:

> Article 1: In compliance with Legislative Decree 1 of 5 December 1928, I peremptorily order the immediate dissolution of any meeting of more than three individuals.

> Article 2: The government forces are ordered, with legal preventions, to strictly comply with this Decree, firing at the multitude [*la multitud*] if necessary.

> Article 3: No person can move after the military bugle sounds.[24]

As the government suspended the rule of law in the banana zone, the capacity to decide who had authority in the particular region was indeed fluid, with strikers impeding the movement of the trains and even deposing the police inspector of Ríofrio, placing labor activist Manuel Campo in charge.[25] The gathering crowd converted Ciénaga's train station into an impromptu amphitheater, with the parked railcars as its main stage. Mahecha and Mayor Fuentes mounted the freight cars to address the workers. Here again, the accounts diverge. Cortés Vargas wrote: "the orators, in incendiary harangues, inspired the people to remain firm, given that the hour of sacrifice had arrived with the declaration of the state of siege." In contrast, several of the workers recall that, as early as 10 p.m., Mahecha began exhorting the strikers to return home. But the workers called Mahecha a coward and told him to go home himself. Mahecha warned them that the military was setting them up.[26]

According to Cortés Vargas's own richly documented and self-exculpatory account, at around 1:30 a.m. on December 6, he ordered all of his troops, "with their machine guns," to march to the train station. Surrounded by armed soldiers, the "mutineers" (*amotinados*) intensified their shouting. The military played the drums for five minutes and then Captain Julio Garavito read both Legislative Decree 1, which placed the region under a state of siege, and Cortés Vargas's own military decree.[27] While the putative reason for reading these decrees before the strikers was to inform them of a legal decision that the government had taken, I would suggest that the public reading of these decrees was not really intended for the workers. Rather, before using violence to reconstitute the social order under the command of the military, the federal government, and the United Fruit Company, the act of reading worked to bind the soldiers together and to the sovereign powers that issued those decrees.[28] In keeping with Walter Benjamin's insight that the sovereign decision is always an act of revolutionary violence that institutes a new juridical order, in the moment just prior to when the military fired upon the rebellious workers, Captain Garavito read the decree that suspended the guarantees of the law and Cortés Vargas's new rule about freedom of assembly and its consequences.[29] With Cortés Vargas still unsure of the loyalty of his troops, the act of reading these decrees served to counteract any remaining affective ties that the infantrymen may have felt toward their old buddies and fellow *magdalenenses*, organizing the men into proxies of the sovereign.[30]

Unperturbed, the workers refused to disperse and instead shouted out to the soldiers to come over and join them. Cortés Vargas ordered the bugler to call the troops to attention. In a scene that sat dormant in Cortés Vargas's 1929 memoir until 1967, when Gabriel García Márquez pulled it out of a past that threatened to be forgotten, the captain ordered the crowd: "You have five minutes to disperse." The workers stayed put. Five minutes later, the bugle sounded again. "One more minute and we will open fire." Another bugle call. No one moved. General Carlos Cortés Vargas described the scene:

> During the course of this last minute, we shouted: "People, disperse, we will open fire!"

"We'll give you the remaining minute!" a voice shouted from the tumult.

We had complied with the penal code. The last bugle call ripped through the air; the multitude seemed stuck in the ground. It was necessary to comply with the law, and we complied: "Open fire!!" we shouted.

The human mass fell like a single man, the clash of the discharge drowned out the shouting.[31]

In *One Hundred Years of Solitude*, García Márquez altered this scene by adding one word, so that the voice from the crowd addressed the soldiers directly: "*Bastards*, we'll give you the remaining minute!"

***

In the dark of night, the firing guns were like so many flash bulbs, illuminating the plaza and arresting the movement of those at the other end of the barrel. Those who could flee, fled. They moved beyond the gun sights, outside the frame lit up by the discharges of the Lewis semiautomatic machine guns.[32] Those who were cut down lay dead or wounded in the plaza at the railroad terminus. Photography is a script of light. The traces of the bullets through the plaza etched a new script that went straight from the muzzle flash, burned through the early morning in this public space, and tore apart the body of a person who had gathered to change how he was treated by the banana company.[33] "They fired on anything that moved. They even killed donkeys that night," recalls Adán Ortiz.[34] This writing with light went on for several minutes, inscribing the sovereign decision upon the bodies of the workers.

When Cortés Vargas called a halt to the firing, the dark of night returned. As Hernando Varela Oliveros remembers, "We heard the garbage truck going by in front of our house and then the boat tooting its horn. The next day, we realized that the truck had been transporting the dead bodies behind the hospital, where they loaded them onto the *Pichincha* barge to throw them into the sea."[35] Another witness, Santander Alemán, recounts what happened at daylight: "At six in the morning, I was witnessing (*presenciando*) the gathering up of the cadavers. The soldiers tried to prevent the townspeople from seeing, but the people wouldn't go away. The people wanted to see."[36] But of the hundreds that the people of the banana zone insisted that the military killed that night, when daylight broke, there were, according to popular memory, just nine dead bodies lying in the plaza. Josefa María, who worked from Ciénaga to support the strike, noted that the military deliberately left each body as a signifier: "They had only left nine dead bodies, equal to the nine demands that the workers made."[37]

***

Nine demands and nine corpses. A mass movement but no photos that would allow the masses to see images of themselves acting in concert. Flashes from machine guns. Memories of the massacre written upon bodies and minds but not on photographic paper. A photograph with numbers written upon it and a memo that reads like a hit list. Bodies disposed of under the cover of darkness. Archives with thousands of photos but none of the strike. These are the mechanisms through which sovereign violence constituted a field of vision. What we cannot see in the documentary and photographic record, we cannot use to generate knowledge of the past. The violence of December 6, 1928, reversed the strike and reestablished the Colombian government's control over the region. The law-making violence of December 6 was then covered up. Bodies were buried in mass graves and hundreds of people were never seen again. In the archives, the violence of that night mutates into law-preserving violence.[38] Official archives contain little to no record of the massacre and the private archives that may contain records of this neo-colonial violence remain inaccessible to researchers. By imagining the photos that could have been taken and by reconstructing the story of the Ciénaga massacre around the few photos that we do have, we might begin to restore the potentiality of the archive and the contingency of history. Arresting these images of the past as they flit by, thereby taking up the task that Benjamin set before us, we might radically historicize a moment in which sovereignty and demands for recognition were truly in play in early-twentieth-century Colombia.

***

While the United Fruit Company and the Colombian military had incessantly raised the specter of violence from the workers, it was not until the declaration of the state of siege that the banana zone was converted into a space outside the law. By eight in the morning of December 6, the military destroyed Mahecha's printing press, burned three thousand copies of the daily newspaper *La Nación*, and began stealing from the cooperative store and ransacking the houses of labor leaders.[39] The U.S. Consulate in Santa Marta cabled Washington to request "the presence within calling distance of an American war ship."[40] Many workers fled the banana zone to find refuge in the mountains. But some stayed and sought to avenge the killing of their companions.

The workers exacted the heaviest price in Sevilla, as recounted by the chief of police, Salvador Fuentes. When Fuentes got word that the workers had just looted the company store in Orihueca, he met with the UFC's superintendent in Sevilla to see how they could defend the company's property. They decided that Fuentes and twelve policemen would move into the UFC's engineering quarters, where twelve North Americans and three Colombians were already hiding out. Soon, the workers arrived, armed with machetes, rifles, and revolvers. Fuentes and Lieutenant José María Quintero begged the workers to stay calm, but they would not listen, for just as with the workers' speech, in which the United Fruit Company heard only "blah, blah, blah" and not meaningful words spoken by people who deserved recognition, now the workers heard only "blah, blah, blah" from the authorities. Fuentes continued: "A voice from the multitude ordered: 'Fire!' Immediately shots were fired and Lieutenant Quintero fell at my side, mortally wounded."[41]

According to the official report, the police fired back at eight hundred workers. They killed several, and the workers began to take cover behind the railroad cars while also looting the company store and setting the company's other buildings on fire. A couple hours later, the military arrived and the workers dispersed. The workers had killed Lieutenant Quintero, while the military and police had killed twenty-nine workers, including "Erasmo Coronel, the communist ringleader."[42] Years later, Álavo Girón reminisced: "Erasmo Coronel was a *muchacho* that we raised here. He was simple and good."[43] The next day, soldiers managed to shoot Mahecha, wounding him as he escaped.[44]

***

On December 7, the U.S. Embassy in Bogotá reported: "Situation outside Santa Marta City unquestionably very serious: outside zone is in revolt; military who have orders 'not to spare ammunition' have already killed and wounded about fifty strikers."[45] Violence exercised through Colombian proxies would be sufficient to restore the status quo. But first, U.S. citizens had to be removed from the zone so that when the military repressed the strikers via a "general offensive," there would be no danger of "repercussions."[46] On December 9, a troop train arrived in the banana zone of Santa Marta "with all American citizens," according to a telegram from Vice Consul Lawrence F. Cotie. He continued: "No Americans killed or wounded. Guerilla warfare now continuing in the zone but military forces are actively engaged in clearing the district of the Communists. [. . .] All danger to American citizens is now past."[47] Americans are protected. Communists are banned and excluded. Sovereign authority is being restored.

Vice Consul Cotie reported that "property belonging to the United Fruit Company, Colombian employees of the Company and private planters was destroyed." Furthermore, he described how the striking workers had been discursively transformed into the enemy: "The troops are still vigorously pursuing the main bands of communists—as the strikers are now called by the military—and excepting for occasional sniping by small groups throughout the entire zone, the situation is controlled by the army."[48] The sovereign's power, which had been briefly suspended, was now being vigorously reasserted. But the photograph of the Colombian labor leaders testifies to the fact that the laborers envisioned another way of being, thinking, and working.

And so it was in Santa Marta, as a crowd formed in response to the sovereign's attempt to reassert his (and it was always "his") power. The U.S. State Department narrated this crisis of authority, noting that "looting and killing was carried on from the moment the announcement of a state of Martial Law was made and the fact that the American residents in the Zone came out of it alive is due to the defense they put up for six hours when they held off the mob that was bent upon killing them."[49] The U.S. consular officer rightly traces the popular indignation at the state's extraordinary reaction—the suspension of the rule of law—to the workers' demands that the company obey Colombian laws. The workers had forced the imperial model of the United Fruit Company into crisis. The sleight of hand by which the company pretended that it was not really in charge had to be abandoned. The actions of the workers made this neocolonial enterprise unstable precisely because their very presence always threatened to call into question the most fundamental political and economic relations that underpinned foreign-controlled commodity production. Thus, the strike exposed and upset the relations of imperial sovereignty that normally obtained in the banana zones.

The U.S. consular officer continued: "Santa Marta was a stretch of territory that was under the control of mobs of armed men and women."[50] In other words, the workers had succeeded, for two days, in creating an autonomous zone that was not subject to the authority of sovereigns in Boston, Bogotá, or Washington. This is the constant threat that constituted power sees in the constitutive energy of a multitude. This is the threat that the United States saw in the "mob" that threatened to rearrange a "soft" colonial relationship, forcing the United Fruit Company to choose between obeying the laws of the host country or openly revealing that this political and economic order rested not on consent, or even compliance, but on the barrel of a gun.

Proper power relations were restored through state violence, as conveyed by the U.S. Embassy: "The legal advisor of the United Fruit Company here in Bogotá stated yesterday that the total number of strikers killed by the Colombian military authorities during the recent disturbance reached between five and six hundred; while the number of soldiers killed was one."[51] A few weeks later, U.S. officials upped the estimate: "The Bogotá representative of the United Fruit Company told me yesterday that the total number of strikers killed by the Colombian military exceeded one thousand."[52]

In spite of the unrelenting violence directed against the laborers, many remained defiant. The workers continued to publicly denounce banana imperialism by displaying the connection between the Colombian government, its military response to the strike, and the way that banana production was now associated with death. The fruit company had fashioned itself as an agent of science bringing progress to the backward tropics. But through the strike, the workers forced the multinational corporation and the Colombian government to take the instrumental reason that underwrote industrial banana production to its absolute limit. The workers openly challenged the company's representations of itself as an engine of progress. As the U.S. Embassy noted: "The manifestations against the Government of yesterday and the day before were conspicuous for the number of inscriptions carried by manifestants relating to the fruit workers' strike, denouncing the Government and especially General Cortés Vargas for the manner in which the strike was put down; also, skeletons and skulls adorned with bunches of bananas were freely displayed."[53] The public linking of death and bananas was not the branding that United Fruit would have chosen for itself. By making that link, workers publicly laid claim to their space and to the local meaning of cultivating this fruit. The strike was about dignity. But even more fundamentally, it was *political*, in accord with Jacques Rancière's description of politics as the staging of a dispute by those who have no recognized part in the community.[54] That is, the workers were deidentifying as *déclassés* who could be expected to tolerate any abuse and to continue working without being recognized as rights-bearing employees. By repeatedly raising the issue of direct contracts, the workers went through a process of subjectification *as workers*, with the same rights as any other workers, and *as citizens*, with the same rights as any other citizens in Colombia.

Even after the massacre, the military had yet to disperse the laborers and their families. Workers continued to gather. They continued to contest the treatment they were receiving. The banana workers showed that although they had been placed into a state of exception, they refused to stay in that juridical space of abandonment. For demanding recognition that they were indeed UFC employees and that the company should obey Colombian laws and provide better compensation, the United Fruit Company marshaled the repressive force of the Colombian military. In other words, the company was the de facto sovereign in this region of Colombia and its local power was contested by labor, which proposed that banana plantation workers be incorporated into the political community of the nation by making the "radical" demand that the laws of the country be enforced.

Imagining a Civil Archive

The United Fruit Company Photograph Collection at Harvard University contains more than 10,400 photos, at least 369 of which are from the company's operations in Colombia. Absent from this official archive is the photograph of the five strike leaders and the memorandum that

Colombia, 10 December 1928. *Courtesy of the United Fruit Company Photograph Collection, Harvard University.*

accompanied that image. Also absent are photographs of the 1928 strike. But there are several photos in the official UFC archive that do document the destruction that workers wrought upon the company's stores, living quarters, bodegas, and telephone lines.

So, what to make of the presence of the photos of the burnt company stores and engineering quarters in the UFC archive at Harvard? Let me respond by recalling that the photo of the five workers that was circulated among company managers does not contain any violence in the image itself. It is the memo that suggests the violent purposes to which that image was put. That image-text initiates a movement of prosopopoeia in which the figures of the labor leaders depicted in the photo are put forth only to efface them, to disfigure them as they are withdrawn by the managers' recontextualization of the subjects depicted and by the numbers and the word "out" written onto the surface of the image. The photo memo distances the company from violence, taking the load off of the communicator by placing the unfavorable ascriptions of "leaders of the recent disturbances," "serving a term of fourteen years in the federal penitentiary," and "one of the most dangerous communistic leaders" onto the men whose class status is disguised by the genre of studio portraiture. And then the UFC kept this photo out of its official archive.

In contrast, the photos of the burnt commissaries document violence—the violence that the workers carried out. The photo of the burnt company store also shows how the workers rejected the constituent violence of the Colombian military and the United Fruit Company. Hiding the photo of the five workers and the memo is one aspect of an ongoing law-preserving violence. Hence, this photograph needs to be read in conjunction with the photo of the five labor leaders. The death that links them is the presence of Erasmo Coronel in the first and the absence of any life in the second, which is more like a crime scene photo, devoid of life and establishing evidence. The way that these two images appeared in the two UFC archives—one *not* intended to be seen by the public and the other donated for researchers—suggests the ways that photos can be used to perpetuate violent sovereign acts that continue to regulate the visual field. By rescuing one of the photos from an archive of power and by reading it in conjunction with an uncensored image, we exercise what Azoulay calls "civil imagination" and begin to transcend the points of view of the United Fruit Company and the Colombian government.

Before closing, I would like to introduce another iteration of the studio portrait of the five labor leaders. It is the same exact portrait as the one that Philippe Bourgois found in the UFC's archive in Panama. But the numbers and the penmanship vary from one photo to the other. In 1929, General Cortés Vargas published a book in which he gave his official account of the strike and the role of the military in Magdalena. The original 1929 edition of his book contained several photographs, including the studio portrait of Bernardino Guerrero, Nicanor Serrano, Pedro M. del Río, Raúl Eduardo Mahecha, and Erasmo Coronel. Although the order of the numbers varies, both photos were captioned such that each number correctly corresponded to the person denoted in the picture. Here's my supposition: At one of the meetings between Cortés Vargas and the UFC manager, each of them had a copy of the photo. The company had its own photographers and they could easily make copies of

Principales dirigentes de la huelga de 1928 en la Zona Bananera: 1. Raúl Eduardo Mahecha, el jefe indiscutido de todo el movimiento obrero de la Zona. 2. Erasmo Coronel, quien murió en el enfrentamiento de la Superintendencia de la United Fruit Company en Sevilla. 3. Pedro M. del Río, uno de los delegados obreros que discutió el pliego de peticiones en la Gobernación del Magdalena. 4. Bernardino Guerrero, secretario permanente de Mahecha. 5. Nicanor Serrano, otro de los delegados obreros que, también en asocio de Coronel, deliberó sobre las solicitudes de los trabajadores en la Gobernación. Esta fotografía fue tomada antes de iniciarse la huelga.

Photo from Cortés Vargas's 1929 book.

photos. Then, Cortés Vargas and Bradshaw sat down together and identified each of the subjects in the photo. I also surmise that the writing on the image in Cortés Vargas's book is his own and that the writing on the UFC's image is Bradshaw's. I would guess that the two men talked about this photo together and that with the photo, they devised a plan for defeating the strike, for driving out Mahecha and the other labor leaders.

Beyond the fact that the same image was put forth in 1929 as part of a public attempt by Cortés Vargas to clear his own name, and then

After the military opened fire on the striking workers in Ciénaga, the workers destroyed several of the UFC's buildings, including the engineers' quarters in Sevilla. This is where Erasmo Coronel was killed. *Courtesy of the United Fruit Company Photograph Collection, Harvard University.*

emerged more than fifty years later, from a secret company archive in the early 1980s, there is one more visual link worth highlighting. Cortés Vargas also provided a photograph of the engineers' quarters in Sevilla after those buildings were destroyed in the fighting on December 6, 1928. That exact same image now sits in the United Fruit Company Photograph Collection at Harvard University. As the company documented the destruction of its property, it evidently made extra prints, some of which Cortés Vargas obtained. The same picture, in two different places and times, marks the place where Erasmo Coronel was killed. His corpse is not in the image. The only violence that the image depicts is that perpetrated by the workers. Erasmo Coronel was buried separately from the other workers killed in Sevilla. But he was also buried in the studio portrait and marked "*out.*" He was then entombed in a company archive in Panama. Anthropologist Philippe Bourgois began a process of exhuming his body, breaking the pact that kept the photo memo, and the violence it suggested, hidden from public view. By retracing the violence that buried this image and by imagining the other photos that we don't get to see, we might begin to interrupt the law-preserving violence that keeps such images secret. In that way, we might begin to bring back the dreams and possibilities that the five men who posed for this picture held fast. We might restore the potentialities of the archive and put it toward more civil ways of being together. But even after the massacre and despite the fact that the archive of it has been mutilated, the striking workers still managed to inscribe equality into a radically unequal neocolonial order. That inscription continues to be cited by Colombian workers and *campesinos* struggling to be seen and heard in a political community that often refuses to recognize them and dismisses their speech as noise.

Labor Exposes Spatial Exceptions

In closing, I would like to explain how my reading of this photograph from 1928 recasts basic historiographic questions about the intersection between labor and empire. By tracing the itinerary of this photo, I have attempted to offer some transportable analytics and methods that scholars of imperial constellations in other places—from South Asia to sub-Saharan Africa—might engage to radically historicize moments when sovereignty was in play.

Historian Paul A. Kramer called for "a U.S. historiography of spatial exceptions: extraordinary power exercised at and through the interstices of sovereignty, often underwritten by essentialisms of race, gender, and civilization."[55] The American Zone in Magdalena was just such a spatial exception. The banana zone decoupled a section of Colombian territory from its national laws, carving out a juridical space in which the company effectively ruled. By protesting the fact that the company flouted Colombian legal codes, the workers challenged the continued existence of an exceptional space that was designed to extract their labor under the guise of bringing modern, scientific agricultural techniques. After being placed into a state of exception and being subjected to extreme violence carried out by the company's surrogates in the Colombian state, the workers physically assaulted UFC property, burning a company store that sold them the material objects of Euro-American consumption. The enclave and its emblematic "American Zone" had long represented themselves as harbingers of progress that kept tropical disease at bay to purportedly establish a model of modernity in the heart of backwardness. But the strike not only challenged the legality of UFC labor practices and the fabrication of an extrajudicial imperial hamlet, it also challenged the moral and aesthetic codes that preserved this spatial exception.

The photo of the strike leaders, the strike itself, and the company's writing over the strike leaders: each illustrates the ways that the spatial exception was a legal netherworld that is characteristically *visual*. Hence I would suggest that the spatial exception is best understood as a theatrical stage created by imperial power. It creates that stage to extract natural resources and labor, on the one hand, and to perform its self-declared civilizational virtues on the other. But most importantly, it is an exceptional space precisely because it is where decisions are made. It is a space in which neither the laws of the metropole nor the laws of the colony are in full force. In the spatial exception, the United Fruit Company created a stage upon which it could freely exercise its will, unencumbered by local laws, which it saw as mere obstacles, like swamps, that it could rework in the service of increased profits from banana production. But this also meant that Colombia's banana-exporting region was also a stage upon which all of the actors could improvise, occasionally doing something unexpected.

In the spatial exception, the company and the workers, as well as the U.S. and Colombian governments, were each actors, producers, and spectators. In this space between law and its absence, each actor/producer/spectator had a degree of freedom about how to hurl oneself into the future. The powerful company felt entitled to force the objectively less powerful workers to accept the terms of employment that it laid out. But the workers felt that the company owed them something more, that they had become its creditors, and it, their debtor. When the company failed to repay them for their work with wages that they considered fair and treatment that they considered decent, the workers decided to seek compensation. In doing so, they forced the company up onto the stage. But this time, the company was no longer playing the role of a collective enterprise of U.S. scientists and engineers whose reworking of local

landscapes and livelihoods was legitimated by a discourse of modernization. With the strike, the workers forced the company and its production
methods to take center stage, visible for all to see. But just as the workers
put the spotlight on the company's imperial labor practices, the United
Fruit Company exited, bringing the Colombian military into the picture.

Thus U.S. imperialism worked most brutally and definitively in the
very moment in which the United Fruit Company and the U.S. government attempted to recede from view, allowing the Colombian government to reassert its sovereignty and to become a more effective surrogate
of U.S. power. Thinking through this photograph has allowed us to see
how the 1928 strike tested whether or not the United Fruit Company
had a reproducible model for how the American imperial state could
continue to exert power through its ad hoc network of corporations,
missionaries, and mercenaries backed by the military and diplomatic
power of the U.S. government. Excavating the making of this photo of
five workers, along with the subsequent uses to which this image was
put, has allowed me to argue that this picture should be seen as an al-
legory for the internal contradiction between self-forging and imperial
overwriting that always stirred within U.S. neocolonial projects. Despite
the rhetoric of liberalism, universality, and modernization, the Boston-
based United Fruit Company created a vertical corporate structure that
allowed it to exploit labor and natural resources throughout the tropics
of Latin America and the Caribbean. But doing so entailed negotiating
not only with various local and national claims to sovereign authority, it
also meant repeatedly interacting with individual workers who had their
own ideas about how they should be treated and how they wanted to live
their lives and provide for their families.

Vast material inequalities, local aspirations to self-government, ex-
ternally imposed corporate discipline, and discourses of race and modernity that cast locals as representatives of barbarism in need of the
UFC's civilization: for each of these reasons and more, workers could
suddenly emerge to assert another sense of themselves and to claim their
rights. The actions of the workers and even the local merchants made
the company-administered spatial exceptions unstable and unworkable,
nearly prompting the U.S. Navy to intervene. In short, the workers' demand that the company operate within the framework of Colombian
labor laws was radical precisely because it prompted an extraordinary

response, one that revealed that violence maintained order in the spatial exceptions carved out by the company.

Retrieving this photo from a violence that is preserved in the archive allows us to rescue the history that puts these workers—Raúl Eduardo Mahecha, Nicanor Serrano, Bernardino Guerrero, Pedro M. del Río, and Erasmo Coronel—in the center of a struggle over local and national sovereignty that exposed the violence exercised by the United Fruit Company and the governments of Colombia and the United States. The photo allows us to hear what the company tried to silence, to see what the company sought to keep invisible. Reclaiming this photo allows us to tell a story of worker-driven self and national forging that banana progress tried to obliterate.

NOTES

1. Philippe Bourgois, "One Hundred Years of United Fruit Company Letters," in *Banana Wars: Power, Production, and History in the Americas*, ed. Steve Striffler and Mark Moberg (Durham, NC: Duke University Press, 2003), 107.

2. Ariella Azoulay, *The Civil Contract of Photography* (New York: Zone Books, 2008), 85–136, 137–186, 413–471.

3. Ariella Azoulay, *Civil Imagination: A Political Ontology of Photography*, trans. Louise Bethlehem (New York: Verso, 2012), chapter four.

4. For example, see: United Fruit Company Headquarters, Boston. "Circular No. 32-17. Boston to Tropical Division Managers," Memorandum, September 19, 1932; "Circular No. B-21" Memorandum, November 15, 1929, United Fruit Company Letters, Bocas del Toro Division.

5. Miguel Urrutia, *The Development of the Colombian Labor Movement* (New Haven, CT: Yale University Press, 1969), 82–83, 93–96; Ignacio Torres Giraldo, *Los inconformes: Historia de la rebeldia de las masas en Colombia*, vol. 3 (Bogotá: Margen Izquierdo, 1973), 199–206.

6. Torres Giraldo, *Inconformes*, vol. 4, 15–16; on Torres Giraldo, see Klaus Meschkat, "Helpful Intervention? The Impact of the Comintern on Early Colombian Communism," *Latin American Perspectives* 35, no. 2 (2008): 39–56.

7. On the socioeconomic conditions in the banana zone on the eve of the strike, see Catherine C. LeGrand, "Living in Macondo: Economy and Culture in a United Fruit Company Banana Enclave in Colombia," in *Close Encounters of Empire: Writing the Cultural History of U.S.-Latin American Relations*, ed. Gilbert M. Joseph, Catherine C. LeGrand, and Ricardo D. Salvatore (Durham, NC: Duke University Press, 1998), 333–368.

8. Carlos Arango Z., *Sobrevivientes de las bananeras* (Bogotá, Colombia: s.n., 1981), 38–39, 49.

9. Ibid., 55.

10. Marcelo Bucheli, *Bananas and Business: The United Fruit Company in Colombia, 1899–2000* (New York: NYU Press, 2005), 125–126.

11. Catherine C. LeGrand, "Legal Narratives of Citizenship, the Social Question, and Public Order in Colombia, 1915–1930 and After." *Citizenship Studies* 7, no. 5 (2013): 530–50.

12. Arango Z., *Sobrevivientes*, 53; Catherine C. LeGrand, "El conflicto de las bananeras," in *Nueva historia de Colombia*, vol. 3, ed. Alvaro Tirado Mejía (Bogotá: Planeta, 1989), 202.

13. LeGrand, "Bananeras," 202.

14. "Hoja suelta," reprinted in Carlos Cortés Vargas, *Los sucesos de las bananeras* (Bogotá: Imprenta "La Luz," 1929), 6–7.

15. Arango Z., *Sobrevivientes*, 54; Cortés Vargas, *Sucesos*, 37.

16. Cortés Vargas, *Sucesos*, 8; Arango Z., *Sobrevivientes*, 60, 58.

17. Jorge Eliécer Gaitán, *La masacre en las bananeras* (Colombia, n.d.), 70–72.

18. LeGrand, "Bananeras," 207.

19. Arango Z., *Sobrevivientes*, 60; for additional examples of UFC-Colombian military conviviality, see Gaitán, *La masacre*, 72–80.

20. Arango Z., *Sobrevivientes*, 61.

21. "Delicada situación," *La Prensa* (Barranquilla, December 3, 1928).

22. "La situación de la huelga," *La Prensa* (Barranquilla, December 4, 1928).

23. Arango Z., *Sobrevivientes*, 54; Cortés Vargas, *Sucesos*, 49.

24. Cortés Vargas, *Sucesos*, 64.

25. Arango Z., *Sobrevivientes*, 61.

26. Cortés Vargas, *Sucesos*, 64; Arango Z., *Sobrevivientes*, 66, 70.

27. Reflecting confusion about who had the constitutional authority to decide on the use of emergency powers, it is significant that Cortés Vargas first notes that the declaration of a state of siege was done through "*Legislative* Decree 1" and then, two pages later, cites "*Executive* Decree 1." See Cortés Vargas, *Sucesos*, 63 and 65.

28. I take inspiration from Jon Beasley-Murray's rereading of the *Requerimiento* in *Posthegemony: Political Theory and Latin America* (Minneapolis: University of Minnesota Press, 2010), 5.

29. Walter Benjamin, "Critique of Violence," in *Reflections: Essays, Aphorisms, Autobiographical Writings*, 1st ed. (New York: Harcourt Brace, 1978), 277–300.

30. Cortés Vargas, *Sucesos*, 65; the U.S. consulate in Colombia also reported: "Feeling against the Government by the proletariat which is shared by some of the soldiers is high and it is doubtful if we can depend upon the Colombian Government for protection," Gray, "Telegram from U.S. Consulate in Santa Marta," December 6, 1928. I have posted digital copies of the original declassified U.S. State Department cables that I cite in this chapter on my website; see http://kevincoleman.org/the-1928-massacre-of-banana-workers. They were originally available at http://www.icdc.com/~paulwolf/columbia/cotie6dec1928.jpg.

31. Cortés Vargas, *Sucesos*, 65.

32. Ibid., 65–66.

33. My analogy between muzzle and camera flashes is drawn from Eduardo Cadava's discussion of Ernst Jünger's "Photography and the 'Second Consciousness,'" in *Words of Light: Theses on the Photography of History* (Princeton, NJ: Princeton University Press, 1997), 53.
34. Arango Z., *Sobrevivientes*, 79.
35. Ibid.
36. Ibid., 91.
37. Ibid., 97.
38. Azoulay theorizes this process in *Civil Imagination*, 230–231.
39. Arango Z., *Sobrevivientes*, 92; LeGrand, "Bananeras," 215.
40. Gray, "Telegram from U.S. Consulate in Santa Marta," December 6, 1928, http://kevincoleman.org/the-1928-massacre-of-banana-workers.
41. Cortés Vargas, *Sucesos*, 96.
42. Cortés Vargas, *Sucesos*, 96–97 and 103–104.
43. Arango Z., *Sobrevivientes*, 33.
44. Cortés Vargas, *Sucesos*, 97–104.
45. Jefferson Caffery, "Telegram from Bogotá Embassy," December 7, 1928, http://kevincoleman.org/the-1928-massacre-of-banana-workers.
46. Ibid.
47. Lawrence F. Cotie for Gray, "Telegram from U.S. Consulate in Santa Marta," December 9, 1928, http://kevincoleman.org/the-1928-massacre-of-banana-workers.
48. Cotie, "Despatch from Santa Marta Consulate," December 11, 1928, http://kevincoleman.org/the-1928-massacre-of-banana-workers.
49. Ibid.
50. Ibid.
51. Jefferson Caffery, "Despatch from Bogotá Embassy," December 29, 1928, http://kevincoleman.org/the-1928-massacre-of-banana-workers.
52. Jefferson Caffery, "Despatch from Bogotá Embassy," January 16, 1929, http://kevincoleman.org/the-1928-massacre-of-banana-workers.
53. Jefferson Caffery, "Despatch from Bogotá Embassy to Secretary of State," June 8, 1929, http://kevincoleman.org/the-1928-massacre-of-banana-workers.
54. I thank Sebastián Carrasai for bringing this point to my attention. See Jacques Rancière, *Disagreement: Politics and Philosophy* (Minneapolis: University of Minnesota Press, 1999), 36.
55. Paul A. Kramer, "Power and Connection: Imperial Histories of the United States in the World," *American Historical Review* 116, no. 5 (December 2011): 1356.

PART II

Intimacies in Colonial Spaces

5

Sexual Labor and the U.S. Military Empire

Comparative Analysis of Europe and East Asia

SEUNGSOOK MOON

In June 2013, SBS, a major South Korean media network, reported trouble between U.S. military authorities and owners of entertainment clubs catering to American soldiers in the city of P'yŏngt'aek. For several years, many of these owners had been taken to U.S. bases where they were interrogated about prostitution involving their clubs' women employees.[1] While news reports focused on how U.S. authorities had violated the Korea-U.S. Status of Forces Agreement (SOFA) by seizing and interrogating Korean citizens, they also cast unwanted light on the persistent problem of "prostitution" coupled with the U.S. military presence in South Korea. As late as December 2012, MBC, another major media network, described migrant Filipina "juicy girls" working in "foreigners-only" entertainment clubs located near the U.S. bases in P'yŏngt'aek. These women sold drinks to GI customers at 30,000 Korean won per glass, accompanied by conversation and dance performances. These "juicy girls" were subject to regular gynecological examinations for detecting venereal disease.[2] Through their labor migration from the older outposts of the U.S. colonial empire to the new postwar U.S. military empire, these women continue a longer history of the sexual labor of empire. Founded and still dependent upon military cantonments, the U.S. empire has combined a quiet tolerance and even active supply of sex workers with the overt and covert examination of women's working bodies.

The media spotlight on P'yŏngt'aek reflects this city's ongoing transformation into one of two major hubs of U.S. military bases in South Korea, after their extensive relocation away from the DMZ and to the south of Seoul.[3] These unsettling reports, a glimpse into the dark side of the U.S. military presence, reveal as well the persistent nexus between men's military labor and women's (hetero)sexual labor. This nexus, fostering the mobilization of female workers, often across different imperial spaces, demonstrates another continuity, this time across empires. As the British colonial empire employed women's paid sexual labor, the U.S. empire with its global network of military bases has produced remarkably similar sexual labor demands and strategies for its regulation. Sexual labor encompasses both the paid and unpaid reproductive labor of caring and entertaining, which various groups of women and men perform to deal with sexual and ideological needs. In the sexual and military encounters of empire, imperial authorities have tolerated or even encouraged in-between practices of casual and romantic sexual encounters and cohabitation alongside more formalized prostitution. Both the British empire and the U.S. empire have relied on sexual labor—directly or indirectly remunerated—to manage the core agents of their imperial power, including soldiers, workers, and administrators. To the extent that these agents have been masculinized, women have performed (hetero)sexual labor not only as sex workers, but also as wives, lovers, domestic servants, and camp followers.

In the political and military economy of the U.S. empire, what overt and covert functions does women's paid (hetero)sexual labor perform, who are the women involved, and how is their sexual labor mobilized and organized? Women's paid sexual labor or sex work can be reframed as a specific form of reproductive labor, parallel to and intrinsically linked to productive labor and military labor, which empire as a political entity relies on for its expansion and reproduction both physically and discursively. Such a recognition is particularly important in understanding the interactions and relationships between U.S. military and local societies in the contexts of war, occupation, and long-term deployment in various countries, notably in East Asia and Europe.[4] The U.S. military empire, even since the end of male conscription in 1973, has mobilized and organized prostitution and cohabitation, and the boundary between the two was and remains ambiguous.

The more recent history of Filipina sex workers in P'yŏngt'aek provides an entry into a longer genealogy of medically supervised prostitution that stretches from the British colonial empire to the U.S. empire, from the World War II military occupation of France and Britain through the postwar military occupation of South Korea, Japan/Okinawa, and

Germany to the continuing U.S. military presence after occupation. Initially, there were more similarities than differences in the organization and mobilization of sexual labor in these countries. However, the politics diverged as they recovered politically and economically and, later, as globalization in the post–Cold War context contributed to a transnational migration of sex workers.

The divergence of sexual labor economies can be explained by the different power relations between host countries and the U.S. military and the type of personnel that predominated (single or family-sponsored). The nature of the host country's regime, whether authoritarian or democratic, has also been a significant factor. Across the life cycle of the U.S. empire, women's sex work, in satisfying (largely male) soldiers' (hetero) sexual needs, has structured heteronormative discourses of imperial superiority linked to racial and cultural hierarchy.

Empires and Women's Sexual Labor

Studies of social relations of sexuality in colonial empires have demonstrated that the regulation of imperial agents' sexual encounters and relationships was integral to establishing and maintaining empire as a *political entity.*[5] Women's (hetero)sexual labor shares certain emotional and physical features with other types of intimate labors, including child rearing, personal assistance, and long-term care of the sick, the old, and the disabled, which domestic servants performed in colonial societies (and beyond). Insofar as the sex work and intimate labors are not reciprocally performed, social relationships between givers and receivers of these labors are always unequal. The inferior in terms of *social status* structured by ethnicity/nation, race, gender, and class provides the superior with these service labors. Givers and receivers of these labors are also marked as members of inferior and superior social groups, respectively. However, sex work is distinct from other intimate labors because it focuses on sexuality as the tool of human reproduction and as a crucial marker of respectability.[6] Potential and actual pregnancy and childbirth have serious and lasting consequences not only for the individuals involved but also for their communities. Children of interracial or other transgressive sexual relations are very likely to complicate boundaries of citizenship and other collective membership.[7]

The U.S. empire inherited European colonial practices of sexual labor regulation, in particular from the British. Until the nineteenth century, colonial empires generally restricted immigration of white women to colonies and condoned and even encouraged concubinage—cohabitation between white men and local women.[8] During earlier stages of colonial expansion, these empires commonly perceived such cohabitation as an effective means of acculturation and coping with loneliness and boredom; during later stages of colonial rule when their dominance was relatively weakened, however, these empires commonly discouraged cohabitation and promoted white endogamy to safeguard European lifestyles associated with respectability and moral superiority.[9] In British India, concubinage became popular after intermarriage between British men and Indian women (or Anglo-Indian women), which was once common across social statuses, was discouraged by the late eighteenth century.[10] At the same time, the British Empire generally viewed prostitution as less threatening to its racialized imperial order than concubinage, which would produce offspring.[11] In contrast, the Dutch Empire considered concubinage more suitable than prostitution to maintain the political order and health of the populations in its colonies, though over time it became concerned that the children of concubinage were demanding economic resources and political rights and creating alliances with organized opposition to its rule.[12] Despite moral qualms about prostitution and cohabitation, both the French Empire and the Dutch Empire defended them as "necessary evils" in the male-dominant contexts of cantonments, trading posts, mining compounds, and plantations to guard against male homosexuality, which was considered a greater evil.[13]

Of particular significance to the regulation of sexual labor in the U.S. empire was the model of medically supervised prostitution that major colonial empires and modern nation-states adopted as a "rational" technology to rule the specific population of female sex workers. The British Empire established and managed licensed brothels coupled with regular medical examination of sex workers and confined treatment of infected sex workers. By the mid-nineteenth century, this form of prostitution was preferred to concubinage as a means to regulate sexual relations between white men and local women, especially in the regimented context of cantonment.[14] Indeed, the medical supervision and confined treatment of sex workers were manifestations of the larger trend in European city planning to isolate socially unacceptable groups, including people with contagious or mental illnesses. This model of prostitution became an essential element of public health legislation and spread to Europe, including Austria, Belgium, Germany, Great Britain, Italy, Norway, Spain, and Sweden. All these countries had licensed prostitution, that is, legalized bordellos administered by the police and medical personnel.[15] The model also spread globally in the era of colonial expansion and settlement,[16] and, in the 1870s, was adopted by Japan.[17]

However, the normalization of medically supervised prostitution generated local and international movements against it under the rubric of the anti–white slavery campaign. In Britain, Victorian feminist Josephine Butler (1828–1906) began and led the long campaign to repeal the Contagious Disease Acts, the legal sanction for this model of prostitution in the empire. Once considered a "modern" and "scientific" way of controlling venereal disease, it was now criticized as inhumane and immoral. In 1927, the League of Nations published a report on white slavery around the world. While this globalized campaign contributed to the decline of prostitution in Europe and Latin America by the mid-twentieth century, it also exposed the fact that such prostitution was deemed unacceptable only when white European women were involved. As indicated by the rubric of "white slavery," the campaign focused on the trafficking of white European adult women and girls into medically supervised prostitution in South America, where a large number of white Europeans settled.[18] This attitude highlights the underlying rule of racial hierarchy in womanhood: women of color in colonies were suitable for performing sexual labor in prostitution because of their inferior culture and moral depravity, but white European women were not because they were suitable for respectable marriage as the guardians of family and anchors of white communities.[19]

When the U.S. colonized the Philippines in 1898, the European model of medically supervised prostitution had been well established as one of the trappings of a modern colonial empire. Despite the local and global campaigns against this system, the U.S. was not shy of adopting it in its colonies. The U.S. version of licensed prostitution included such features of the British model as registration of sex workers, issuance of individual certificates in connection to regular genital examination (conducted by a U.S. Army surgeon), and incarceration of infected sex workers for treatment in hospitals guarded by the police.[20] When this system of prostitution alarmed critics at the turn of the century, including social purity activists, suffragists, and anti-imperialists, they still had limited influence over practices on the ground in remote colonies.[21] Hence the U.S. military continued to mobilize and regulate women's sexual labor for their soldiers later during World War II when the U.S. emerged as a military empire and in the postwar era when it expanded its global network of bases.

The Politics of Sexual Labor and the U.S. Military Empire during World War II and Postwar Occupations

Toward the end of World War II, the U.S. military, the bulk of Allied forces, occupied France. Despite shared racial identities and France's position as a major colonial empire, there was a significant power disparity between it and the United States. While France had been defeated and occupied by Nazi Germany, and became impoverished during the war, the U.S. was an emerging superpower with impressive wealth and enormous military power. In the context of power disparity and perceived cultural differences, France, in the American mind, was no longer a member of the imperial family. Instead, American GIs commonly viewed the French, especially the women they encountered, as primitive, immoral, and sexually loose. Reflecting the convergence of popular and official perceptions of France, the U.S. military authorities unequivocally promoted the Normandy campaign as an erotic adventure for young soldiers away from home. They depicted France as an eroticized feminine other to be rescued by masculine GIs. Hence abundant sex was the reward for liberation.[22] These perceptions underscore that race was not an automatic unifier; apparent racial similarity could be undermined by more specific cultural differences and power disparities. Indeed, GIs behaved imperiously in France; they drank excessively, drove recklessly, chased women aggressively, and got into fights frequently..[23] This was a prototype of the relationship between the U.S. military and local women in South Korea, Japan/Okinawa, and to a lesser extent West Germany during their periods of military occupation.

Given the unequal relationship between France and the U.S. and sexualization of the military campaign in France, the "[a]verage Joe equated

France with brothels and pretty women."[24] In the context of ongoing war and the mass impoverishment of the French, the boundary between prostitution and fleeting romance was often ambiguous. Sex between U.S. soldiers and French women commonly involved the exchange of U.S. Army goods for sexual favors from women in desperate need of food, fuel, and other items crucial to their and their families' survival. This type of unregulated (private) prostitution exploded as a massive number of GIs deployed with a poisonous alchemy of an imperious attitude, abundant Army goods, and money to spend. In fact, the U.S. military did not rely on the kind of licensed prostitution already familiar to the French. While French authorities proposed licensed brothels in the face of ubiquitous sexual encounters between local women and U.S. soldiers, U.S. military authorities, alarmed by the rampant spread of venereal disease among GIs, instead officially closed some bordellos. The U.S. military rejected the proposal because it would have been difficult to set up such a system in the midst of a mobile military campaign and the U.S. authorities did not foresee long-term military occupation. Above all, the military sought to keep prostitution invisible after its experience in the colonial Philippines and in accordance with the War Department policy to suppress it.[25] Even so, in the absence of licensed prostitution, the military still medically inspected sex workers, distributed condoms, and organized prophylactic stations. Military authorities also enforced racial segregation in brothels.[26]

The French case provides some noteworthy evidence about the politics of women's sexual labor. First, it confirms that the military continued to view women's sexual labor as a necessity for soldiers, especially during wartime when they had to be kept loyal and motivated to fight in the face of injury and death. As General George Patton said: "if they don't fuck, they don't fight."[27] Patton's unabashed frontline view was reflected in a significant change in the veterans' affairs policy. Prior to the repeal of Section 2 of the Veterans Regulation Act, approved on May 17, 1926, U.S. soldiers who contracted venereal disease "due to misconduct" and subsequently lost their service hours forewent their pension and compensation. This punishment was in line with the 1941 May Act, which affirmed that prostitution was illegal. In September 1944, however, the War Department amended the regulation concerning veterans' claims to disability and benefits. Now, a VD-infected veteran would not be penalized for time lost during treatment "if the person in service complies with the Army or Navy regulations requiring him to report and receive treatment for such disease." The military had come to treat venereal disease as an exception to a principle that a veteran was barred from receiving pensions "for any disability due to the claimant's own willful misconduct or vicious habits." [28] This exception continued during the U.S. military occupation of South Korea, Japan/Okinawa, and Germany, despite the resistance of venereal disease control councils.[29]

The French case also confirms the latent function of women's sexual labor embedded in prostitution. The persistent attempts to monitor and regulate the sexual labor had a significance beyond coping with venereal disease; they were at the heart of the very politics of military occupation. Notably, the military targeted for medical examination not only professional prostitutes but also any women associated with GIs. Such attempts to control—and scapegoat—unidentified masses of women helped the U.S. confront the social and political anxiety associated with its new global power. Within its ranks, the racially segregated military reinforced racial boundaries through the segregation of prostitutes. Like their British counterparts, U.S. military authorities were anxious about the spread of homosexuality in the military's homosocial context. Women's sexual labor seemed to them necessary to keep male homosexuality at bay.[30]

The wartime U.S. military presence in Britain from the summer of 1942 to the summer of 1945 shows a striking counter-case to the occupation of France. The major site in the politics of women's sexual labor in wartime Britain was not so much prostitution as pervasive romance between British woman and GIs. Young women's sexual ventures were at the center of widespread social anxiety about the presence of American soldiers whose number reached roughly a million. Official and social agencies monitored the activities of young women who consorted with GIs and organized various social events to ensure race and class boundaries. British authorities tried to make sure that white GIs dated women from "respectable" middle-class or upper-class families rather than "promiscuous" working-class women. At the same time, authorities discouraged white women, regardless of class, from associating with black GIs. Instead, formal agencies and informal groups brought black British women to social gatherings separately organized for black soldiers.[31] Such racial and classed regulation of women's sexual labor fit easily within the history of sexuality in the British Empire.[32] The stark difference between wartime sexual regulation in France and Britain is attributable to the sense of affinity that underlay the relationship between Britain and the U.S., based on such shared attributes as language, the religious predominance of Protestantism, and basic social values. Nor was Britain defeated and occupied by Nazi Germany. As a result, the U.S. did not turn Britain into its inferior other. It remained a genuine ally.

The end of World War II terminated the U.S. occupation of France, but it began the U.S. occupation of the southern part of the Korean Peninsula. Replacing the Japanese colonial state, the U.S. Army set up a military government. During this occupation from 1945 to 1948, the U.S. encountered South Korea not only as a former colony of Japan, the defeated enemy, but also an unfamiliar "Oriental" country with vast racial and cultural differences. In the name of "democratizing" Korea, the U.S. occupiers, in 1947, abolished medically supervised (licensed or public) prostitution, which the Japanese established during their rule. While Koreans initially viewed Americans as liberators, GIs understood liberation in sexual and even imperial terms. They expected sexual rewards in this "exotic" Asian country they had saved from Japanese fascism.[33] In turn, military authorities condoned unregulated (private) prostitution on the grounds of cultural difference and accepted GIs' sexual entitlement. In fact, they did not criminalize Korean prostitutes as long as they remained free from venereal disease. As in occupied France, unregulated private prostitution mushroomed and the military government became alarmed by the rampant spread of venereal disease among soldiers. In response, it established in May 1947 the Venereal Disease Control Section under the Department of Public Health and Welfare and introduced periodic medical examinations of "entertaining girls" and incarcerated treatment of infected women.[34]

The U.S. occupation of Japan (1945–52) involved an even more severely unequal relationship as a consequence of unconditional surrender. At the same time, Japan had been the major colonial power in Asia; the U.S. viewed it as a potential major ally in the new Cold War order and was committed to the reconstruction of democratic Japan. Like their

French but unlike their Korean counterparts, Japanese elites were willing to provide occupying U.S. forces with licensed prostitution to protect "respectable" women. After all, the Japanese Empire had made active use of the sexual labor of prostitutes and "comfort women" throughout its colonial expansion. Fearing the mass rape of Japanese women by GIs, the Tokyo Metropolitan Police Board enlisted owners of sex industries and restaurants to set up the Recreation and Amusement Association (RAA) and established a system of regulated brothels, known as "comfort" facilities, catering exclusively to American soldiers.[35] In the face of the rapid spread of venereal disease among GIs and concerned about the military's image, however, U.S. authorities abolished RAA brothels in 1946. Subsequently, women working for these brothels became private streetwalkers known as "pan-pan."[36]

The U.S. occupation of Germany, by contrast, began with a formal expression of hostility and caution in a policy of "nonfraternization." Although this policy sought to prevent GIs from interacting with Germans verbally and physically, it failed to curb soldiers from aggressively pursuing sexual contact with German women. Many German women were in turn attracted to healthy GIs in the context of dire impoverishment and the scarcity of young German men.[37] Given the large number of Americans of German ancestry and racial affinity, the social distance between GIs and German women must have been less than that between GIs and Korean or Japanese women. Unregulated private prostitution exploded as women in many different walks of life joined professional prostitutes to eke out livings by exchanging sexual favors for gifts or money. Given the ubiquity of sexual liaisons between GIs and German women, German authorities proposed licensed brothels but the U.S. military refused, citing the War Department's official ban on prostitution and public scrutiny back home.[38]

Despite local differences in these diverse postwar contexts, certain commonalities are striking. First, in the absence of licensed prostitution, U.S. military authorities made informal arrangements with local businesses to set up entertainment facilities, including dance halls, bars, night clubs, and restaurants as well as brothels, and condoned prostitution as a necessity. GIs were given condoms and prophylactic kits before they left their units. This contradicted the War Department's official policy on prostitution and authorities tried to keep such practices invisible to the public back in the United States. Second, the authorities ensured that these entertainment facilities were racially segregated. Third, the military ended up regulating the sexual labor of various categories of women beyond professional sex workers who consorted with U.S. soldiers. Borrowing from the colonial model of medically supervised prostitution, they imposed regular medical examinations on barmaids, dancers, hostesses, waitresses, coffee girls, typists, nurses, and other women who had regular contact with GIs.[39] Fourth, the military carried out random or periodic "vice raids" to round up women for medical examination. In occupied Japan, arrested women were charged for their medical examinations, a practice that the U.S. military had first introduced in colonial Philippines. [40]

Cohabitation, colloquially called "shacking up," also emerged as a common context for the sexual labor local women provided for GIs. Soldiers, their women, and military authorities generally preferred steady and monogamous relationships to prostitution. Women favored this arrangement to working in clubs, bars, or brothels because of its relative stability and the lack of stress from dealing with employers, managers, and multiple customers. GIs also benefited because cohabitation provided easy sexual access to a steady partner at a lower price than prostitution, along with unpaid domestic labor and even emotional ties. The authorities recognized that cohabitation was less likely to spread venereal disease than prostitution and could contribute to soldiers' emotional stability and morale. In addition, individual soldiers were financially responsible for cohabitation, and the authorities did not have to provide a set of benefits and social services reserved for marriage. Military regulation of cohabitation in these occupied countries remained minimal and overshadowed by concern with venereal disease control and prostitution.[41] Yet, especially in Korea and Japan, U.S. authorities worried about the birth of mixed-race children. In Germany, the authorities were concerned about mixed children of black GIs and white German women.

These common features of U.S. military policy from Korea and Japan to Germany reproduced an older colonial view of women's sexual labor as merely a source of venereal disease and threat to soldiers' health, rather than as formal employment, a crucial source of livelihood. Such a view justified the widespread, intrusive practices that subjected women to regular genital examinations and incarcerated treatment of the infected. Yet, as in the colonial era, these medical practices proved ineffective in containing or preventing venereal disease outbreaks.[42] Despite the serious health threat and moral hazard it posed, the U.S. military accepted prostitution as a necessity for male agents of imperial power. On the surface, the privileging of men's (hetero)sexual desire over the public issue of women's health turned women's sexual labor into a mere instrument of soldiers' satisfaction. At a deeper level, however, a contradiction remained between official discouragement of prostitution and its acceptance on the ground. Sex workers, as the abject and marginalized other, embodied societal anxieties about the stability and strength of the racialized imperial order—covert prostitution functioned as a mechanism to deal with such anxieties. In addition, this form of sexual labor, particularly in racially segregated entertainment facilities, was less likely than cohabitation or marriage to produce mixed-race offspring.

The Politics of Sexual Labor and U.S. Military Bases in the Cold War and Post–Cold War Eras

After the postwar U.S. occupation ended, the trajectories of women's sexual labor diverged in South Korea, Japan/Okinawa, and Germany. In South Korea, as the U.S. expanded its military bases during and after the Korean War (1950–53), camptowns naturally grew around them. In the poverty-stricken postwar decade, camptown prostitution grew at an explosive rate. In 1958, for example, there were an estimated 300,000 sex workers in Korea, approximately 180,000 of whom were in the camptowns. To tighten control over sex workers and curb venereal disease, the U.S. military and the Korean government agreed to concentrate sex workers in several areas where U.S. troops were stationed. In 1957, the military established a score of designated clubs and dance halls in large cities hosting U.S. bases, and for the first time permitted its soldiers to stay overnight outside their barracks. In the same year, the Ministry of Health and Social Affairs also established 89 venereal disease clinics throughout Korea, 43 of them clustered on major U.S. bases in Seoul, P'aju, Pusan, Pyŏngt'aek, Taegu, and Yangju.[43] These arrangements streamlined camptown prostitution into an avatar of the colonial model of medically supervised prostitution.

This system of camptown prostitution had its heyday in the 1960s.[44] Early in the decade, Park Chung Hee's military regime further consolidated the system by designating "special districts" where prostitution was allowed despite its criminalization in Korean law and the U.S. Uniform Code of Military Justice. This spatial separation expediently contained the unseemly side effect of the foreign military presence. Additionally, under the Tourism Promotion Law, enacted in 1961, camptown clubs catering exclusively to U.S. soldiers became "special tourism facility businesses." Each club was required to deposit $500 per month in its savings account to contribute to the accumulation of capital necessary for the economic development of the country. Noncompliance with this regulation could lead to the withdrawal of business approval by the government. By the mid-1960s, roughly 10,000 camptown sex workers were employed in the Tongduchŏn area alone, staggering figures in light of the total number of U.S. troops in South Korea, which fluctuated from 50,000 to 85,000 between 1955 and 1970.[45] The 1980s saw the economic significance of the camptown sex industry decline and the nationality of sex workers shift. Since the late 1980s, migrant women from the Philippines and the former Soviet Union have replaced young Korean sex workers in the camptowns.[46] As MBC reported in its exposé, these foreign women came to Korea on "entertainment" visas but have been incorporated into the long-established camptown prostitution system.

In Japan/Okinawa, the politics of sexual labor bifurcated because Okinawa, which housed the bulk of U.S. military bases and its troops in Japan, remained under direct U.S. military rule until 1972.[47] In the main islands, pan-pan girls and entertainment facilities catering to GIs declined as postwar Japan became prosperous—many Japanese women moved out of the sex industry and the remaining sex workers became too expensive for U.S. soldiers. Young Japanese women became available, instead, as potential dates for GIs.[48] In contrast (but similar to South Korea), Okinawa witnessed the rapid spread of special entertainment districts filled with what were called "A-sign" (for "Approved") bars and clubs around U.S. military bases . In 1950, military authorities established four such special entertainment districts to serve U.S. military personnel.[49] The bars and clubs were in some cases constructed on land the U.S. military had seized from local farmers for the construction of its bases.[50] Since 1957, the working-class district of Henoko in Nago City has hosted U.S. Marine Corps Camp Schwab and provided "recreation" and "entertainment" facilities for U.S. soldiers.[51]

The sexual industry in Okinawa boomed during the Korean and Vietnam Wars. The archipelago became a major destination for combat-fatigued soldiers who were enjoying their rest and recreation leaves. At the height of its entertainment district's popularity, Henoko's 74 acres bustled with more than 200 bars, restaurants, and brothels.[52] As many as one out of every 30 Okinawan women worked in these types of entertainment districts. As on the main islands, this sex industry declined significantly after Okinawa was returned to Japanese control and became relatively affluent with massive economic support from Tokyo and the collection of rent on the bases.[53] These political and economic changes have also divided local communities into those, generally working class, who benefit from the continuing presence of the U.S. military and those, generally middle class, who oppose it on ideological grounds.[54] While many local women still marry GIs, migrant Filipinas, entering Japan on "entertainment" visas since the late 1970s, have replaced local sex workers.[55] Today, some 7,300 Filipinas work in the diminished sex industry catering to U.S. military personnel and civilian tourists in Okinawa.[56] In addition, the spatial division and power difference between mainland Japan and Okinawa continues to encourages mainland women to travel to Okinawa to find GI boyfriends.[57]

In Germany, the entertainment industry in base towns shrank considerably in the 1960s; as in Japan, economic recovery and the dissolution of the gold standard made German sex workers too expensive for GIs. Moreover, because the U.S. viewed Germany as a "favored ally" at the frontlines of Cold War Europe, the U.S. military was relatively accommodating of relationships between soldiers and local civilians, and promoted social gatherings between them. Military authorities allowed, even helped, GIs to rent apartments outside military barracks. In this new social and political context, many German women dated and married GIs.[58] Germany also developed a thriving sex industry, particularly after a 2002 reform that raised the social and legal status of sex workers, guaranteeing such benefits as health insurance and pensions. In the current era of globalization, more than two-thirds of sex workers in Germany hail from impoverished East European countries, including Bulgaria, Hungary, and Romania.[59] It is estimated that 400,000 sex workers serve one million men per day,[60] Germans and U.S. soldiers alike. This situation is quite different from the one in South Korea, where a category of foreign sex workers that mostly caters to GIs exists alongside a sex industry mainly catering to domestic customers.

The comparative discussion of individual countries demonstrates convergence and divergence in how the U.S. military empire approaches women's sexual labor. In Germany, the postwar model of covert prostitution quickly disappeared as the country gained economic and political power in the 1960s. The more respectable practices of dating and marriage between German women and GIs became an integral part of the strategic cooperation between Germany and the U.S. as equal partners with cultural and racial affinity. In contrast, an equivalent degree of progressive change has not taken place in South Korea and Okinawa despite the considerable economic and political transformations in these host societies. The situation on the main islands of Japan can be placed between the German and Korean/Okinawan patterns.[61] The difference suggests that racialized Orientalism mediates the shifting economic and political power relations between the U.S. and these host societies that are culturally and racially different from the (mainstream) United States. South Korea and Okinawa are still seen as racialized sexual playgrounds for hard-working, stressed GIs. This lingering perception is reflected in the persistence of camptown prostitution in South Korea and the recurring incidents of sexual violence against women and young girls both there and in Okinawa.[62]

The nature of a host society's political regime and the intensity of its masculinist view of women's sexual labor also matter a great deal to the perpetuation of the colonial model of medically supervised prostitution. Delayed democratization in South Korea and Okinawa facilitated the U.S. military's employment of this model. Under the Japanese Empire, South Korea and Okinawa had been fully exposed to the institution of state-organized "comfort women" and "comfort stations." That legacy contributed to the acceptance of a system in which poor and marginalized women were used to entertain U.S. soldiers, thereby protecting the wives and daughters of respectable families. This is a striking contrast to postwar Germany, which, like many other European societies, also had a history of licensed prostitution.

Divergences in the politics of women's sexual labor are also affected by the specific composition of U.S. troops—military branch, marital status, and type of deployment, whether family-sponsored or single. To this day, for example, roughly 90 percent of U.S. soldiers stationed in South Korea serve one-year terms of duty without their families. These short-term-duty soldiers are mostly young and serve in the Army. In Okinawa, families do accompany some soldiers, but the overwhelming portion of those stationed there are young Marines being trained for warfare elsewhere. In Germany, close to half of U.S. soldiers serve family-sponsored long-term duty.[63]

In the post–Cold War era, as the numbers of local Okinawan and Korean women in the special entertainment industry catering to GIs declined, their roles were increasingly filled by transnational migrant women from impoverished countries. Another noteworthy development in the politics of women's sexual labor in these societies is the overt condemnation of prostitution by the U.S. military since the early 2000s. In the summer of 2002, an Ohio television station broadcast a hidden-camera recording of a "courtesy patrol" in Tongduchŏn, South Korea, interacting with migrant foreign women trafficked into camptown clubs. The same year, *Time* magazine published an article about Filipinas and Russian women trafficked into these clubs. In response, the U.S. Department of Defense introduced a zero-tolerance policy on human trafficking and prostitution.[64] In South Korea and Okinawa, U.S. soldiers were subjected to new curfews and entertainment bars and clubs catering to GIs were made off limits. (The SBS report about the interrogation of camptown business owners mentioned at the beginning of the chapter took place in this context.) These measures, in turn, have triggered growing rates of cohabitation between foreign entertainers and GIs to avoid prostitution charges. Resembling the colonial practice of concubinage, this type of sexual relationship commonly results in offspring. When GIs complete their service and leave, these women are often abandoned while they are pregnant or have already given birth. Due to power differentials in general and unequal Status of Forces Agreements (SOFAs) with South Korea and Okinawa in particular, these women face very difficult battles to secure basic child support from their GI partners.[65] In contrast, the Germany-U.S. SOFA recommends U.S. soldiers bear financial responsibility for children they father in Germany even after they leave the country, making it much easier for their partners to demand child support if they are abandoned or separated.[66] Such a minimum recommendation, let alone a mandatory child support regulation, does not exist in the SOFAs between the U.S. and Japan or South Korea.

Conclusion

The comparative analysis of how the U.S. military empire has dealt with women's sexual labor draws attention to the pervasive and persistent pairing of men's military labor and women's (hetero)sexual labor—primarily in the form of prostitution and secondarily in the form of cohabitation. While the military has officially criminalized prostitution and at times explicitly condemned it in response to public controversy, it has relied on sex workers' labor and been directly and indirectly involved in mobilizing and managing them in occupied and host societies. Women's sexual labor maintains, entertains, and motivates men in their work as agents of imperial power and is therefore necessary for soldiers venturing away from their families and women. The U.S. military has long naturalized men's heterosexual desire and entitled soldiers' access to women's sexual service. It has generally kept this covert because it goes against not only the positive masculine image of self-control and discipline, but also respectable and white (middle-class) collective identity. The masculinist view of men's heterosexuality is irrational to the extent that it exposed soldiers to the deadly threat of venereal disease in the past and continues to expose the military in general to the ethical and moral problems tied to prostitution. Internationally, U.S. soldiers who have committed sexual violence against sex workers and other women and girls in unequal host societies like South Korea and Okinawa have often received little or no punishment.[67] This irrationality is also poignantly revealed by the current crisis of the military leadership in addressing sexual violence committed by male soldiers against female soldiers, integrated into the U.S. armed forces since 1973.[68] According to an analysis of sex crime allegations filed between mid-2005 and early 2013, military authorities handled such crimes with "random and inconsistent judgments."[69]

Unlike productive labor but like other reproductive labor or care work, women's sexual labor is directed to other human beings and therefore is the source simultaneously of unmediated physical pleasure and violence. Additionally, women's sexual labor not only can reproduce human beings and thereby allow for the continuity of community, it is also one of the primary behaviors human beings share both with each other and with other animals; sexual behavior, as a result, becomes a crucial measure of respectability tied to a collective identity. In contrast, soldiers are trained as agents of armed and organized violence to defend "our" community against "other" communities that "attack" or "threaten" it. There is a powerful symbolism in the contact or union between sexual labor, which can give life and reproduce a community, and military labor, which can take life in the name of protecting our community. In *Imperial Leather*, pairing sex workers as the abject with soldiers as agents of abjection, Anne McClintock suggests that military labor and women's sexual labor are primordially coupled. It remains to be seen how this connection will change as a result of the growing presence of female soldiers and the recent acceptance of gays in the U.S. military.

The prevalence of homophobia in the U.S. military reflects underlying social and individual anxieties about the ambiguity and, porousness of the boundary between heterosexual and homosexual men,[70] evidenced by the numerous men who have married women while taking male lovers. Given the plasticity of human sexuality, male soldiers in largely homosocial settings need to be reminded by the very authorities to whom they report that they have a natural desire for women's sexual labor.

Despite the striking persistence of the masculinist view that has dominated the U.S. military empire's relations to women's sexual labor, there have been significant variations in how that view has been translated into policies and practices on the ground. The specific power relationship between the U.S. and an occupied or host country profoundly shapes the specific ways the military approaches women's sexual labor. At the same time, what remains fairly consistent is that women of marginalized and therefore low-social-status groups perform paid sex work. In occupied France, these were impoverished and othered French women whose racial affinity with the white identity of the U.S. empire was diminished by the magnification of cultural difference. In occupied South Korea and Japan/Okinawa, they were impoverished women whose racial otherness was unmistakable. In occupied Germany, they were impoverished women of a former enemy whose cultural and racial affinity restored their humanity. In post–Cold War South Korea and Okinawa, they are migrant women from the Philippines and other impoverished countries.

NOTES

1. Chae-yong Ch'oi, "Chuhanmigun kijiro sang'indŭl pullŏduryŏ pulbŏpsusa" (Taking business owners to U.S. military bases, conducting illegal investigation), June 15, 2013 (Seoul: Seoul Broadcasting System).

2. Ŭn-sang Ko, "Hyŏnjang rŭp'o: kijich'onmada p'ilip'in 'jusigŏl'" (A field report: Filipina juicy girls in every camptown), December 11, 2012 (Seoul: Munhwa Broadcasting Corporation).

3. For an extensive discussion of this relocation, see Seungsook Moon, "Protesting the Expansion of U.S. Military Bases in Pyeongtaek: A Local Movement in South Korea," *South Atlantic Quarterly* 111:4 (Fall 2012): 856–867.

4. For an overview of this comparative discussion, see Maria Höhn and Seungsook Moon, "Introduction: The Politics of Gender, Sexuality, Race, and Class in the U.S. Military Empire," in *Over There: Living with the U.S. Military Empire from World War II to the Present*, ed. Maria Höhn and Seungsook Moon (Durham, NC: Duke University Press, 2010), 1–36.

5. Alain Cobin, *Women for Hire: Prostitution and Sexuality in France after 1850*, trans. Alan Sheridan (Cambridge, MA: Harvard University Press, 1990); Ronald Hyam, *Empire and Sexuality: The British Experience* (Manchester, UK, and New York: Manchester University Press, 1990); Paul Kramer, "The Darkness that Enters the Home: The Politics of Prostitution during the Philippine-American War," in *Haunted by Empire: Geographies of Intimacies in North American History*, ed. Ann Laura Stoler (Durham, NC: Duke University Press, 2006), 366–404; Philippa Levine, *Prostitution, Race, and Politics: Policing Venereal Disease in the British Empire* (New York: Routledge, 2003); Anne McClintock, *Imperial Leather: Race, Gender, and Sexuality in the Colonial Context* (New York: Routledge, 1995); Anne Laura Stoler, *Carnal Knowledge and Imperial Power: Race and the Intimate in Colonial Rule* (Berkeley and Los Angeles: University of California Press, 2002); Robert Young, *Colonial Desire: Hybridity in Theory, Culture, and Race* (London and New York: Routledge, 1995).

6. Regarding the connection between sexuality and respectability, Norbert Elias's *The Theory of Civilizing Process*, trans. Edmund Jephcott (New York: Urizen Books, 1978) is insightful. He argues that histories of manners in Europe point to a broad trend of humans distancing themselves from what they share with other animals, in particular from naked violence, which has been considered a law of nature. Because sexual acts exemplify the commonality among humans and between humans and other animals, societies tend to develop fine hierarchical gradations concerning the respectability of various sexualities and sexual behaviors.

7. Anne McClintock in her psychohistory of imperialism, *Imperial Leather*, explains the anxiety around sexuality and respectability tied to perceptions of the imperial self. She identifies the ambivalence of megalomania and paranoia as the underlying mechanism of imperial rule over the colonized. This dual feeling suggests "a

crisis in masculine imperial identity, suspended between a fantasy of conquest and a dread of engulfment" and also "between rape and emasculation" (27). She links this ambivalence to the "paradox of abjection," a concept that captures a fundamental dynamic of modern, industrial imperialism. The abject is everything that the self attempts to expunge in order to become socially acceptable and desirable but nevertheless haunts at the margins. Abject peoples are those whom empires reject and suppress but cannot do without, including prostitutes, domestic workers, slaves, and the colonized. While prostitutes are a socially abject group in empire, soldiers are socially appointed agents of abjection (71, 72).

8. Stoler, *Carnal Knowledge and Imperial Power*, 48.

9. Stoler, *Carnal Knowledge and Imperial Power*, 51, 68.

10. Hyam, *Empire and Sexuality*, 116. As a result, concubinage became pervasive across the global network of colonies, where British men found themselves isolated and lonely with few opportunities for entertainment and intellectual stimulation. It persisted as a commonpractice throughout the nineteenth and well into the twentieth century (107–108). In Hong Kong, concubinage continued to be legal until 1970. See Kerrie L. Macpherson, "Health and Empire: Britain's National Campaign to Combat Venereal Diseases in Shanghai, Hong Kong, and Singapore," in *Sex, Sin, and Suffering: Venereal Disease and European Society since 1820*, ed. Roger Davidson and Lesley A. Hall (London and New York: Routledge, 2001), 183.

11. Levine, *Prostitution, Race, and Politics*, 179.

12. Stoler, *Carnal Knowledge and Imperial Power*, ch. 3.

13. Stoler, *Carnal Knowledge and Imperial Power*, 2.

14. See Levine, *Prostitution, Race, and Politics*, 179. This model of medically supervised prostitution was not a British invention; it can be traced to the licensed bordellos in European cities—whether ruled by a monarch, noblemen, or the Catholic Church—that became common during the fifteenth century. By the early nineteenth century, medically regulated bordellos, complete with mandatory registration of female prostitutes, their regular genital examination, and isolated treatment of infected prostitutes, were widespread in France. A series of contagious disease acts and ordinances passed in the 1850s and 1860s in Britain and its colonies were the most official expression of how the empire viewed prostitutes' sexual labor—as the exclusive source of venereal disease and therefore a health threat to male agents of imperial power. See M. Satish Kumar, "'Oriental Sore' or 'Public Nuisance': The Regulation of Prostitution in Colonial India, 1805–1889," in *(Dis)placing Empire: Renegotiating British Colonial Geographies*, ed. L. J. Proudfoot and M. M. Roche (Burlington, VT: Ashgate, 2005), 159–161.

15. Donna J. Guy, "Medical Imperialism Gone Awry: The Campaign against Legalized Prostitution in Latin America," in *Science, Medicine, and Cultural Imperialism*, ed. Teresa A. Meade and Mark Walker (New York: St. Martin's Press, 1991), 18, 19; Philip Howell, "Prostitution and the Place of Empire: Regulation

and Repeal in Hong Kong and the British Imperial Network," in *(Dis)placing Empire*, ed. Proudfoot and Roche, 176.

16. Ronald Hyam describes the centrality of sex work to the managing of the British Empire : "The empire was as much a system of prostitution networks as it was (in Kipling's famous phrase) a web of submarine cables. The extraordinary movement of 'proletarian globe-trotters' and indentured labourers which the British superintended had its essential parallel in the migration of pimps and prostitutes, who readily took the whole world as their oyster every bit as much as missionaries regarded it as their parish. The brothels of Cairo, Port Said, Bombay and Singapore routinely provided sexual initiation for young Britons travelling east of Suez" (*Empire and Sexuality*, 212).

17. Sarah Kovner, *Occupying Power: Sex Workers and Servicemen in Postwar Japan* (Stanford, CA: Stanford University Press, 2012), 11.

18. Guy, "Medical Imperialism," 27, 29.

19. The prostitute's sexual labor was deeply racialized in the British Empire. Unlike the French, the British never took their own prostitutes to their colonies, because they considered the presence of white prostitutes damaging to their imperial prestige. Whenever British prostitutes were found in India and other colonies, they were sent home. See Hyam, *Empire and Sexuality*, 142.

20. Applying an entrepreneurial spirit to financing the system, the authorities charged sex workers compulsory fees for medical examinations and fines when they violated rules. They also replaced certificates with "inspection books" for recording weekly medical examinations and individual histories of venereal disease. See Kramer, "The Darkness that Enters the Home," 372, 374.

21. One obvious change in response to the critical campaigns was the formal introduction in 1901 of regular medical examinations of soldiers. See Kramer, "The Darkness that Enters the Home," 393.

22. Mary Louis Roberts, *What Soldiers Do: Sex and the American GI in World War II France* (Chicago: University of Chicago Press, 2013), chs. 1 and 2.

23. Roberts, *What Soldiers Do*, 74.

24. Roberts, *What Soldiers Do*, 63.

25. Roberts, *What Soldiers Do*, 184, 185.

26. Roberts, *What Soldiers Do*, 40.

27. Roberts, *What Soldiers Do*, 160.

28. U.S. War Department Memorandum, "Claims—Disability—Section 2, act 17 May 1926, repealed; Veterans Regulation Number 10 amended." October 17, 1944, NARA RG 554, Box 147.

29. Seungsook Moon, "Regulating Desire, Managing the Empire: U.S. Military Prostitution in South Korea, 1945–1970," in *Over There*, ed. Höhn and Moon, 47.

30. Roberts, *What Soldiers Do*, 174.

31. Sonya Rose, "Girls and GIs: Race, Sex and Diplomacy in World War II Britain," *International History Review* 19 (February 1997): 146–160.

32. See Howell, "Prostitution and the Place of Empire"; Hyam, *Empire and Sexuality*; Kumar, "'Oriental Sore'"; Levine, *Prostitution, Race, and Politics*; Young, *Colonial Desire*.
33. Moon, "Regulating Desire," 44, 45.
34. Moon, "Regulating Desire," 45.
35. Mire Koikari, "Rethinking Gender and Power in the US Occupation of Japan, 1945–1952," *Gender & History* 11:2 (1999): 321.
36. Kovner, *Occupying Power*, 30.
37. Maria Höhn, "'You Can't Pin Sergeant's Stripes on an Archangel': Soldiering, Sexuality, and U.S. Army Policies in Germany," in *Over There*, ed. Höhn and Moon, 114.
38. Höhn, "'You Can't Pin Sergeant's Stripes on an Archangel,'" 123.
39. This attempt to monitor various categories of women echoes a British approach to prostitution. Curiously, despite the legalization of regulated prostitution throughout her global imperial network, the British Empire did not formally define prostitution for a long time. The consequent ambiguity gave the colonial authorities immense discretionary power in convicting women as prostitutes; such convictions were based not on a clear definition but on establishing certain patterns of behavior. See Levine, *Prostitution, Race, and Politics*, 189.
40. Koikari, "Rethinking Gender and Power," 323, 324.
41. See Moon, "Regulating Desire"; Höhn, "'You Can't Pin Sergeant's Stripes on an Archangel,'"; Michiko Takeuchi, "'Pan-Pan Girls' Performing and Resisting Neocolonialism(s) in the Pacific Theater: U.S. Military Prostitution in Occupied Japan, 1945–1952," in *Over There*, ed. Höhn and Moon, 78–108.
42. This was also the case with the British Empire, as the anti–contagious disease movement highlighted. In British India, for example, medically supervised prostitution failed to curb the spread of venereal disease and instead entailed excessive medical inspections of various categories of women who were not registered prostitutes, including courtesans, hereditary prostitutes, and any women suspected of being prostitutes. See Kumar, "'Oriental Sore,'" 166–167.
43. See Moon, "Regulating Desire," 55.
44. Moon, "Regulating Desire," 56–68.
45. Moon, "Regulating Desire," 40. The ratio of prostitutes to soldiers was evidently much higher than those in the British and Japanese empires. In the regimental brothels of the British Indian Army, "there was a highly favourable ratio of about one prostitute to every forty-four men. . . . The "ideal" ratio aimed at by the Japanese Army during the Pacific War was putatively one to forty" (Hyam, *Empire and Sexuality*, 212).
46. Seungsook Moon, "Camptown Prostitution and Imperial SOFA: Abuse and Violence against Transnational Camptown Women in South Korea," in *Over There*, ed. Höhn and Moon, 337–365. For an extensive study of Filipina entertainers in contemporary Korea, see Sealing Cheng, *On the Move for Love: Migrant*

Entertainers and the U.S. Military in South Korea (Philadelphia: University of Pennsylvania Press, 2010).

47. Okinawa represents merely 0.6 percent of Japan's entire land mass, but it hosts 75 percent of the U.S. military facilities and almost two-thirds of American troops in Japan. See Inoue S. Masamichi, *Okinawa and the U.S. Military: Identity Making in the Age of Globalization* (New York: Columbia University Press, 2007), 2. Fourteen U.S. military installations occupy approximately 20 percent of the main island of Okinawa. See David McNeill, "Special Report: US Troops are Stationed in Japan to Protect the Nation, but to Sex Workers in Okinawa, They Bring Fear Not Security." *Independent*, June 17, 2013.

48. Takeuchi, "'Pan-Pan Girls,'" 104.

49. See Setsuko Tachikawa, "Okinawans Angry with Hashimoto Say Sex Services Don't Curb Crime," *Asahi Shinbun*, May 24, 2013.

50. "Okinawa: Effects of Long-Term U.S. Military Presence," *Women for Genuine Security*, 2007, www.genuinesecurity.org/partners/report/Okinawa.pdf.

51. See Masamichi, *Okinawa and the U.S. Military*, chs. 3 and 4.

52. Masamichi, *Okinawa and the U.S. Military*, 17.

53. Suzuyo Takazato, "Report from Okinawa: Long-Term U.S. Military Presence," *Canadian Woman Studies* 19:4 (2010): 42–48.

54. See Masamichi, *Okinawa and the U.S. Military*, chs. 6 and 7.

55. See Rebecca Forgash, "Military Transnational Marriage in Okinawa: Intimacy across Boundaries of Nation, Race, and Class" (Ph. D. diss., University of Arizona, 2004).

56. See "Okinawa: Effects of Long-Term U.S. Military Presence."

57. Chris Ames, "Crossfire Couples: Marginality and Agency among Okinawan Women in Relationships with U.S. Military Men," in *Over There*, ed. Höhn and Moon, *179–180*.

58. Höhn, "'You Can't Pin Sergeant's Stripes on an Archangel,'" 125, 136.

59. Jason Overdorf, "Germany's Legalized Sex Industry Is Booming," *Global Post*, November 26, 2013, http://www.globalpost.com/dispatch/news/regions/europe/germany/131125/berlin-sex-workers-prostitution-law.

60. "Prostitution in Germany: A Giant Teutonic Brothel," *Economist*, November 16, 2013.

61. See Höhn and Moon, "Introduction," in *Over There*, ed. Höhn and Moon.

62. For compilations of crimes committed by American soldiers against Korean civilians, including sexual violence, see Headquarters of the Movement to Eradicate American Soldiers' Crime, ed., *Migunbŏmjoiwa han-mi SOFA* (American soldiers' crime and the Korea–U.S. SOFA) (Seoul: Turimidia, 2002); National Campaign to Eliminate Crimes Committed by U.S. Forces in Korea, ed., *Kkŭnnaji anŭn ap'ŭmŭi yŏksa: Migunbŏmjoe* (A history of pain that has not yet ended: crimes committed by U.S. Forces in Korea) (Seoul: Kaemasŏwŏn, 1999).

    One of the most publicized incidents of sexual violence in Okinawa was the 1995 gang rape of a 12-year-old school girl by three U.S. soldiers. This led to a series of public apologies by U.S. leaders, including President Bill Clinton, Secretary of State Warren Christopher, Secretary of Defense William Perry, and Ambassador to Japan Walter Mondale. For a scholarly analysis, see Linda Isako Angst, "The Sacrifice of a Schoolgirl: The 1995 Rape Case, Discourses of Power, and Women's Lives in Okinawa," *Critical Asian Studies* 33:2 (2001): 243–266.

63. Höhn, "'You Can't Pin Sergeant's Stripes on an Archangel,'" 137.

64. Moon, "Camptown Prostitution," 346.

65. Moon, "Camptown Prostitution"; Suzuyo Takazato, "Report from Okinawa: Long-Term U.S. Military Presence and Violence against Women," *Canadian Woman Studies* 19:4 (1999): 42–47.

66. Takazato, "Report from Okinawa," 46.

67. Okinawan Women Act Against Military Violence, an NGO organized by Harumi Miyagi, has compiled annual statistics on sex crimes committed by U.S. military personnel. See Tachikawa, "Okinawans Angry." According to a *Military Times* article, between 2005 and early 2013 in Japan, "[o]ut of 473 sexual assault allegations within Navy and Marine Corps units, just 116, or 24 percent, ended up in courts-martial. In the Navy, one case in 2012 led to court-martial, compared to 13 in which commanders used nonjudicial penalties instead" (Richard Lardner and Yuri Kageyama, "Documents Reveal Chaotic U.S. Military Sex-Abuse Record in Japan," *Military Times*, February 9, 2014,http://www.militarytimes.com/article/20140209/NEWS06/302090001/Documents-reveal-chaotic-U-S-military-sex-abuse-record-Japan).

68. See the documentary *Invisible War* (San Francisco: Independent Lens Films, 2012), directed by Kirby Dick, for the pervasiveness of sexual violence against female soldiers (and a minority of male soldiers) in recent years in the U.S. military. In 2010, 108,121 veterans screened positive for military sexual trauma, and 68,379 had at least one Veterans Health Administration outpatient visit for related conditions. Also in 2010, the Department of Defense processed reports of 3,198 new assaults and estimated the actual number to be closer to 19,000. Only 244 perpetrators were convicted. It is important to note that these figures were collected after controversy erupted over the issue. See "Department of Defense Annual Report on Sexual Assault in the Military: Fiscal Year 2010," *U.S. Department of Defense*, March 2011, http://www.sapr.mil/public/docs/reports/DoD_Fiscal_Year_2010_Annual_Report_on_Sexual_Assault_in_the_Military.pdf.

69. See Lardner and Kageyama, "Documents Reveal."

70. For studies of homophobia and misogyny in the U.S. military, see Stan Goff, *Sex and War* (s.p.: Lulu Press, 2006); Elizabeth Lutes Hillman, *Defending America: Military Culture and the Cold War Court-Martial* (Princeton, NJ: Princeton University Press, 2005), Steven Zeeland, *The Masculine Marine: Homoeroticism in the U.S. Marine Corps* (New York: Harrington Park Press, 1996).

6

Making Aloha

Lei and the Cultural Labor of Hospitality

VERNADETTE VICUÑA GONZALEZ

In her landmark essay on the tourism industry's prostitution of Native Hawaiian culture, feminist indigenous activist Haunani-Kay Trask critiques the reduction of Hawaiian culture, lands, and people into attractions, destinations, and entertainers.[1] Attending to the rise of mass tourism in Hawai'i that began in the 1950s and 1960s, Trask identifies the commodification of the islands and its indigenous culture by corporate tourism as a primary cause of the social problems that shape the lived realities of the islands' Native population. Her manifesto strikes two particularly dissonant notes: a pointed critique of Native Hawaiians who allow their cultural practices to be "prostituted" and alienated from the values of indigenous life, and a clear message disinviting the tourist. The first condemns the participation of Native Hawaiians in a tourism industry that depends on them as exotic symbols of aloha, yet that limits their participation to isolated and limited service roles. The second is a rejection of the gendered and sexualized imagination of the hospitable, welcoming Native woman: "If you are thinking of visiting my homeland, please do not. We do not want or need any more tourists, and we certainly do not like them."[2] Drawing from and disavowing long-sedimented images of feminized landscapes and bodies awaiting the action of masculine explorers, Trask condemns tourism's erotics of service, availability, and accessibility as legacies that do not fall far from the colonial tree. These moments of dissonance provide the two linked lines of inquiry about the cultural labor of hospitality with which this chapter contends.

Insisting on hospitality as a commodity that is produced through labor makes possible multiple interventions. It denaturalizes the link between hospitality and the putatively friendly native and makes room for questions about the ideological work of hospitality in the service of empire—that is, the cultural labor enabled through the manufacture of aloha.[3] Adria Imada describes how Kanaka Maoli—the indigenous term for Native Hawaiians—are "instrumentalized" through the translation of indigenous practices into a tourist economy, masking imperial displacements and dispossessions through the use of Native culture as an alibi and invitation to empire.[4] Hawaii's tourism industry would have no coherence were it not for the cultural labor of Native Hawaiians who formed its early workforce. Framing hospitality in terms of labor also expands the traditional analytical category of labor studies to include the often overlooked work of affect, and brings attention to the gendered and sexualized character of the laborers who manufacture the feeling of hospitality. While Trask castigates Native Hawaiians in the tourism industry, her rhetorical use of the stigmatized term "prostitution" can dismiss the workers whose livelihoods depend on the service industry in Hawaiʻi. Yet "prostitution" also gestures to the rich and provocative feminist scholarship on the labor politics of sex work, the most useful of which rejects a simplistic understanding of women in the sex industry as oppressed victims and explores the "prostitute" as an underexamined category of labor.[5] Trask rightly and provocatively argues that the erotics of hospitality share the same sexual logics as prostitution, particularly in the porno-tropical terrain of empire, but this observation leaves underexamined the ways in which Native Hawaiians who took part in a hospitality industry did so in a context of intense sociocultural change and were themselves agents of that change.[6] By rendering their work with more nuance, I hope to understand how they made aloha for sale even as that work was instrumental in their ongoing dispossession.

This genealogy of hospitality in Hawaiʻi grapples with Trask's reframing of tourism as a nonconsensual relationship through a close study of the labor behind its primary symbol, the lei. While the making, giving, and wearing of the lei is a significant part of Native Hawaiian culture, its association with Hawaii's tourism industry is a modern phenomenon that emerged at the turn of the century with the advent of the islands' first significant groups of leisure travelers. This historical period, not coincidentally, also marked the consolidation of U.S. rule in the island. The 1875 Reciprocity Treaty granted the sugar oligarchs of Hawaiʻi favorable status and also granted the U.S. military access to Pearl Harbor. Then in 1893, U.S. business elites, aided by the U.S. Navy, overthrew the Hawaiian Kingdom. The short-lived Republic of Hawaii, led by one Sanford Dole, was adroitly annexed by the United States five years later through the specious shorthand of a Congressional joint resolution, just in time to serve as a fueling station for American expansionist wars in the Philippines. The Territorial Era (1898–1959) saw the concept of hospitality gain cultural traction as a way to allay the anxieties occasioned by these suspect and contested maneuvers.[7] Hand in hand with a sustained campaign by white elites to consolidate settlement by attracting more of their own, lei selling and other gestures of welcome manufactured a narrative of consent to imperial governance.[8]

During this period, the lei, as a tangible symbol of Native Hawaiian aloha, carried a great deal of ideological weight: its fragile, fragrant blooms went a long way toward recasting imperialism into a relationship characterized by a longed-for welcome and benevolent friendship. As Imada so concisely argues, aloha has been perverted under the U.S. colonial regime in Hawai'i: "Imagined and deployed as a mutuality, intimacy and hospitality, aloha has managed to mask U.S. imperial expansion in Hawai'i."[9]

This chapter examines how Native Hawaiians navigated the tourism industry's will to exploit Native Hawaiian culture. Native Hawaiian desires for financial survival and the kind of labor they undertook in shifting economies operated alongside their investments in sustaining community bonds and indigenous practices even as these bonds and practices were being pulled into the orbit of capitalist and imperialist regimes. What does it mean to produce a Native Hawaiian–inflected hospitality in occupied territory? What kinds of work does it entail? To answer these questions, I use English-language print media from Hawaii's Territorial Era, which tended to be produced by white American settlers who often used a travelogue tone when writing about indigenous culture in Hawai'i.[10] While one-sided, these representations also yield important insights into some of the detail of the work done by lei sellers, and how they, in turn, understood the kinds of colonial desires that motivated the reporters even as the sellers used them for a kind of free advertising. Likewise, an oral history of eleven longtime lei sellers (many of them second and third generation) conducted in the mid-1980s yields a rich lode of material about family businesses in the lei-selling industry, but these interviews also have their limitations. The lei sellers themselves initiated the oral history project, because they wanted to record their experiences for posterity, particularly in a booming tourism industry that was rapidly marginalizing their more individual approaches to hospitality entrepreneurship in favor of mass-produced lei. While the lei sellers clearly had investments in a kind of authenticity that was good for business and public relations, their oral histories also provide personal "insider" recollections of the lei industry from the early decades of the twentieth century. The fact that the lei sellers share memories that are fifty or sixty years old, or are second-hand stories passed down, should also be put into the context of Hawaii's oral history tradition of "talking story," the sharing of personal narratives and memories, even as these memories are subjective, incomplete, and always changing, particularly in a time of late capitalism.

Transforming the Lei

Native Hawaiian expressions of aloha illuminate how the lei's meanings vary according to context: aloha is not only used as a greeting or farewell, but also as a signifier of "Hawaiian ethics, the very core of Hawaiian life" that can "encompass love, sympathy, pity, joy, compassion, affection, veneration and mercy."[11] For Native Hawaiians, the giving of the lei is a symbol of aloha, the profoundly vital force that binds together people, families, and communities. Lei can range from humble to elaborate: woven, strung, wound, or mounted, they were historically made from materials as diverse as feathers, shells, seeds, flora, and even human hair. The object of the lei is imbued with significance through the acts of making and giving: stringing together flowers by hand, chewing tough maile leaves to soften them for tying, and investing effort and thought into its design—these mark the corporeal and affective investments in an object of aloha.

Potently enlisted by emergent tourism during the Territorial Era, these expressions and extensions of reciprocity and love were repurposed to soften the stark story of illegal overthrow and annexation. Elite-owned and -run media naturalized and recast colonial relations as travel encounters. In these narratives, the idioms of tourism were particularly effective in deflecting the ongoing theft of land and sovereignty.[12] In the interim between the 1893 overthrow and the 1898 U.S. annexation of the islands, the *Paradise of the Pacific*, the primary magazine for the islands' white American elite or haoles, described the "picturesque group of flower or lei women" in their "happy lazy life . . . perfectly content . . . dreaming away the long hours under the soft skies of this tropical paradise."[13] This early framing of Hawai'i as a destination that welcomed guests was essential to the colonial fantasy of hospitality, so crucial especially in the anxious years after the overthrow, when the deposed Queen Lili'uokalani inspired an interisland petition drive to return sovereignty to the Kingdom of Hawai'i, and the so-called Republic of Hawaii foiled attempts at armed insurrection. Representations of lei women happily and contentedly lazing their days away became a shorthand for the intimate and amicable relations of consent that occluded the tensions of empire, and continued to appear in the *Paradise of the Pacific* in the early years after the United States officially annexed the islands.[14]

Under the regime of early tourism in the islands, the indigenous practice of lei giving shifted to lei selling, monetizing a transaction of aloha even as the invocation of a feminized soft primitivism lent the practice a sense of island open-heartedness and generosity, obscuring the labor of making aloha.[15] Part of the reason that the lei retained the romantic luster of the tropics was that lei selling was the particular domain of Native Hawaiian women; it was therefore understood to be natural to them, and therefore was not work. In 1901, the thirty Native Hawaiian lei women who regularly sold lei on Hotel Street in Honolulu confirmed this association of feminine indigeneity with a natural talent for hospitality.[16] Despite tourism's emergence as a viable industry in this period, and in particular, the commercialization of lei making and selling, the labor of tourism looked more like leisure: hula dancers, lei makers, and even the beach boys of Waikīkī were all understood to be just doing what came naturally. Overdetermined by representations of island life and culture as "happy" and "lazy," the feminized work of hospitality disappears. In contrast, the plantation laborer is more easily identified as the quintessential subject of labor history in Hawai'i—immigrant, male, Asian.[17] The much more flexible though no less regimented labor of hospitality remains underexamined, invisible as labor. Over the next few decades, the much-publicized voyages of steamers and ocean liners solidified the practice of giving lei to arriving and departing tourists, generating more work for lei vendors.

With the emergence of tourism as a small but significant industry in the islands and the decline of traditional modes of communal land relations, many Native Hawaiians opted to monetize their cultural practices and translate them into an American register of capitalism. Lei selling, unlike plantation labor, gave Native Hawaiians who were entering a heightened capitalist system a modicum of labor sovereignty and a livelihood that lay outside the discipline of plantation work. While educated and urban Native Hawaiians benefited from an alliance with a white elite Republican Party, which funneled a disproportionate number of government and private sector jobs to them courtesy of a political patronage system, at least half of Native Hawaiians refused to assimilate into the developing plantation economy, staying isolated in remote rural areas, where their livelihoods were defined by subsistence farming and fishing.[18] The lei sellers epitomized the working-class urban Native Hawaiians with few marketable skills who were navigating the shifting currents of U.S. governance and capitalism in order to survive.[19] For them, the self-exoticization of tourism provided a preferable kind of employment to the sugar and pineapple plantation economy that was manned by imported Asian labor. Elizabeth Buck contends that early tourism's "trivialized version of Hawaiian culture" provided limited roles for Native Hawaiians as entertainers and service workers, citing racism as a primary reason for why they were excluded from upper management even as the tourism industry "made profitable use of their culture as well as their labor."[20] While tourism was coercive and exploitative of indigenous people and their culture, in the end, lei sellers and other Native Hawaiians who served in the tourism industry preferred its flexibility to the regimented, backbreaking work of extracting sweetness from sugarcane.

The lei's association with hospitality also worked to further distance lei making and selling from labor as evidenced by the transformation of May Day to Lei Day. In 1929, Lei Day—the brainchild of Don Blanding, an American writer who was much enamored with the islands—became an official holiday after the idea was published in the *Honolulu Star-Bulletin* and enthusiastically received. For Blanding, "[t]he beautiful Hawaiian custom of presenting visitors with lei has possibly done more than anything else to add to the natural charm of our lovely islands by its token of welcome and aloha, thus creating the longing to return."[21] It was also probably no accident that May Day, which, in the modern era, was associated as much with the International Workers of the World as with a traditional European celebration of spring, leaned more toward a hybridized form of the latter in a plantation-era Hawai'i that was, in the 1920s and 1930s, wracked by labor violence.[22] In fact, 1920 marked a massive six-month interethnic strike by Filipino and Japanese plantation workers. Four years later, thirteen thousand Filipinos struck in Kaua'i. Insisting on a Lei Day that bore closer resemblance to a nostalgic spring ritual than a commemoration of worker rights in a Hawai'i where union organizing was robust and threatened the racialized economic hierarchy, the elite interlocutors of *Paradise of the Pacific* and the *Honolulu Star-Bulletin* mapped the lei and the working-class Native Hawaiian women onto their vision of a friendly tropics. Domesticating labor conflict, covering it over with tropical flora, and inventing a new holiday, white American settlers consolidated their claim to Hawai'i as kama'aina (a term that haoles and white American residents claimed to describe their rights to Hawai'i).[23] The invocation of the lei as a form that would hold a simplistic content of celebration moved it away from indigenous expression and solidarity and closer to a symbol that would reflect a white American vision of modernity and a commodified, manageable indigeneity for the tourism market.

Lei sellers at the waterfront, Honolulu Harbor, 1901. *Courtesy Hawaii State Archives.*

By the 1920s and 1930s, all these efforts worked together to produce a Hawai'i that early tourists would associate with happy islanders. Smiling Native Hawaiian lei sellers eagerly awaiting the arrival of the next steamer from California confirmed the message of welcome upon which kama'aina claims to Hawai'i were built.[24]

By the 1930s, the Hawai'i Tourist Bureau estimated that there were two hundred lei sellers in the territory, making evident that lei selling was a recognizable, regulated profession.[25]

While Blanding identified the lei as that "beautiful Hawaiian custom" that extends hospitality to visitors and promotes tourism, he wrote from a tourist-settler perspective that romanticized the conditions of his presence on the islands. What was for Blanding and other new arrivals the "pretty sight" of all the lei sellers wearing "muumuus and their big pāpales" and "leis on their hats" was rather a conscious staging by the lei sellers to create "an attractive sight" for tourists on steamships.[26] From the oral histories of longtime lei sellers, it is clear that lei vendors understood that tourism's commodification of aloha was remaking the lei into a souvenir, a thing that was an alienable object rather than a symbol of indigenous reciprocal social relations. Gail Burgess, a lei seller of Hawaiian-Chinese-Spanish descent born in 1922, distinguished the lei as souvenir from the lei she might make for family: "That's the thing that was made mostly for these boats that came and the ships that came. These President ships or the Dollar line, like that. They were all made for those people like that because they used it as souvenirs. See, when they bought it, they took it back with them to whatever country they were going to."[27] For many vendors, the scene at the docks was the first time they had actually sold lei: Peggy McKenzie, writing a series for the *Honolulu Advertiser* on "People of Paradise" in the 1960s, interviewed "Mama" Wright, an old-timer lei seller who was born in Hilo in 1893. Wright claimed that she did not sell lei until she came to Honolulu in 1914: "When they say 'dollar,' I think, dollar, that's plenty enough."[28] Once assigned a dollar amount, lei as souvenirs became commodities, ushering in and symbolizing the transformation of Hawaii's economy according to the dictates of capitalism.

Made expressly for sale, these lei symbolized an aloha that was transacted in a monetized exchange, rather than the kind of "beautiful custom with a beautiful thought" imagined by Blanding, early tourists, and settlers.[29] On Honolulu's steamer days, "practically everyday in Hawaii," lei vendors lined up early at Irwin Park near the Aloha Tower to position themselves for new arrivals.[30] Born in 1933, lei seller Harriet Kauwe was involved in the lei-selling business from childhood, and remembered the scene that her Native Hawaiian mother negotiated at the waterfront when ships arrived: "My mother, very aggressive. . . . So, she can go in here and just get at it. . . . I couldn't see myself plowing in, going right to the tourist. And you gotta be fast because . . . if you can get your arm of leis into this guy's arm of leis, you've made a sale. But if you're slow, and the other lei seller get her armful of leis on top of his arm, then you're out of luck, you know."[31] Kauwe's recollections of the early steamer days at the waterfront highlighted her mother's aggression and the ways it benefited her in selling lei. Unsettling Blanding's fantasy of intimate hospitality, Kauwe instead substituted a scene of competition—of having to "plow" in to sell the lei. The jostling and eager crowd of lei sellers that greeted steamer passengers in the 1930s saw tourists as a source of income, and the lei they bestowed en masse were less about Native Hawaiian generosity and expressions of aloha than competition and survival. The generosity of the gift that tourists were experiencing— and the ridiculously low price of the lei—which lent itself to the charm (and affordability) of a tropical holiday, should be understood instead as stemming from desperation and determination. As Gail Burgess put it, "When they started selling leis, when the boat came in and the customers started coming in, there was no such thing as courtesy. It was sell or take it home and eat it. (Laughter)."[32] Yet tourist and kama'aina narratives transformed aggression and desperation on the part of the lei sellers into a generosity or openness, eliding the hardships of the new subsistence economies of small entrepreneurship.

Love's Labor

Gifts of lei had value because they translated the giver's time and effort into material evidence of love for the receiver. Describing a gift from Queen Ka'ahumanu, a missionary's wife in 1825 notes the intricate "neatly formed triple wreath of orange coloured [sic] flowers, the blossom of the 'ilima" that "probably cost the persons who made it almost, if not quite as much time and patience as many . . . an expert milliner, in more polished nations."[33] As objects given in welcome, these elaborate lei evoked reflections on the labor it took to make them, eliciting an analogy of skilled artisanship to portray what was later described as non-work.

Yet of course tourism heralded the standardization of the lei and subjected the labor of lei making to a new kind of calculus. Recollecting how their parents entered the lei business in the early part of the century, some lei sellers tracked the transition from lei giving to lei selling through the ways in which once "free" things, like flowers and plants, as well as labor, became monetized. Once lei sellers started making lei in larger volumes for tourists, going out into the country to pick greenery and wild flowers or using the materials from one's yard was no longer sufficient. Native Hawaiian Martina Macalino, a second-generation lei seller born in 1917, recalled how her parents "used to go up the mountain, pick up all the greeneries."[34] As the lei-selling business grew, lei sellers went from solely raising their own flowers, collecting them from neighbors, or gathering them from the mountains to also buying them.[35] Moana Umi, another second-generation lei seller of Hawaiian-Chinese-Irish descent, remembered that "it took a little bit of time, but where we [were] staying (in Kalihi) had flowers. So pick it over there. Then [my mother] bought some."[36] By the 1930s, migrant Japanese growers started to supply the lei sellers with wholesale carnations, gardenias, and plumerias, which had become standard for tourist lei. When flowers had to be paid for, lei selling became even more subject to the regime of profit.

With tourism, the point was to "make lei fast, not hard."[37] This meant stringing flowers, minimizing the use of more elaborate and time-consuming techniques such as weaving, braiding, or sewing, and eliminating the use of more traditional materials. Martina Macalino recalls how lei making was more labor intensive prior to this standardization: "My father used to cut the hala, toonk-toonk-toonk. . . . [M]y poor dad used to sit down on the floor with his big bag of maile, and chew, chew, chew. Oh, yeah, chew, chew. (Chuckles)."[38] Tourism's demands streamlined and simplified the process, which meant choosing flowers for their fragrance and ease of assembly. Stringing flowers together was the fastest way to create these simpler lei. After gathering, flowers and greens were sorted for quality and matching color and size, then prepared according to the type of flower. Many flowers required peeling off the tough green sepals to ease the long needle through the center of the flower and speed up the process of stringing. Lei makers strung blooms together on the needle, fitting them snugly front to back, then slid them down the string until the approximately two to three feet of length was filled. Certain flowers lent themselves to quick stringing and became more popular, like plumerias: "Fill up the needle in no time, all pau!"[39] Other flowers, such as gardenias and carnations, became more favored because fewer were needed to make a simple lei.[40] Flowers that were easy to string took as little as two to three minutes to assemble once the flowers were prepared for stringing.

While tourist lei were of the less elaborate variety, the sheer demand for them intensified the labor of their manufacture. Moana Umi's description of the "hard job" of lei selling specifically contradicted the relaxed tropical image associated with lei giving: "Lots of people feel, well, oh, we sit down all day. Oh, we just wrapped around flowers. We smell good all day. But it really isn't. It's a tedious, tired job. Now, they say, 'Anybody can sell leis. Anybody can go pick up flowers and string it.' But it's the time you give it. Now, some of them pick it up and they string it. Feels good the first few times that you do it. But then, if you stay with it, it isn't. It's a tiresome—lot of the old folks drop out because they can't handle it."[41]

Family members were conscripted into the lei-making business, many of them while still quite young. By 1935, the growth of the lei industry reflected the growth of the tourism industry. According to Margaret Kalinchak, the first president of the Hawaiian Lei Sellers Association, the lei industry provided a living for approximately four hundred families in Honolulu alone.[42] Gail Burgess depicted a childhood dictated by the demands of lei selling: "But most of those leis, I stayed up day and night and morning, stringing, so that my mother would have most of the flowers strung before she left. . . . I was only, what? Eleven, twelve. And then, get up. You know, just fall asleep, stringing like that. And then get up again. Have to string it or else if I don't string, if she don't string, the leis is not going to get done by itself. So I would string, string, string, string, fall asleep. And then, wake them up, I throw it down. String, string, and fall asleep until all around the clock."[43] Burgess's experience was a typical childhood initiation into the family business.[44] In 1940, there was an estimated production of two thousand lei per day on O'ahu, with the vast majority being sold to arriving and departing tourists.[45] Hotels also began to order lei for their customers. Moana Umi remembered her late night efforts of making one thousand to twelve hundred lei a night for the Kaiser Hawaiian Village's luaus in the 1950s.[46] The recruitment of unpaid family members and lei making's domination of family time reflected the shift of Hawaii's economy in the 1950s to a model increasingly oriented toward outside investment in mass tourism.

The labor that was a significant part of the expression of aloha was devalued, even as it was also monetized. Part of this devaluation was at the hands of the lei sellers themselves; after all, this was an object that had previously been free. Assigning a price to lei contradicted the very concept of lei giving. This might explain how for many of the "old-time" lei sellers like Gail Burgess's mother, labor was not factored into the price of the lei: "A lot of 'em would get ruined because they didn't sell it then for the boat, that would all have to be thrown away. Because it's all smashed and ruined already. So that's why they sold it cheap. They would yell their head off. 'Quarter. Here's fifty cents. Two for quarter. Three for quarter. Here, ten for dollar.' Just imagine, 'Here, ten for dollar.' . . . You might just as well throw it away. But they was only interested in the dollar. So that means they picked they own flowers, they strung their own. They didn't care about—their time was nothing. It didn't matter anything. It's only as long as they got a dollar, they figured they made money."[47]

What tourists might take pleasure in—the beauty and bargain of a souvenir—was part of a calculus that looked, above all else, to extract any kind of money from them for an object that had never been assigned a price. Moana Umi put it thus: "When the ship come in already, you get whatever they have in their arm for a dollar. . . . They threw the leis in their arms and stuff and collected the dollar."[48] The undervaluation of the sellers' own labor in this transaction meant little as long as the overall exchange resulted in money to feed their families.

Camouflaging Militarism

The advent of Pan American's Hawai'i Clipper service in 1936, opening up the route from San Francisco to Honolulu, signified the beginnings of mass tourism, which was then interrupted by World War II. On the eve of the Japanese attack on Pearl Harbor, Hawaii's lei sellers were doing a brisk business that produced an estimated one million lei annually and generated $150,000–$200,000 total sales.[49] A significant and growing clientele in the years leading up to the war was the increasing numbers of soldiers and construction workers that accompanied the military buildup of Hawai'i. With the war's onset, the first wave of wealthy tourists to Hawai'i ended, curtailing lei-selling practices and demonstrating the dangers of depending on a volatile industry.

Motivated by the economic hardships and shortages of wartime, lei sellers were forced to look elsewhere for their livelihoods, and the military had work for them. Martina Macalino remembers that many elderly lei sellers struggled until her "mother went and asked to have the lei sellers to work in the camouflage for the army. That's how they had all the lei sellers go."[50] The recruitment of Native Hawaiians into the war effort and the emphasis on the military utility of Native Hawaiian culture and labor operated to manufacture consent among islanders by including them in military life.[51] About fifty lei sellers were employed making nets to hide gun emplacements and air raid warning stations from airborne enemy surveillance and attack, transferring their lei-making skills to weaving camouflage.[52] Harriet Kauwe remembers that while her mother continued to sell lei during war time, she had to supplement her income by working as a defense worker at Pearl Harbor.[53] Sliding into a militarized workforce, these lei sellers, in some ways, corroborated U.S. rule and occupation. While their new work arose out of wartime exigencies, the military had long been a presence on the islands, and had indeed been one of the key actors in the United States' annexation of Hawai'i. The lei sellers' wartime work put in stark relief how the labor of hospitality operated to camouflage the islands' historical militarization.

The war and this recruitment of Native Hawaiians into the militarized economy marked the shift from a civilian tourist clientele to a militarized one, which also helped to facilitate an image of military personnel as welcome guests, even if their generosity created new tensions. The lei sellers who did continue to sell lei during wartime learned to negotiate unfamiliar kinds of spaces such as military clubs and bars, putting themselves in potentially risky situations. Harriet Kauwe recalls that in the evenings, her mother sold lei during dances at Fort DeRussy or Pearl City Tavern while she, her siblings, and her father strung lei in the station wagon.[54] Kauwe describes the whole family effort that nonetheless put her mother front and center as the salesperson: "When she run short of leis, she comes to the car, and my dad used to say, 'Hurry up, hurry up, your mommy needs some more leis.' We used to string in the car and give it to her."[55] The entrance of Native Hawaiian women once again into recreational spaces dominated by young white men looking for pleasure extended the erotics of hospitality to the military. Martina Macalino described how her mother also began to sell lei at night: "She goes from bar to bar to sell. She's done that for years. She work till about three, four o'clock in the morning."[56] The gendered labor Macalino's and Kauwe's mothers undertook solidified the military as a new clientele that lei sellers had to learn to traverse.

Even with the end of the war and the resumption of commercial air flights to Hawai'i, soldiers continued to be a significant source of income for lei sellers. Sisters Charlotte Fuller and Queenie Dowsett, lei sellers who also inherited the business from their mother, recalled that immediately after the war, they were selling lei out of their station wagon around the clubs in Waikīkī, but also at the airport, where the military transports would arrive.[57] In addition, their mother, who had established good relations with the military during the war, enjoyed their postwar patronage: "The military guys, if they needed 1,000 leis for something because they were coming or going overseas, we strung the leis that she gave (with her heart)."[58] The gratitude engendered by the military for wartime protections thus structured the postwar relations between soldiers and lei sellers. Harriet Kauwe described how the rhythms and new spaces of lei selling were dictated by the itineraries of navy flights: "That used to carry a lot of military people back and forth. That happened one time, my uncle went. I think he did put up a stand and he made money.... And had all these jalopies. We just built a stand on. No more electricity over there [Lagoon Drive]. Just a dark road and don't even have street lights. What we have is gas lanterns. We hang it onto the stand, maybe two gas lanterns per stand. This is how it started."[59] The lei sellers on Lagoon Drive rebuilt their business around the arrivals and departures of the military, working within the realities of an increasingly militarized Hawai'i. Maile Lee, a Hawaiian Caucasian lei seller who was just a child during the war, reiterated how the military schedule dictated her family's lei selling: "The military plane would come in every afternoon, oh, 3:00, 3:30, and that's when we had the majority of our business would be the military people then."[60] The military business at Lagoon Drive attracted a distinct group who would park on the side of the road in an established order and wait for their customers. The transformation of soldiers into a new kind of tourist in this postwar moment illustrates how military logics came to define the everyday realities of working Hawaiians during this time. It also illuminates how the lei operated to defuse the politically charged question of Hawaii's increasingly martial identity. This seemingly inevitable militarization held little menace for lei sellers, whose relations with the military had been translated through a monetized tourist idiom.

Keeping Some Aloha for Themselves

Translating the lei to a capitalist economy was never a complete and exact process. At the turn of the century, even as the lei sellers were adapting to the new regime of tourism, competition was suspended once the tourists were gone. Gail Burgess noted that after the heat of competition, when scrabbling for customers at the piers resulted in ill feelings and the occasional desire "to give 'em one punch," once the boats departed, lei sellers reverted to "resting around sitting on their mats on the grass like that, they're all friendly, happy and laughing. (Laughs)."[61] Indeed, Burgess suggested that selling lei, while it brought out "the greed," also "taught lot of those people how to get along or even to survive."[62] Negotiating the rifts of market competition, lei sellers also insisted on holding on to the kind of aloha that would sustain their connections during good and bad times. Sophia Ventura, a member of another multigenerational lei selling family, remembered that at the waterfront, the women were connected, even as they were competitors: "We all sit down, string our leis. My mother was there, too. And she'd make food and call (chuckles) everybody."[63]

The postwar boom in mass tourism regularized lei selling and further intensified the commodification of indigenous culture. Lei sellers, while increasingly enmeshed into relationships of dependence on tourism and militarism, were well aware of the trivialization and commodification of Native Hawaiian culture, and their own strategic—and even occasionally oppositional—participation in it. Reorienting themselves to serve the middle-class American tourists who came en masse with the revolutions in commercial aviation, lei sellers in the 1950s located themselves squarely within the territory's tourism strategy. They struggled to balance the image and reality of Native Hawaiian culture with having to operate within an economy of scale that further commodified aloha and dictated new temporal and familial pressures.

Lei sellers were at the very bottom of the corporate tourism ladder, and they struggled to adapt to a tourism economy that looked and felt quite different from its prewar incarnation. Along with infrastructural investments to ease the path of multinational investors, Hawaii's territorial government sought to utilize Native Hawaiians as a unique element of a tropical holiday. Taking advantage of the ways that the cultural work of hospitality operated during the war, in which luaus and hulas were deployed in familiar eroticized modes to welcome and succor soldiers, the tourism industry was primed to transform fantasy into reality for the masses.[64] The recollections of lei sellers illustrate how they maneuvered the revival of their livelihoods, the exploitative work rhythms it engendered, and the wish to sustain their own cultural practices within the new regime of mass tourism. For instance, lei sellers, while enjoying music and hula in their everyday lives, also used them as incentives to sell lei. Gail Burgess and her sister Lillian Cameron recalled how at Beachwalk Park after the war, lei sellers and their families who were in the entertainment industry drummed up business for themselves by working together to create the ambience that tourists desired: "They would play music, then sell leis there with their lanterns. They had all these station wagons here and there parked along Kalākaua [Avenue]. They would hang their leis and their flowers, whatever they had."[65] Playing to and with expectations of authentic Hawaiianness, their brother and his friends would then teach tourists to dance to the music, but with a caveat: "Well, of course we tell, 'Oh, but you gotta wear a lei. You have to dance. All the dancers have to wear a lei.' So, they go to our little corner wagon we had there."[66] In addition, by weaving Native Hawaiian cultural practices into opportunities to further monetize aloha, these lei sellers transformed the ways that tourism appropriated the labor of the family into new opportunities for family connection, albeit within the regimes of tourism.

The conscious use and appreciation of Native Hawaiian cultural iconography and performance was something that lei sellers understood as part of the rhetoric of tourism that would benefit them. At the same time, within the accelerated rhythms of mass tourism, their desire for "Hawaiiana" exceeded the ways in which Native Hawaiian culture could be commodified by tourism. Both lei sellers and the state, for instance, used Native Hawaiian forms, such as music, hula, and even architecture to encourage the tropical fantasy of hospitality. At the new airport, constructed in 1962, booths constructed in "Hawaiiana" style helped to foster a nostalgia for old-style tourism, even among the lei sellers themselves.[67] Lillian Cameron described the "grass shacks" that the territory built for the Lagoon Drive lei sellers: "it looked like a flower village with all the greenery and the shack. And the area was so nice, like a typical village like you see now in the Polynesian Cultural Center."[68] Maile Lee concurred, reminiscing about the "wonderful atmosphere at the old airport" that was "full of aloha spirit," which for her embodied the "typical" and "authentic" Hawai'i.[69] These sentiments are perhaps colored by the lei sellers' own nostalgia for a space where they were centralized and valued as symbols of aloha, as opposed to what they perceived as their waning status at the time of the interviews in the 1980s. At that point, subsequent renovations of the airport and the relocation of lei sellers away from the main terminal had cut down on business and marginalized them as the purveyors of aloha. In addition to having to compete with florists, contend with package tours that provided their own lei, and pay rent, the airport lei sellers found that they were pushed aside even as more and more tourists arrived. At the "old" grass huts, they remembered a kind of community similar to the waterfront days. Lillian Cameron recalled that even as the airport stall's demands on her time increased, her work there was also entwined with the pleasures of connecting with family and friends: "Everybody came. 'Cause then, my brother and them would play music. They started to play in the back. You know, because when they have the rehearsal, when they have to do a show or something, so they go in the back and practice with all the instruments. . . . So, that'll get all the tourists. You know, they hear the music. From in the front, when the buses used to stop. Take pictures, they all go in the back. Everybody goes in the back. Pretty soon, everybody's dancing. (Laughs). We had a big crowd over there."[70] Noting that the music would "get" tourists, Lillian Cameron also laughed when recollecting the pleasures of having "everybody" present and "dancing," pointing to the ways in which lei sellers navigated the monetization of

Native culture. Selling aloha for mass tourists, the lei sellers nonetheless also kept some for themselves.

The lei as tourist souvenir was but a shallow approximation of what it meant to these working women. Lei seller Queenie Dowsett, Sophia Ventura's daughter, explained how the lei's monetization existed alongside the kinds of relationships made possible in tourism economies: "We made good leis. We made beautiful leis. They're worth every penny. Yes. The lei business has been great for us. It gave us independence, which is great for Hawai'i. It gave us a lot of wisdom of people. (And we enjoyed meeting people. We made many, many friends through the lei business.)"[71] For Dowsett, the legacy of lei selling has filtered down in terms of the beauty and value of the lei, the wisdom of intergenerational and community knowledge, financial independence, and connectedness. They also continued the practice of giving lei for free to consolidate relationships within their entrepreneurial and cultural communities. For Harriet Kauwe, lei giving helped cement the customer relationships upon which her business was built, but the gift of the lei simultaneously bestowed the gift of conviviality and company to both giver and receiver, and helped to remind her and the recipient of the bonds of friendship and love that connected them. Sophia Ventura's philosophy corroborated the continuing importance of the lei in Native Hawaiian culture when she weighed the gift of a lei against the money it could otherwise bring in:

> But otherwise, if there's plenty, I think plenty, oh, well, we all share. (Laughter). . . . You know, the old folks, "Ha'awi, ha'awi. Ha'awi a pau loa (Give until it's all gone.)" (Laughs). Well, I don't know. I guess if they made us not Hawaiian, maybe something else, maybe little better, but putting that Hawaiian blood in us (chuckles), that the worse blood they could put inside anybody because they can't ever forget to be generous. No can. They want to be mean sometimes. You get a strong feeling, eh. But (chuckles) you end up giving.[72]

While both Kauwe and Ventura joke about the capitalist handicap of being Native Hawaiian, and the inevitability of giving until it is all gone, this notion of aloha engendered community ties that also nurtured the lei sellers and helped them to negotiate the changing social landscape of territorial Hawai'i.

Lei selling was and is a hard business. Moana Umi described a long day that started at 5 a.m. and ended at midnight, with "times [when] you get a little bit heartbroken, a little bit depressed," which was a typical day for lei sellers.[73] However, many of the lei sellers also acknowledged that the business, with all its stress, gave multiple generations of their families a way to make a living and educate their children.[74] The importance of the new ties among fellow lei vendors was paramount and represented the shifting and adaptable communities that emerged under new regimes. No less important than their family ties, these new relations between lei sellers sustained them as they entered into a volatile and uncertain capitalist economy. The lei thus represented economic survival as well as a continuing cultural practice under the shifting conditions produced by tourism and capitalism. Even as lei sellers sold lei as souvenirs, the giving and even the wearing of the lei continued alongside and sometimes even through its sale in tourism circuits. The lei sellers continued to delineate the occasions by which they made lei for giving, even if in the spaces of tourism, giving lei was already imbricated in the commodification of Native Hawaiian hospitality.

Retaining and remaking the pleasures of lei making and giving in the economy of lei selling was a point of pride, as if to say that the beauty of freshly picked flowers and their vibrantly hued and fragrant petals, the gratification of giving and receiving lei from friends and family, the tactile reminder of a wreath of love—all these cannot be bought or sold (even as they also are). The cultural labor of making aloha for sale is never quite so complete.

NOTES

1. Haunani-Kay Trask, "These Lovely Hula Hands: Corporate Tourism and the Prostitution of Hawaiian Culture," in *From a Native Daughter: Colonialism and Sovereignty in Hawai'i* (Honolulu: University of Hawai'i Press, 1999), 136–47.

2. Trask, "These Lovely Hula Hands," 146. Trask's rhetoric follows that of Jamaica Kincaid, who likewise addresses the tourist to Antigua and illuminates life on a supposedly postcolonial British West Indies island in *A Small Place*. Jamaica Kincaid, *A Small Place* (New York: Farrar, Straus and Giroux, 1988).

3. On cultural labor, see Michael Denning, *The Cultural Front: The Laboring of American Culture in the Twentieth Century* (New York: Verso, 1998).

4. Adria L. Imada, *Aloha America: Hula Circuits through the U.S. Empire* (Durham, NC: Duke University Press, 2012), 266.

5. See, for example, M. Jacqui Alexander, "Erotic Autonomy as a Politics of Decolonization: An Anatomy of Feminist and State Practice in the Bahamas Tourist Economy," in *Feminist Genealogies, Colonial Legacies, Democratic Futures*, ed. M. Jacqui Alexander and Chandra Talpade Mohanty (New York: Routledge, 1997), 63–100; and Kamala Kempado, ed., *Sun, Sex, and Gold: Tourism and Sex Work in the Caribbean* (Lanham, MD: Rowman & Littlefield, 1999).

6. For more on porno-tropics, see Anne McClintock, *Imperial Leather: Race, Gender and Sexuality in the Colonial Conquest* (New York: Routledge, 1995).

7. Noenoe Silva, *Aloha Betrayed: Native Hawaiian Resistance to American Colonialism* (Durham, NC: Duke University Press, 2004).

8. See Christine Skwiot, *The Purposes of Paradise: U.S. Tourism and Empire in Cuba and Hawai'i* (Philadelphia: University of Pennsylvania Press, 2010).

9. Imada, *Aloha America*, 9.

10. This is due to a language limitation on my part, but also because English-language newspapers had an investment in a certain type of coverage of Native Hawaiians in which this research is interested. See Silva in *Aloha Betrayed* for an analysis of Hawaiian-language newspapers and their politics of representation and resistance.

11. Reverend Aikaiko Akaka, as quoted in Imada, *Aloha America*, 8.

12. See, e.g., Paulette Feeney, "Aloha and Allegiance: Imagining America's Paradise" (Ph.D. dissertation, University of Hawai'i at Mānoa, 2009); Skwiot, *The Purposes of Paradise*.

13. Frank L. Hoogs, "Flower Women of Honolulu," *Paradise of the Pacific*, August 1896: 121.

14. Josephine C. Barber, "Lei Women," *Paradise of the Pacific*, April 1901: 13; William M. Langton, "The Lei," *Paradise of the Pacific*, August 1900: 8.

15. Jane Desmond, *Staging Tourism: Bodies on Display from Waikiki to Sea World* (Chicago: University of Chicago Press, 1999).

16. Barber, "Lei Women," 13.

17. Ronald Takaki, *Pau Hana: Plantation Life and Labor in Hawaii, 1835–1920* (Honolulu: University of Hawai'i Press, 1983).

18. Noenoe K. Silva, "I Ku Mau Mau: How Kanaka Maoli Tried to Sustain National Identity within the United States Political System," *American Studies* 45(3): 9–32; Davianna Pōmaika'i McGregor, *Nā Kua'āina: Living Hawaiian Culture* (Honolulu: University of Hawai'i Press, 2007), 44.

19. McGregor, *Nā Kua'āina*, 196.

20. Elizabeth Buck, *Paradise Remade: The Politics of Culture and History in Hawai'i* (Philadelphia: Temple University Press, 1993), 174.

21. Don Blanding, as quoted in Steven J. Friesen, "The Origins of Lei Day: Festivity and the Construction of Ethnicity in the Territory of Hawaii," *History and Anthropology* 10(1) (December 1996): 19.

22. See also Donna T. Haverty-Stacke, *America's Forgotten Holiday: May Day and Nationalism, 1867–1960* (New York: New York University Press, 2008), for a parallel account of how labor drove the birth and evolution of May Day.

23. "Orchids May Be Grown with Ease in Hawaii, Expert Says," *Honolulu Advertiser*, April 2, 1934.

24. DoSoto Brown, *Hawaii Recalls: Selling Romance to America: Nostalgic Images of the Hawaiian Islands, 1920–1950s* (Honolulu: Editions Limited, 1982).

25. "About 20 Lei Sellers Carry on Old Hawaiian Custom," *Honolulu Star-Bulletin*, November 21, 1931: 1, 3.

26. Harriet Kauwe, 93. Unless indicated otherwise, the oral histories used in this chapter are from *Ka Poʻe Kau Lei: An Oral History of Hawaiʻi's Lei Sellers*. Oral History Project, Social Science Research Institute, University of Hawaiʻi at Mānoa, 1986. All interviews for this project were conducted by ʻIwalani Hodges, a researcher at the Center for Oral History.

27. Gail Burgess, 398. The racial/ethnic terms that describe these lei makers are from the original oral histories.

28. Peggy McKenzie, "Hawaii's Lei Sellers," *Honolulu Advertiser*, May 1, 1960: 10.

29. Charles W. Kenn, "Hawaii's Wreath of Love," *Paradise of the Pacific*, May 1935: 7.

30. McKenzie, "Hawaii's Lei Sellers," 10.

31. Harriet Kauwe, 92.

32. Gail Burgess, 401.

33. Jeanne Booth Johnson, "Everybody Wore Leis Every Day in Old Hawaii," *Honolulu Advertiser*, September 4, 1960: 10.

34. Martina Macalino, 133.

35. Martina Macalino, 135.

36. Moana Umi, 301.

37. "About 200 Lei Sellers Carry on Old Hawaiian Custom": 1.

38. Martina Macalino, 155.

39. "Mama" Wright, as quoted in McKenzie, "Hawaii's Lei Sellers," 10.

40. McKenzie, "Hawaii's Lei Sellers," 10; "Flower Lei Keeps Alive Custom Of Friendliness," *Honolulu Advertiser*, August 29, 1948: 1. In addition, tourists increasingly wanted lei as souvenirs that would not spoil and would not violate agricultural rules, so paper flowers also became popular.

41. Moana Umi, 303.

42. *Honolulu Star-Bulletin*, February 9, 1935: 10.

43. Gail Burgess, 415.

44. Harriet Kauwe, 90–92.

45. Anne Oberlin, "Millions of Flower Leis," *Paradise of the Pacific*, November 1940: 9.

46. Moana Umi, 303.

47. Gail Burgess, 402.

48. Moana Umi, 304.

49. Oberlin, "Millions of Flower Leis," 9–11.

50. Martina Macalino, 139.

51. Imada, *Aloha America*, 219–20.

52. *Honolulu Star-Bulletin*, February 26, 1943: 6.

53. Harriet Kauwe, 97.

54. Harriet Kauwe, 97.
55. Harriet Kauwe, 97–98.
56. Martina Macalino, 140.
57. Charlotte Fuller, 358; Queenie Dowsett, 369. See also Irene Asing Sims, 213.
58. Queenie Dowsett, 374.
59. Harriet Kauwe, 99.
60. Maile Lee, 258. I use "Caucasian" here even though it is problematic and bears the imprint of the politics of social science eugenics because the original source uses this term. Particularly in Hawai'i, where the colonial politics of blood quantum has land and sovereignty at stake, such terms need problematization. See J. Kēhaulani Kauanui, *Hawaiian Blood: Colonialism and the Politics of Sovereignty and Indigeneity* (Durham, NC: Duke University Press, 2008).
61. Gail Burgess, 408.
62. Gail Burgess, 408.
63. Sophia Ventura, 378.
64. See Imada, *Aloha America*, 213–54.
65. Gail Burgess, 413.
66. Lillian Cameron, 421.
67. Sandra Santimer, 14.
68. Lillian Cameron, 427.
69. Maile Lee, 259.
70. Lillian Cameron, 426.
71. Queenie Dowsett, 375.
72. Sophia Ventura, 377.
73. Moana Umi, 327, 332.
74. Maile Lee, 263.

7

The Advantages of Empire

Chinese Servants and Conflicts over Settler Domesticity in the "White Pacific," 1870–1900

ANDREW T. URBAN

Introduction: Cultural Calculations and the Political Economy of Empire

Over the course of eighteen days in the fall of 1876, the United States Congress's Joint Special Committee to Investigate Chinese Immigration conducted hearings in San Francisco's Palace Hotel. During the proceedings, a testy exchange about domestic labor arose between Aaron Sargent, the vehemently anti-Chinese Republican senator from the state of California who would write the majority report for the committee, and the Reverend Otis Gibson, a leading Methodist missionary involved in Protestant outreach to Chinese immigrants in the city. The dispute centered on whether the employment of male Chinese servants prevented white women from being hired to those positions. Witnesses and elected officials estimated that seven thousand Chinese servants were working for white households in California, with a minimum of three thousand Chinese domestic laborers employed in San Francisco alone.[1] Sargent concluded that this meant that three thousand white women in San Francisco had been denied jobs as servants, a calculation that portrayed occupational gains for Chinese immigrants as invariably resulting in white laborers' losses through direct competition.

Gibson's own experiences, however, suggested otherwise. He testified that he and his wife had tried three or four times to "get the white ones in" when searching for servants in the preceding years, but had not found a white woman willing to meet their needs. He had not substituted Chinese for white labor, but had hired Chinese servants as the only available option. Was this, Sargent speculated, a reaction to Gibson's "hard" ways with his servants and his well-known public support for Chinese immigration, which cast his character as an employer in doubt? Gibson curtly responded, "That may be."[2] Undaunted, Gibson stated that he could hire a Chinese servant for sixteen dollars a month, whereas a white servant would cost him twenty-five dollars. In addition, a white "girl" defined her job duties with explicit limitations, insisting, for example, that the laundry be sent out. Gibson felt obligated to repeat that if white workers would contract as servants on the terms he set, he would employ them over the Chinese, but that he could not be blamed for navigating the labor market in a way that any prudent capitalist would respect. Gibson and Sargent's impasse reflected a broader debate about domestic labor and to what extent white women workers had the right to establish sovereignty over the home as a workplace. Whether servants deserved to socialize in their employers' homes and outside them, reject assignments that they had not specifically agreed to do, or implement their managerial prerogatives over how the labor was to be completed had become a national obsession.

Gibson argued that basic "political economy" proved that the presence of "a few thousand unskilled laborers" would ultimately function to attract skilled laborers, merchants, financiers, and the clergy—groups that in his opinion were essential to economic and social advancement—to San Francisco and other growing Western cities. The better classes of settlers, Gibson implied, had an expectation that domestic services such as cooking, cleaning, and laundering could be reasonably obtained from the labor market, so that they could devote themselves to work of a higher purpose. If this meant relying on a new and seemingly exotic source of labor in the Chinese, Gibson concluded, so be it.

Sargent was not swayed by Gibson's theory of the complementary role that Chinese labor could play in augmenting the quality of Western settlement. He challenged Gibson to explain his comfort in letting male Chinese servants care for white children as nurses, an area of domestic work that went beyond cooking and cleaning, and involved even more intimate exchanges between capital and labor. Sargent was undoubtedly aware that the direct participation of Chinese immigrants in physical care work was a concern even for employers who were otherwise predisposed to hire Chinese servants. He pointed out that Gibson, in the course of recalling his experience as a missionary in China earlier in the hearing, had testified that infanticide was one of the practices that prevailed among the Chinese in their native country, and was a marker of the savagery that he and other evangelicals had traveled abroad to eradicate.[3] Sargent's allusion to the potential vulnerability of white children reminded the public that Gibson's detached and clinical discussion of supply and demand failed to account for how cultural and moral values would be imparted to the domestic spaces that white settlers wanted to produce in their rapidly growing towns and cities, and how those spaces would be occupied and worked in terms of race and gender.

In historian Patrick Wolfe's well-known formulation: "invasion is a structure not an event." The social theorist Lorenzo Veracini adds, "Settlers, unlike other migrants, 'remove' to establish a better polity, either by setting up an ideal social body or by constituting an exemplary model of social organisation."[4] Continued occupation transformed invasion into settlement and presented opportunities to produce and consume services born out of the greater division of labor. In California and other Anglophone Pacific societies, the white population maintained the belief that the social and market relations taking shape represented an experiment in settlement, in which the variables at play departed sharply from previous iterations of white "civilization." Trying to determine the course of this experiment brought white settlers of different classes into frequent conflict.

While Sargent's stance would carry the day legislatively—in May 1882, Congress passed the Chinese Restriction Act, barring Chinese laborers on the grounds that they were economically and culturally unassimilable—Gibson's description of how markets for Chinese domestic labor operated in practice received its own forms of validation.[5] In the decades that followed, Anglophone settlements across the Pacific world would legislate or strengthen existing restrictions on Chinese migration.[6] Wherever initiatives to extend gatekeeping to the borders of businesses and private homes materialized, divides among white settlers arose in concert. In an editorial that appeared in the *Sydney Morning Herald* on June 12, 1888, during Australia's Intercolonial Conference on the issue of Chinese immigration, the newspaper—despite supporting the Australian colonies' renewed efforts to establish sovereignty over migration in the form of more stringent restrictions on the entry of

Chinese laborers—cautioned white Australians to temper their desire to purge the country of Chinese labor altogether.[7] Noting word of a proposal by Newcastle miners to initiate a boycott campaign against all Chinese businesses and any white employers that hired Chinese labor, whether as part of their trade or for personal service, the *Herald* warned that such approaches would make "society an aggressive and censorious institution, and it will stir up feeling not only between Chinamen and Australians, but between Australians and Australians."[8] Whereas the governance of national labor markets could be allowed to reflect the popular will, as manifested through legislators' actions, this same popular will had to respect the right of private capital, within the law, to hire whom it chose. A letter from a member of the Federated Seamen's Union to the newspaper the next day disagreed staunchly, noting that, in light of the entry rights granted to the more than one million Chinese British subjects of Hong Kong and the Straits Settlements, the boycott was the only really effective option. "I would sooner keep John as a pauper," he concluded, "than keep my brother as pauper."[9]

Settlement, Global Trade, and Debates about Chinese Domestic Labor

In late-nineteenth-century debates about Chinese immigration, how to establish the right demographic composition of the population was a governing concern of settlement that was never just about the present, but always geared at ensuring and actively orchestrating an imagined future. Historians' emphasis on the establishment of nations' "right" to control immigration through regulations governing entry has obscured the sharp conflicts that persisted between white employers and white laborers over how to govern and use the alien Chinese labor that remained, and continued to arrive, legally or illegally.[10] In the minds of many white participants in the immigration debates, whether alien Chinese labor deserved a place in the United States West and in Anglophone settlements across the Pacific hinged less on whether these laborers might be made into citizens, and more on whether their labor could be harnessed to abet the settlement and development goals of the white majority.[11] Free market advocates insisted that alien Chinese labor could be used—and granted a physical space of inclusion—as a capital tool for white settlement. Anglophone settler societies, as they continued to move toward economies oriented around industrial capitalism and trade rather than the extraction of mineral wealth, were squandering the unique competitive advantage that Chinese labor, when carefully confined and relegated to menial labor, afforded to regions in close proximity to Asia.

Anti-Chinese activists claimed that domestic service best functioned as a temporary occupation for white women, in which they deserved to be treated as social equals and not as menials, while awaiting the opportunity to marry. White laborers understood domestic service in the context of their own aspirations to possess the gendered domestic labor and care work of women through marriage, which they accused greedy capitalists of subverting through their experiments with Chinese men. Absent such opportunities, white women would be discouraged from relocating to remote Pacific outposts, since there would be limited options for unmarried women to work as wage earners, or would be forced to seek out disreputable work. Henry George, testifying in front of the Congressional Joint Committee in 1876, predicted that Chinese immigration would gradually transform California into British India, "where the few white men who are there ride in palanquins, and are waited on by dozens of servants."[12] By surrendering control over how domesticity was produced, white laborers risked seeing the state transformed from a settlement representing the expansion of republican institutions into new territory, to a planter colony of dependents ruled by plutocrats. In rationalizing their violent expulsions of Chinese communities during the 1880s, white Westerners maintained that their purges supported the more exalted purpose of making way for renewed white settlement. A white tailor in Tacoma, Washington, who had played an active role in expelling the city's Chinese community in 1885 testified to Congress that prior to the Chinese being forced out there were only two or three white women working as servants in the entire city. Since then, he added, white women had not only settled in the town due to the availability of domestic work, but had improved the town "socially" by providing working men with respectable female counterparts to court and marry.[13]

The movement of human capital in the form of labor power needs to be understood in relationship to the unique regulatory concerns it raised and the fierce antagonisms it generated between white settler laborers and white settler capitalists. Unlike other configurations of free trade, such as access to capital, credit, and markets, which all classes of settlers championed in general terms—even while disagreeing fiercely over how such access was to operate—there was no consensus about how settler trade in human labor, especially when linked to China and Asia, was to be pursued. While historians such as Kristen Hoganson have highlighted how the late-nineteenth-century growth of global commerce that Americans enjoyed as consumers constituted "an imperial buy in," less attention has been devoted to how Americans reacted to the consumption of foreign "goods" in the form of labor classified as alien, and to what extent consumers, representing diverse class backgrounds, were willing to accept immigrant labor as part of an imagined domestic economy.[14] Chinese servants represented the physical embodiment of the new possibilities that global consumerism allowed, and, as an exchange, its most intimate and animate embrace. Campaigns to halt the immigration of Chinese and drive them out of domestic service industries reveal that white laborers in the late-nineteenth-century United States guarded against what the historian Mae Ngai has called the "imported colonialism" of laborers barred from naturalizing.[15] When federal courts and representatives of the State Department selectively intervened to adjudicate boycotts, riots, and expulsions directed at Chinese communities, they did so not out of concern for the rights of laborers and merchants, but in order to ensure that the policy of free trade with China was maintained.

Finally, while struggles over whether or not to boycott Asian labor had distinctly local resonances and contexts that reflected the differing sovereign statuses of the United States, Canada, and Australia, it is clear that the debates about the long-term wisdom of using or not using Asian labor connected these regions' political economies. As historian Kornel Chang observes, "the development of the North American West would not have been possible without overseas Asian labor and markets, which were made accessible and forced open by Euro-American imperial incursions into East Asia and the South Pacific. As such, frontier expansion and overseas empire-building were inextricably intertwined—the development of one being utterly dependent on the other."[16] The political sovereignty that white settlers claimed as the privileged occupants of "white men's countries" could not eradicate dependencies on Chinese labor that were already an established feature of expansion.[17] Nor were white capitalists in newly settled Anglophone areas willing to concede sovereignty over the individual and familial market behavior that such dependencies had conditioned. Settlers with capital doggedly persisted in defending what they understood as market and contractual liberties to hire whomever they wished, even if such employment practices meant relying on labor power derived from imperial networks of trade, rather than from the traditional sources of white settlers and citizens. This was their "White Pacific."

The Biopolitics of Domestic Labor Consumption: The Right to White Reproduction

Following the Panic of 1873, rising interest rates starved newly formed industries in San Francisco and other California cities of financial capital. By 1877, one-fifth of San Francisco's labor force was unemployed.[18] On July 23, 1877, San Francisco erupted in anti-Chinese violence. Protests that had begun as a show of sympathy for the ongoing national railroad strike turned instead against Chinese immigration. For three days, mobs razed Chinese laundries and dry goods stores, and targeted the offices and docked ships of the Pacific Mail Steamship company, which transported the majority of Chinese immigrants. A Committee for Public Safety, bankrolled by the city's elite, formed to bolster the ranks of the city's police and fire departments. A year after his testimony, Otis Gibson's Methodist Mission on Washington Street came under attack by the mob, which stoned the building and tried to set it on fire. In the aftermath of the so-called "July Days," Denis Kearney, an Irish immigrant and journeyman laborer most recently employed as a drayman, took charge of the California branch of the Workingmen's Party, transforming it into an anti-Chinese political party.

The rally song "Twelve Hundred More," with its reference to "twelve hundred pure and virtuous girls," forced to "barter away their virtue, to get a crust of bread," featured prominently at the protests of white laborers and their families during this period.[19] Twelve hundred was the number of Chinese immigrants each steamship arriving in San Francisco purportedly discharged, each ready to take a job that would otherwise belong to the community of white laborers. Whereas white women entered labor markets for domestic service selectively during boom times, the onset of economic depression in California made previously undesirable situations more coveted. Male "breadwinners," who in more prosperous times kept wives and daughters from wage-earning positions and in unpaid domestic labor instead, relented as well, as more and more male wage laborers became vulnerable to fluctuating levels of production.[20] This is not to suggest that women wage earners held only symbolic positions in anti-Chinese demonstrations. Anna Smith, for example, was a leading orator for the Workingmen's Party of California, and a fixture at its rallies. Into the twentieth century, women like Charlotte Odlum Smith, the founder of the National Women's Industrial League, held leadership roles in the anti-Chinese movement. Petitioning Congress in 1902, Smith reminded legislators that due to the prevalence of Chinese labor in domestic industries, "women have more to fear from this class of undesirable immigration than the wage-men."[21]

As much as women were actors in exclusion movements, they also enlisted themselves—and were enlisted by their white male counterparts—as subjects in a biopolitical discourse that targeted Chinese labor as a threat to reproduction. The production of knowledge that undergirded white laborers' demands for immigration restrictions was not scientific as much as it was moralistic and sensationalistic, a point that political economists, whose theories referenced the "natural" laws of supply and demand, rarely hesitated to point out. Historian Martha Mabie Gardner notes that during the period, "Stories of white women workers unsuccessfully competing with Chinese workers, finding themselves unemployed, and eventually forced into prostitution, were so common in the labor press as to comprise a virtual genre"—a genre primarily concerned with evoking empathy for the right of white Californians to labor.[22] Calls for racial allegiance in employment and for state intervention on behalf of white workers referenced the traditions and practices of pursuing a moral economy, in which employers had ethical and social obligations to use their capital in ways that benefited the good of the white community as a whole.[23] In Henry Grimm's 1879 anti-Chinese immigrant drama *The Chinese Must Go!*, Ah Coy, a male Chinese servant, is depicted as remarking that white men were "damn fools" for having wives and children, who "cost plenty money."[24] If biological reproduction was reduced to a decision about how to "rationally" use whatever surplus value could be accrued from wages, civilization could hardly flourish.

Anti-Chinese laborers and their allies invoked a vision of settlement where white employers perpetuated the frontier ethos of the past, and rejected "the few would-be aristocrats who like to put on frills," as Arthur Bunster, the brewer and workingmen's politician in Victoria, British Columbia, called employers who hired Chinese servants. [25] Whites might hire each other on egalitarian terms, despite the unequal power dynamic of the exchange. Even more utopically, white settlers might return to the germinal days of the late 1840s—nostalgically portrayed by Jessie Benton Frémont in her 1878 text *A Year of American Travel*— when even the governor, Bennett Riley, had no choice but to serve as his own gardener.[26] By and large, however, the anti-Chinese activists in late-nineteenth-century Pacific world Anglophone societies were not the settlers that Karl Marx enthusiastically described in volume one of *Capital*, who upon arriving in Swan River, Western Australia, as part of a colonization company set up by Edward Gibbon Wakefield, refused to enter into relationships of servitude altogether. As Marx noted, glossing over the settlers' own role in dispossessing aboriginal peoples, "Wakefield discovered that in the Colonies, property in money, means of subsistence, machines, and other means of production, does not as yet stamp a man as a capitalist if there be wanting the correlative—the wage-worker, the other man who is compelled to sell himself of his own free will. He discovered that capital is not a thing, but a social relation between persons, established by the instrumentality of things."[27] Anti-Chinese restrictionists in the Anglophone Pacific world of the late nineteenth century were determined to assert control over the social relations that urban market exchanges for labor had brought to settler societies, rather than repudiate them altogether.

Much in the way that it can be argued that the United States and American corporations had no reservations about extending sovereign rule and private ownership over lands that could not be worked immediately, white laborers—as one cohort of settlers in this era—asserted control over sites of labor in the forms of homes, boarding houses, and restaurants, even when physically absent. White employers continually expressed their infuriation with white women's relative refusal to enter into domestic service, even after Congress had provided them with legislation designed to reduce job competition. Economist Peter Philips documents that after the 1882 Restriction Act, the total percentage of white women and Chinese men working as servants in San Francisco relative to the total paid domestic labor workforce remained the same, even though the former's numbers continued to increase, while the latter's declined.[28]

In "Meat vs. Rice," the anti-Chinese manifesto published by the American Federation of Labor in 1902, the refusal of white women to enter into service—despite the decreased competition—was explained in part by what the authors claimed was the lasting legacy of Chinese exploitation. Twenty years after the initial Restriction Act, "the white domestic servant was expected to live in the room originally built for John, generally situated in the cellar and void of all comforts, frequently unpainted or unpapered, containing a bedstead and a chair." Acknowledging that the shortage of white servants in San Francisco and other Western cities persisted, the authors concluded, "Absolute servility was expected from those who took the place of the Chinaman, and it will take years to obliterate these traces of inferiority and reestablish the proper relations of employer and employee."[29] If white women were unwilling to work as servants, they argued, it was because certain features of how servants were treated—such as their relegation to spartan and concealed rooms—denoted racialized labor relations at odds with republican citizenship. The degraded status of Chinese servants, and the dehumanizing treatment that their employment as domestic laborers permitted, was built into the architectural design of Western homes, the manifesto alleged, and could not be easily—to use an appropriately racial metaphor—whitewashed.

Middle-class publications, by contrast, exhorted white laborers to accept the presence of Chinese labor as a benefit of foreign trade that could tangibly improve the lives of industrious wage-earning individuals and their families, so long as they aspired to social mobility. To make this happen, white workers had to admit that there were distinct market advantages to employing alien labor, and that the wages taken away from white individuals denied the opportunity to perform the work were offset by the purchasing power that the white community as a whole received. There is some evidence that white women servants did embrace or at least accept the role that Chinese laborers played in making their own jobs easier by freeing them from some of the more oner-

George Frederick Keller, "The Chinese Must Go, but Who Keeps Them?" *San Francisco Illustrated Wasp*, May 11, 1878, 648–49. *Courtesy of the Bancroft Library, University of California, Berkeley.* White laborers are depicted conducting business with a Chinese laundryman, fishmonger, and cigar manufacturer, while Denis Kearney—appearing in the center of the cartoon as a braying donkey—advocates for exclusion. Targeting the divide between rhetoric and action, the cartoon implies that the services wage earners utilized would either be unavailable or no longer affordable if their attempts to bar Chinese immigration proved successful.

ous household tasks. Ann Jane Sinclair, for instance, wrote in 1879 from San Francisco to her cousin in Ireland that she had "not much work" to do for the family that employed her, since "all the Cloths is washed out" and "the China men do all the washin." This left her to have only to tend to the home's fires, cook the meals, and make the beds.[30]

Proponents of Chinese labor cited how enterprising white laborers who were able to put aside narrow-minded bigotry learned the benefits of employing Chinese servants once they acquired capital. Rather than resist the racial and imperial division of labor, they accepted it as a rational way of sparing citizens from the most arduous and menial of tasks. In accounts that circulated throughout the White Pacific, the transition from settler laborer to capitalist was portrayed as a process of personal growth in which white workers learned to cast aside irrational fears of becoming dependent on menial labor performed by the Chinese. Edward Roper, the English travel writer and illustrator, emphasized that when thrifty white laborers in British Columbia earned opportunities to dispose of the capital they had accumulated and became employers hiring labor for the first time, they had no qualms using Chinese servants whatever their previous stances may have been.[31] The author Joaquin Miller, writing in the *North American Review* in 1901, stated that it was common sense that there was "work for all who really want to work." Miller wrote that "the real labore[r] of our Pacific Empire . . . whether he has a little shop or a little farm, does not want his wife and growing children to cook, wash, and do chamber work, when he can get a silent and submissive little Mongolian to do it for a song. For our ambitious and splendid white boy or girl cannot get on nearly so well at school if kept at home to do washing, do chamber work, and help mother."[32] By blurring the lines between laborers and capitalists in settler societies, and invoking the same republican spirit that workers marshaled, proponents of the Chinese servant made him into a marginalized source of labor upon which whites could collectively receive social benefits, as a shared racial privilege.

Personal Conflicts: Los Angeles, 1886

Federal restrictions on Chinese immigration, which many trades' organizations denounced as ineffective and insufficient, failed to satisfy white laborers' desire to control how the labor market operated. Boycotts over alien participation in domestic service industries occurred regularly in myriad cities and towns throughout the Anglophone Pacific world, and were ways in which white laborers tried to eliminate the settlement of Chinese altogether by denying them the ability to earn wages, both before and after restrictive legislation was passed. In urging boycotts against Chinese labor, restrictionists attempted to intimidate and shame white employers who hired Chinese laborers as race traitors. The Order of Caucasians, a secret society founded in Sacramento in 1876, appears to have first developed this tactic by sending letters that threatened violence if employers failed to dismiss Chinese employees. Beginning in May 1878, *Thisleton's* published a weekly list that featured the names and addresses of businesses employing Chinese servants and cooks, and of private families with Chinese servants working in their homes.[33] In the effort to drive Chinese immigrants out of Seattle in February 1886, the suffragist and People's Party organizer Mary Kenworthy led a women's committee that went door to door urging middle-class women not to hire Chinese servants or to use Chinese laundries, calling those who did members of a "dog-salmon aristocracy" who selfishly bolstered their own fortunes by relying on an inferior substitute.[34]

In 1879, the California Constitutional Convention—at which representatives of the Workingmen's Party constituted a majority of the delegates—presented a new constitution for the state, which included a ban on both private and public corporations employing any "Chinese or Mongolian." This "victory" for white labor was short-lived. When Tiburcio Parrott, the president of the Quicksilver Mining Corporation, was arrested and imprisoned for employing Chinese laborers, he filed a writ of habeas corpus. Hearing his case, the Ninth Circuit Court ruled that the state's employment ban infringed upon the corporation's freedom of contract, and violated the treaty rights guaranteed to Chinese immigrants in the United States as agreed upon in the 1868 Burlingame Treaty and extended to them as "persons" residing in the United States under the Fourteenth Amendment.[35] In 1886, the United States Supreme Court ruled in *Yick Wo v. Hopkins* that an 1880 San Francisco statute requiring all laundries operating out of wooden buildings to apply for a permit from the Board of Supervisors was unconstitutional, on the grounds that it too violated the Equal Protection Clause, due to its selective enforcement against Chinese businesses. As the legal scholar Gabriel Chin has argued, *Yick Wo* and similar cases should not be misread as early defenses of civil rights. The court invalidated the statute not because it represented racial discrimination against Chinese laborers and businesses as a class, but only because treaties negotiated with China, and the Fourteenth Amendment, recognized noncitizens' right to property.[36]

Denied the use of legislative tools in driving out Chinese businesses and residents, Western cities and towns instead ramped up boycotts that relied—ostensibly—on persuasion alone. On February 20, 1886, the Trades and Labor Council of Los Angeles, comprised of various unions affiliated with the Knights of Labor, passed a resolution calling for the boycott of businesses directly owned and operated by Chinese residents—citing vegetable gardeners, restaurants, and laundries specifically—as well as all businesses that employed Chinese labor.[37] In addition, the Council called for the boycott of any establishment that subcontracted goods and services produced by Chinese labor, such as hotels that sent out guests' clothes to Chinese laundries or purchased produce cultivated by Chinese gardeners, and of individual realtors and businessmen who leased or sold land to Chinese residents as part of their commercial enterprises. The Council's list of layered provisions explaining the boycott speaks to the important role that Chinese labor played across a range of different enterprises that served domestic needs. As was the case in boycotts occurring elsewhere throughout the West, the Trades Council introduced a financial penalty to be levied against union members who violated the resolutions. Finally, the Council "recommended"—making sure not to run afoul of the law by threatening more forceful tactics—that families discharge all Chinese "servants" in favor of American "help," again deploying this shift in language to highlight the presumed difference between the circumstances under which Chinese domestics labored, and the terms by which white women entered into the occupation. A week later, during a massive demonstration on February 27, the resolution was publically endorsed by an estimated 10 percent of Los Angeles's population. Individual employers and businesses were given until May 1, the workers' holiday, to adjust their practices accordingly.

The Council stated that it was "in favor of a legal and peaceful solution to the Chinese question."[38] This was likely an attempt to convince the city's leaders that the events of October 24, 1871, during which seventeen Chinese immigrants were executed by lynching and two knifed to death, would not be repeated.[39] It was also included to assure Los Angeles's citizenry that the city would not follow the example set in places like Rock Springs, Wyoming, where in September 1885 at least twenty-eight Chinese immigrants were murdered by a white mob attempting to drive them out. From early 1885 through the summer of 1886, the United States West experienced what historian Jean Pfaelzer describes as a wave of "ethnic cleansing" campaigns against Chinese communities, often coordinated by the Knights of Labor, in which boycotts aimed at workers and businesses occurred in concert with pogroms aimed at expelling entire populations.[40] As had been the case with anti-Chinese campaigns in the late 1870s, the Los Angeles boycott unfurled against the backdrop of a larger struggle between white workers and the railroads, in this case a strike that had begun in March 1886 and led more than two hundred thousand workers to walk away from jobs on the Union Pacific and Missouri Pacific lines in response to the corporations' union busting. Chinese servants and vegetable gardeners, while hardly the tools of monopolistic capital, were nonetheless targeted due to the racial animosity that the confrontation with the railroad stoked.

In a letter to the *Los Angeles Times* on March 1, 1886, Jordan Cox, a builder and member of the Knights of Labor, urged the citizens of Los Angeles to treat the boycott as an ethical choice that they could make as consumers. Cox asserted that the actions of the Council were rooted in a defensive posture that merely sought to redistribute a finite amount of capital to the laborers who, on account of being white citizens, were more deserving. Put more simply, Cox stated to his fellow citizens that "when you employ Chinese you are boycotting Americans, to the same extent!"[41] A letter from "An Old Miner" in response to Cox two days later took time to both validate the principles of this stance—the author noted that in his experience, "there is perhaps no American in this county that would prefer a Chinaman to an American"—but questioned whether this common interest could be actualized in practice. The author shared the example of a West Los Angeles family who had searched for a white servant girl for more than a month, only to be rebuffed repeatedly on account of having small children who added to the workload.[42] Loyalties to race and nation were sound maxims, the Old Miner concluded, but made no sense as market behavior. A profile that appeared in the anti-boycott *Times* on May 1, the date by which all white employers were supposed to have dismissed their Chinese employees, enthusiastically highlighted further inconsistencies between rhetoric and action. The newspaper took particular aim at the Trades Council's contention that 80 percent of the city's white population was complying with its resolutions. The *Times* cited as a common example an employer who had initially acceded to the boycott and fired the Chinese laundryman his family contracted with, whom he paid one dollar a week, only to rehire him when the white laundress he engaged as a replacement charged him $3.75 a week to do the same job.[43]

There was a consensus among whites that the importation of female laborers from Europe was the best safeguard against Chinese labor monopolizing gendered industries, although pro- and anti-Chinese activists disagreed on whether this could be effective as a policy on short notice. In Los Angeles, boycott supporters took measures to alleviate the shortage of white women laborers willing to enter into domestic service. This was imperative to resolving a basic contradiction in their argument, which alleged that it was competition with Chinese workers that kept whites out of the occupation. The Immigration Association of Southern California, which Los Angeles's Board of Trade had chartered in 1884, announced on March 21, 1886, that it would be dispatching an additional agent to England to recruit more servants to come under contract to California, with the promise of fifteen to twenty dollars a month in wages, to check any labor scarcities that the boycott might cause.[44] Despite the extension of prohibitions on the labor migration of contracted workers from Europe under the 1885 Foran Act, Congress exempted the recruitment of immigrants for personal or domestic service from the legislation. The efforts of the Los Angeles immigration bureau—and bureaus that existed in other cities and towns where boycotts were taking place, like Chico—remained, therefore, legal.[45] Whatever the successes of the association's recruitment efforts in England, as a state-sanctioned intervention it was neither efficient, given the unavoidable delays that accompanied the transport of English women to the California labor market, nor realistically capable of immediately altering what was, by that point, the deeply embedded role of Chinese immigrant labor in the service sector of the economy. And the wages the association pledged were well below the prevailing rates of the era.[46]

Some employers had no compunctions about defying the boycott openly. To them, whatever the imperial threat that alien Chinese labor posed to the *herrenvolk* republic, losing sovereignty over the use of their own capital would be far worse. Capitalists suggested that they were reasonable to fear becoming dependents of labor. W. T. Strobridge, the proprietor of the St. Charles Hotel, conceded that while he had lost the business of a number of his regular boarders, who had left in response to his refusal to fall in line and dismiss his Chinese cooks, waiters, and servants, he would as soon close his establishment altogether than be "dictated to" by outsiders. Robert Heffner, a realtor who employed two Chinese servants in his home, pledged that the "sentiments" of white laborers—a phrase that emphasized the emotional rather than rational qualities of the trade unionists' stance—would have no effect on how he conducted his private business.[47] The boycott seemed to anger white middle-class women in particular, who had in previous decades been among the most stalwart defenders of Chinese labor, a role that many would continue to occupy well into the twentieth century. The Women's Club of Los Angeles, for example, attacked the boycott for proceeding with the assumption that white families would be able to survive the loss of Chinese domestic labor by exploiting the unpaid labor of wives and daughters instead.[48] Consumer self-interest, as the eventual failure of the 1886 boycott indicates, was stronger than abstract appeals to racial solidarity. If anything, it hardened the commitment of white settler capitalists to freedom of trade and contract, since they saw their own plight as one in which Chinese domestic labor had a key place.

Conclusion: Expelling the "Hewers of Wood and Drawers of Water"

For strident exclusionists, the import of white women, and the reproductive human capital they furnished, was always on the horizon. D. S. Cowan, a special agent hired by the U.S. Department of Treasury in 1888 to investigate the smuggling of Chinese from Canada into the American Pacific Northwest, waxed biblically on how the Chinese laborers found in the region's homes, laundries, and hotels were "hewers of wood and drawers of water," adding that "there are no whites on the coast to take their places." The Canadian head tax of fifty dollars on their entry was not sufficient to stop them from subsequently sneaking into the United States, since they could earn that in wages as cooks and servants in cities like Seattle and Portland within a month.[49] Like many vehemently anti-Chinese immigration officials, Cowan did not see Chinese labor—despite filling a shortage that he readily acknowledged—as a boon, crucial to completing work that would otherwise go undone. Instead, he worried about what the establishment of Chinese labor in these industries would portend for the future, when regions that were currently too distant to lure white labor became more accessible. His vision of settler ownership extended well beyond control of land and political institutions, and into the realm of labor markets and their very constitution.

NOTES

1. One witness placed the number of Chinese servants in San Francisco at five to six thousand, based on extrapolation from a six-block sampling. The figure of three thousand Chinese servants in San Francisco was used more commonly during the hearing. It is unclear whether these estimates were also intended to include Chinese servants working for Chinese employers. With the hearings focused on job competition between racial groups, the employment practices of Chinese merchants went virtually unnoticed, except when they involved alleged incidents of female enslavement. United States Congress, Joint Special Committee to Investigate Chinese Immigration, *Report of the Joint Special Committee to Investigate Chinese Immigration*, 44th Cong., 2d sess., S. Rept. 689 (Washington, DC: GPO, 1877), 253 (herein cited as Committee, *Report*). The 1880 Census tallied San Francisco's population at 233,959, making it the ninth-largest city in the United States. Of that population, there were 21,745 residents enumerated as members of the Chinese race (no distinction was made between Chinese immigrants and American-born Chinese residents), approximately 9.3 percent of the total population. Using the lower figure of three thousand Chinese servants, this would have meant that close to 14 percent of all Chinese residents of San Francisco worked in domestic service. George E. Waring, Jr., *Reports on the Social Statistics of Cities, Part II* (Washington, DC: GPO, 1887), 800.

2. Committee, *Report*, 424.

3. Committee, *Report*, 427. In an 1876 article in *Scribner's*, for example, Sarah Henshaw noted, "No matter how good a Chinaman may be, ladies never leave their children with them, especially little girls." Henshaw, "California Housekeepers and Chinese Servants," *Scribner's Monthly* 12 (August 1876): 739. Photographs from California in the late nineteenth century, however, routinely show children accompanied by male Chinese nurses, in compositions not unlike those used to visually frame the deferential role of the black servant and "Mammy."

4. Patrick Wolfe, *Settler Colonialism and the Transformation of Anthropology: The Politics and Poetics of an Ethnographic Event* (New York: Bloomsbury Academic, 1999), 2; Lorenzo Veracini, *Settler Colonialism: A Theoretical Overview* (London: Palgrave Macmillan, 2010), 4. The political scientist Aziz Rana similarly extends the temporality of settlement, arguing that, throughout the nineteenth century, the promises of settler colonialism and its articulation as a political ideology continued to structure debates about citizenship and republicanism. Rana, *The Two Faces of American Freedom* (Cambridge, MA: Harvard University Press, 2010), 176–235.

5. Despite the fact that the voices of Chinese immigrants and witnesses appear nowhere in the more than twelve hundred pages of testimony that the federal government published, Daniel Tichenor notes that the committee's report provides an early example of the way in which the United States sought to rationalize policies of inclusion and exclusion through "expert" evaluations of conditions on the ground. See Tichenor, *Dividing Lines: The Politics of*

Immigration Control in America (Princeton, NJ: Princeton University Press, 2002), 100. Alexander Saxton describes the committee's conclusions as representing a "strategic victory" for Western restrictionists, since it put Congress on the record as officially recommending a policy of exclusion. Saxton, *The Indispensable Enemy: Labor and the Anti-Chinese Movement in California* (Berkeley: University of California Press, 1971), 132.

6. My use of "Anglophone" here, as a term describing settlements and societies with English-speaking majorities, does not mean that the inhabitants of these regions identified ethnically as English. In the United States West, as well as in Canada and Australia, migrants brought with them Irish, Scottish, Welsh, Scandinavian, and German ethnic identities and did not speak English exclusively. I avoid using "white settlements" since the racial composition of communities that included Chinese aliens, black migrants, and indigenous populations did not reflect the racial stability that this phrase implies. For further discussion of the phrase "Anglophone settlement," see James Belich, *Replenishing the Earth: The Settler Revolution and the Rise of the Angloworld, 1783–1939* (New York: Oxford University Press, 2009), 58–59.

7. On prefederation exclusion efforts in Australia, see Marilyn Lake, "'Lowe Kong Meng Appeals to International Law: Transnational Lives Caught between Empire and Nation," in Desley Deacon, Penny Russell and Angela Woollacott, eds., *Transnational Lives: Biographies of Global Modernity, 1700–Present* (New York: Palgrave Macmillan, 2010), 223–37.

8. *Sydney Morning Herald*, June 12, 1888.

9. "To the Editor of the Herald," *Sydney Morning Herald*, June 13, 1888.

10. As Erika Lee argues, the narrow focus on exclusion debates has often come at the neglect of "the six decades of the exclusion era itself." Lee, *At America's Gates: Chinese Immigration During the Exclusion Era, 1882–1943* (Chapel Hill: University of North Carolina Press, 2003), 24.

11. Moon-Ho Jung, *Coolies and Cane: Race, Labor, and Sugar in the Age of Emancipation* (London and Baltimore: Johns Hopkins University Press, 2006), 76–106. Among missionary communities, there were advocates of granting citizenship to Chinese immigrants who had proved their Christian worth. See Joshua Paddison, *American Heathens: Religion, Race, and Reconstruction in California* (Berkeley: University of California Press, 2012), 35–56, and Derek Chang, *Citizens of a Christian Nation: Evangelical Missions and the Problem of Race in the Nineteenth Century* (Philadelphia: University of Pennsylvania Press, 2010).

12. Committee, *Report*, 287. As Paul Kramer notes, in American republican thought, "Empire was the tragic fate of republics that, in pursuit of expansionary power, crushed their own definitional freedom and virtue. The republic that became an empire had congealed irreversibly into something fundamentally unlike itself." Kramer, "Power and Connection: Imperial Histories of the United States in the World," *American Historical Review* 116:5 (2011): 1358.

13. U.S. House of Representatives, Select Committee on Immigration and Naturalization, *Report on Chinese Immigration*, 51st Cong., 2nd Sess., Report No. 4048, 1891, 182.

14. Kristin Hoganson, *Consumers' Imperium: The Global Production of American Domesticity, 1865–1920* (Chapel Hill: University of North Carolina, 2007), 11. Prior to the middle part of the twentieth century—with the exception of campaigns for tariffs against foreign manufactured goods—few white American wage laborers spent their time protesting the consumption and circulation of commodities that came from abroad, especially when they were the beneficiaries. Dana Frank, *Buy American: The Untold Story of Economic Nationalism* (Boston: Beacon Press, 1999), 33–55, and Woodruff D. Smith, "Complications of the Commonplace: Tea, Sugar, and Imperialism," *Journal of Interdisciplinary History* 23:2 (1992): 259–78.

15. Although Ngai uses the term to describe the plight of Mexican guestworkers brought to the United States as a flexible and disposable alien labor force under the *bracero* program and its predecessors, it aptly characterizes Chinese laborers' legal status in the late nineteenth century. Mae Ngai, *Impossible Subjects: Illegal Aliens and the Making of Modern America* (Princeton, NJ: Princeton University Press, 2004), 129.

16. Kornell Chang, *Pacific Connections: The Making of the U.S.-Canadian Borderlands* (Berkeley: University of California Press, 2012), 12.

17. As Marilyn Lake and Henry Reynolds argue, "white man's countries" in the Pacific world identified with each other's mission, traded in policy expertise, and constructed an imagined cultural and racial community linked by a collective goal of shoring up Anglophone settler societies against an Asian influx and the perceived perils of multiracial democracy. Lake and Reynolds, *Drawing the Global Colour Line: White Men's Countries and the International Challenge of Racial Equality* (Cambridge, UK: Cambridge University Press, 2008). As Chang notes, connections between white communities in Australia, Canada, and the United States were undergirded by more tangible exchanges as well, in the form of exclusionists and labor leaders who traveled a transpacific circuit. Chang, *Pacific Connections*, 89–116.

18. For an overview of the causes that contributed to the economic depression in San Francisco and the "July Days," see Michael Kazin, "The July Days in San Francisco, 1877: Prelude to Kearneyism," in David Stowell, ed., *The Great Strike of 1877: New Perspectives* (Urbana: University of Illinois Press, 2008), 136–63. On the railroad strikes of 1877 in a national context, see Philip Foner, *The Great Labor Uprising of 1877* (New York: Monad Press, 1977).

19. The lyrics for "Twelve Hundred More" are printed in Lewis H. Carlson and George A. Colburn, *In Their Place: White America Defines Her Minorities, 1850–1950* (New York: John Wiley and Sons, 1972), 170–77. The song followed the tune of an Irish nationalist ballad, "The Wearing of the Green," which dates back to at least 1798.

20. As historian Amy Dru Stanley argues, the economic downturns of the 1870s led Congress to investigate whether a marriage crisis existed among male wage laborers, since their ability to earn enough money to support a family was increasingly being called into question. Stanley, *From Bondage to Contract: Wage Labor, Marriage, and the Market in the Age of Slave Emancipation* (Cambridge, UK: Cambridge University Press, 1998), 154–56.
21. "Petition from the Woman's National Industrial League of America," Records of the Committee on Immigration and Naturalization, 53d–79th Congresses (1893–1946), Petitions and Memorials, Box 197, HR52A-H28.2.
22. Martha Mabie Gardner, "Working on White Womanhood: White Working Women in the SanFrancisco Anti-Chinese Movement, 1877–1890," *Journal of Social History* 33: 1 (Autumn 1999): 74.
23. On the "moral economy" and workers' invocation of their right to be protected from the market, see, most notably, E. P. Thompson, "The Moral Economy of the English Crowd in the Eighteenth Century," *Past and Present* 50 (Feb. 1971): 76–136.
24. Henry Grimm, *"The Chinese Must Go." A Farce in Four Acts* (San Francisco: A. Bancroft & Co., 1879), 3.
25. Bunster went on to suggest that the Indians native to Vancouver Island were perfectly capable servants and available to do this work, but that elites in Victoria chose Chinese domestic laborers instead as a luxury item. *British Colonist*, November 4, 1879.
26. Jesse Benton Frémont, *A Year of American Travel* (New York: Harper & Brothers, 1878), 102–3. Library of Congress. *California as I Saw It: First-Person Narratives of California's Early Years, 1849–1900*, Volume 192 (Washington, DC: Library of Congress, 2000 [database online]).
27. Marx, *Capital, Volume One*, ch. 33 (online version of the 1887 English translation, http://www.marxists.org/archive/marx/works/1867-c1/ch33.htm); H. O. Pappe, "Wakefield and Marx," *Economic History Review*, New Series 4:1 (1951): 88–97.
28. Peter Philips, "Capitalism Absent the Family: Distortions in the Labor and Marriage Markets that Led to a Confrontation of Chinese Men with White Women over Domestic Servant Work in Post–Gold Rush California" (provided by the author).
29. Samuel Gompers and Herman Gutstadt, *Some Reasons for Chinese Exclusion— Meat vs. Rice—American Manhood against Asiatic Coolieism—Which Shall Survive?* (Washington, DC: GPO, 1902), 15.
30. Ann Jane Sinclair to Mary Ann Graham, December 1879. Sinclair Letters, Public Relations Office of Northern Ireland, D1497/4/2. I am grateful to Kerby Miller for making a copy of this letter available.
31. Edward Roper, *By Track and Trail: A Journey through Canada* (London: W.H. Allen & Co., 1891), 255.
32. Miller, "The Chinese and the Exclusion Act," *North American Review* 173 (December 1901): 784.

33. See, for example, "Some of the Citizens Who Employ John Chinaman," *Thistleton's Magazine*, May 4, 1878. On the Order of the Caucasian boycotts, see Jean Pfaelzer, *Driven Out: The Forgotten War against Chinese Americans* (Berkeley: University of California Press, 2008), 66.

34. Gardner, "Working on White Womanhood," 73. John Putman, "Racism and Temperance: The Politics of Class and Gender in Late-19th-Century Seattle," *Pacific Northwest Quarterly* 95: 2 (2004): 76–77. "Dog salmon" was a reference to the least desirable species of "chum" salmon, and a play on the description of New England's elite as a "codfish aristocracy" that sought to hide the more humble sources of their wealth.

35. *Re Tiburcio Parrott*, 1 F. 481 (C.C.D. Cal. 1880). On the legal background to the case, see Charles McClain, *In Search of Equality: The Chinese Struggle against Discrimination in Nineteenth-Century America* (Berkeley: University of California Press, 1994), 79–92. See also Paul Kens, "Civil Liberties, Chinese Laborers, and Corporations," in Gordon Morris Bakken, ed., *Law in the Western United States* (Norman: University of Oklahoma Press, 2001), 499–502.

36. *Yick Wo v. Hopkins*, 118 U.S. 356 (1886). Gabriel J. Chin, "Unexplainable on Grounds of Race: Doubts About *Yick Wo*," 2008 U. ILL. L.REV., 1359. For a critique of Chin's interpretation, see David Bernstein, "Revisiting Yick Wo v. Hopkins," ibid., 1393.

37. The boycott was proposed only after an initiative brought before the Los Angeles City Council in July 1885 to remove the Chinese from city limits was deemed by the city attorney as likely to be judged unconstitutional, and therefore tabled. Everett Hager Gordon, *An 1886 Chinese Labor Boycott in Los Angeles* (Pasadena, CA: Castle Press, 1982); Grace H. Stimson, *Rise of the Labor Movement in Los Angeles* (Berkeley: University of California Press, 1955), 60–67.

38. "The Boycott: How the Anti-Chinese Movers Propose to Start Their Campaign," *Los Angeles Times*, February 23, 1886.

39. Scott Zesch, *The Chinatown War: Chinese Los Angeles and the Massacre of 1871* (New York: Oxford University Press, 2012).

40. Pfaelzer, *Driven Out*, 253.

41. Jordan Cox, "A Boycott Both Ways," *Los Angeles Times*, March 2, 1886.

42. "An Old Miner's Words," *Los Angeles Times*, March 4, 1886.

43. "The Boycott," *Los Angeles Times*, May 1, 1886.

44. "Trained Servants—The Best Way to Boycott the Chinese," *Los Angeles Times*, March 21, 1886.

45. On the Chico boycott, which middle-class white women fervently protested against, see Michele Shover, "Chico Women: Nemesis of a Rural Town's Anti-Chinese Campaigns, 1876–1888," *California History* 67: 4 (1988): 228–43. On Westerners' fears of contract labor, see Gunther Peck, *Reinventing Free Labor: Padrones and Immigrant Workers in the North American West, 1880–1930* (Cambridge, UK: Cambridge University Press, 2000). As Donna Gabaccia argues, it was Southern and Eastern European men's association with unfree labor, and

with the formation of bachelor, sojourner communities, which led them to be categorized as a threat and a type of "yellow peril." Donna Gabaccia, "The 'Yellow Peril' and the 'Chinese of Europe': Global Perspectives and Race and Labor, 1815–1930," in Jan Lucassen and Leo Lucassen, eds., *Migration, Migration History, History: Old Paradigms and New Perspectives* (Bern: Peter Lang, 1997), 177–96.

46. *Los Angeles Times*, February 28, 1886.

47. "The Boycott," *Los Angeles Times*, May 1, 1886.

48. Raymond Lou, "The Anti-Chinese Movement in Los Angeles, 1870–1890," in Robert Asher and Charles Stephenson, eds., *Labor Divided: Race & Ethnicity in United States Labor Struggles, 1835–1960* (Albany: SUNY Press, 1990), 58–59.

49. D. S. Cowan to Charles S. Fairchild, Secretary of Treasury, August 30, 1888. National Archives, Record Group 85, Custom Case Files no. 3358d, 1877–1891, Box 2, Folder 12.

8

Empire and the Moving Body

Fermin Tobera, Military California, and Rural Space

DOROTHY B. FUJITA-RONY

Fermin Tobera's story began much like those of the thousands of other Filipino men who flocked to the United States in the early twentieth century for work and educational opportunity. He was born on July 5, 1908, to Valentina Ibarra and Mariano Tuvera of Sinait, Ilocos Sur. His mother reported that although the family could not afford to send him to public school, he learned how to read and write. As she commented, "From childhood, Fermin had always shown himself gentle, courteous to the old and always ready to obey."[1] In 1928, Tobera followed other young Filipino men migrating to Hawai'i and the U.S. West Coast with the goal of sending needed remittances to his family back in the Philippines.

On January 23, 1930, however, Tobera's story took a sudden and tragic turn: his body was found shot through the heart in his bed on the Murphy Ranch outside Watsonville, California, in a bunkhouse that had been attacked by white male rioters. His death would unleash a fierce debate among political leaders on both sides of the Pacific over the position of Filipina/os in relation to U.S. empire. These arguments drew attention to the young Filipina/os who circulated through the United States, physically vulnerable due to animosity based on race, gender, and class. Tobera's mother asked for his body to be sent home to the Philippines so they could have a funeral. She later reported, "Everyday, ever since I heard of the horrible news, I have been weeping because he, who had been my strength, he upon whom I had to depend died in a manner that is not sanctioned by God." Ibarra called upon the Philippine government to seek justice for her son's death: "I appeal to the government of my country, if it has any power at all, to demand that the murderers of my son be made to pay his damages, for, because of them, I a poor woman, have been deprived of the help of my son."[2] Ibarra's comments are revealing—not only her expression of profound grief over the loss of her son and the condemnation of his murderers, but also her questioning of the Philippine government's ability to secure justice and economic restitution for his death.

Tobera's case is widely known in Asian American studies for exemplifying the antipathy directed toward Filipina/os during the Great Depression as well as the perceived racial and sexual threat posed by young male Filipino workers prior to the 1934 Tydings-McDuffie Act, which closed down colonial migration and set the Philippines on the path to independence. His case has been widely referenced by many authors, from Bruno Lasker's 1931 report to the Institute of Pacific Relations about the then current state of Filipina/o migration to more recent works like Rick Baldoz's *The Third Asiatic Invasion*, which analyzes how discourse around Tobera's untimely death illuminated national debates around citizenship and race.[3]

My intent is to add to these discussions by taking a new vantage point: assessing how Tobera's death provides us with a lens for understanding the significance of rural California to U.S.-Philippines relations. For Filipina/o workers in rural California, empire was not only a formal *political* space in which they were incorporated as U.S. nationals, it also signified a *military* space for U.S. ambitions in the Pacific region and a *laboring* space through which they moved and worked for California's corporate economy. Rather than being peripheral to the "real" locus of political activity in urban metropoles like Washington, D.C., New York City, and Manila, rural California was a central arena of empire for Filipina/o workers that embodied larger patterns of imperial confrontation and regular violence, as exemplified by Tobera's death.

A detailed mapping of Tobera's story demonstrates that the geography of empire was more complex than the common binaries of "core and periphery" and "urban and rural" would suggest. In their anthology *Mobile Subjects*, Tony Ballantyne and Antoinette Burton call for a mobile kind of analysis, "one where the ground or space itself is ever moving, and those operating on it find themselves routinely adjusting themselves—whether by choice or otherwise—to its perpetual motion."[4] Their discussion encourages us to examine Tobera's death in light of the flow of workers following multiple labor circuits in California's rural economy, an economy also organized by its proximity to the Pacific metropole of San Francisco. All of these factors shaped the ways in which Tobera's death was understood and discussed in local, regional, transpacific, and empire-wide contexts. On a material level, this was represented by the coverage of the Watsonville riots in newspapers from the United States' largest cities such as the *San Francisco Chronicle*, the *New York Times*, and the *Washington Post*, in Philippine newspapers like the *Manila Bulletin* and the *Philippine Herald*, and in the local Watsonville community newspaper, the *Evening Pajaronian*. The public attention granted to anti-Filipina/o rioting in California in these newspapers enables us to chart the impact of empire in sites we often overlook as central to the formation of U.S. empire, such as Watsonville and the Pajaro Valley in the rural crossroads of California.

California Agriculture and the Migrating Body

Filipina/o laborers followed complex, multidirectional migratory networks under U.S. empire, including routes across the Pacific that served a Philippine colonial export economy as well as U.S. interests in securing strategic military sites for expansion and passage to California's corporate farming areas and adjacent cities. By entering Watsonville and the Pajaro Valley, Filipina/os moved in the regional orbit surrounding the international and militarized port city of San Francisco, which was a critical sending and receiving site in support of war in the Pacific. Sites like the Presidio, Alcatraz, Fort Baker, Fort Funston, and the Mare Island Naval Shipyard consolidated the military nature of the Bay Area, an integral part of the region's growth.[5] The War of 1898 further spurred San Francisco's militarization, as well as greatly expanded business, manufacturing, and trade opportunities.[6] Another precipitating factor was the United States' increasing rivalry with Japan, whose power was growing in the early twentieth century after colonizing Korea and defeating Russia in the Russo-Japanese war. Japan regarded its overseas population in California as crucial to its expansionary plans, even as exclusionary legislation like the 1913 Alien Land Act underscored the fierce opposition in white California to Japanese permanent settlement.[7]

The bulk of California's agricultural industry comprised huge, industrialized businesses that relied upon massive outputs, large-scale irrigation, and corporate ownership to produce an enormous variety of fruits, vegetables, and other crops like cotton. Despite San Francisco's emerging role in global U.S. militarism, however, rural California in the era between World War I and World War II typically was cast as "domestic." As it featured a sizeable number of permanent white residents, whiteness—which connoted Americanness—was one factor in this characterization. Furthermore, its major corporate industry, agriculture, was firmly in the hands of a white oligarchy. California agribusiness made handsome profits from migratory workers of color by upholding a racially segregated labor market and fiercely tamping down on workers' efforts to unionize, and it benefited as well from the regular expansion of the labor force through new groups of mobile laborers.[8]

In this scenario, colonial workers like Filipina/os were essential. When exclusionary legislation curtailed the numbers of incoming workers, as in the case of Chinese immigrants in 1882, Japanese immigrants in 1906, and Mexican immigrants in 1924, the population of Filipina/o workers—who were U.S. nationals—grew. From 1925 to 1929, 24,123 Filipina/os arrived in California, the vast majority of them men under thirty.[9]

As U.S. nationals, Filipina/o workers formed a special category. While Mexicans could become U.S. citizens or, conversely, be deported as aliens, Filipina/os could not become citizens or be deported. In this age of immigration with its heavily scrutinized restrictive legislation and well-monitored borders, Filipina/os could not be controlled in the same way as other immigrants because their mobility was determined by imperial laws, a point that was not lost on observers. For instance, while condemning mob violence on its editorial page, the *San Francisco Chronicle* declared, "There is a serious immigration problem involved in the introduction of large numbers of persons who are unassimilable yet who are given a status little short of full citizenship." While the *Chronicle* did not see the Philippines becoming a state, it also said that Filipina/os could not "be permanently held as chattels."[10]

The presence of Filipina/o workers elicited deep anger and fear due to their ambiguous political status and their resistance to social boundaries. By engaging in mixed-race socialization, Filipina/os were seen as defying conventional racialized etiquette. As Fred Hart, a farmer from Salinas, commented, "The Filipinos will not leave our white girls alone. . . . Frequently they intermarry."[11] Such perceptions struck deep at the heart of polarizing concerns about white privilege, whether or not U.S. colonials were fit to be citizens, and if the future of the United States was to remain white. As Peggy Pascoe notes regarding the fundamental nature of these matters, "projects of white supremacy and white purity" such as anti-miscegenation policies were encoded in political and judicial bureaucracies.[12] Hence, the ambiguous social positioning of Filipina/os threatened entrenched racial hierarchies.

The danger thus symbolized by Filipina/os was multiple in form: they represented a so-called foreign invasion that challenged Americanness, as non-whites they were a threat to whiteness, and as a mobile workforce who did not need U.S. passports they were regular competitors for employment. Furthermore, as a predominantly male population who sought interaction with white women, Filipino men were a social threat, and these relationships would have permanent consequences for U.S. society if Filipino men and white women married and had U.S.-citizen children. As Philippine Resident Commissioner Pedro Guevara stated in the House of Representatives, because Filipina/os "are under the American Flag, we feel entitled to come here and engage in the same kind of work as Americans, and we will expect the full protection of the law."[13] However, this Filipina/o sense of belonging rankled those intent on maintaining white privilege.

Scholars Marilyn Lake and Henry Reynolds write in their analysis of the global color line that "the assertion of whiteness was born in the apprehension of imminent loss."[14] And indeed, the reaction to the Filipino men in rural California during this period was also an indication of the measure of their threat in this regard. As young male workers of color coming in large groups to sparsely populated, largely white American rural areas, any influx of Filipinos quickly changed the composition of a community and challenged its racial politics. These Filipino men were racial others in a state that had well-established exclusionary legislation targeting Asians, including stringent barriers to immigration and citizenship, and laws preventing aliens ineligible for citizenship from owning land.[15] Daniel E. Bender reminds us that observers of the growth of immigrant "colonies" in the United States portrayed these sites as "places and sites of conquests," in which foreign migrants were seen as invasionary forces.[16] If the arriving Filipina/os were seen as a type of conquering military force from that kind of xenophobic standpoint, an especially ironic perspective given their colonial status, then whites' abhorrence of Filipino men and white women's social mixing becomes even more clear. Whether or not long-term residents in the Watsonville area saw Filipina/os in these terms, tensions were further heightened by the relatively recent history of colonization. By 1930, the year of Tobera's death, the United States' imperial control of the Philippines had been in place for just over thirty years. While many of the young male Filipino workers in California were likely born after the U.S. entered the Philippines, they certainly would have grown up with communal knowledge of the U.S. occupation and the long war of resistance waged against the Americans. Indeed the Bureau of Insular Affairs, which oversaw the government in the Philippines and the welfare of Filipina/os in the continental United States, was housed under the War Department, befitting the military origins of the relationship.[17]

Furthermore, these Filipino men were especially threatening because they were *here* and not *over there*. As opposed to being thousands of miles away across the Pacific, these U.S. nationals literally were in the same communities as the white speakers who deplored their labor migration. Republican congressman Arthur Monroe Free from San Jose denounced the Filipino men as sexual predators, and went so far as to justify anti-Filipina/o violence on the basis of Filipinos' reputed moral depravity. Free rationalized that "the alleged killing of a Filipino in a riot was in reality the forceful expression of a community craving to rid itself of vice dens run by the Filipino colonists" and condemned "the vicious practices of members of the Filipino colony in luring young white girls into degradation."[18] By raising the lurid spectacle of "vice dens" and young white women being enticed "into degradation," Free was utilizing stereotypes commonly associated with Chinese immigrants in U.S. mass popular culture. However, unlike Chinese laborers, whose migration had been curtailed by the 1882 Chinese Exclusion Act, the "Filipino colony" continued to migrate freely under U.S. imperialism.

The Violence Materializes

On January 21, around two hundred white American men tried to raid the Northern Monterey Filipino Club owned by the Paddon brothers, where nine white women were working as entertainers.[19] The violence expanded, as the numbers of white men swelled to five hundred, and the following night the mob attacked a Filipina/o community with pistols and clubs. At one house, the mob threw rocks and fired shots, as Filipinos tried to flee through an orchard. Asserting his authority in claiming U.S. national territory and reminding the crowd of the difference between foreign and domestic space, Chief of Police Robert Hastings placed his men around the house and told the crowd, "Remember this is an American house. We'll have to shoot the first man that comes near." While the mob began to disperse, the officers took thirty Filipina/os to City Hall for safety. Then another mob attacked a Filipina/o house on Van Ness Avenue, and shots were fired on both sides until the police arrived.[20]

Perceptions that these events were sparked by foreign intrusion intensified as leftists became involved. Ever alert to the spread of communism from outside sources, local leaders watched carefully when literature from the Young Communist League and the Communist Party appeared shortly after in Watsonville, calling for white American and Filipina/o laborers to band together to combat agricultural owners, law enforcement, and the American Legion. This concern about the spread of communism among Filipina/os in California paralleled the U.S. government's monitoring of leftist organizations in the Philippines by the Bureau of Insular Affairs, and was indicative of the kinds of government surveillance applied to Filipina/os.[21]

Fred Majors, one of the participants in the riot that led to Tobera's death, later said that young people's anger was provoked by Filipino "insolence": "In groups of four and five," Majors declared, "they push white people off the sidewalks. If a woman walks the streets alone they make suggestive or slurring remarks at her."[22] According to statements given to the district attorney, Raymond Smith, another participant, reported that a Filipino man had insulted his female companion, Elsie Trevison of Reno, when they were out walking and "broke into a torrent of vile epithets." Smith then hit the man in the mouth, and he and the Filipino began fighting. Here, there were multiple perceived transgressions: Filipinos gathered in collective numbers and infringed upon the free movement of white people. Furthermore, they contaminated the space with improper speech, rendering it "unsafe" for white women and goading their white male protectors into action.

The fight between Smith and the Filipino man could very well have concluded without inciting further violence. However, Smith met up with nine other young men from Watsonville and searched for the alleged Filipino culprit to bring him into the police. Later, in investigating the events that led to Tobera's death, the police reported that one of the cars used by Smith and another white man fit the description of a car seen near Murphy ranch, where Tobera was killed. The police then arrested Smith and six other young white men for participating in the riot (an eighth man was later arrested), all of whom came from "prominent families."[23]

Smith's initiative in enforcing social boundaries was applauded by other local residents. One individual who wrote to the *Evening Pajaronian* decried what the writer perceived as a lack of support for the local white "boys" who were arrested for rioting, saying, "If you don't help these boys it is going to make the Filipinos braver, gamer, more conceited, etc." The writer invoked the importance of unifying different groups in support of the political project of whiteness and continued, "You will notice that I used the term of 'white Americans' because I mean, 'white' at heart, whether you be black, yellow, or white." The writer continued, "And also because I noticed in one of the papers that the Filipinos of this community are citizens! Well, if those boys are sentenced to jail, it will prove to the Filipino that he is a respected citizen and has equal rights, and can go with our daughters and sisters to dances, auto riding, petting parties, etc."[24] While the writer called for the support of people of color who were "white at heart," the writer's conception of mutual sociality fell short of accepting Filipina/os as entitled to the same social freedoms as white people. The writer noted with dismay the potential temerity of Filipina/os who might come to think of themselves as political equals, especially regarding socially intimate relations with white American women.

The violence and political unrest quickly spread to other sites in California, around locations frequented by Filipino workers. In San Jose, the day after Tobera was killed, five white American men emerged from an automobile and assaulted two Filipinos. Half an hour later, a group of white San Jose men attacked two Filipinos, and a twenty-two-year-old bystander, Alfred Johnson, was stabbed twice in the back.[25] The police arrested twenty-year-old Leonard Bresette for threatening to organize

riots in response to Johnson's stabbing, to attack Filipina/o lettuce laborers, and to dynamite Filipina/o homes.[26] Then, on January 29, unknown
persons blew up the Stockton headquarters of the Filipino Federation of
America, where several Filipina/os were sleeping. The violence shook
the Filipina/o community, although Police Chief James C. Dewey and
District Attorney Guard C. Darrah attributed the bombing to a feud
between two Filipina/o groups, as opposed to being the work of white
Americans.[27] Local officials nonetheless kept a close eye on establishments that promoted social interactions between whites and Filipina/os,
and that might set off more hostilities.[28] Law enforcement was especially
concerned that the unrest would spread to Los Angeles, in particular to
the city's Filipino dancing clubs, which employed approximately three
thousand white American women. In the Filipino dance halls along Los
Angeles's Main Street, white female entertainers said they had heard of
the possibility of retaliatory attacks against white American men who
came to the area. Riot-squad cars and police patrolled the neighbor-
hood, alert to any violence that might occur.[29]

Empire and Militarism at "Home"

Tellingly, reaction to the anti-Filipino events reinforced both private
and public military networks in California. In January 1930, local police
joined with two veterans' groups, the American Legionnaires and another
comprised of Spanish-American War veterans, to keep the area under
surveillance. According to one rumor, Filipina/os were organizing a raid
on San Francisco's Presidio to secure ammunition and weapons and set
it on fire. Another San Francisco rumor maintained that thirty thousand
California Filipina/os aimed to take U.S. military supplies and to fire
upon any "Americans" they saw.[30] The Watsonville *Evening Pajaronian*
reported on the unfolding events. Underscoring the community's preoccupation with colonial affairs, a January 23 editorial in the paper warned
about the need to contain violence to avoid the mobilization of U.S. soldiers on the scene and the declaration of martial law. It further cautioned
about the possible repercussions for "Americans" in the Philippines.[31]

Filipino offficials, part of an independence mission, met with U.S.
military government officials such as the secretary of war and the head
of the Bureau of Insular Affairs. Commissioner Guevara noted the dan-

ger faced by Filipina/os on the West Coast, and contended that if the situation were reversed and "Americans" were attacked in the Philippines, U.S. authorities "would call 'battleships and armies' into action." From Manila, the *Philippine Herald* similarly pointed out, "For offense less serious than what these American[s] in California did, the American Army made savage reprisals against the Moros. . . . And when American marines shoot Nicaraguans and kill Negroes in Haiti, it is all right."[32] Commentators on both sides of the Pacific stressed the importance of containing events. Manila Chief of Police Columbus E. Piatt asserted that the fights in Watsonville were "purely local" and would not extend to Manila, despite reports of possible activity by Filipinos seeking retaliation against Americans in the Philippines.[33] On behalf of Filipina/os in the region, community leaders in the Pajaro Valley put out a statement "assuring the people of Santa Cruz county the settlement would give no further offense to the whites."[34]

While the incidents began in a local context, they quickly took on importance at the statewide and national levels because of their imperial nature, reaching all the way to Washington, D.C. and New York City, as well as to Honolulu and Manila. Filipino leadership in Washington sent a group telegram to Filipino labor leaders in California to "avoid trouble, do your utmost to prevent any recurrence of the riots and always obey the officers from whom you should seek protection."[35] Pablo Manlapit, a Filipino lawyer based in Los Angeles who had been a union leader in the deadly 1924 strike in Hawai'i, communicated with California governor C. C. Young about a resolution calling for an investigation of the riots and the prosecution of their instigators, which was approved by a thousand Los Angeles Filipina/os.[36] In Washington, D.C., the riots spurred debates about exclusion and independence in the U.S. Congress, especially as a congressional immigration committee was considering Filipina/o exclusion through amendments to the Jones Law, which regulated U.S. governance of the Philippines.[37]

Both critics and proponents of Filipina/o migration saw independence as the best solution for the political upheaval: in one fell swoop, the United States could demonstrate its strength and democracy by "giving" the Philippines its independence, and Filipina/os could be declared "alien," their bodies excised from the United States' national body politic. These issues had special relevance to Californians, as demonstrated by the Watsonville critics who joined the fray, commenting on the imperial events literally at their doorstep. For example, on January 21 the *Evening Pajaronian* editorial advocated independence so that the Philippines would get its comeuppance from Japan: "When they do get their independence, it will be no time ere they get sassy with Japan. Then the Japanese will sail over, lick the life out of them, take over the country, and turn it into a second Korea."[38] This editorial evidenced not only the paper's patronizing attitude but its presumed authority regarding colonial political events, as well. By characterizing Philippine nationalist sentiment as "sassy," the writer diminished Filipina/os' ambitions for justice. The writer implied that they should grateful to be under the U.S. empire rather than under the allegedly more repressive rule of the Japanese. These comments also underscored the dual impact of Japanese and U.S. empire upon Filipina/os on two fronts: the U.S. West Coast and the Philippine Islands. These issues would be dramatically magnified in the next decade during World War II, when the U.S. and Japan would be at war, and Japan would occupy the Philippines.[39]

In the face of the growing controversy, Philippine officials traveled to California to investigate the situation. Apolinar Velasco, who had participated in the resolution of recent labor disturbances in the San Joaquin Valley, gave the opinion that the Watsonville events were provoked by migratory laborers "who don't represent the best type of American citizen. Not only the American Legion, but the good citizens of Watsonville and southern California generally are doing everything possible to protect Filipinos. I don't look for further trouble."[40] Filipina/o community leaders in San Francisco attempted to minimize the disturbances, stressing that Filipina/os behaved as dutiful colonials: "all Filipinos in the United States are anxious only to live peacefully and unmolested. They admit that irresponsible ruffians in all cases have been to blame for overt acts against Filipino workers. They also admit that in every case officers of the law have been swift to protect the Filipinos and apprehend and prosecute the hoodlums." President Gabriel Arellano of the Philippine Civic League in San Francisco further remarked, "The people making the attacks don't represent the American people, but the hoodlum class. We put our faith in the better class of American people."[41] By contrasting "irresponsible ruffians" and "hoodlums" with "the better class of American people" and law enforcement officials, these Filipino leaders were publicly voicing their "faith" in U.S. colonial rule. This position was unsurprising given the political power imbalance and the investment of Filipina/o leaders in California in cultivating public and government support in the continental United States.

The Body of Fermin Tobera Returns

It was a journey of reverse migration: Tobera's body was sent from California to Honolulu, to Manila, and finally to Tobera's home province of Ilocos Sur. In Manila, Filipina/os organized a protest against what they saw as racialized violence against Flipina/os in the United States. Their public demonstrations were orderly, clearly evoking the same tropes as a military funeral, and their ceremonial flourishes drew a pointed contrast with the white mob violence in Watsonville. Prior to Tobera's body arriving, Filipina/o organizers comprising academics, legislative members, and newspaper editors met at City Hall, and decided to hold a day of "national humiliation" on February 2 to draw attention to the California riots and Tobera's death. Organizers planned to have workers and other laborers at the pier when the boat with his body arrived. A procession would then march to the Luneta, where political leaders would give speeches.[42] By these kinds of public performances, organizers sought to claim political space with the appropriate level of gravity—even the cockfights around the city would take a holiday. However, Manila mayor Tomas Earnshaw denied a parade permit to University of the Philippines students, so they kept their protest to campus, which was attended by over one thousand students from various schools.[43]

Law professor and dean Jorge Bocobo wrote a manifesto decrying Tobera's death and the continued violence faced by Filipino workers across the Pacific: "He went there as thousands of others have done because the American Flag flies over this Archipelago." Bocobo called for a peaceful protest and advocated "separation," as Filipinos "cannot enjoy the same rights and opportunities as American citizens."[44] At the "National Humiliation Day" ceremony, he queried, "Despised as an inferior race and deprived of equal economic opportunities, how can we Filipinos accept our present status under the American flag?"[45]

The protests were covered by newspapers from Manila to New York City, and back again in Watsonville, with crowd estimates varying widely.

While the *Evening Pajaronian*, reported ten thousand attendees, a front-page story in the *New York Times* offered much lower figures, "scarcely 1,500", and sardonically commented, "The expected '100,000' laborers went to the racetrack instead."[46] The *Manila Daily Bulletin* reported that no community programs were organized in California for "National Humiliation Day," although Filipino dance halls in Los Angeles where white American women worked stayed shut, as requested by Filipino leaders.[47] This self-regulating move sought to preempt the possibility of violence, at the cost of economic loss. In a development not covered by other papers, the *Evening Pajaronian* reported on February 3 that ten thousand veterans who had participated in the Philippine Revolution gathered for a meeting in Manila the day after "National Humiliation Day," including nationalist leader Emilio Aguinaldo, who criticized the Quezon administration, underscoring the political turmoil in the Philippines.[48]

On February 13, California Filipina/o leaders made another attempt to contain the unrest and, arguably, mitigate the U.S. political backlash. The Filipino Emergency Association, a group of Filipina/o leaders that organized in response to the political unrest, requested "leniency" for the eight young men arrested for their involvement in the Watsonville riot, who were headed for a superior court trial presided over by Judge D. W. Rohrback. As the Filipina/o leaders noted, "The association is cooperating with state and county officials in order to maintain harmony and good will between Filipino and American citizens."[49] In the end, the eight men pled guilty to charges of inciting to riot and breaking into Filipina/o homes and each was sentenced to two years in San Quentin penitentiary. However, the court largely or entirely suspended the sentences—the four convicted men who were twenty-one years or older were jailed for thirty days. Under the suspension stipulation, the *Evening Pajaronian* reported, the convicted men were required to remain in the local region, avoid pool halls and alcohol, "never molest Filipinos," and maintain "sober and industrious lives."[50] Whether or not the leaders of the Filipino Emergency Association who had called for leniency were relieved with the outcome of the case is unclear. After all, there were an array of formal and informal measures that constrained Filipina/os, especially in the depths of the Great Depression. Given the obvious severity of the violence, the light sentences attest to the limitations of the protections granted Filipina/os as they moved through the U.S./Philippines colonial geography.

On March 12, Tobera's body finally arrived in Manila, completing the final stage of a solemn journey from California to the Philippines. His body lay in state, overseen by members of labor groups and Ilocano students. Despite his mother's expressed wish to the Philippine government that the culprits in his murder be made to pay damages, nothing in the historical records indicates that they did so.[51]

Conclusion

As the anti-Filipina/o riots in California unfolded at the beginning of 1930, a January 27 Manila Daily Bulletin editorial argued, "Many of the Filipino laborers in California are of a low class, largely the ones who have not made good in Hawaii. In the lines of work to which they gravitate they come into contact with a correspondingly low class of American laborers. It is very largely a matter of riff-raff on both sides. The class of woman to be found as dance hall girls catering to that class of laborer is well known." The editorial continued, "He who for political reasons promotes the spirit of ill feeling which prolongs or spreads the rioting is doing nothing more than trying to have the Philippine question settled in the California lettuce fields and the dance halls of the vegetable gardening districts by floater laborers."[52]

As it happened, working-class politics in rural California would indeed have a tremendous impact on how people answered "the Philippine question," as demonstrated by the political furor after Fermin Tobera's death. Empire, as embodied by rural Filipina/o workers, was a moving phenomenon capable of transforming the most local of circumstances. As a result, rural California was a central arena for actions and discussions around politics, militarism, and labor. While Watsonville and Pajaro Valley might popularly be considered domestic spaces within the continental U.S., these sites also represented a meeting ground for colonials and noncolonials in a region that oversaw military and economic movement across the Pacific.

The disturbances to Filipina/o labor migration had a cascading effect upon government analysis and legislation. The next few years would bring numerous legislative bills and court cases that challenged the evolving political status of Filipina/os.[53] These would culminate in the 1934 Tydings-McDuffie Act, which promised independence to the

Philippines and virtually closed U.S. borders to Filipina/o immigration, although the Philippines would not gain its independence from the United States until 1946. By that time, the borders had been redrawn, leaving Filipina/os on the other side of the boundary line as aliens to the United States.

Less than a decade after the Tydings-McDuffie Act, however, government actions would once again show the permeability of the border when U.S. military interests were at stake, as well as the integration of rural California into the U.S. empire. Under Franklin Delano Roosevelt's administration, the military draft law changed in 1942 to make Filipinos in the United States "draft and volunteer eligible" for all branches of the armed forces, even if they were not citizens. This led to the organization of the U.S. Army's First and Second Filipino Regiments. Reflecting the prominence of the Filipina/o community in California as well as their future deployment across the Pacific, these units initially trained in military installations in rural California. Ironically, some of these men would occupy the Salinas Rodeo Grounds shortly after they were vacated by Japanese Americans en route to inland concentration camps, heading away from the Pacific. From these rural California sites, the Filipino soldiers too would be migrating, heading west across the ocean in service of U.S. military campaigns. Many of these men were of Fermin Tobera's cohort, born in the early years of U.S. colonization in the Philippines. For these Filipinos, U.S. citizenship was easily obtainable at last—in 1943, mass naturalization ceremonies ushered thousands of these soldiers into the embrace of American citizenship. On one day alone in February, twelve hundred Filipinos became U.S. citizens.[54] This chapter of their lives underscores once again the significance of military California within the U.S. empire, especially as defined by the Filipina/o workers who circulated in its space.

NOTES

1. Jose G. Flores, "Tobera's Mother Seeks Damages for Death of Son in Hands of American Ruffians in Watsonville," *Philippines Herald*, 16 February 1930, 3.
2. Ibid.
3. Bruno Lasker, *Filipino Immigration to Continental United States and to Hawaii* (Chicago: University of Chicago Press, for the American Council of the Institute of Pacific Relations, 1931), 14–15, 358–365; Rick Baldoz, *The Third Asiatic Invasion: Empire and Migration in Filipino America, 1898–1946* (New York: New

York University Press, 2011), 139–142; Dawn Bohulano Mabalon, *Little Manila Is in the Heart: The Making of the Filipino American Community in Stockton, California* (Durham, NC: Duke University Press, 2013), 93–95.

4. Tony Ballantyne and Antoinette Burton, *Moving Subjects: Gender, Mobility, and Intimacy in an Age of Global Empire* (Urbana: University of Illinois Press, 2009), 3.

5. Gray Brechin, *Imperial San Francisco: Urban Power, Earthly Ruin* (Berkeley: University of California Press, 2006), 123–130.

6. Ibid., 135.

7. Ibid., 142–144; T. Fujitani, *Race for Empire: Koreans as Japanese and Japanese As Americans during World War II* (Berkeley: University of California Press, 2011), 6–28; Eiichiro Azuma, *Between Two Empires: Race, History, and Transnationalism in Japanese America* (New York: Oxford University Press, 2005), 22–24, 25–26; Yuji Ichioka, *The Issei: The World of the First Generation Japanese Immigrants, 1885–1924* (New York: Free Press, 1988), 150–156.

8. Carey McWilliams, *Factories in the Field: The Story of Migratory Farm Labor in California* (Santa Barbara, CA, and Salt Lake City: Peregrine Smith, 1971), 11–65; Devra Weber, *Dark Sweat, White Gold: California Farm Workers, Cotton, and the New Deal* (Berkeley: University of California Press, 1994), 27–29; David R. Roediger and Elizabeth D. Esch, *The Production of Difference: Race and the Management of Labor in U.S. History* (New York: Oxford University Press, 2012), 197–198; Mabalon, *Little Manila*, 69–73.

9. Camille Guerin-Gonzales, *Mexican Workers and American Dreams: Immigration, Repatriation, and California Farm Labor, 1900–1939* (New Brunswick, NJ: Rutgers University Press, 1994), 16–24; Weber, *Dark Sweat, White Gold*, 34–35, 37; McWilliams, *Factories in the Field*, 103–133. One of the best resources available regarding a Filipina American's participation in California agriculture is Angeles Monrayo, edited by Rizaline R. Raymundo, *Tomorrow's Memories: A Diary, 1924–1928* (Honolulu: University of Hawai'i Press, published in collaboration with the UCLA Asian American Studies Center, 2003).

10. "Immigration Only One of the Problems Dewey Brought to Us," *San Francisco Chronicle*, 24 January 1930, 24.

11. "Filipino Laborers Are Criticised," *Manila Daily Bulletin*, 1 February 1930, 4.

12. Peggy Pascoe, *What Comes Naturally: Miscegenation Law and the Making of Race in America* (New York: Oxford University Press, 2009), 14.

13. "Army Acts in Watsonville Race Riots, Martial Law Threat Made in Message to Governor, Police Given Name of Man Believed to Have Slain Filipino," *San Francisco Chronicle*, 25 January 1930, 1.

14. Marilyn Lake and Henry Reynolds, *Drawing the Global Colour Line: White Men's Countries and the International Challenge of Racial Equality* (New York: Cambridge University Press, 2008), 2.

15. Mae Ngai, *Impossible Subjects: Illegal Aliens and the Making of Modern America* (Princeton, NJ: Princeton University Press, 2005), 39–50.

16. Daniel E. Bender, *American Abyss: Savagery and Civilization in the Age of Industry* (Ithaca, NY: Cornell University Press, 2009), 72–74.
17. Alfred W. McCoy, *Policing America's Empire: The United States, the Philippines, and the Rise of the Surveillance State* (Madison: University of Wisconsin Press, 2009), 43.
18. "Filipinos Scored by Free in House," *San Francisco Chronicle*, 26 January 1930, 2.
19. "2 Shot as Mob Storms Club in Watsonville Race Riot," *San Francisco Chronicle*, 22 January 1930, 1.
20. "Race Riots Sweep Valley, Scores Saved from Mobs as Counties Rush Police Aid, Filipino Guarded in Watsonville City Hall after Labor Outbreak," *San Francisco Chronicle*, 23 January 1930. 1.
21. File 28342–2 with "Bolsheviki Press Clippings"; File 28342/10+ with "Bolsheviki, misc. P.I. cor., cables, etc." Record Group 350, Bureau of Insular Affairs, U.S. National Archives (NARA).
22. "Race Riot Menace Spreads to LA, Ringleaders Vanish from Watsonville Investigation, Filipinos in Southern City Reported Planning to Make Reprisals," *San Francisco Chronicle*, 26 January 1930, 1.
23. "New Race Riot Outbreak Threatens, Armed Guards Check Mob from Attack on Filipinos, Body of Wednesday Night Victim Found in Ranch Bunkhouse," *San Francisco Chronicle*,24 January 1930, 1.
24. "People's Forum: Calls on Rioters to Help Boys Out of Jail," *Evening Pajaronian*, 13 February 1930, 6. The writer likely was conflating U.S. national status, which the Filipinos held as colonial workers, with U.S. citizenship.
25. "White Man Stabbed, 4 More Filipinos Wounded in Race Riot; Legion Patrolling City," *Manila Daily Bulletin*, 25 January 1930, 1.
26. "2 Filipinos in Frisco Brawl, Police Squads Called Out as Youths Battle White Crowd," *Manila Daily Bulletin*, 29 January 1930, 1.
27. "Blast Tears Off Front of Filipino Club in Stockton, Street Riots Follow New Labor Outbreak in California, Presidio Upset, San Francisco Stirred over Rumored Military Plot," *Manila Daily Bulletin*, 30 January 1930, 1; "White Girl, 16, Disappears in Watsonville Filipino War," *San Francisco Chronicle*, 30 January 1930, 1.
28. "Communists Attempt to Disrupt Industry to Make Labor Row," *Evening Pajaronian*, 25 January 1930, 1; "Race Riot Menace Spreads to LA."
29. "Race Riot Menace Spreads to LA."
30. "Monterey Filipino Plot Hinted, Bomb Thrown in Stockton," *Evening Pajaronian*, 29 January 1930, 1.
31. "Should Be Suppressed," *Evening Pajaronian*, 23 January 1930, 1.
32. Fernando Leano, "That Watsonville Incident, Local Writers Hit American Government for Recent California Incident; Indorse [*sic*] Mourning Day Idea (A Symposium)," *Philippine Herald*, 2 February 1930, 8.
33. "Seek Action, Filipinos Envoys Confer with Hurley, Parker; Assured Protection, Talk in Congress, Guevara, Osias Address House; Exclusion Move Revived,"

Manila Daily Bulletin, 27 January 1930, 1; "Americans Threatened," *New York Times*, 27 January 1930, 20.

34. "Race Riots Sweep Valley."

35. "Seek Action."

36. "Threat Note Sent Judge in Filipino Row, Search for Watsonville Girl Futile; U.S. Opens Inquiry," *San Francisco Chronicle*, 31 January, 1930, 3.

37. "Plan in House, Committee Studies Means of Making Exclusion Constitutional, Congress Stirred, Senate and House Turn Attention to Riots in California," *Manila Daily Bulletin*, 31 January 1930, 2.

38. "Alternating Currents (Dictated by J.G.P.)," *Evening Pajaronian*, 21 January 1930, 6.

39. Daniel B. Schirmer and Stephen Rosskamm Shalom, *The Philippines Reader: A History of Colonialism, Neocolonialism, Dictatorship, and Resistance* (Boston: South End Press, 1987), chapter 3 ("War, Collaboration, and Resistance"), 69–84.

40. "Seek Action."

41. "Blast Tears Off Front."

42. "Big Demonstration to Greet Remains, Labor Organizations to Stage Protest," *Philippine Herald*, 15 February 1930, 1.

43. "Plans Laid for Manila Observance," *Manila Daily Bulletin*, 31 January 1930, 1.

44. "Manifesto on U.S. Riots Sets Mourning Day, Leaders, Educators Meet, Decry Mobbing of U.S. Filipinos, Laid to Labor, Trouble Not Racial but Merely Local, Says Roxas in Cable," *Manila Daily Bulletin*, 28 January 1930, 1, 4.

45. "Tears Flow at Luneta, 'Humiliation Day' Fete Draws Expressions of Sentiment," *Manila Daily Bulletin*, 3 February 1930, 1.

46. "10,000 Attend 'Humiliation' Meet in Manila," *Evening Pajaronian*, 3 February 1930, 1; "Filipinos Shun Riot Protest, But Flock to Manila Races," *New York Times*, 3 February 1930, 1.

47. "Filipinos Are Back on Farms," *Manila Daily Bulletin*, 3 February 1930, 1; "Filipino Dance Halls Closed," *Manila Daily Bulletin*, 3 February 1930, 1.

48. "10,000 Attend 'Humiliation' Meet in Manila." These veterans were likely Filipino, although it is possible that there also were non-Filipino veterans who had decided to remain in the Philippines after the war.

49. "U.S. Filipinos Ask Leniency for 8 Alleged Riot Leaders, Write Prosecuting Attorney They Are Eager to Cooperate to Establish Harmony," *Philippine Herald*, 15 February 1930, 9.

50. "12 Rioters Plead Guilty; 30 Days, California Court Slaps on 2 Years; Suspended," *Manila Daily Bulletin*, 27 February 1930, 12; "Eight Rioters Get Probation, 4 Wait in Jail," *Evening Pajaronian*, 25 February 1930, 1.

51. "Fear Rioting when Filipinos Gather at Bier of Riot Victim," *Evening Pajaronian*, 12 March 1930, 1.

52. "Settlement by Riots," *Manila Daily Bulletin*, 27 January 1930, 16.

53. Will J. French, California Department of Industrial Relations, *Facts about Filipino Immigration into California* (San Francisco: State Department of Industrial

Relations, 1930; republished, San Francisco: R and E Research Associates, 1972); RG350, Records of the Bureau of Insular Affairs Special Records Relating to the Philippine Islands, Stats. Conc. Filipino Immigration into the United States, 1910–1932, Entry 51, Box 1, "Filipino Immigration into the Continental United States and Occupations Followed by Filipinos in the States of California, Oregon, and Washington and in the Continental United States as a Whole, Appendix C, Bills and Resolutions Introduced in Congress to Exclude or Limit Filipino Immigration into the Continental United States and Action Taken Thereon Prior to Opening of 72d Congress, 1st session" (December 7, 1931), 1–3; representative articles include "Citizenship Case May Go to High Court, Lawyer of Filipino Deprived of Papers Will Fight Ruling," *Manila Daily Bulletin*, 26 February 1930, 14; "Filipinos Are Mongolians, Los Angeles Judge Rules; Ban Against Marriage Broadcast All Over State," *Manila Daily Bulletin*, 27 February 1930, 1.

54. Filipino American National Historical Society, Manilatown Heritage Foundation, and Pin@y Educational Partnerships, *Filipinos in San Francisco* (Charleston, SC: Arcadia Publishing, 2011), 9; Noel Dizon, dir., *An Untold Triumph: America's Filipino Soldiers* (ICT Productions, 2002); "Salinas Assembly Center, California," in Jeffrey F. Burton, Mary M. Farrell, Florence B. Lord, and Richard W. Lord, "Confinement and Ethnicity: An Overview of World War II Japanese American Relocation Sites," *National Park Service*, July 2000, www.nps.gov/history/online_books/ anthropology74/ce16j.htm.

9

Slavery's Stale Soil

Indentured Labor, Guestworkers, and the End of Empire

CINDY HAHAMOVITCH

This is not a question of more or less, of this or that safeguard, of an occasional defect here, or excess there. But it
is that of a monstrous, rotten system, rooted upon slavery,
grown in its stale soil, emulating its worst abuses, and only
the more dangerous because it presents itself under false
colours, whereas slavery bore the brand of infamy upon its
forehead.
—Chief Justice Joseph Beaumont (1863–68) on the indenture system in British Guiana[1]

On October 11, 2013, I sat on a human rights commission assembled to
hear four Jamaican workers testify to the ways they had been exploited
during the months they had spent cleaning luxury hotels and condos
on Florida's Emerald Coast.[2] All four Jamaicans—one man and three
women—had arrived in the U.S. on legal, temporary—guestworker[3]—
visas that bound them to a company called Mr. Clean for a nine-month
period. Promised forty-hour workweeks and furnished apartments,
they paid $2,000 each to the company, flew to the U.S. at their own
expense, and then arrived in Destin, Florida, to find that they were
expected to sleep on the floor of a completely bare apartment already
crowded with twelve other guestworkers, each of whom was paying
$300 a month in rent. No one got anything like forty hours of work a
week. The workers alleged that Mr. Clean used several crowded apartments as informal hiring halls from which the company selected only a
few workers each day. At the end of each fortnight, the workers would
receive checks for only a few dollars each, in some cases for no dol-

lars. Some received handwritten notes indicating the amount they owed Mr. Clean. When six of the Jamaicans (including the four I met in New York) complained to a supervisor, all the guestworkers received a memo warning them that anyone who didn't show up for work would be immediately evicted, reported to immigration authorities as AWOL, and taken to the airport for deportation with an Okaloosa County Sheriff's Department escort.[4]

Mr. Clean certainly seemed dirty, but I was struck during the commission meeting by the fact that the assembled trade union leaders, legislators, human rights activists, and academics repeatedly referred to the Jamaicans' experiences as slavery. Nor were they the first observers to make such a connection. The Southern Poverty Law Center's report on guestworker programs is titled "Close to Slavery," and Kevin Bales, founder of Free the Slaves, says the U.S. guestworker program "delivers men and women into slavery."[5] I listened, infuriated by the workers' tale and moved by their courage, but the slavery analogy rankled. Guestworkers in the United States and elsewhere in the world are too often treated in a way that emulates slavery, to paraphrase Chief Justice Beaumont. The Mr. Clean story, unfortunately, is not even a particularly extreme case of abuse. Guestworkers have been locked in, immobilized by the confiscation of their travel documents, even beaten and raped. Nonetheless, calling guestworkers "slaves" elides more than it reveals. Slavery has taken different forms at different times and in different places, but the fact that in 1992 alone Filipino guestworkers sent home $4.3 billion (U.S.), a figure far larger than their country's $3 billion foreign debt, should make it clear that guestworker programs are something else entirely.[6] Slaves don't send home remittances.

This chapter suggests that my fellow commissioners would have come far closer to the truth had they compared guestworker programs, the temporary labor migration schemes that began in the late nineteenth century and continue on a massive scale today, to indentured servitude, the labor migration system by which employers bound workers for a period of years. This was how more than half of all European migrants to Britain's American colonies made their way across the Atlantic in the seventeenth and eighteenth centuries, and it was how Asians, Pacific Islanders, and some Africans found their way to the Caribbean, Mauritius, Australia, and beyond in the nineteenth.

Guestworker programs are best compared not to that first phase in the history of indentured servitude but to the second, which began after Britain's 1807 slave trade ban, when British leaders and planters sought an alternative source of labor for Britain's far-flung sugar colonies.[7] In the early nineteenth century, indentured servitude was reborn, not as a means to move Europeans across the Atlantic, but as a way to supply British sugar planters with a new source of cheap and (ostensibly) controllable workers of color. Known as the "coolie trade,"[8] this resurgent system of indentured servitude came under fire almost immediately as "a new system of slavery."[9] Those allegations stung because Great Britain was promoting indentured servitude as part of its attempt to eradicate slavery in its colonies. Thus British officials in the Colonial Office and those who ran India's government responded by creating a massive system of laws, local ordinances, and immigration agents known as Protectors of Immigrants to ensure that indentured laborers were indeed volunteers.

Unlike slavery then, both indentured servitude and guestworker programs were supposed to be voluntary labor migration schemes, designed to mobilize and then immobilize "free labor" but on a temporary basis. The fact that workers signed contracts—if only by making a mark—means that at some point along the way they consented to their migration. That moment of consent—the instant when a man or woman followed a recruiter, answered an ad, submitted to a physical examination, boarded a boat or plane, even bribed an official—represents migrants' hopes for opportunities abroad, opportunities that some migrants realized, and that were almost never possible for slaves. That element of choice—however fragile—separates these schemes from slavery in fundamental ways.

That element of consent also made indentured servitude and guestworker programs particularly hard to police. As the Mr. Clean story illustrates, the fact that workers labored under the rubric of legal contracts doesn't mean they got what their contracts promised. Consent could be based on patently false promises. And even when workers knew what they were getting into, they were often *compelled* to make the leap by poverty, war, debt, and lack of opportunities at home. The line between consent and coercion was, and remains, very blurry. But in an era that gradually deemed slavery abhorrent, the element of consent could be a distinct disadvantage because it legitimized both indentured servitude and guestworker programs as "free labor" systems, disguising their frequent use of coercion. As Chief Justice Beaumont said of indentured servitude, forced labor schemes could fly under "false colours."

For these reasons, this chapter abandons the oft-made comparison between slavery and guestworker programs and instead compares one modern American guestworker scheme—the nation's oldest—to the system of indentured servitude that the British spread around the world in the nineteenth century. The H-2A program (formerly known as just H-2 and before that as the Emergency Labor Importation Program) has since World War II supplied over a hundred thousand men from the British Caribbean—most of them Jamaicans—to American farms, especially sugar plantations in Florida. It is particularly useful as a case study because it was initially created in 1943 when the British Empire was still in existence and when the United States was expanding its presence and influence in the wartime Caribbean. Because the H-2A program recruited British subjects for American employers, it allows us to see what happened when an imperial labor system passed into American hands.

This is not a simple story, however, of one empire replacing another. Although the U.S. was undoubtedly an imperial power in many parts of the world—as we can see from the other essays in this book—the postwar American role in Jamaica looked strikingly unimperial. No marines landed. No gunboats floated in Kingston's harbor. No Yankee bureaucrats ran Jamaica's customs house or appointed its governor. This American imperialism lacked all the trappings of empire. Instead, the United States handed American agricultural employers a colonial labor program to run as they saw fit. The result was a new sort of internal empire in which American employers imported a captive labor force but, to paraphrase Kipling, felt no burden to serve those captives' needs.

As we'll see, Britain's benevolent bureaucracy wasn't so benevolent either. As Beaumont suggests, it was capable of rectifying a "defect here" and an "excess there," but it could not or would not uproot "a monstrous, rotten system" that had been planted in slavery's "stale soil." As a result, by the end of the coolie trade in the early twentieth century, despite British officials' reform efforts, indentured servants were subject to the same violence and deprivation that their predecessors experienced in the early nineteenth century. If many coolies ultimately prospered in their host countries it was not because Britain's Protectors of Immigrants were successful but because ex-indentured servants could stay on after their indentures had expired, take advantage of other opportunities, and, as permanent residents, mobilize politically to demand an end to the coolie trade.

H-2A workers had no such advantages. By definition, guestworkers, like the Mr. Clean recruits, have no right to stay at the end of their contracts. Those who did usually remained without authorization and thus could not mobilize politically as ex-coolies did. American employers quickly learned that they could deploy guestworkers' deportability as a tool of labor discipline. That lesson, learned just months after Jamaicans began arriving as guestworkers in 1943, inspired the U.S. to abandon the regulatory system that it and British officials had imposed on the wartime movements of Caribbean men. In the following decades, Jamaicans continued to travel under the rubric of contracts that theoretically protected their interests, but their deportability made those contracts meaningless. The Mr. Clean workers were living proof of that point; addressing the Human Rights Commission as new members of the National Guestworker Alliance, their visas were about to expire.

Bound Labor Reborn

The most tragic thing about the history of nineteenth-century indentured servitude is not the widespread use of flogging, or the increased use of penal sanctions to punish desertion, or even the shockingly high mortality rates among indentured laborers, but the fact that the deadly and coercive system of indentured servitude in the nineteenth century was the result of a sincere effort to end slavery. In fact, it seemed for a brief time that bound labor in all its forms might founder on the shoals of revolutionary sentiment. At the turn of the nineteenth century, revolutionary notions of equality and liberty seemed to call all forms of bondage into question: many slave owners manumitted their slaves; legislatures in the northern states of the new American republic abolished slavery; Haitian slaves revolted, declaring the first black republic; and both Britain and the new United States banned the transatlantic trade in slaves in 1807 and 1808, respectively. British naval squadrons policed the Atlantic, towing slave ships to "mixed commission courts"—the first international human rights courts—and freeing their human cargo. Americans refused to let their new republic serve as a dumping ground for Great Britain's criminals (whereupon the British rerouted convict transportation to Australia), and "at will" employment (in which employees could quit or be fired) rapidly replaced indentured servitude. These were heady times.

Unfortunately, reports of forced labor's demise were premature. The impending slave trade ban and the cotton gin caused slave values to sky-rocket, and so, even as indentured servitude died in the United States, slavery was born again in what historians call the "Second Slavery."[10] In contrast, Britain ended slavery throughout its empire, except in India, transforming slaves into "apprentices" of their masters and then into free men and women a few years later. At the same time, however, the British gave indentured servitude a new lease on life as a legal alternative to the buying and selling of Africans. That was the moment at which the United States and Great Britain's paths diverged: in the U.S., indentured servitude died and slavery was reborn; in the British Empire, slavery died and indentured servitude was reborn. Not all migrants of color were "coolies," but the binding of Europeans on contracts was decreasing even as it was increasing for people of color.[11]

The spread of indentured servitude across the British Empire began almost accidentally in the years following Britain's 1807 slave trade ban as the captains of the anti-slavery squadrons patrolling the Atlantic struggled to find some safe haven to disembark the slaves they liberated. Fearing that freed slaves would be reenslaved if they were released on the west African coast, the Navy transported them to British sugar colonies in the Caribbean, where they worked as indentured servants, alongside slaves. Given the fact that the Africans were not given the opportunity to accept or reject this decision, it was an inauspicious beginning.

Inspired, perhaps, by the Navy's example, plantation owners in British colonies began scrambling for indentured laborers in 1833, when the British Parliament voted to end slavery.[12] In 1834, the year the apprentice system began, planters in British Mauritius and the French colony of Bourbon (both Indian Ocean islands off the coast of Madagascar) began importing Indian laborers on five-year contracts, and two years later planters in Demerara (part of British Guiana) began experimenting with African contract laborers from the Azores and the Madeiras. Here too the migrants' consent mattered little if at all. Thus in 1836, John Gladstone, a Liverpool merchant with sugar plantations in Demerara and the father of the future prime minister, wrote to the Calcutta firm supplying Indians to Mauritius to inquire into the possibilities of securing "young, active, able-bodied" Bengalis for Demerara. He was assured, he reported gleefully, that Indian migrants could be supplied, "the natives being perfectly ignorant of the place they go or the length of the voyage they are undertaking."[13]

Planters weren't seeking migrants because they lacked labor, we should note; enslaved workers didn't vanish in a poof of smoke when emancipation took effect. Rather, the planters' problem was a dearth of labor that they could control by their usual means. Gladstone makes that clear in his initial letter to Calcutta: "You will probably be aware that we are very particularly situated with our Negro apprentices in the West Indies," he wrote, "and that it is a matter of doubt and uncertainty how they may be induced to continue their services on the plantations after their apprenticeship expires in 1840." Coercion was a necessity, he implied; high wages an impossibility (although Gladstone would eventually receive £85,600 in compensation for the 2,183 slaves he was required to free). Concerned a few months later about a new British Guianan ordinance that limited labor contracts to only three years (Gladstone was holding out for seven), he wrote to Lord Glenelg, the secretary of state for the colonies, expressing his worry that, at the end of the apprentice period, women would withdraw their labor from the fields and the men would be "very likely to form combinations for the purpose of restricting the ordinary and necessary periods of labour, as well as to compel the planters to pay them wages, at rates much above their means or ability to comply with." "Under these circumstances," Gladstone wrote, planters needed to obtain "other free labourers, to such an extent *as may excite competition*, and induce our present apprentices to believe that it may become practicable to carry forward the cultivation on a moderate scale independent of their aid."[14] Thus Gladstone sought Indian migrants less to replace Africans than to undercut their ability to bargain. "Several importations from the Madeiras and Azores have taken place into Demerara," he noted, "so far with good effects on the minds of the blacks."[15]

In the meantime, planters stuck to coercion as a means of persuasion. Floggings and other punishments increased during the apprenticeship period. In Mauritius, for example, foremen punished fully one quarter of apprentices between 1835 and 1836, more than half by flogging. Freedom turned out to be so brutal, in fact, that the British public, stirred up by abolitionist pressure groups, demanded an end to the apprenticeship period two years ahead of schedule.[16]

Denied their private right to command black labor, planters throughout the empire, who dominated colonial legislatures, enacted master-servant codes, including vagrancy laws, pass laws, and desertion laws. In nineteenth-century England penal sanctions were still in force but decreasingly used to punish laborers who quit their jobs, struck, escaped, or simply slept in; planters in the colonies could rely on them in the aftermath of emancipation.[17] As Paul Craven and Doug Hay put it, planters used every means at their disposal to impress upon the freedmen that "freedom of contract" did not mean freedom "to abandon one's contract."[18]

By the time planters had succeeded in creating legal ways of controlling black labor, they had already launched a full-scale effort to supplement African laborers with Indian "coolies." In some colonies, like Barbados and St. Kitts, where there was virtually no available land, and thus few alternatives for freed people to do anything but cut cane, plantation owners had little cause for concern about labor supply, and few sought migrant laborers. But in colonies like Jamaica, British Guiana, Mauritius, and the Cape Colony—where there was arable land to which freed people could withdraw—planters scrambled to muster labor from Britain's most populous colony. Seventy-five indentured laborers landed in Mauritius in 1834; 451,000 followed over the next seventy-five years. Nearly 301,000 Indians landed in British Guiana, 158,000 in Trinidad, 36,000 in Jamaica.[19]

The Mauritius venture began as a private enterprise, although the government of India and of the colony quickly stepped in to impose rules. Gladstone therefore proceeded more carefully, writing to London's India Board (of the East India Company) in February 1837 to make sure that he didn't need any special dispensations or charters to remove laborers from India for work in British Guiana. He was assured that "there is no reason to apprehend that the Indian Government would interfere with the project" so long as the hiring was voluntary, and that "due care" was "taken of the labourers so hired whilst at seas, and to prevent their subsequent abandonment."[20] By the time Gladstone's ships were ready to depart Calcutta, however, the secretary of state for the colonies was far less sanguine about the scheme, having just rejected Mauritius's new labor ordinances as "scarcely less rigid, and in some material respects even less equitable, than that of slavery itself." Opposition to Gladstone's scheme had also exploded in Britain's anti-slavery press. Gladstone got his Indian laborers but, John Scoble, a representative of the British Anti-Slavery Society, arrived in British Guiana on the contract workers' heels, and just in time to witness the flogging of several laborers who had tried to escape and walk back to Calcutta.[21] Sensitive to the accusation that it was allowing planters to recreate slavery, the India Office officials issued rules that required the supervision of government agents, the inspections of ships, and free passage home after five years for any ex-servant who wanted to return. Two years later, the governor of Mauritius reported that 8 to 11 percent of indentured servants in Mauritius were dying annually, and British Guiana's governor admitted that "rather more" than one in eight Indian laborers had died.[22] The India Office suspended all recruiting.

As years passed without new recruits, plantation owners lobbied fiercely for the resumption of emigration. The fact that sugar production had declined in the British Empire after emancipation while it increased dramatically in Brazil and Cuba, where slavery remained legal, bolstered their case. Abolitionists were increasingly of two minds. The most militant, who had reorganized as the British and Foreign Society for the Universal Abolition of Negro Slavery and the Slave Trade (BFASS), argued forcefully that contract labor was slavery in sheep's clothing. But others accepted contract labor as a consensual system of servitude, little different from the apprenticeship contracts used in England. Such a system was necessary, they argued, if England was to convince other colonial powers that plantation societies could be run profitably without slaves and if free traders were going to succeed in removing the preferred duty status that British sugar enjoyed in England.[23]

In 1842, Lord Stanley, the secretary of state for the colonies, crafted a compromise that got emigration going again but under stricter rules. The new rules imposed limits on the number of emigrants ships could carry; allowed emigrants to take their wives and children with them, free of charge; permitted emigrants to choose among employers on their arrival; limited their contracts to a year only; and required employers to pay laborers' return fares after five. Most importantly, Stanley's plan put emigration squarely under the control of government agents rather than private recruiters. Immigrant agents were expected to interview migrants before their departure to ensure that they had consented to their indenture, and a Protector of Immigrants was appointed in each receiving colony to survey conditions and investigate complaints.[24] The coolie trade continued both as an imperial project and as an object of imperial scrutiny.

Ironically, the triumph of free traders' 1854 equalization bill, which equalized tariffs on sugar whether it was slave or freely made, resulted in massive state subsidies for the transportation of bound indentured labor. When West Indian planters howled in protest at the new law, Parliament voted to loan them £1,500,000 to expand the migration scheme, and allowed them to pay the remaining cost by taxing freed slaves. Bechu, a highly literate Bengali indentured laborer, who made a name for himself in late-nineteenth-century British Guiana by excoriating the coolie trade in the press, noted the irony that "the suffering Negro and Creole labourers" were taxed to "flood the labour market" with coolies, who kept down wages for all plantation workers to a "starvation point."[25]

It was on this basis that indentured servitude spread around the globe to, within, and beyond British colonies. As other empires and nations abolished slavery (France and Denmark in 1843, Holland in 1863, Portugal in 1869, Latin American countries as they declared independence), they too adopted indentured servitude as a means to populate new territories or to force native-born workers to compete with imported "coolies" in old ones. Employers' fervent desire for cheap and complacent labor quickly drew migrants beyond the pathways of empire and beyond sugar plantations. So Pacific Islanders scraped guano out of Peruvian caves and Chinese men mined gold in the Transvaal, combinations no imperial logic can explain. Nonetheless, "slavery and sugar" remained European empires' "mutually cultivating curses," as Jason Parker puts it.[26] The more Europeans and Americans sweetened their tea and coffee with sugar and spread their toast with jam, the more colonial subjects sailed the currents of empire, paying their oceanic passage with fixed terms of labor. In all, millions of indentured servants moved intercontinentally between the 1840s and the 1920s.[27]

The most striking feature of this second phase in the history of indentured servitude and the first was the primacy of color. In the nineteenth century, indentured servants were recruited in India, China, the Pacific Islands, and the African continent. Europeans crossed oceans in the same period, of course—some fifty million crossed an ocean in the long nineteenth century—but they rarely did so on contracts that required them to work off their fare. In fact, when British colonial officials wanted to settle British people in far-flung territories like Australia or Canada in the nineteenth century, they offered subsidies with no strings attached. Even maligned and degraded Irish tenant farmers dumped in Quebec or New York during the potato famine weren't required to work off the cost of their passage. Later in the nineteenth century, Europeans trying to make it to the United States to work often bound themselves to recruiters and companies, but Congress tried to ban the practice by passing the Alien Contract Labor (or Foran Act) in 1886.[28] In contrast, people of color increasingly moved under the rubric of indentured servitude contracts. And even those who didn't—like the Chinese fortune seekers who joined California's and Victoria's gold rush migrations—were maligned as "coolies."[29]

Despite the widespread assumption that "coolies" were slavish and degraded, bound migrants proved to be far less compliant than employers had anticipated. Indentured laborers deserted, went on strike, assaulted plantation officials, set buildings and cane fields afire, and lodged complaints for assault, irregular rations, late or nondelivery of return fares, lack of adequate medical care, and nonpayment of wages. In British Guiana, indentured servants brought 624 complaints against their bosses between 1874 and 1895, winning 208 convictions. Employers clamped down, using the master-servant codes they had passed to control black workers. In Mauritius, fully 9 percent of indentured laborers were arrested for vagrancy each year between 1861 and 1871. In British Guiana, between 1874 and 1895, 65,084 laborers were convicted of offenses against their bosses.[30]

Given these constraints on indentured workers, historians have long debated how voluntary this ostensibly free system of labor supply was. Writing in the 1970s, historian Hugh Tinker sided with the antislavery activists who declared the coolie trade "a new system of slavery."[31] For Tinker, as for Beaumont, the system was rotten at its core and no amount of "reform" could have fixed it. "[F]or a period of seventy or eighty years," he wrote, "British statesmen and administrators were being confronted with evidence that the planting interest was exploiting Indian workers in ways which could not be tolerated by a decent, humane society: and yet they continued to assure themselves that these wrongs were mere abuses and irregularities which could be amenable to reform."[32] David Northrup considers this hyperbole, warning that many kinds of labor conditions were condemned as "slavery" in the nineteenth century—waged labor among them. He agrees that death rates on coolie ships and conditions on plantations were abysmal at the start but, he argues, colonial regulators made a difference. Richard B. Allen and Marina Carter condemn conditions for coolies in Mauritius, but argue that, after their indentures expired, Indian immigrants made considerable gains as small farmers, peddlers, shopkeepers, and even professionals.

All these views can be reconciled if we recognize that indentured servants could begin as volunteers and then become captives and that indentured servitude could be incredibly exploitive *and* a means to greater opportunities. Indian laborers' own testimony reveals both the range of experiences as well as how quickly what began as a voluntary act of migration could slip into human trafficking. A Bengali woman named Djoram, for example, was out of work and sitting in a tailor's shop in Calcutta when a "duffadar" (a recruiter or labor gang leader) told her she "could get ten rupees a month wages, food and clothing," as a servant to a gentleman and lady who were traveling by ship to "Meritch" (Mauritius). She was promised that it was a "five days' journey, and that if I pleased I could remain in service there or return." "They thus deceived me," she said, "and got me on board." The journey took three months. Other migrants noted that they signed on with the understanding that the "company" they were going to work for was the East India Company, not some place overseas. Some sought to go to one location and ended up in another. One recruit, who sought to follow friends to Mauritius, followed a duffadar to a place he called the "new Mauritius depot," only to discover that he was in Demerara in South America. Another man returned from Mauritius to recruit for his masters "as they were very kind to me," only to discover that his brother had been "enticed away by an arkotty [also a recruiter] who took him to the Trinidad depot."[33]

However often migrants were tricked into the hold of coolie ships, the fact that most agreed to follow a recruiter made the regulatory process far more difficult than the simultaneous British effort to interdict slave ships. It was easy enough for British naval officers to presume that any ship sailing from the African coast with a hold full of Africans was violating the slave trade ban (although mixed commission courts made the final determination), but it was not so easy to determine whether particular travelers among hundreds on a ship bound for Trinidad or the Transvaal had been tricked or coerced into the hold. Even by the end of the century, Bechu noted, the immigrant agents on the docks often didn't speak the languages of their charges. "It seems passing strange," he noted wryly, "that the ignorant *uneducated* coolie should be required to learn a foreign language," but that "the *educated* European should save himself a little trouble to acquire the language of the people with whom he has so much to do."[34] British officials who couldn't communicate with the migrants had to rely on underlings whose loyalties they couldn't control. Thus a Mauritius sirdar (driver) named Matadoo complained that he had to pay a bribe to get the seventeen men he had recruited into the emigration depot at Madras. The contractors there, he explained, "divide and engage the men as they like. Mr. Burton [the emigration agent] knows nothing about their doings. He employs them and pays them; but he probably does not know how they ill-treat and cheat the emigrants who pass through his office."[35]

Even if British officials in receiving colonies made some difference, for example in enforcing regulations preventing the auctioning of laborers on the docks, regulating what happened on the plantations was another matter. Local officials had to live among the planters they sought to regulate (and often stayed in planters' houses when they came to do inspections). Which regulations pertained was not even clear. Regulations flowing from England were often ignored by planters or countermanded by colonial legislatures, which were dominated by planters and merchants. This was the case for the 1842 rule that limited indenture contracts to a year. In 1849 the Mauritian government authorized three-year contracts, and in 1862 extended that to five years. Local ordinances like these were supposed to be approved by the Colonial Office, but by mid-century officials in Britain tended to allow colonial ordinances a trial period and then neglected to access how the trial went. Local rule usually prevailed.[36]

As a result, British regulations were inconsistently enforced and only sporadically effective. Death rates on ships declined over the course of the century, but that was likely because ships got much faster. In Mauritius, living conditions seemed to improve as a result of reforms but wages went virtually unchanged for sixty years. As late as the early twentieth century, death rates on plantations in Malaya were as high as 25 percent and indentured servants were subject to "systematic flogging."[37] In fact, Bechu, the thorn in the side of British Guiana's planters, began his career as an editorialist in 1896, when a clash between laborers protesting wage decreases and planters resulted in five workers dead and fifty-nine wounded.

Bechu's own story clearly demonstrated how weak enforcement mechanisms were in the receiving colonies. Orphaned at a young age and raised by a Scottish Presbyterian missionary in India, Bechu had fallen on hard times some years after her death. In 1894, at the age of thirty-six, he accepted a recruiter's offer to take him to Trinidad for a three-year indenture. "I was in reduced circumstances and I met a recruiter who told me he would put me in the way of making a living if I was willing to cross the sea." His debt to the recruiter grew as he waited to depart the Calcutta Depot. After several days, the recruiter presented him with a bill for food and other expenses, telling him he could pay it or go to British Guiana for five years. Unable to pay, Bechu reluctantly agreed to change his destination. Highly literate, he could read his contract on his arrival in Demerara, but, he noted, no one explained it to the illiterate workers with whom he arrived. It made little difference, in any case, because employers ignored the contract. Field laborers worked twelve-hour-plus days for one shilling a day, although their contracts limited them to seven hours for a shilling. As sugar prices tumbled at the end of the century, growers increasingly required that laborers switch to task work, which meant the task had to be completed to earn the same shilling. The tasks assigned were so large that completing them often took two days, which meant that wages were effectively cut in half. The immigrant agent did not investigate. "[A]lthough I am nearly two years on this estate," Bechu noted, "neither I nor any of my shipmates have had the honor of appearing before Mr. Gladwin [the immigrant agent]." "[I]t is useless seeking the assistance of [the Protector]," he argued, "*for such officials are virtually the protector of the planters.*" "Men do not gather grapes from thorns," Bechu wrote perceptively, "nor do they get reforms from officials and the system that created the need of reform. . . . I have no hesitation that our immigration system cannot be made clean without a new broom."[38]

That new broom eventually came not as a result of colonial reforms, as Northrup suggests, but as a result of the activism of ex-indentured settlers in receiving countries and nationalists in sending countries who eventually succeeded in cutting off the coolie trade at its source. The migrants' time under indenture might have been a bitter experience for most, but significant numbers of those who survived the experience settled in their host colonies and made economic gains. The Protector of Immigrants in Mauritius noted in 1860, for example, that "old immigrants" were setting themselves up as small landowners, shopkeepers, peddlers, and craftsmen. Indians made up less than 3 percent of professionals in 1851 but were 25 percent of professionals in 1881.[39]

Former coolies' ability to stay and advocate for themselves generated resentment among white settlers and free black or "creole" populations, who feared the growing economic and political power of ex-coolie communities. Thus colonial legislatures often passed discriminatory legislation, such as the Cape Colony's 1894 ordinance imposing a tax on ex-coolies who settled rather than recontracting or leaving. It was these discriminatory laws that Mohandas Gandhi challenged in Durban before returning to India and transforming what had become a campaign to end the coolie trade into a leading issue for Indian nationalists.

As a result of that campaign, India's government terminated migration to Natal in 1908, and migration to Mauritius and Malaya ended soon after. By that time, China's government had already ended indentured migration out of China after an official investigation into conditions in Cuba, Peru, and the United States. World War I brought "a stark reappraisal of coolie emigration" and, in the war's aftermath, the British participated in the creation of the International Labour Organization (ILO), which condemned and worked to end the coolie trade (which explains why, as we'll see later, the British secretary of state during World War II was so reluctant to endorse a contract labor scheme designed to move British subjects from the British Caribbean to the United States).[40]

Coolies Redux?

By the time the coolie trade had breathed its last, guestworker programs were well under way. Strikingly similar to the nineteenth-century bound labor schemes, they were nonetheless designed to avoid precisely the sort of ethnic conflicts that would make Gandhi a nationalist icon. From the perspective of white settlers in Britain's colonies, the problem with the coolie trade was that ex-coolies stuck around. The migration paths of European and non-European labor migrants in the nineteenth century were usually separate, but where they intersected in the settler colonies Marilyn Lake and Henry Reynolds call "white men's countries" sparks flew.[41] Thus in Queensland, Natal, and the Cape Colony, early guestworker programs were produced by European "settlers'" refusal to compete with "migrants" of color who chose to stay at the end of their indentures (as was their right).[42]

In the 1880s, in the first case, mine managers in the Kimberley diamond complex in Britain's Cape Colony wanted to import labor without generating the sort of white opposition that was already wracking Natal (and that would later produce the anti-Indian ordinances that Gandhi contested). Instead of importing indentured servants, therefore, mine managers imported miners from Portuguese East Africa (now Mozambique) but under new terms. Managers kept the migrant miners immobile like indentured servants by locking them into "closed compounds" and paying them every six months instead of weekly, but they forced them to become mobile again at the end of their contracts. Instead of being allowed to stay and settle, as indentured servants often did, the migrant miners were required to return home before recontracting again.[43] This was indentured servitude with a difference.

A similar process transformed indentured servants into guestworkers in turn-of-the-century Australia, where late-nineteenth-century sugar planters had been "blackbirding" (kidnapping) Melanesians for use as cane cutters when they were denied indentured servants from India. The Melanesians generated little comment from white Australians until the worldwide depression of the 1890s forced unemployed white workers to seek jobs in the cane fields. White Australians' anger at having to compete for work with nonwhites fed the popular campaign to unify the continent's British colonies into a single, independent, "White Australia." Almost immediately on its formation in 1901, Australia's new Commonwealth Parliament expelled Melanesians and passed an Immigration Restriction Act that required immigrants to pass a "dictation test" in a European language. Two years later, the 1903 Commonwealth Naturalization Act limited the right of naturalization to European immigrants. Only then did Australia's parliament allow sugar planters to reimport Melanesians, and then only on temporary visas and in very small numbers.[44]

Indentured servitude allowed empires to move people from colony to colony, populating ostensibly labor-poor regions with workers from labor-rich ones. In contrast, guestworker programs became a way to bring the periphery to the metropole, while sparing the latter from having to integrate the former. So, for example, during World War I, France recruited workers from Italy, Spain, Indochina, Madagascar, North Africa, and China on six-month contracts, directing the workers of color to jobs and housing deemed "unsuitable for Frenchmen." When the war ended, the European immigrants were encouraged to settle; the non-white workers were deported. The U.S. suspended immigration restrictions during the war to allow railroads and farmers access to contract workers from Mexico and the Bahamas, but required employers to promise that they would deport those workers when the war ended.[45]

American farm employers (who represented a tiny minority of U.S. growers) soon had cause to regret those deportations when the farm economy boomed again during World War II. This time, however, their frantic lobbying didn't immediately result in the creation of a guest-worker program. World War II came on the heels of twenty years of agricultural depression (the agricultural economy had crashed a full decade before 1929), during which the agricultural labor force was glutted with labor. As a result, New Deal officials were worried less about labor scarcity than labor surplus. On the eve of Pearl Harbor, they were still building temporary and permanent migratory labor camps to house homeless farmworkers and their families. Yet the war was having an effect on labor supply. The combination of the draft, base construction, and war jobs had reduced unemployment somewhat, but unevenly. Wages rose very little if at all for farmworkers, but the shrinking of the massive oversupply of labor gave them some measure of power in negotiations with growers, and they were using it. Black farmworkers in Belle Glade, Florida, decided collectively to refuse to leave their federal labor camp for the fields when growers dropped the piece rate for bean picking.[46] As in apprenticeship-era British Guiana, Jamaica, and Mauritius, then, American growers' problem was less a dearth of labor than a dearth of compliant labor.

Growers' own words belied the notion that farmworkers were unavailable. "I want 6 Bahama [*sic*] Laborers and need them now," wrote
Mrs. William J. Krome, a South Florida orchard owner, on January 29,
1943, in a telegram to the U.S. secretary of agriculture; "Bahamians are
far better help than riffraff now walking our roads and shooting craps in
our fields." "1,000 farm laborers idle in the communities and a majority
of those working effectively employing delaying tactics," wrote another.
"Negroes have to be bossed," added a third. "You can't boss them when
they make that kind of money and when they can get another job anywhere they want it. I haven't fired a Negro in I don't know when. They
quit first."[47] Black farmworkers weren't idle; they were simply taking advantage of farmers' growing desperation to bargain up their wages. A
few growers solved their own problem by paying more, building better
housing, and even engaging in collective bargaining with farmworkers—
Seabrook Farms in South Jersey, which produced Birds Eye vegetables,
was the most notable of these—but like sugar planters in Demerara and
Jamaica, most growers refused to adapt to new circumstances, prefer-
ring to import other workers of color from abroad to negotiating with
the workers they had at hand.

The conflict between growers and newly militant farmworkers was
particularly fraught in Clewiston, Florida, where U.S. Sugar—the nation's largest sugar cane company—was under investigation by the U.S.
Department of Justice. The company was indicted in 1942 for enslav-
ing black workers who migrated in response to false promises of free
transportation and high wages and then having those who tried to leave
beaten and allegedly murdered. The charges were dismissed on a tech-
nicality but U.S. Sugar's managers had learned their lesson. Banned from
imprisoning local black workers, they demanded foreign workers.

Like apprenticeship-era plantation owners who tended to see any
contraction of the black labor force or increase in wages or workers'
militancy as a crisis of labor supply, white growers in the U.S. South were
particularly outraged at the idea that black workers could bargain. Unlike in nineteenth-century British plantation colonies, however, American farmers faced a New Deal government that was skeptical of their
dire predictions of labor scarcity. The New Deal had done very little
for farmworkers during the Depression beyond building a handful of
temporary shelters; in fact Congress had excluded farmworkers from

all the signal labor legislation of the 1930s, including minimum wage law, collective bargaining law, and social security. But federal officials remained unconvinced that a labor crisis was imminent. Growers' problem, federal officials concluded, was that they had grown accustomed to a great "over-supply of workers" and had thus "come to consider . . . any reduction in the surplus supply as a shortage."[48] The interagency committee charged with estimating labor needs and supply noted, moreover, that the growers complaining the loudest about labor scarcity and spiraling wages were those who paid the least. Instead of heeding growers' demands for foreign workers, federal officials began moving American workers from areas of surplus to areas of relative scarcity, which only infuriated growers in areas deemed glutted with labor.

U.S. growers demanding Caribbean farmworkers were also up against Oliver Stanley, the British secretary of state for the colonies (and the great-great-grandson of Lord Stanley, the secretary of state for the colonies who had restarted emigration from India in the 1840s), for whom the idea of a temporary labor migration scheme between Britain's Caribbean colonies and the U.S. smacked of indentured servitude.[49]

Making little progress through official channels, Florida growers took matters into their own hands, much as Mauritius planters had done in the 1830s. Joining together under the tireless leadership of a tomato farmer and self-appointed diplomat named Luther L. Chandler, Florida vegetable, fruit, and sugar producers formed a formidable foreign labor lobby. "[T]housands of these Negroes in the Bahama Islands are without employment," Chandler wrote to the U.S. Immigration and Naturalization Service (INS), "and it would really be a favor to them if permitted to simply fill in the slack." He promised that growers could guarantee the return of any Bahamians they imported, provided (in a little shout-out to South Africa) growers were "allowed to protect themselves by holding the laborers behind an inclosure [sic] during their leisure hours."[50]

When the INS was unmoved, Chandler took it upon himself to open private, diplomatic negotiations with none other than Edward VIII, the Duke of Windsor and former king of England, who had abdicated his throne to marry an American divorcée. Appointed governor of the Bahamas to get him out of the way and out of the news, the duke and his controversial duchess whiled away their time entertaining wealthy war refugees while the Bahamian unemployment crisis grew. In 1941, just before the Japanese attack on Pearl Harbor, Chandler arrived in Nassau with a delegation of Florida growers who offered to take the duke's unemployment problem off his hands. A few months later, he helped the duke secure a meeting with President Roosevelt. According to Chandler, Edward contributed "very good ideas" to the migration plan, including the suggestion that a part of each man's pay be withheld and deposited in the Bahamas to guarantee his return to the colony (which became and remains a feature of the U.S. agricultural guestworker program).[51]

Chandler never did convince the head of the INS—the only agency with the power to declare a labor shortage and waive immigration restrictions—that American growers needed foreign labor. Growers simply did an end run around the INS by lobbying Congress and the president. In early 1942, President Roosevelt ordered the U.S. secretary of labor to negotiate a guestworker program with the government of Mexico, the governor of the Bahamas, and the British secretary of state for the colonies on behalf of Jamaica.

Oliver Stanley remained unenthusiastic about Chandler's proposed scheme, both because it so resembled indentured servitude and because he feared what might befall West Indians working in the Jim Crow South. Stanley noted that making the workers pay their own way—as Chandler had proposed—contravened International Labour Organization conventions on the migration of indigenous workers that Britain had helped author merely a decade earlier. (American officials shot back that black people were not "indigenous" to the Caribbean and that it didn't matter if they were because the United States hadn't signed the ILO conventions.)[52] Stanley continued to dig in his heels, noting that Jamaicans—unaccustomed to formal segregation—might react virulently to racial discrimination and get themselves lynched as a result (he had none of the same concerns for Bahamians because the Bahamas imposed similar sorts of restrictions on black Bahamians' use of hotels, restaurants, and cinemas, and because Bahamians had long experience working in Florida).[53]

Finally, in January 1943, after drawing out negotiations for months, Stanley relented, allowing up to five thousand Bahamians and fifty thousand Jamaicans to travel to the U.S. He was convinced not by U.S. negotiators, but by Caribbean poverty. Largely a society of farmers who owned little of the land they worked, Jamaica was devastated by the Great Depression and the war that followed. The crash inspired nativist movements that forced many Jamaicans working in Cuba or Latin America to return home. Unemployment on the island skyrocketed.[54] In 1938, Jamaican plantation workers, dockworkers, and the urban unemployed had launched full-scale rebellions for pay hikes, collective bargaining rights, and the franchise, but their protests were violently crushed. Labor leaders were thrown in jail as a result, but news of the uprisings and the repression that followed invigorated anti-imperial forces in England and around the world, and had resulted in the 1940 Colonial Development and Welfare Act, which promised Jamaicans reform and an infusion of British aid.

The aid didn't come, however, and Jamaica's economy only got worse. The outbreak of World War II, which lifted the U.S. economy out of depression, but made matters much worse for Jamaicans because U-boat warfare and shortages of ships disrupted what was almost entirely an export economy. "Conditions there are terrible," remarked one man, "the government is not interested in the poor man."[55] In fact, Jamaica's government, which was partly appointed and partly elected—but by a voting pool limited to the 6 percent of the population that owned property—was not interested in the poor man. The white oligarchy's response to the wartime economic crisis was to restore public flogging for men caught stealing vegetables and fruit. It invoked the statute nearly seven hundred times over the next three years.[56]

Unable to send the aid that Britain's parliament had promised, Stanley demanded that Jamaica institute universal suffrage by 1944 and he relented on the question of sending Caribbean workers to the United States. He did so, however, only after winning several protections for the workers who would "reach over" from the Caribbean. He insisted that U.S. officials abide by ILO conventions, which barred indebting international labor migrants by charging them for their transportation. The Bahamas would pay for Bahamian migrants' short flight to Florida and the U.S. would pay for Jamaicans' journey by sea. West Indian liaison officers—white employees of the Colonial Office—would accompany both groups and be paid for their services by the United States. And, at Stanley's insistence, Jamaicans would be placed north of the Mason-Dixon Line only. Here were the vestiges of the old benevolent empire at work.

Jamaica's white politicians worried that the program would create labor shortages for them, but they welcomed the prospect of currying favor with fifty thousand future voters. Although Jamaica's white oligarchs had little hope of holding on to power after universal suffrage took effect, they formed a new political party, which they disingenuously named the Democratic Party, and doled out recruitment tickets themselves.

Jamaican men were thrilled with the prospect of working in the U.S. (women were too, but they weren't included).[57] Recruits cheerfully lined up to apply, stripped naked for medical examinations, traveled in cow cars to the capital, and boarded troop carriers to the United States. They were unquestionably volunteers and not slaves by any definition.

"Going to Foreign"

Because Mexico's government and the British secretary of state for the colonies had insisted that the U.S. take responsibility for Caribbean and Mexican guestworkers, the Emergency Labor Importation Program began as a publicly run scheme and foreign workers arrived in northern states covered by what may have been the best contracts any migrant farmworker anywhere had ever seen. The U.S.-Bahamian and U.S.-British agreements required that growers pay a minimum wage (set at thirty cents an hour in 1943) or the prevailing wage, whichever was higher. It guaranteed free transportation, free housing in government camps or preapproved private facilities, even a nondiscrimination clause. Workers were covered by a "three-quarter guarantee" that promised work or wages for three-quarters of the contract period, an unprecedented benefit for agricultural workers who frequently lost days and even weeks of work to bad weather. The migration program was publicly not privately run, with U.S. officials recruiting, screening, transporting, housing, feeding, and generally insuring that foreign workers were well treated. In the hopes that these remarkable contracts would elevate conditions for U.S. farmworkers, federal officials also required that growers who wanted foreign workers had to offer the same terms to domestic workers. Here was a New Deal for farmworkers brought to the U.S. from south of the border.

Traveling on U.S. warships that had to outrun German submarines, Jamaicans landed in whatever American port the Navy could get them to quickest, even if that meant disembarking in the South. On arrival, they were processed and fingerprinted before being sent north by train, each recruit bearing a pamphlet written by J. Harris, Jamaica's labor adviser, and Herbert MacDonald, chief of the liaison officers, who assured them that they would be "among a friendly English-speaking people" and that "the word 'Negro'" was used in the United States not "to offend," "but . . . in the same way as the word 'coloured'" was used in Jamaica. "Respect the 'Star Spangled Banner,'" they admonished, and "try to recognize it whenever it is played . . . remember it is as sacred to Americans as 'God Save the King' is to us."[58]

For a few months, the guestworker scheme seemed to work better than anyone had anticipated. Sent to northern communities from Iowa to Connecticut, Jamaicans were welcomed by farmers, fêted by rural communities, greeted by marching bands, given the "keys to New York," even taken to church by white locals who were bemused by the sight and sound of black farmworkers with "almost Oxfordian" accents. On their arrival in Michigan, Jamaicans received the princely sum of $100 as a cash advance.[59] Many northern farmers seemed willing to entertain the notion that Jamaicans were, if not quite their equals, at least an exotic and superior sort of "Negro," who required special treatment.

Whether "God Save the King" was in fact "sacred" to Jamaicans, they were quick to play on their Britishness in their interactions with white Americans. Stanley Amritt, a self-appointed spokesman for the Jamaican guestworkers of Le Sueur, Minnesota, insisted that they had come to the United States because of their patriotism, not their destitution. "[O]ur income in normal times is in most cases equal to the wages we earn in the United States," he wrote to the *Minneapolis Sunday Tribune*, though the war had caused "some economic stringency" that made it necessary to "seek work in your country." Still, he insisted, "it should always be borne in mind that we are induced to come here to do our part in the war effort. . . . We are happy to make the sacrifice if it hastens the victory which every loyal Britisher longs for."[60]

Jamaicans' willingness to assert themselves as British subjects or at least as not African Americans led some to protest discrimination, just as Oliver Stanley had feared. George Hudson, sent to Connecticut as a farmworker, insisted that "[m]any of the discrimination barriers were broken down by us," and recounted an incident in which a theater called the Strand refused to admit him and fellow workers. "[W]e showed up in force," he recalled, "and demanded they let us in. . . . The [African] Americans were scared to challenge these places, but because we had numbers of us who traveled together we were not afraid."[61] Another group of Jamaicans jumped a counter in a South Jersey restaurant and began breaking dishes when they realized that they were being refused service. What these war workers failed to note in their recollections is that British and U.S. officials and even growers stepped in to protect them. For example, when the manager of the South Jersey restaurant called Seabrook Farms to ask what to do about Jamaicans' dish-breaking protest, John Seabrook told him, "Feed them." It is difficult to imagine many farm employers doing the same for African Americans in 1943.[62] For a few months, Jamaicans were able to assert themselves precisely because they were British subjects under Britain's protection. Or at least so it seemed. The honeymoon didn't last.

The downward slide began in Florida. U.S. Sugar had expected to have its labor needs filled by Bahamians, but the Bahamians knew Florida and thus knew they could do less dangerous and better paying work picking beans (they were no doubt familiar with U.S. Sugar's practice of locking black workers in at night and threatening those who tried to leave with violence). U.S. Sugar sought alternatives. Recognizing that their 1942 indictment on slavery charges would repel many African American migrants, the company's managers put their formidable political muscle into demanding that the War Manpower Office supply Jamaicans, despite Stanley's ban.

Even while the first Jamaican recruits were still arriving in the U.S., American officials backed up U.S. Sugar by refusing to send more ships to Jamaica to transport migrants until Stanley had lifted his ban on sending Jamaicans to the Jim Crow South. If Jamaicans couldn't work in Florida, they wouldn't work in the U.S. at all. With Jamaicans at home clamoring for the program's resumption, Jamaican newspapers touting the remittance monies already sent home, and U.S. growers beginning to recruit in Puerto Rico, Stanley reluctantly relented. In September 1943, Jamaicans began arriving in Florida, at which point the wartime guest-worker program slipped right back into the nineteenth century.

Deportable Coolies

Jamaicans arriving in Florida in the fall of 1943 were greeted not by marching bands and mayors bearing the keys to Clewiston, but by labor camp bosses bearing rifles and blackjacks. In some areas, tent cities set up to accommodate them were surrounded by barbed wire, in others men needed passes to leave and bells summoned them to daily roll calls. All the federally run camps were segregated by color and citizenship (African Americans and West Indians were housed separately). And, despite the nondiscrimination clause in their contracts, new arrivals to Florida were required to sign a "Jim Crow Creed" in which they pledged to abide by the customs of southern segregation.[63]

Where northern papers had referred to the recruits as Jamaicans, noting that they were British subjects and unlike African Americans in many respects, Florida papers referred to them as "Negroes," "West Indian Negroes," or, in one case, as "alien negro laborers." In the South, race trumped citizenship.[64]

The first Jamaican arrivals from the North rejected this new treatment, refusing to get off the buses and generally abusing "everyone & everything in sight," as the chief liaison officer put it. But instead of relocating the men who objected to local conditions as officials had been doing in the North, or flogging them as plantation managers would have done in the nineteenth century, U.S. and sugar company officials shipped off protesting guestworkers to the Dade City jail and from there back to Kingston, Jamaica. In the following weeks, eight to nine hundred Jamaicans were imprisoned and then deported for refusing "to sign the Jim Crow agreement forced upon them."[65] Suddenly, the workers' foreignness, which had shielded them in the North, became their Achilles' heel. Using the threat of deportation and sometimes actual repatriation to deal with workers' protests persists to this day, as the Mr. Clean workers discovered.

Years later, after Jamaicans had been coming to the U.S. to harvest sugarcane for over two decades, a section foreman for the Florida Sugarcane Growers' Cooperative succinctly explained the significance of guestworkers' continued deportability (tellingly, he calls them "offshores"): "We bring the Jamaican here under contract. If he violates his contract we can send him home. So we've got leverage over that West Indian that we don't have over American workers. When that offshore comes in here, he's either going to cut cane or get sent home—or if he violates his immigration status and runs away from his employer, the law will get him."[66]

Employers' power to deport immediately undercut the colonial liaison officers' authority to regulate the program. Fitzroy Parkinson recalled that when a white supervisor threatened to kick "one of our boys" "everybody stopped working" and demanded redress. Instead, the local liaison officer told them their options were to finish the sugar harvest and then go north or return home immediately.[67] In 1946, Jamaica's Labour Party, victorious after the advent of universal suffrage, tried withdrawing Jamaican migrants from Florida to protest racist practices, but when the government of Barbados offered to take up the slack, the Jamaican officials relented. With jobs, remittances, and patronage at stake, Jamaica would assert little influence over the program.

Those who were deported were quickly replaced by prerecruited men who were standing by for a call to go to Kingston and from there to the U.S. With Jamaica's population swelling by 30 percent between the census of 1943 and the next in 1960, the countryside was crowded with willing recruits. Ten men would arrive at recruitment stations for every job available.[68]

No longer was the promise of deportation just a sop to nativists, as in the Transvaal or Queensland; the threat of deportation was now firmly established as a form of labor discipline and so it has remained, despite black majority rule in Jamaica in 1944 and independence from Great Britain in 1962.

Making Impermanence Permanent

Unlike nineteenth-century British indentured servitude, which started out anarchic and ended up at least somewhat regulated, U.S. guestworker programs went in the other direction. They began as publicly run programs during World War II and ended up in the hands of growers within two years of the war's end (although, officially, the Mexican program remained government run until it ended it 1964). Federal officials extended the Caribbean programs twice and then withdrew from their operations in 1947, selling federal labor camps to growers for a dollar a piece and allowing growers to run them on their own, as long as the INS certified the existence of a labor shortage (which it almost invariably did). In 1952, Congress institutionalized the consolidated Caribbean guestworker schemes as a privately run but state-sanctioned affair.

The consequences of privatization coupled with workers' deportability were immediately clear. U.S. Sugar slashed tonnage rates in half at the war's end, driving all its remaining African American workers from the company's fields. West Indians replaced them. New guestworker contracts, which growers' associations renegotiated directly with Caribbean governments, passed on the costs of travel, housing, food, recruitment and management expenses, medical insurance—even the liaison service—to the workers themselves.[69] An additional 10 percent of workers' pay was withheld in Jamaican banks (without interest) to ensure their departure. Growers could handpick men they liked and personally deport and blacklist those they didn't. In the following decades, lawsuits, investigations, and all manner of exposés would allege timecard fraud, embezzlement of medical insurance premiums, false arrest, and other abuses. The sort of violence that indentured servants routinely experienced was rare, but only because deportation had replaced the whip as the principal tool of labor discipline.

Roll Back, Britannia

It is not terribly surprising that the U.S. withdrew from the daily affairs of the Caribbean guestworker program, given the Republican majority's rollback of New Deal programs in the late 1940s.[70] What is surprising is how rapidly the British Empire faded from the scene. Certainly, the Colonial Office had its hands full in the late 1940s with Indian nationalists, apartheid South Africa, and the British occupation of Palestine. British officials may simply have recognized that they lacked the funds to fulfill the promises they had made to Jamaica in 1940 and thus figured that jobs in the U.S., even on U.S. growers' terms, were better than nothing. Whatever the reason, the Colonial Office dropped out of the guestworker program's operations soon after the war's end, without so much as a by-your-leave. Before doing so, it tried to increase the influence of the various islands' liaison services by consolidating them into one West Indian Central Labour Organization (other British West Indians having joined Jamaicans in the U.S. in the last year of the war), but that was about it. The liaison officers stayed on in the postwar period, but they represented the sending islands' governments rather than the Colonial Office, and they spent far more time trying to retain guestworkers' jobs than they did advocating for fair treatment.[71]

Yet if Jamaica began its fall out of the British Empire as early as 1947, it didn't exactly tumble into the U.S.'s orbit. Americans were interested in Jamaican bauxite in the postwar period, but U.S. officials remained wary of Jamaican migrants as potential settlers. In the restrictionist immigration climate of the 1940s, Congress was not inclined to let European refugees or even concentration camp survivors into the U.S., let alone Jamaican farmworkers. In 1952, it became more difficult for Jamaicans to gain permanent entry to the U.S. (the McCarran-Walter Act having reduced Jamaica's annual immigration quota from one thousand immigrants a year to just one hundred).[72] Unable to settle in the U.S. as permanent, authorized immigrants, Jamaicans who had money saved from their wartime experience often boarded banana boats to England, taking advantage of their Britishness to settle in the metropole, at least until Britain's 1962 Commonwealth Act barred that gate as well. So much for the embrace of empire.

Jamaica occupied no strategic position for the United States, except eventually as a bulwark against communist Cuba. It was not a source of gold or oil or even sugar (the U.S. Sugar Act having divided the U.S. sugar market almost evenly between American and Cuban producers). Jamaica did, however, remain a source of guestworkers—"hired hands" with strong backs—who were willing to work in the United States for six months out of the year, some for twenty years running, without their families alongside them, any prospect of permanent residency, or a pension to retire on in their old age. "I work there," Samuel Brown said flatly of his years in the U.S., "and it grow them up."[73] This was a new sort of imperial dependency between two grossly unequal nations, one that permitted the U.S. to obtain labor from an imperial labor pool, without having to make good on any imperial responsibilities.

Jamaica's post–oil shock debt crisis only reinforced Jamaicans' dependence on temporary jobs in the United States. Never having received the aid Britain had promised in the thirties, the island's postindependence government had to borrow money to build high schools, a university, hospitals, and infrastructure projects neglected by Britain's waning Colonial Office. In the 1970s, however, the skyrocketing cost of oil, which Jamaica had to import, made those debts impossible to pay. The structural adjustment programs imposed since then by the U.S., the World Bank, and the IMF have forced Jamaica to devalue its currency and cut social spending. They required free trade agreements that opened Jamaican markets to cheap, subsidized farm products from the United States.

The glut of American milk, chicken, and fruit—while perhaps a boon to consumers—has left many Jamaican farmers without a livelihood, and thus with a desperate need to secure a recruitment ticket to "reach over" to the U.S. as guestworkers. Jamaica has been a captive economy. Its rural men are mobile and yet captive servants of U.S. agriculture.

From Belle Glade to Dubai

The similarities between guestworker programs and indentured servitude remain striking. Both allowed imperial powers to move people of color around the world—sometimes over great distances. Both offered opportunities for poor people to earn a livelihood abroad while also creating enormous opportunities for exploitation. Both prompted workers to travel under the rubric of temporary contracts that were rarely enforced.

At the same time, the differences seem just as striking. Britain's imperial bureaucracy may not have been particularly effective in protecting indentured servants, beyond giving migrants some sense of their rights as "loyal Britishers," but the guestworkers "reaching over" to the U.S. from Jamaica were protected neither by their own government nor by their host nation. "What do you get . . . when you go up there and work?" a Jamaican waitress/guestworker who worked in Virginia asked me. "Nothing," she continued, answering her own question. "[T]hey work everything to go back to them and you don't come home with nothing. . . . Everything they say is how it goes. They no negotiate nothing."[74] American officials had far more interest in enforcing the terms of foreign workers' contacts than colonial legislatures did in the nineteenth century, but they didn't. Sending governments have been just as toothless. The Raj and the supposedly feeble Ch'ing Dynasty wielded more power to protect their countrymen abroad than Jamaica did after World War II. In the end, though, it was what happened after workers' contracts expired that seems to have mattered most. The fact that guestworkers couldn't build up a permanent, legal, settler population meant they couldn't wield the rights of subjects or citizens in their own defense, as Indians in Natal did. Because they did not create politically mobilized and legally settled *immigrant* populations that could advocate for migrants, guestworker programs might even be said to be more exploitive than indentured servitude ever was.

And yet guestworker programs have spread around the world in recent years and in some places represent the principle way that nations admit workers. By 1985, for example, four Persian Gulf states had majority guestworker workforces, and the United Arab Emirates' population was over 90 percent guestworkers.[75] These new programs seem to have taken the privatized U.S. programs as their model. In the Middle East and the Pacific Rim, as in the U.S., guestworkers often pay large fees to recruiters for temporary visas, surrender the titles to their homes and their travel documents to recruiters or sponsors, and pay first-class rents for steerage housing. The yawning wealth gap between sending and receiving countries has only made it harder for sending countries to influence conditions.

The routes guestworkers travel, moreover, have strayed even further from imperial pathways. Today Filipinos work on temporary contracts from Tel Aviv to Montreal; South Asians migrants outnumber Arabs in some parts of the Middle East; and, although Mexicans once again dominate the American guestworker population, guestworkers come to the United States from as far away as Thailand and Peru. Modern contract labor schemes respect no imperial boundaries, nor traditional connections between metropole and periphery. Nor do nation-states or international courts have much say over the terms under which international labor migrants work. In the dying days of the British Empire, the U.S. adopted an imperial system of labor supply, freed it from the constraints of imperial regulation, and set it loose upon the world.

NOTES

1. Joseph Beaumont, *The New Slavery: An Account of the Indian and Chinese Immigrants in British Guiana* (London: W. Ridgway, 1871), 14.
2. The author would like to thank the National Humanities Center, the College of William & Mary, and all the scholars who read and commented on this article, including Reynolds Nelson Hahamovitch, Gunther Peck, Sumathi Ramaswamy, Tracy Banivanua Mar, Lucy Davies, Amelia Butler, Shellion Parris, Dwight Allen, Denise Camero and participants in the DC Working Class History Seminar, the Race, State, and Empire Seminar at the National Humanities Center, the Labor Seminar at UC Santa Barbara, Sally Deutsch's graduate class at Duke University, Sven Beckert and Christine Desan's classes at Harvard University, and the Social Science Research Seminar at Wake Forest University.
3. The term "guestworker" is a euphemism that rarely describes the way foreign contract workers are treated. It is a translation of the German "*gastarbeiter*," which was coined in the post–World War II period when millions of foreign

workers labored on contracts in West Germany. The new term was, no doubt, an attempt to distinguish Germany's postwar labor importation program from its very nasty prewar, Nazi-sponsored predecessors, in which foreign workers were known as *"fremdarbeiter,"* or "alien workers." See Cindy Hahamovitch, "Creating the Perfect Immigrants: Guestworkers of the World in Historical Perspective," *Labor History* 44, 1 (January 2003): 69–94.

4. Employer's memo in author's possession.

5. "Close to Slavery: Guestworker Programs in the United States," Southern Poverty Law Center, http://www.splcenter.org/get-informed/publications/close-to-slavery-guestworker-programs-in-the-united-states# (accessed June 1, 2013); Ron Soodalter and Kevin Bales, *The Slave Next Door: Human Trafficking and Slavery in America Today* (Berkeley: University of California Press, 2009), 263.

6. Jason DeParle, "A Good Provider is One Who Leaves," *New York Times*, April 22, 2007, Section 6, Column 1, Magazine, 50.

7. By signing an indenture bond, European migrants had their way paid, but they then owed their benefactor their labor and obedience for a period of years (usually five) during which they couldn't quit, leave, or marry without their masters' say-so. They could be resold and disciplined like slaves, but they had recourse to justices of the peace if they objected to their sale or if their punishment was excessive. At the end of the indenture period, they normally received some payment; men usually received a small plot of land in the early colonial period, and a suit of cloths and perhaps a musket toward the end. Enforceable in court, the indenture system kept arrivals, who might otherwise have squatted on whatever land they could find or sold their labor to the highest bidder, at work for the particular masters who had paid their way. Indentured servants' numbers kept rising until the American Revolution, although by that time the number of indentured servants had long been eclipsed by African slaves. David W. Galenson, "The Rise and Fall of Indentured Servitude in the Americas: An Economic Analysis," *Journal of Economic History* 44, 1 (1984): 1–26; Howard Lamar, "From Bondage to Contract. Ethnic Labor in the American West, 1600–1890," in Steven Hahn and Jonathan Prude, eds., *The Countryside in the Age of Capitalist Transformation. Essays in the Social History of Rural America* (Chapel Hill: University of North Carolina Press, 1985); Aaron S. Fogleman, "From Slaves, Convicts and Servants to Free Passengers: The Transformation of Immigration in the Era of the American Revolution," *Journal of American History* 85, 1 (June 1998): 43–76.

8. The origins of the word "coolie" are uncertain. One possibility is that the word referred to the Indian ethnic group Koḷī, since members of this group frequently worked as laborers or performed menial tasks. The Portuguese, who established a viceroyalty in India in the early sixteenth century, used *"cule"* to describe the labor they hired there and later in China. Some think the Tamil word *"kūli,"* which means "hire" and also payment for occasional work, is the most likely source. In all these usages, the word seems to refer simply to labor or at worst

menial labor, but in the nineteenth century the word "coolie" came to mean degraded or enslaved Asian labor and was often used offensively to describe Asians as a group. See *Oxford English Dictionary*, http://www.oed.com.proxy.wm.edu/view/Entry/40991?redirectedFrom=coolie#eid (accessed July 24, 2013).

9. Lord John Russell, February 15, 1840, cited in Hugh Tinker, *A New System of Slavery: The Export of Indian Labour Overseas, 1830–1920* (London: Oxford University Press, 1974), frontispiece.

10. See Anthony Kaye, "The Second Slavery: Modernity in the Nineteenth-Century South and the Atlantic World," *Journal of Southern History* 75 (August 2009): 627–50.

11. David Northrup says that most Europeans traveled freely and most Asians were bound, but Adam McKeown notes that indentured servants were only a fraction of Asian migrants in the nineteenth century. David Northrup, *Indentured Labor in the Age of Imperialism, 1838–1914* (Cambridge, UK: Cambridge University Press, 1995), 8–9; Adam McKeown, *Melancholy Order: Asian Migration and the Globalization of Borders* (New York: Columbia University Press, 2008), 45.

12. In 1843 Indian slavery was "delegalized" but not abolished, which meant masters no longer had rights but nothing changed unless slaves took the initiative to free themselves. Richard Huzzey, *Freedom Burning: Anti-Slavery and Empire in Victorian Britain* (Ithaca, NY: Cornell University Press, 2012), 178.

13. Madhavi Kale, *Fragments of Empire: Capital, Slavery, and Indian Indentured Labor Migration in the British Caribbean* (Philadelphia: University of Pennsylvania Press, 1998), 16. See also Richard B. Allen, *Slaves, Freedmen, and Indentured Laborers in Colonial Mauritius* (Cambridge, UK: Cambridge University Press, 2006), 13–17;

14. My italics. Kale, *Fragments of Empire*, 13–19. The quote is on 14.

15. Kale, *Fragments of Empire*, 14.

16. Kale, *Fragments of Empire*, 14–16; Tinker, *A New System of Slavery*, 17.

17. Douglas Hay notes that British labor wasn't entirely free either in the nineteenth century. Penal sanctions were under attack by trade unions by the 1840s but they were still invoked. However, British workers found to have violated labor contracts were far more likely to be held responsible for damages than imprisoned or flogged. "England, 1562–1875: The Law and its Uses," 59–116, in Paul Craven and Douglas Hay, eds., *Masters, Servants, and Magistrates in Britain and the Empire, 1562–1955* (Chapel Hill: University of North Carolina Press, 2004), 103.

18. "Introduction," in Craven and Hay, eds., *Masters, Servants, and Magistrates*, 24–26. The quoted material is on 26.

19. Allen, *Slaves, Freedmen*, 17; Walton Look Lai, *Indentured Labor, Caribbean Sugar: Chinese and Indian Migrants to the British West Indies, 1838–1918* (Baltimore: Johns Hopkins University Press, 1993), 19.

20. Kale, *Fragments of Empire*, 17–18.

21. Kale, *Fragments of Empire*, 20–22, 27; Huzzey, *Freedom Burning*, 179–80.

22. Howard Temperley, *British Antislavery: 1833–1870* (London: Longman Group, 1972), 124–27.

23. Huzzey, *Freedom Burning*, 1–20.

24. Tinker, *A New System of Slavery*, 73–74; Temperley, *British Antislavery*, 130–31; Suzanne Miers, *Slavery in the Twentieth Century: The Evolution of a Global Problem* (New York: Altamira Press, 2003), 6–7.

25. Clem Seecharan, *Bechu: "Bound Coolie"Rradical in British Guiana, 1894–1901* (Kingston, Jamaica: University of the West Indies Press, 1999), 51.

26. Jason C. Parker, *Brother's Keeper: The United States, Race, and Empire in the British Caribbean, 1937–1962* (New York: Oxford University Press, 2008), 5.

27. How many millions is a matter of dispute. Northrup's estimate of two million is conservative, according to Jayetta Sharma, because it counts only the official indentures approved by British officials in India. Her estimate of ten million includes informally recorded arrangements and migration from other places. The number would be higher still if we included indentured servants who did not cross oceans, like the one million laborers moved by the British from central India to tea plantations in Assam. See Jayeeta Sharma, *Empire's Garden: Assam and the Making of India* (Durham, NC: Duke University Press, 2011); Northrup, *Indentured Labor*, 44.

28. The best discussion of contracted European labor in the United States is Gunther Peck, *Reinventing Free Labor: Padrones and Immigrant Workers in the North American West, 1885–1930* (Cambridge, UK: Cambridge University Press, 2000).

29. Northrup, *Indentured Labor*, 8–9; Tyler Anbinder, "From Famine to Five Points: Lord Lansdowne's Irish Tenants Encounter North America's Most Notorious Slum," *American Historical Review* 107 (April 2002): 351–87.

30. Secharran, *Bechu*, 28, 40–41; Allen, *Slaves, Freedmen*, 68.

31. Kale, *Fragments of Empire*, 22; Tinker, *A New System of Slavery*, frontispiece.

32. Tinker, *A New System of Slavery*, xiv–xv, 247.

33. Marina Carter and Khal Torabully, *Coolitude: An Anthology of the Indian Labour Diaspora* (London: Anthem Press, 2002), 17–44.

34. Secharran, *Bechu*, 71.

35. Carter and Torabully, *Coolitude*, 34–35.

36. Allen, *Slaves, Freedmen*, 60; M. K. Banton, "The Colonial Office, 1820–1955," 251–302, in Craven and Hay, eds. *Masters, Servants, and Magistrates*

37. Tinker, *A New System of Slavery*, 109, 314–16.

38. Deemed too weak to cut cane, Bechu assisted the driver for over a year but he experienced repeated bouts of fever. Eventually, he was made a house servant, during which he "availed himself 'of every opportunity to read,'" with his employer's permission. Secharran, *Bechu*, 2–92.

39. Allen, *Slaves, Freedmen*, 72–73.

40. Barred from recruiting indentured servants, Caribbean employers again sought new sources of labor once again, which led to a strange reversal of migration trends by the turn of the twentieth century. Thus Black West Indians built the Panama Canal, cleared forests for railroads in Central America, drilled for oil in Venezuela, and worked on all manner of plantations in Central America,

including the banana plantations owned by United Fruit, described in this volume by Jason Colby. Interestingly, wherever they worked, they would assert their rights as British subjects in the face of discrimination and exploitation, and, as Lara Putnam shows, when the British failed to defend those rights, they crafted a new pan-African and anti-imperial identity. Elizabeth Thomas-Hope, "The Establishment of a Migration Tradition: British West Indian Movements to the Hispanic Caribbean in the Century After Emancipation," in Colin G. Clarke, ed., *Caribbean Social Relations*, Monograph Series, No. 8 (Liverpool: Centre for Latin American Studies, 1978), 68; Lara Putnam, *The Company They Kept: Migrants and the Politics of Gender in Caribbean Costa Rica, 1870–1960* (Chapel Hill: University of North Carolina Press, 2002), and *Radical Moves: Caribbean Migrants and the Politics of Race in the Jazz Age* (Chapel Hill: University of North Carolina Press, 2013); Julie Greene, *The Canal Builders: Making America's Empire at the Panama Canal* (New York: Penguin Publishing, 2009).

41. Marilyn Lake and Henry Reynolds, *Drawing the Global Colour Line: White Men's Countries and the International Challenge of Racial Equality* (New York: Cambridge University Press, 2008).

42. A third early program was born in Prussia in 1890 as a state-brokered compromise between planters, who demanded renewed access to Polish workers, and nativists who demanded the exclusion of Poles from German society. The solution Bismarck crafted allowed for the Poles' return but only on temporary contracts that cycled them in and out of the country and discouraged their integration into German society. Race would seem to have nothing to do with the Prussian example but Germans described Poles in much the same terms that European settlers described "coolies." See Ulrich Herbert, *A History of Foreign Labor in Germany, 1880–1980: Seasonal Workers, Forced Laborers, Guest Workers* (Ann Arbor: University of Michigan Press, 1990); Hahamovitch, "Creating the Perfect Immigrants."

43. Rob Turrell, "Kimberley's Model Compounds," *Journal of African History* 25, 1 (January 1984): 59–75; Francis Wilson, *Labour in the South African Gold Mines, 1911–1969* (London: Cambridge University Press, 1972), 1, 3–5, 10–14; Jonathan Crush, Alan Jeeves, and David Yudelman, *South Africa's Labor Empire: A History of Black Migrancy to the Gold Mines* (Boulder, CO: Westview Press, 1991), 1–32.

44. See Tracey Banivanua Mar, "Bulimaen and Hard Work Indenture, Identity and Complexity in Colonial North Queensland" (Ph.D. dissertation, University of Melbourne, 2000); Edward Wybergh Docker, *The Blackbirders: The Recruiting of South Seas Labour for Queensland, 1863–1907* (Sydney: Angus & Robertson, 1970); James Jupp, *Immigration* (New York: Oxford University Press, 1991), 41–51; *Cairns Morning Post*, March 9, 1906, and January 8, 1907.

45. Hahamovitch, "Creating the Perfect Immigrants."

46. For other examples, see Cindy Hahamovitch, *The Fruits of Their Labor: Atlantic Coast Farmworkers and the Making of Migrant Poverty, 1870–1945* (Chapel Hill: University of North Carolina Press, 1997), 171–72.

47. Telegrams, Office of Labor, FSA Correspondence, 1943–44, box 75, file: 4-FLT-R57, RG 224, NARA.

48. Albert A. Blum, "The Farmer, the Army, and the Draft," *Agricultural History* 38, 1 (January 1964): 40; Hahamovitch, *Fruits*, 138–39; Cindy Hahamovitch, *No Man's Land: Jamaican Guestworkers in America and the Global History of Deportable Labor* (Princeton, NJ: Princeton University Press, 2011), 37.

49. Stanley's resistance may also have been partly motivated by politics as the U.S. and the British were in the midst of a war of wills over the future of the Caribbean. British imperialists, among them Winston Churchill and Stanley himself, were determined to hold onto Britain's empire in the aftermath of the war. Already discomfited at having to accept American bases in the British Caribbean and cranky about the U.S.'s refusal to silence West Indian anti-imperial activists in New York, Stanley would have been happy to point out American failings in the Jim Crow South and the absence of formal segregation in Jamaica. Parker, *Brother's Keeper*, 41.

50. Raymond H. Beers, Immigration Inspector, to Inspector in Charge, INS, Miami, December 9, 1941, NARA, RG 85, 85–58A734, Box 2087, File 56078/477.

51. L. L. Chandler to Senators Claude Pepper, Charles O. Andrews, and Representative Pat Cannon, June 24, 1942, 85–58A734, File 56078 /477, Box 2087, RG, 85, NARA.

52. ILO conventions weren't international laws but rather guidelines that individual countries were urged to endorse. The U.S. has endorsed few. Telegram from Secretary of State for the Colonies to Barbados, Windward Islands, Leewards, Trinidad and Jamaica, April 20, 1943, PRO, CO 859, 12261/1/43, Conditions of Employment and International Labour Conventions, West Indies; AACC to Secretary of State for the Colonies, March 20, 1943, PRO, CO 318, 448/10, Recruitment of Labour for U.S.; *Daily Gleaner* (Kingston, Jamaica), 1 April 1943.

53. Telegram from Secretary of State for the Colonies to Barbados, Windward Islands, Leewards, Trinidad and Jamaica, April 20, 1943, PRO, CO 859, 12261/1/43, Conditions of Employment and International Labour Conventions, West Indies; AACC to Secretary of State for the Colonies, March 20, 1943, PRO, CO 318, 448/10, Recruitment of Labour for U.S.; Cindy Hahamovitch, "'In America Life Is Given Away': Jamaican Farmworkers and the Making of Agricultural Immigration Policy," 134–60, in Catherine McNicol Stock and Robert D. Johnston, eds., *The Countryside in the Age of the Modern State: Political Histories of Rural America* (Ithaca, NY: Cornell University Press, 2001).

54. Half of all the cultivated land in Jamaica was divided among just fourteen hundred mostly foreign landowners, the bulk of them American and British corporations. Eric Williams, *The Negro in the Caribbean* (Washington, DC: Associates in Negro Folk Education, 1942), 49; Frank Fonda Taylor, *To Hell with Paradise: A History of the Jamaican Tourist Industry* (Pittsburgh: University of Pittsburgh Press, 1993), 37–43.

55. *Amsterdam News*, June 5, 1943, p. 13; James W. Vann, August 1942, general correspondence, box 16, file RP-M-85–183, monthly reports, RG 96, NARA; correspondence, 1943–44, box 75, file 4-FLT-R57, RG 224, NARA.

56. Parliamentary debates (Hansard), Great Britain, Parliament, House of Lords, v. 166, p. 475.

57. Jamaican women were excluded because by the time the Jamaican program was approved, some of the Bahamian women who had been allowed to participate had become pregnant in the United States. Not wanting to allow temporary workers' children to be born U.S. citizens, the INS had moved to deport them, which inspired several to seek abortions. Horrified, the INS banned women. Hahamovitch, *No Man's Land*, 3.

58. AACC to Secretary of State for the Colonies, March 20, 1943, PRO, CO 318, 448/10.

59. Leaford C. Williams, *Journey into Diplomacy: A Black Man's Shocking Discovery—A Memoir* (Presque Isle, ME: Northeast Publishing House, 1996), 76–78, 60.

60. Transcript of July 2, 1944, letter to the editor in PRO, CO 318, 460/1.

61. Fay Clarke Johnson, *Soldiers of the Soil* (New York: Vantage Press, 1995), 63–64.

62. Hahamovitch, *No Man's Land*, 64.

63. *Amsterdam News*, November 6, 1943, p. 7-B.

64. See *Panama City* (Florida) *News Herald*, August 28, 1945; *Stuart News*, September 6, 1945; *Palm Beach Post*, August 29, 1945, p. 2.

65. *Pittsburgh Courier*, October 26, 1943.

66. Kramer, *The Offshores: A Study of Foreign Farm Labor in the U.S.* (St. Petersburg, FL: Community Action Fund, 1966), 39.

67. Johnson, *Soldiers of the Soil*, 38–39.

68. Hahamovitch, *No Man's Land*, 101.

69. Under the terms of the privatized program, Caribbean farmworkers came to the United States on chartered planes and worked off their airfare in the fields. Employers paid workers' return fare, but only if they completed the season without incident, making airfare a tool of labor discipline.

70. The Mexican guestworker program, which lasted only until 1964, remained under U.S. control at Mexico's insistence, however Congress allocated no funds to enforce *braceros*' contracts, so that program too was effectively privatized.

71. Hahamovitch, *No Man's Land*.

72. The act reauthorized the temporary admission of "non-immigrants," but it made no provision for the immigration of foreign farmworkers on a permanent basis, despite growers' insistence that they needed farm labor. The new law excluded all workers unless the Department of Labor deemed them necessary, while simultaneously creating a preference for applicants who had "high education, technical training, specialized experience, or exceptional ability." They and their families were allotted 50 percent of the quota spots. The other 50 percent went to the immediate relatives of citizens and lawfully admitted aliens. Without a special

preference, the unskilled, the category into which farmworkers were regularly lumped, would join a long list of excluded categories, below psychopaths, drug addicts, lepers, professional beggars, polygamists, prostitutes, and convicts. Sec. 203, *U.S. Statutes at Large*, 1952, Vol. 66, 82nd Cong., 163–282.

73. Samuel Brown (name changed by request), interviewed by Cindy Hahamovitch and Lindsey Allen, Effort, Clarendon Parish, Jamaica, July 26, 2003.

74. Sandra Brown (name changed by request), interviewed by Cindy Hahamovitch, Effort, Clarendon Parish, Jamaica, January 26, 2003.

75. I have discussed the massive, post–World War II European guestworker programs, which started out highly exploitive but improved over time, in Hahamovitch, "Creating the Perfect Immigrant."

PART IV

Imperial Labor and Control in the Tropics

10

The Colonization of Antislavery and the Americanization of Empires

The Labor of Autonomy and the Labor of Subordination in Togo and the United States

ANDREW ZIMMERMAN

In the first decade of the twentieth century, the German colony of Togo, in West Africa, employed graduates and a faculty member from Booker T. Washington's Tuskegee Institute as part of an agricultural development program.[1] Their immediate purpose was to transform Togolese cotton growing from a small economic sector that supported local spinning and weaving into a large monocropping sector for the export of raw cotton to European mills. It was thus a classic case of what Andre Gunder Frank called the "development of underdevelopment."[2] The Tuskegee expedition members were the first to develop a cotton varietal that would grow well in Africa and whose fibers could be used along with fibers from the United States in the finely calibrated spinning machinery of European mills.[3] This set the stage for the wave of colonial cotton projects that followed, as well, arguably, as today's West African cotton industry. The cotton project also helped the German state and missionaries break the ability of Togolese households to resist colonial domination by forcing Africans to grow a crop with enormous labor requirements and little value for growers. As an agricultural and as a social experiment, the expedition was, in the view of British, French, Belgian, and South African colonial observers, an extraordinary success. It set the stage for a host of imitations and adaptations of Tuskegee in Africa throughout the first decades of the twentieth century and beyond.

The work of Tuskegee Institute in Togo reveals a geography of U.S. imperialism more broad, and an imperial history more deep, than that of the territories subjected to formal U.S. state sovereignty after 1898.

The overlapping economic, political, and cultural dimensions of empire brought multiple imperial actors into territories formally subjected to a single imperial state. The development and implementation of capitalist labor systems occupied European colonizers on the ground to a greater extent than interimperialist squabbles about colonial borders or even the dubious treaties of protection concluded with local political elites. The United States played a central role in the development of these colonial labor systems in many European colonies and thus had an imperial reach far beyond the territories over which the Stars and Stripes flew. The counterrevolution of 1877, when Reconstruction ended and white elites in states of the former Confederacy recouped much of the power they had lost with the abolition of slavery, represented the global face of the U. S. at least as much as the more celebrated revolution of 1776.

The United States was an especially important colonial model because it had successfully dealt with precisely the problem that brought European colonizers to Africa in the nineteenth century: how to devise forms of coercion that would allow white elites to continue exploiting black labor even after the end of slavery.[4] Slaving had long connected the Americas and West Africa, and the post-emancipation labor regimes devised in the American South were instances of a larger structural reorientation of Atlantic capitalism from bonded to formally free labor. From the founding of Sierra Leone in the late eighteenth century to the British conquest of Lagos in 1861 to the convening of the Berlin West Africa conference of 1884–85, European imperialists claimed to combat slavery in Africa while in fact depending on varieties of coercion, including slavery.[5] Post-emancipation forms of racial coercion were the core of European colonial efforts in Africa, as they were of many white efforts in the American South. While many, both critics and apologists, have frequently suggested that the New South order of segregation, disfranchisement, sharecropping, and racial terror was backward, a holdover from slavery, many others at the time, from New South boosters to European colonial others, saw the region's racial regime of labor control as an admirable modern feature, one that might be profitably applied to parts of the world.[6] Germans were the first to bring the New South to Africa in a literal way, by employing African American educators from Tuskegee Institute to try to reproduce U.S. cotton growing in Togo.

Like post-emancipation labor-coercive regimes in the U.S. South, the European colonial regimes in West Africa did not result from antislavery policy initiatives, but rather from elite attempts to coopt prior successful rebellions against slavery by the enslaved themselves. While the Civil War was perhaps, as Steven Hahn has suggested, "the greatest slave rebellion in modern history," African Americans were not alone in this mid-century worldwide rebellion against unfree labor.[7] It also included Togolese resistance to Asante slaving and, on a larger scale, a wave of slave uprisings that spread from the Niger Delta port town of Calabar in the 1850s.[8] White elites sought to use these uprisings to further their own geopolitical interests by establishing colonial authority in the name of antislavery while ensuring that black freedom from slavery did not mean black freedom from the labor demands of white capital.

European imperialism in Africa thus came to resemble the "counterrevolution of property" that W.E.B. Du Bois identified in the post-Reconstruction United States. This counterrevolution by white elites, according to Du Bois, subverted much of the democratic potential of what he termed the "general strike" by which enslaved workers emancipated themselves during the U.S. Civil War.[9] Similarly, Africans resisting slavery created a variety of noncolonial, noncapitalist economic and political forms that would also prove hostile to the new forms of economic exploitation and political domination that Europeans offered as alternatives to slavery. European imperialism fought much more vigorously against such African forms of economic autonomy than it did against African slavery. The post–Civil War United States was an instance of, a central participant in, and model for this process because, from the perspective of white capitalist elites, the United States had successfully navigated an end to slavery without overturning hierarchies of class or race.

The Tuskegee personnel who came to German Togo did not understand their task in precisely these terms, but rather through a discourse of "racial uplift" that many colonial and U.S. elites nonetheless regarded as accommodation to white supremacy. Leading the expedition was James Nathan Calloway, a faculty member in the Tuskegee agriculture department who had graduated from Fisk University in 1890. John Winfrey Robinson, who had graduated from Tuskegee in 1897, accompanied Calloway. After graduation, Robinson had taught school in Alabama for a year before returning to Tuskegee to do postgraduate work in agriculture, likely with Calloway and George Washington Carver, the famous head of the institute's agriculture department. Robinson would soon become the leader of the expedition. Also on the expedition were Allen Lynn Burks, a recent graduate in agriculture from Tuskegee, and Shepherd Lincoln Harris, who had come to Tuskegee from Union, Georgia, in 1886 to study mechanics, but had never graduated.

The political and other motivations behind the Tuskegee expedition to Togo were as fraught as those behind the creation of Tuskegee Institute itself. Tuskegee imparted a great deal of authority to a few African Americans, especially Booker T. Washington, by seeming, at least, to accept the disfranchisement and economic subordination of the great majority of African Americans. The Tuskegee expedition to German Togo represented an international version of this strategy. For Du Bois, Washington did not simply accommodate himself to the measures by which African Americans were kept economically and politically subordinate, but rather "helped their speedier accomplishment."[10] Some historians have challenged this view, and argued that Washington did in fact seek to improve the situation of the majority of African Americans, albeit in ways constrained by the terrible racism of the American New South.[11] Elsewhere I have argued that his work with German imperialism helped transform Washington from a cautious challenger of white domination into the accommodationist criticized by Du Bois and many others.[12] Tuskegee shares this ambivalence of coercion and liberation with virtually all liberal enterprises, whether colonial or metropolitan, whose founding moment was a defeat and cooptation of prior democratic revolutions.

A transnational labor history of slavery and emancipation reveals a nineteenth-century system of overlapping empires in which the United States played a central role long before its formal colonial acquisitions in 1898. But placing labor at the center of our histories also requires that we decenter empires, for the labor of empire consists not, in the first place, of the machinations of American and European managerial and technical elites but rather of the labor of specific African societies. Writing a labor history of nineteenth-century empire means treating empire as an emergent product of local counterrevolutions of property. African histories were not simply settings for histories of European and U.S. empire; rather, European and U.S. imperialisms were episodes in African histories. To treat the histories of empires apart from the African histories with which they intersected would be to reproduce, rather than to critically comprehend, the categories of empire.[13]

Thus, rather than beginning with American or European imperial concepts and efforts, this essay begins in Tove, the group of six villages about sixty miles from the coast in the German colony of Togo where the Tuskegee expedition would begin its work in 1901. It begins neither with the arrival of Tuskegee personnel in the region, nor even with the 1884 German declaration of sovereignty over Togo, but rather with the longer struggle of Toveers for autonomy, first against Asante and Atlantic slaving and only later against German colonialism and the colonial application of the American New South.

Power and Production in Tove between the Atlantic Slave Trade and Colonial Rule

Tove was a polity of the Ewe, the largest ethnic group in southern Togo and the southeastern Gold Coast (Ghana today). Tove and other Ewe polities were on the western edge of the Bight of Benin, that section of the West African coast between the Volta River and the Niger Delta once known to Europeans as the Slave Coast. The societies of the region shared many social and cultural features and spoke mutually intelligible languages that historians now classify as Gbe.[14] The Gbe suffered the most severe population decline of any region of Africa affected by the Atlantic slave trade. The especially high demand for men, moreover, skewed the gender balance in the region until the second half of the nineteenth century.[15] In spite of this devastation, Gbe societies developed economic, political, and religious practices that facilitated a centuries-long struggle against enslavement and enabled their resistance to colonial rule. Not simply in their enslaved bodies, but also in their political and intellectual practices, the Gbe were as transnational as any European society—arguably more so than the Germans who would later come to colonize them.[16]

Perhaps the best known contribution of Gbe to transnational intellectual and political cultures was the religious practices of Vodun, which slaves brought from the Bight of Benin to the French sugar colony of St. Domingue. In the eighteenth century, slave traders took almost half of those captured from the Bight of Benin to the Caribbean island, where they made up about a quarter of the enslaved population.[17] The Vodun these enslaved Gbe brought with them to St. Domingue proved central to the revolution of 1791–1804, when free and enslaved blacks defeated both slavery and French colonialism and achieved independence for the island under its present name, Haiti.[18] The Ewe, including those in Tove, would later employ other Gbe religious practices, especially the Yewe secret society, to organize and support their resistance against German colonialism.

A decentralized political authority and a diverse and diffuse household economy aided Ewe resistance to both slaving and to colonialism.[19] Several Ewe women shared a single husband and could each possess their own households and fields, which were linked to those of their husbands through gift and market exchange. Missionaries and colonial officials would later remark, mostly with dismay, upon the unusual independence of Ewe women. Labor was divided by gender, with certain crops and tasks considered appropriate for men, others for women. Only women grew, spun, and dyed cotton, while only men could learn to weave the yarn into cloth. (The Ewe cotton textile industry helped lend plausibility to German plans for exporting cotton as a raw material from the colony, an economic transformation that, like many others in colonialism, helped shift high-value production from Africa to Europe.) Ewe households could also hold slaves, although the scale of production made this a society with slaves rather than a slave society. While the Ewe political economy was hardly classless or an idyllic "merrie olde Africa," it did afford many of its members a greater degree of political and economic autonomy than existed in Atlantic slave economies or, arguably, in the capitalist free labor economies of Europe.

The Ewe were able to take advantage of the growing world demand for palm oil to support their economic autonomy, even while, in other parts of West Africa, the new demand led to the expansion of slave labor to produce this valuable cash crop.[20] Oil palms grow freely in much of West Africa, and, while they can be improved by cultivation, oil can also be collected and processed by individuals from wild palms. Palm oil had numerous industrial uses in Europe, from machine lubrication to soap making to the fabrication of smokeless gunpowder. Palm oil also had a great many uses in Africa, both in various manufacturing processes and as an important component of local cuisine. Individual Ewe could harvest palm oil on their own account and choose between consuming it, selling it locally, or selling it to European merchants on the coast, who competed with each other and thus offered a relatively high price.

The political and economic autonomy of Tove was further enhanced by its specialized pottery industry. Earthenware was one of the most important household goods in Togo, used for water collection, storage, washing, and other purposes, and ranging widely in size and price.[21] Because pottery is heavy and unwieldy relative to its value, it was immune from foreign competition from European or Hausa manufacturers. Pottery production in Tove was an industry, moreover, like cotton growing and spinning, dominated by women. Workers in the Tove pottery industry gathered clay locally with relatively few tools, so individuals did not have to acquire particular wealth or hire themselves out to others in order to participate in it. Pottery production thus further supported the diffuse household political economy that would support resistance to outside domination.

The Ewe combatted slave raiding by the Kingdom of Asante, in the neighboring Gold Coast, well before the arrival of the German colonial state in West Africa. Indeed, many of the strategies they employed against Germans may have first been used against the Asante. With the decline of the Atlantic slave trade in the nineteenth century, former slave-exporting African states began exploiting slave labor on their own account, often to produce the staple crops that European colonists and missionaries proclaimed to be the legitimate alternative to slave exports. As the westernmost Gbe group, the Ewe were especially subject to Asante slaving, which continued to demand slaves as tribute even as European demand dwindled. Historian Donna J. E. Maier has described "an escalating battle between popular resistance and Asante retaliation" going back to the 1820s and culminating in the 1869–71 Asante invasion of Eweland.[22] The decentralized nature of their polity and economy made Ewe resistance sporadic and diffuse. Part of Tove's strategy against the Asante also included switching sides several times to avoid ever fighting on the losing side of the war.[23] Protestant missionaries from the North German Mission Society of Bremen, already predisposed against Tove, later registered these moves simply as cowardice or betrayal, but such flexibility also offered some of the few possibilities for resistance to stronger states, whether Asante or German. As one Ewe military leader, Ahoto, reportedly boasted to an invading Asante army demanding surrender: "The tortoise in the bush is an experienced animal, and until now no bird with his beak has been able to affect him. He can break a beak to pieces."[24]

While colonial ethnographies have encouraged us to regard precolonial societies like the Ewe as premodern or autochthonous, they in fact emerged at the same time, and out of the same political economic conjuncture, as many other Atlantic communities and social movements. The Ewe, like many contemporary African, American, and European groups, experimented with economic, gender, and political structures in hopes of deriving a form that would help them achieve and preserve autonomy in an increasingly confining capitalist world. Colonial attacks on Ewe political economy can thus be understood as part of a much larger counterattack by capital and the state on the human freedoms won in the round of revolutions of the late eighteenth and early nineteenth centuries. Ewe organization of power and production proved a relatively strong political order that also preserved much individual and household autonomy. The Ewe, and the Toveers especially, would adapt the political, military, and economic strategies they had employed against Asante slavers for use against German colonists.

The German War on Tove

In contrast to their relatively passive defense against the Asante in 1869–71, Toveers used their position on a major north-south route to offer stiff resistance to German attempts to expand their authority in Togo beyond the coastline. After Germany declared Togo a protectorate in 1884, the Tove villages rarely raised the red-white-and-black imperial flag that would signify their acceptance of German "protection." When the German official Curt von François visited Tove in 1888, the inhabitants welcomed him by brandishing their weapons and firing warning shots at his tent.[25] Later, although the Toveers could not prevent Germans from stopping on north-south journeys, leaders generally refused to greet them and locals charged exorbitant prices for food and lodging.[26]

As the Gbe-derived practice of Vodun facilitated political resistance against European colonialism and slavery in St. Domingue (Haiti), the

Yewe secret society, another Gbe religious practice, facilitated resistance to European colonialism in Tove, as well as in other parts of Eweland.[27] Tove was a stronghold of the Yewe secret society, and, according to local missionaries, villagers shunned the few residents who did not belong to the society.[28] German colonists generally regarded all Ewe religious practices, which they termed "fetishism," as a challenge to their own political authority and economic power, which they termed "civilization." As an early observer declared: "The fetish, an enemy of all civilization [*Kultur*], sees in the intrusion of civilization its own decline. It [thus] has every reason to incense the people against the intrusion of European goods and to place hindrances in the way of foreigners."[29] The Yewe society was an especially challenging religious practice to European political and economic authority. The name "Yewe" referred not to the *trōwo* (gods, or "fetishes") that the society venerated, but rather to the secrecy of the society itself. The Yewe society was thought to have come to the Ewe from Dahomey at the end of the nineteenth century, at the time when newly expansive European colonial states came to compete with local powers. The Yewe society established local compounds or courts that only its initiates could enter. Members received new names, learned to speak a secret language, and were forbidden, on pain of death, to reveal anything that occurred in these compounds. The society, Europeans recognized, posed a challenge to the colonial state.

Even after the German state established a station at Misahöhe, north of Tove, the road connecting Misahöhe to the coastal capital of Lomé remained partly in the control of Toveers, who resisted incursions by Germans into their territory as much as feasible. Hans Gruner, the head of the Misahöhe district for most of the German colonial period, soon found occasion to establish military control of the region.[30] In 1895, Toveers harassed the botanist Ernst Baumann while he conducted research on nearby Mount Agu. Toveers who belonged to the Yewe society believed the peak should be mounted only by their priests. Given the close interconnection of the Yewe society and resistance to colonialism, defending this religious restriction also meant defending a basis of political autonomy. Upon returning to the Misahöhe station, Baumann sent out troops to arrest his tormentors. Residents of one of the Tove villages, Tove-Dzigbe, attacked Baumann's troops and managed to free their prisoners. This led to a full-scale uprising, during which the Toveers controlled the north-south road for several weeks, long enough that supplies ran out at the German station Kete-Krachi, farther to the north.[31]

The German government sent out more troops from the south to join Hans Gruner and his Misahöhe troops. The German force killed many Toveers, wounded many others, destroyed five of the six Tove villages, and laid waste to their farms and houses.[32] Apparently German officers decapitated some of the corpses and sent the heads to Germany. (There they were likely studied by anthropologists, who encouraged such battlefield trophy taking, which provided data and museum displays in support of the racial categorizing that, in part, justified to the European public such massacres in the first place).[33] The Germans meted out punishments to all the men, probably floggings and forced labor, and seized as tribute whatever property they had not already destroyed.

Germans made a particular point of destroying the local pottery industry by breaking ceramics and driving away the villagers. Four years later, a visiting German found the former village of Tove-Dzigbe, where the uprising had begun, consisting only of "ruins jutting forth from the weeds." He did note that some Toveers were returning in hopes of resuming "their handicraft, the pottery that was once known far and wide."[34] For years after the uprising, the destruction was still evident in the area, with collapsing, empty houses and shattered pottery along the road.[35] By 1902 missionaries reported that women no longer earned their livings from pottery, and even in 1974 a visiting British historian reported that "[p]eople still tell in Togo of the smashing of local pottery to create a market for the German imported hardware—and show the broken potsherds to prove it."[36] The Germans established a garrison in the Tove area with a German officer and a hundred African soldiers recruited from other parts of Togo.[37]

Through their superior military force, the German colonial state was able to destroy the pottery industry that had sustained the independence of Tove for decades and hindered the spread of foreign capital and political power north along the caravan route through Tove. In 1896, German merchants set up their first warehouse near Misahöhe, the station that had been cut off by the Toveers during the 1895 war. By 1902 the market offered "flour from Minnesota, ham from Chicago, butter from Denmark, and canned fruits from California."[38] Now that the German state had destroyed a form of labor that had sustained resistance to colonial rule, it sought to bring to the wrecked and abandoned villages of Tove a form of labor that would sustain colonial rule itself. To do so it would turn to the cotton growing labor of the American New South that had been "redeemed" by white supremacists from the black equality promised by the Civil War and Reconstruction.

An American Response to a Colonial Problem

Having destroyed much of Tove, German colonial officials set about recreating it in a manner more suited to their political and economic aims. Hans Gruner, the Misahöhe officer responsible for the massacres in the 1895 Tove war, declared that "the value of a colony" depended upon a "numerous, hard-working population."[39] A "numerous, hard-working population" was precisely what Gruner had helped drive out of Tove, and his understanding of labor was clearly something different from, for example, the pottery industry that he had wrecked. German colonial rule in Togo and elsewhere proceeded at least as much through instituting certain types of labor as it did on military conquest.[40] Indeed, each new military conquest, including the one at Tove, delivered prisoners whom the Germans compelled to work. Gruner expected local leaders to turn over the "work-shy, the vagabonds, the habitual thieves and the like" to German officials who would place them in "reform settlements."[41] One of the watchwords of German colonialism was "educating of the Negro to work" (*Erziehung des Negers zur Arbeit*), and discussions of this topic often cited the postslavery American South as a positive model.[42] One kind of labor had enabled Ewe resistance; a new kind, Gruner hoped, would enable German domination. This was the kind of labor that German colonial officials identified in the post-Reconstruction American South, especially as it was ideally represented by Tuskegee Institute. Thus, Gruner enthusiastically welcomed the four members of the Tuskegee expedition when they arrived in Togo in January 1901 to, in the words of the German who arranged the expedition, "teach the negroes there how to plant and harvest cotton in a rational and scientific way."[43]

Booker T. Washington sent the Tuskegee expedition to Togo from a mistaken, but common belief among many white and black Americans that Africa was primitive in comparison to the United States, and that to make Africa more like the United States, even during one of the worst periods of American racism, was to improve it.[44] Africa, in this view, was so backward in every respect that working with the colonial state to make it more like the American South, for all the obvious racism and other deficiencies of both, was still an improvement. The idea that American slavery, for all its brutality, had improved African Americans both culturally and as workers was common among many policy makers and social scientists, and many hoped that colonialism would impart the supposedly beneficial lessons of U.S. slavery in free labor economies in Africa. For example, the U.S. sociologist and Tuskegee publicist Robert E. Park explained that Africans would have "to serve a long and hard apprenticeship to Europe, an apprenticeship not unlike that which Negroes in America underwent in slavery." Tuskegee might help, Park offered, "to abridge this apprenticeship of the younger to the older races, or at least to make it less cruel and inhuman than it now frequently is."[45] The German Colonial Office shared these sentiments, adding that Africans held in "correct political distance from whites" and directed on a course of "cultural development" with a "practical, economical direction" might actually become better cotton growers than "the more civilized Negro in the United States."[46] While Booker T. Washington and the Tuskegee expedition members surely must have seen through some of this rhetoric about the U.S. South, white belief in this rhetoric also won them a great deal of influence and support. The Jim Crow South was no international embarrassment in the years before the First World War, but rather a model of racial order that was an important element of U.S. global influence.

For many colonial officials in Togo, cotton farming represented an especially effective means of undermining African political and economic autonomy, driving Africans into the state of efficient racial and economic subordination in which they believed African Americans lived and that they hoped to introduce in Togo. The Colonial Economic Committee, the organization sponsoring the Tuskegee expedition, offered that introducing cotton cultivation for the world market would bolster the power of the German state in Togo, making the Togolese "economically dependent upon us," and thus making the Germans "finally the real masters" of Togo.[47] That cotton was not profitable for Togolese growers, especially in comparison to many other opportunities that existed before the onset of colonial rule, would be praised by some as an advantage of the staple. Paul Rohrbach, for example, a colonial liberal, advocated cotton growing for all Africans because, even if African farmers produced as much as colonialists desired, it brought growers so little that it would not provide them with wealth that might become "a means of political resistance [*Widersetzlichkeit*]."[48] Rohrbach singled out the Tuskegee efforts in Togo for special praise in this regard.

The colonial transformation of work in Tove not only changed the products of African labor from those that enriched and empowered Africans to those that impoverished and subordinated them; it also transformed the labor process itself in order to effect changes in Ewe society that would further colonial domination. Most centrally, these colonial interventions sought to undermine the extended, polygynous households that had afforded individual autonomy to African men, women, and children, and had proven so resistant to outside control. This particular household division of labor not only challenged European standards of what counted as good, but also prevented the development of patriarchal chains of command through which colonial authority, in which a tiny white minority ruled a black majority, operated.

Introducing the plow to agriculturalists who had previously worked with hoes, colonial reformers thought, would have the most important social and cultural effects on Africans. Colonial authorities in Germany and elsewhere proposed that, with the introduction of the plow, the work of draft animals would replace the labor of wives and children, transforming polygamous, female-headed households farming with hoes into monogamous, patriarchal family farms.[49] African Americans, one colonial agricultural expert explained, had adopted the plow under the beneficial direction of slavery; Africans would do so under the guidance of colonial authorities.[50] The methods of cotton farming Tuskegee would introduce, Hans Gruner explained to an audience of African notables and missionaries in Tove, allowed a man to live as a "free farmer on his own plot, at home with his family." Men would no longer have to travel long distances to earn money as day laborers or porters and "the women would cease to ramble around." "Orderly family relations," Gruner concluded, "could take hold."[51] For Gruner, "orderly family relations" would settle the population under the control of male heads of households and, ultimately, of his station.

Booker T. Washington, who never visited Togo, echoed these colonial domestic aspirations. Writing in 1904, after several other Tuskegee graduates had moved to Tove with their wives to set up model households, Washington described a domesticity at odds not only with Ewe society but also with the reality of the expedition in Togo. Women in Tove, he claimed, learned sewing, cooking, and housekeeping from the Tuskegee wives. Men, he maintained, built houses with shutters, doors, and bathrooms, and furnished with beds. Men took over all marketing, he ventured, leaving their wives and children in these model households to attend to housekeeping and farm work. This new domesticity, Washington concluded, led to a Christian life, and these Africans observed the Sabbath, dressing in holiday attire on Sundays and attending services at the mission.[52] Such a description would have been a flight of fancy for any part of Togo; it was particularly at odds with reality in Tove, where houses still remained in ruins after the destruction meted out by German colonists; where colonial soldiers forced residents to labor on Tuskegee cotton farms; and where the Yewe secret society, important for resisting these colonial impositions, remained as strong as ever.

The Tuskegee expedition settled in in Tove-Dzigbe, the still devastated village where the 1895 war had first broken out. The Tuskegee men occupied several of the huts in Tove-Dzigbe that had remained empty since the German attacks.[53] Gruner, now able to assert his authority over Tove, had local authorities assemble about two hundred of their subjects to clear the fields and build additional housing. These workers then provided the main labor force for the cotton experiments. The majority, not surprisingly, had no familiarity with the agricultural implements that the expedition had brought from the United States, and John W. Robinson complained that "it was more difficult to train the boys than it was to train the horses."[54] In fact, these "boys" soon found themselves in the harnesses of the horses and oxen, for draft animals died of sleeping sickness soon after they were brought to Togo. Rather than leveraging cotton farming to create patriarchal domesticity, the colonial agricultural project in Togo reduced many men—both literally and metaphorically—to the position of beasts of burden. Indeed, the success of the expedition in increasing the export of cotton from Togo and using this industry to expand German authority in the colony proceeded less from the success of the imagined family plans of Gruner and others than from the coercion that the failure of these plans prompted.

John W. Robinson expressed discomfort with some of the more egregious aspects of this racial order. In 1904, he wrote to the governor of Togo to insist that cotton growing should be taught only where it would make people wealthy; if yams or maize yielded greater benefits to their growers in particular areas, these regions should not be induced to grow cotton. In coastal areas, where commerce was the most profitable pursuit, he suggested that the colonial state should "wish to make them [Africans] better traders," rather than forcing them to become farmers.[55] The government ignored Robinson's sentiments, as Robinson himself was evidently able to do as well, and he continued his work at Tove and went on to found an extraordinarily successful—and coercive—cotton school elsewhere in Togo, which he headed until his death in 1909.

Like German colonial authorities, Robinson saw the forms of coercion applied in Togo as an Americanization of African relations of production. Suggesting in a letter to the German governor of Togo that blacks in both Africa and America "are very improvident and full of childish simplicity" but "submit readily to leadership and are easily encouraged," he thus proposed managing some of the cotton farmers in Togo "halfway as a settler would be treated, and halfway as a laborer or what we call a 'cropper' i.e. one who makes a farm under the direction of another."[56] (The term "cropper" is synonymous with "sharecropper.") Sharecropping in the United States involved different mechanisms of supervision and coercion than those proposed by Robinson, but his point was not to bring share tenancy to Togo but rather to suggest that the colonial "direction of another" borrow techniques from the American South. Suggesting that coercive management of black labor was somehow American lent it credibility in colonial circles and also, it seems, for John Robinson. If he had hoped that this image of the American South would give African Americans a greater role in transforming African agriculture, he was wrong. From at least 1902, the German government of Togo began favoring the expertise of white German American southerners, beginning with the cotton inspector Joseph Buvinghausen, a deputy sheriff from Harris County, Texas. The government had begun to fear that African Americans would bring not only an idealized New South to the German colony, but also practices of resistance to that racial order.

Indeed, the people of Tove resisted German imperialism not only by defending their locality against the imperialist internationalism that brought American agricultural labor practices to bear on Togo; they also created their own internationalisms, including with African Americans opposed to Tuskegee methods. In the years after the arrival of the expedition, a large number of young people left Tove for the Gold Coast, in part because of a drought, but surely also to avoid the labor demands imposed on Tove by the Tuskegee cotton fields. Many of them went to study at an African Methodist Episcopal Zion mission in the British colony. The head of that mission, Thomas B. Freeman, the son of an African American freedman and an English woman, had left the Wesleyans after a long and distinguished missionary career in the Gold Coast. Freeman openly criticized the educational opportunities available in the German colony and attracted many Togolese students to cross the border to his mission school.[57] Apparently young people in Tove believed that Freeman could teach English reading and writing in a single day.[58] English literacy was one of the few avenues for upward mobility within the colonial system, and escaping to this school meant also escaping a life of colonial agricultural labor. By 1904, the AME Zion mission in the Gold Coast had also begun holding what missionaries from the North German Mission described, using the English term, as "revival meetings" where "various people, especially women, comport themselves absurdly, shaking their heads, waving their arms about in the air, and shriek and scream like fetish women."[59] Whatever the actual nature of these observances, missionaries recognized in them an echo of Gbe religion that was an obstacle not just to Christian conversion but also to colonial subordination. Both the Ewe and German colonists had African American allies and adapted the racial politics of post-emancipation United States to their own struggles with each other.

A labor history of imperialism in Africa reveals the multiple, overlapping forms of sovereignties and power involved in what a more conventional political and diplomatic narrative might represent as relatively clear national compartmentalization of the globe. Such a labor history also decenters imperial actors, revealing them as contemporaries of those Africans whom they claimed to be bringing, for the first time, into history. In fact, the Ewe of Tove and the Germans who wished to rule them both had long historical connections to the larger struggle over bondage in the Atlantic world. As Gbe, the Ewe were part of a religious world that was integral to the Haitian revolution and remained relevant to their struggle against German imperialism. As producers seeking both to resist enslavement and other older forms of bondage and also to preserve their autonomy against newer capitalist forms of labor, the Ewe carried on a struggle parallel to thousands of similar ones around the world. German colonizers likewise participated in a much larger capitalist world system that sought to channel these rebellions against old forms of bondage into new political and economic forms that would preserve, and even expand, their ability to exercise control and extract surplus value. Seeing German colonialism as a phase of Ewe history better portrays how imperialism emerged as a reaction against democratic rebellions of the nineteenth century, and thus helps correct the colonizers' view of their own history as having brought something—goods, ideas, progress, whatever—to a relatively passive Africa.

The history of African Americans in the United States plays an especially important role in this expanded, labor history of empire in Africa because the rebellion against bondage and the "counterrevolution of property" in the U.S.—the Civil War, Reconstruction, and the New South—was so large and played such a paradigmatic role for so many. For German officials and their colonial admirers in other nations, African Americans in the New South represented an ideal colonial labor force and ideal black subjects in a white supremacist political order. Booker T. Washington and the Tuskegee Institute expedition members participated in this colonial project because they saw it as part of a global program of racial uplift, even if they rejected some of the most exploitative aspects of colonialism and the U.S. New South. The Ewe of Tove rejected the Tuskegee program, but turned to a different set of African American religious, political, and educational practices represented by the missionary Thomas B. Freeman, whom they evidently found more supportive of their own struggles than the Tuskegee personnel in Tove. The African, the American, and the German histories entangled in colonial Togo represent a recombination of local variants of a common Atlantic history formed, finally, by struggles between the labor of autonomy and the labor of subordination.

NOTES

1. This essay draws on Andrew Zimmerman, *Alabama in Africa: Booker T. Washington, the German Empire, and the Globalization of the New South* (Princeton, NJ: Princeton University Press, 2010).

2. Andre Gunder Frank, "The Development of Underdevelopment," *Monthly Review* 18 (1966): 17–31. There are many important critiques of dependency theory, but no persuasive refutations of its basic thesis of combined and uneven development rather than liberal modernization theory as an explanation of global inequality.

3. Compare Sven Beckert, "Emancipation and Empire: Reconstructing the Worldwide Web of Cotton Production in the Age of the American Civil War," *American Historical Review* 109 (2004): 1405–1438, and Beckert, "From Tuskegee to Togo: The Problem of Freedom in the Empire of Cotton," *Journal of American History* 92 (2005): 498–526.

4. There is a vast literature on post-emancipation labor regimes. One important example is Frederick Cooper, Thomas C. Holt, and Rebecca J. Scott, *Beyond Slavery: Explorations of Race, Labor, and Citizenship* (Chapel Hill: University of North Carolina Press, 2000).). On race and labor before and after emancipation, see David R. Roediger and Elizabeth D. Esch, *The Production of Difference: Race and the Management of Labor in U.S. History* (New York: Oxford University Press, 2012).

5. See Paul E. Lovejoy, *Transformations in Slavery: A History of Slavery in Africa*, 3rd ed. (1983; Cambridge, UK: Cambridge University Press, 2012).

6. See also Natalie J. Ring, *The Problem South: Region, Empire, and the New Liberal State, 1880–1930* (Athens: University of Georgia Press, 2012).

7. Steven Hahn, "Did We Miss the Greatest Slave Rebellion in Modern History," in *The Political Worlds of Slavery and Freedom* (Cambridge, MA: Harvard University Press, 2009), 55–114.

8. Lovejoy, *Transformations in Slavery*, 252–53.

9. W.E.B. Du Bois, *Black Reconstruction: An Essay toward a History of the Part which Black Folk Played in the Attempt to Reconstruct Democracy in America, 1860–1880* (1935; New York: Free Press, 1998). "The General Strike" is the title of chapter four and "Counter-Revolution of Property" the title of chapter fourteen of that book. On Du Bois's *Black Reconstruction* and empire, see also Julie Greene, this volume.

10. W.E.B. Du Bois, "Of Mr. Booker T. Washington and Others," in *The Souls of Black Folk* (1903; Mineola: Dover, 1994), 25–35, 31.

11. See, especially, Robert J. Norrell, *Up from History: The Life of Booker T. Washington* (Cambridge, MA: Harvard University Press, 2009).

12. Zimmerman, *Alabama in Africa*, 45–65.

13. This point is made forcefully in Ranajit Guha, "On the Prose of Counter-Insurgency," in *Selected Subaltern Studies* (New York: Oxford University Press, 1988), 45–86. See also Andrew Zimmerman, "Africa in Imperial and

Transnational History: Multi-Sited Historiography and the Necessity of Theory," *Journal of African History* 54 (2013): 331–40.

14. Robin Law, *The Slave Coast of West Africa, 1550–1750: The Impact of the Atlantic Slave Trade on an African Society* (New York: Oxford University Press, 1991).

15. Patrick Manning, *Slavery and African Life: Occidental, Oriental, and African Slave Trades* (Cambridge, UK: Cambridge University Press, 1990), 66–69.

16. On the international reach of Gbe practices, see James H. Sweet, *Domingos Álvares, African Healing, and the Intellectual History of the Atlantic World* (Chapel Hill: University of North Carolina Press, 2011).

17. Information on the destinations of enslaved Africans from the Bight of Benin comes from David Eltis, Stephen D. Behrendt, David Richardson, and Herbert S. Klein, *The Trans-Atlantic Slave Trade: A Database on CD-ROM* (Cambridge, UK: Cambridge University Press, 1999).

18. John K. Thornton has demonstrated the role Kongo political philosophy played in the Haitian revolution, but also emphasized that this was just one of the African intellectual currents in the revolution. See his "'I Am the Subject of the King of Congo': African Political Ideology and the Haitian Revolution," *Journal of World History* 4, no. 2 (October 1, 1993): 181–214.

19. Unless otherwise noted, my account of Ewe political economy is based primarily on Jakob Spieth, *Die Ewe-Stämme: Material zur Kunde des Ewe-Volkes in Deutsch-Togo* (Berlin: Dietrich Reimer, 1906), and Diedrich Westermann, *Die Glidyi-Ewe in Togo: Züge aus ihrem Gesellschaftsleben* (Berlin: Walter de Gruyter, 1935).

20. See Martin Lynn, *Commerce and Economic Change in West Africa: The Palm Oil Trade in the Nineteenth Century* (Cambridge, UK: Cambridge University Press, 1997).

21. On pottery production in Tove, see Heinrich Klose, *Togo unter deutscher Flagge* (Berlin: Dietrich Reimer, 1899), 160–163; Mary Gaunt, *Alone in West Africa* (London: T. Werner Laurie, 1912), 255; Anthony G. Hopkins, *An Economic History of West Africa* (New York, Columbia University Press, 1973), ch. 2.

22. Donna J. E. Maier, "Asante War Aims in the 1869 Invasion of Ewe," in *The Golden Stool: Studies of the Asante Center and Periphery*, ed. Enid Schildkrout (New York: American Museum of Natural History, 1987), 232–244, 240.

23. Spieth, *Die Ewe-Stämme*, 34–40.

24. Maier, "Asante War Aims," 243.

25. Curt von François, *Ohne Schuß durch dick und dünn: Erste Erforschung des Togohinterlandes*, ed. Götz von François (Esch-Waldems: Eigenverlag Dr. Götz von François, 1972), 19.

26. Klose, *Togo unter deutscher Flagge*, 164.

27. On the Yewe society, see Sandra E. Greene, *Gender, Ethnicity, and Social Change on the Upper Slave Coast: A History of the Anlo Ewe* (Portsmouth: Heinemann, 1996), 81–99; "Erstes Regen in Tove," Monats-Blatt der Norddeutschen Missions-Gesellschaft, 3rd series, vol. 6 (1894): 98–100; Carl Spiess, "Die Landschaft Tove

bei Lome in Togo," *Deutsche Geographische Blätter* 25 (1902): 75–79; Spiess, "Religionsbegriffe der Evheer in Westafrika," *Mitteilungen des Seminars fuer Orientalische Sprachen* 6 (1903): 109–127, 124–127.

28. Spiess, "Die Landschaft Tove bei Lome in Togo," and "Religionsbegriffe der Evheer in Westafrika"; H. Schröder, Lomé, to Missionsinspektor, 24 July 1905, Lomé, Briefe Berichte, Bd. 5, 1905, Norddeutsche Missionsgesellschaft, Staatsarchiv Bremen, 20/3.

29. Klose, *Togo unter deutscher Flagge*, 164.

30. Hans Gruner, *Vormarsch zum Niger: Die Memoiren des Leiters der Togo-Hinterlandexpedition 1894/95*, Peter Sebald, ed. (Berlin: Edition Ost, 1997). Except where noted, the account of the battle comes from Klose, *Togo unter deutscher Flagge*, 160–168.

31. Klose, *Togo unter deutscher Flagge*, 407–408.

32. Hans Gruner asserts that he killed thirty people in his report on the "Tove-Unruhen," Misahohe, 1 April 1895, K. 7, Mappe 34, Nachlass 250 (Hans Gruner) in Staatsbibliothek Berlin, 5–7. In a 1981 interview, one of Gruner's African soldiers, Fritz Togbe, recalled the battle as particularly fierce with many deaths. See Dadja Halla-Kawa Simtaro, "Le Togo 'Musterkolonie': Souvenir de l'Allemangne dans la société togolaise," 2 vols., Ph.D. diss., Universite de Provence, Aix-Marseille I, 1982, vol. 2, 601.

33. The decapitations are reported in "Kwittah Terrible Revelations," *Gold Coast Chronicle*, 26 July 1895, 3. The author of this article did not discuss the anthropological use of the heads. On this colonial anthropology, see Andrew Zimmerman, *Anthropology and Antihumanism in Imperial Germany* (Chicago: University of Chicago Press, 2001), ch. 7.

34. Klose, *Togo unter deutscher Flagge*, 160.

35. Spiess, "Die Landschaft Tove bei Lome in Togo," 75, and Klose, *Togo unter deutscher Flagge*, 163.

36. C. Osswald, Jahresbericht der Station Lome, 20 January 1902, Lomé, Norddeutsche Missionsgesellschaft, Staatsarchiv Bremen, 20/1; Marion Johnson, "Cotton Imperialism in West Africa," *African Affairs* 73 (1974): 178–187, 184.

37. James N. Calloway, "Tuskegee Cotton-Planters in Africa," *Outlook* 70 (March 29, 1902): 772–776.

38. Calloway, "Tuskegee Cotton-Planters in Africa."

39. "Entwurf einer Dienstanweisung für Bezirksleiter," n.d. (printed), K. 7, Mappe 36, Nachlass 250 (Hans Gruner) in Staatsbibliothek Berlin, Bl. 171–182.

40. For a transnational history of German ideas of labor and colonialism, see Sebastian Conrad, *Globalisation and the Nation in Imperial Germany*, trans. Sorcha O'Hagan (2006; Cambridge, UK: Cambridge University Press, 2010).

41. Gruner, Miksahöhe, "Pflichten und Rechte der Häuptlinge, " n.d., K. 7, Mappe 36, Nachlass 250 (Hans Gruner) in Staatsbibliothek Berlin, Bl. 150. Togo's penal colony was in Chra, near Atakpame.

42. For a discussion of this colonial literature, see Anton Markmiller, 'Die Erziehung des Negers zur Arbeit': Wie die koloniale Pädagogik afrikanische Gesellschaften in die Abhängigkeit führte (Berlin: Dietrich Reimer, 1995).

43. Beno von Herman to Booker T. Washington, 3 September 1900, in Louis R. Harlan, ed., The Booker T. Washington Papers, 14 vols. (Urbana: University of Illinois Press, 1972–1989), 5:633–636.

44. See Tunde Adeleke, UnAfrican Americans: Nineteenth-Century Black Nationalists and the Civilizing Mission (Lexington: University Press of Kentucky, 1998).

45. Robert E. Park, "Education by Cultural Groups," Southern Workman 41 (1912): 369–377, here 369–370, 377.

46. Reichskolonialamt, Die Baumwollfrage: Denkschrift über Produktion und Verbrauch von Baumwolle Massnahmen gegen die Baumwollnot (Jena: Gustav Fischer, 1911), 131–132.

47. Kolonialwirtschaftliches Komitee, "Baumwoll-Expedition nach Togo" [1900], Togo National Archives (microfilm copy), Bundesarchiv Berlin, R150, FA 1–332, Bl. 88–102.

48. Paul Rohrbach, Deutsche Kolonialwirtschaft: Kulturpolitische Grundsätze für die Rassen- und Missionsfragen (Berlin: Hilfe, 1909), 41–42.

49. This view was elaborated by the German sociologist Eduard Hahn, Die Entstehung der Pflugkultur (unsres Ackerbaus) (Heidelberg: Carl Winter's Universitätsbuchhandlung, 1909).

50. Otto Warburg, "Einführung der Pflugkultur in den deutschen Kolonien," Verhandlungen des Kolonial-Wirtschaftlichen Komitees (1906): 4–9.

51. Minutes of a meeting at the Misahöhe Station between Gruner and local African leaders, the missionary Schosser, two teachers from the mission at Agu ,and five teachers from the Catholic mission, 15 April 1904, Bundesarchiv Berlin (hereafter BArch) R1001/8222, Bl. 140–141.

52. Booker T. Washington, Working with the Hands (1904; New York: Negro Universities Press, 1969), 226–230.

53. Gruner, Station Misahöhe, to the Government of Togo, 1 August 1900, Togo National Archives, microfilm copy in BArch (hereafter TNA), FA 1–332, Bl. 110.

54. John W. Robinson to Booker T. Washington, 26 May 1901, in Harlan, ed., Booker T. Washington Papers 6:126–129.

55. John W. Robinson to Governor Zech, 17 January 1904, TNA, FA 1–332, Bl. 295–301.

56. See John W. Robinson, Notsé, to Governor Zech, 12 December 1904, TNA FA 1/303, Bl. 255–258, and the copy of this letter sent by the future Governor Zech to Atakpame District Office, 29 December 1904, TNA FA 3/1008, Bl. 114–118. See the positive response to this proposal in Station Atakpame [to the Government of Togo], 25 September 1905, TNA FA 1–304, Bl. 60–63.

57. "Die African Methodist Episcopal Zion Church in Keta," Monats-Blatt der Norddeutschen Missions-Gesellschaft, 3rd series, 14 (1902): 101–103. On Freeman,

see also J.H., review of Thomas B. Freeman, by John Milum (London, n.d.), *Evangelisches Missions-Magazin* (Basel) 38 (1894): 174–175; Edwin W. Smith, *Aggrey of Africa: A Study in Black and White* (1929; New York: Books for Libraries, 1971), 30, 43.

58. E. Anrima [?], Lehrer, Tove, to A. W. Schreiber, Inspector of the North German Mission, Bremen, 2 March 1904, NDM 20/2.

59. "African Methodist Episcopal Zion Church," *Monats-Blatt der Norddeutschen Missions-Gesellschaft*, 3rd series, 15 [*sic*—should be 16] (1904): 53.

11

Progressive Empire

Race and Tropicality in United Fruit's Central America

JASON M. COLBY

In 1914, U.S. writer and inventor Frederick Upham Adams published *Conquest of the Tropics*, a triumphalist account of the United Fruit Company (UFC). Crafted in close consultation with company officials, the book called on readers to praise the U.S. banana "pioneers" whose hard work was bringing order and progress to Central America. In contrast to earlier visitors, who often portrayed Central America as a land of natural abundance and easy living, Adams depicted a harsh and perilous landscape where white men proved their manhood and extended U.S. civilization. Combatting the "seen and invisible dangers of the tropical fastnesses," Adams declared, these hardy banana men exemplified "that instinctive spirit which ever has urged the American to face and conquer the frontier." The story of UFC, he asserted, "is a record of a monumental constructive work performed amid surroundings so difficult that the plain narrative seems more like a romance than the account of deeds actually performed."[1]

Yet embedded in this imperial narrative was surprising recognition of the company's black labor force. The issue of work and workers figured prominently throughout the book, not only in Adams's treatment of UFC operations but also in his portrayal of the company's host nations. "The labor question is a vital one in the American tropics," he explained. Although UFC boasted of wages higher than "ever before offered" in the region, it had proven "almost impossible to tempt the average native of Central America to work, and many of them are physically incapable of sustained manual labor." As a result, UFC, like the U.S. government's canal construction in Panama, had come to rely on British West Indians. These black migrant laborers cleared and planted UFC farms and harvested and loaded its bananas. Indeed, Adams concluded, "the Jamaica negro is the workman who has made possible the wonders which the United Fruit Company has achieved in Central America."[2]

This seems a remarkable admission. In an age of ascendant white supremacy, a white American author, whose avowed purpose was to celebrate UFC's imperial work in Central America, acknowledged that the firm's accomplishments depended upon black migrant laborers. Nor were such observations unique: throughout the 1910s and early 1920s, UFC officials, U.S. diplomats, and pro-company authors routinely emphasized the importance of West Indians in the company's operations. Yet as inexplicable as this praise might appear, it served an imperial objective. Rather than challenging the assumptions of racial hierarchy that UFC officials espoused and practiced, public recognition of West Indian workers in fact bolstered the company's imperial narrative concerning Central America, as well as its resistance to anti-black immigration restrictions in the region. This chapter examines this link between race, work, and discourses of imperial progress in the context of UFC operations in Central America. In doing so, however, it explores questions with comparative application to colonial encounters elsewhere, particularly regarding the relationship between tropicality, work, and imperial narratives. First, how did perceptions of tropical landscapes and peoples influence imperial labor recruitment and control strategies? Second, how did the employment of migrant laborers, in this case, black West Indians from the British Empire, actually strengthen and legitimize the imperial authority of an American company? Finally, how did the shifting makeup of the labor force alter imperial representations and evaluations of laborers and their work?

Historians have addressed some aspects of these questions. Scholars such as Mary Louise Pratt, Fredrick Pike, and Nancy Stepan have traced common themes in European and American writings on Latin America. Beginning in the early nineteenth century, Pratt notes, European writers and artists approached Latin America with "imperial eyes," depicting the new nations as lands of abundant resources and feckless "natives." In a similar vein, Pike has shown how the U.S. tendency to view Latin Americans as indolent yet mercurial children of nature served as a justification for imperial expansion. For her part, Stepan has revealed the common tropes of "tropicality" that pervaded the written and visual representations of Latin America in the nineteenth century.[3] Other historians have explored the cultural and institutional development of the U.S. Caribbean empire in its governmental and corporate manifestations. This includes a number of studies of the two largest U.S. enterprises in the region: the Panama Canal and UFC. Julie Greene's study of Panama Canal workers, for example, offers insight not only into the experience of laborers in the Canal Zone but also the impact of canal construction on the U.S. imperial imagination.[4] Likewise, historians such as Aviva Chomsky, John Soluri, and myself have examined the racial, ecological, and imperial implications of the American banana industry. Yet no scholar has explored the relationship between the discourse of tropicality often associated with travel writing and the labor practices of U.S. corporate colonialism.[5]

The process of building, and the necessity of legitimizing, the U.S. empire caused Americans to shift their depiction of Central America from an idyllic, tropical Eden to a rugged, perilous frontier. Yet conversely, this same process reinforced widely held stereotypes of the region's residents. Frustrated by their inability to recruit local Central Americans in the 1870s and 1880s, U.S. railroad contractors and banana entrepreneurs turned to British West Indians to fill their labor needs. Following its founding in 1899, UFC expanded upon this system, in the process often praising black workers publicly for their role in bringing order to Central America's tropical chaos. In addition to encouraging West Indian loyalty to UFC, this emphasis on the need for, and the merits of, its black migrant labor force bolstered the firm's claims to imperial authority in Central America, implying that the region's inhabitants lacked not only the capital and expertise but also the character and work ethic necessary to bring progress to their nations. By the early 1910s, however, resistance from those migrant workers forced a change in company strategy. In response to West Indian strikes, UFC began hiring a growing number of Spanish-speaking Central Americans, in large part to help discipline its black laborers. In the following years, UFC officials continued their public praise of West Indians, partly in response to rising calls for immigration restriction within Central America. As its workforce became increasingly Central American, and as anti–West Indian sentiment in its host nations mounted, however, UFC shifted its rhetoric. While company officials continued to celebrate the firm's role in taming the tropics, they placed less emphasis on the contributions of its workforce, for logical reasons. Whereas earlier recognition of West Indian migrants had strengthened UFC's claims to authority in the region, acknowledgement of its now predominantly Central American workforce threatened to legitimize the rising labor demands confronting the company. Instead, during the 1920s, UFC espoused a Fordist emphasis on corporate benevolence. As in the case of domestic U.S. industries, this strategy aimed to appropriate the mantle of Progressivism as well as to cultivate labor quiescence. Because UFC operated in the U.S. imperial sphere, however, it faced additional challenges, particularly with the rise of anti-imperial and anti-black Central American nationalism. As a result, while the company's progressive discourse of the 1920s retained its earlier currents of tropicality, it increasingly attempted to distance itself from the history of U.S. imperialism and black labor migration in the region. It was a difficult task, for UFC has emerged from that history.

Americans projected fantasies and fears onto Central America long before the advent of UFC. This included consistent depictions of the region as a backward realm of race mixing and Catholic "superstition." Until at least the 1890s, a consistent trope in U.S. travel writing and government correspondence on Central America was that of the improvident "native" lounging amid tropical abundance. Viewing the landscape through "imperial eyes," much like their European predecessors, North American visitors interpreted the lushness of the Central American jungles as clear evidence that locals had failed to exploit rich soil and subsoil resources. Only North American ambition and effort could develop the region properly. The ease of life in Central America, symbolized by the profusion of tropical fruit, had dissuaded Central Americans from exerting themselves, they reasoned.[6] To be sure, U.S. writers acknowledged the danger of tropical disease, particularly in the Colombian state of Panama. Yet this discourse, contrasting native indolence and tropical luxury with North American tenacity and progress (itself formed by the severity of the North American temperate zone) remained remarkably consistent throughout the second half of the nineteenth century. Central Americans had been blessed with a land of plenty but were too lazy to develop it.[7] In his 1887 travel account, *Guatemala, Land of the Quetzal*, for example, New Englander William Brigham marveled at the region's fecundity, but noted that "of all countries I have seen, Guatemala, in common with the other States of Central America, makes least use of her natural advantages, and does least to overcome those obstacles Nature has thrown in her way." With labor, and American capital, he mused, the region's Caribbean coast could become "the great fruit-producing orchard of the United States."[8] Famed journalist Richard Harding Davis was even blunter in his 1896 account, *Three Gringos in Venezuela and Central America*. Observing that "there is no more interesting question . . . than that of what is to be done with the world's land which is lying unimproved," he described Central Americans as "a gang of semi-barbarians in a beautifully furnished house, of which they can understand neither its possibilities of comfort nor its use." If the region was to progress, Davis concluded, "it will have to be some other man than a native-born Central-American who is to do it."[9]

Yet these bold claims circulated in tension with the actual experience of Americans working in the region. Between 1850 and 1855, for example, the New York–based Panama Railroad Company confronted severe climatic challenges and labor shortages in the construction of a rail line across the Colombian province.[10] Two decades later, U.S. railroad contractors in Central America, including Minor C. Keith, likewise discovered that taming the tropics was no easy task. During his two-decade struggle to build a railway through Costa Rica's Caribbean lowlands, Keith confronted not only yellow fever, which killed three of his brothers, but also the rapid plant growth and unpredictable flash floods that stymied rail construction in the region. His correspondence from this period frequently featured complaints about both the landscape and the residents of the American tropics. In an 1876 letter to creditors at W. R. Grace, for example, he bemoaned the challenges of working "in all kinds of weather" and "amongst the worst class of people."[11]

As such statements hinted, while work experience in the region disabused Keith and other U.S. entrepreneurs of the myth of the gentle tropics, it tended to reinforce negative views of Central Americans themselves, whom they demeaned both for failing to develop local resources and for refusing to work for wages. Indeed, a standard complaint among U.S. employers from the time of the Panama Railroad Company through UFC's early decades was the unwillingness of local residents to work. In reality, labor shortages stemmed primarily from the nature of these enterprises, most of which were located in remote areas. The small number of local inhabitants refused to abandon their subsistence economies for irregular wage labor, and residents of the highlands had no desire to work in disease-ridden railroad camps in the Caribbean lowlands. For American contractors, however, frustration with labor shortages reinforced the stereotype of the lazy Central American.

By necessity, then, as well as by preference, U.S. enterprises drew the bulk of their workforce from outside their zones of operation. Chinese, Irish, and West Indian laborers, as well as migrants from other parts of Colombia, constructed the Panama railroad. Elsewhere in Central America, they experimented with a number of labor sources before turning to black immigrant workers. In Costa Rica, for example, Keith came to rely on Jamaican laborers; his counterparts in Guatemala, on the other hand, hired mostly African Americans and Belizeans, as well as some laborers from the Caribbean islands.[12]

The U.S. government's leap into overseas empire accelerated U.S. businesses' dependence on West Indian labor from the British empire. In particular, President Theodore Roosevelt's decision to detach Panama from Colombia in late 1903 had a profound impact on regional labor flows and, subsequently, U.S. perceptions of the tropics and the disparate labor capacities of West Indians and Spanish-speaking residents. Over the following decade, the construction of the Panama Canal became the iconic symbol of the U.S. empire's progressive work in the world. Roosevelt proudly depicted the project as a white American triumph over tropical disorder, and U.S. citizens celebrated their determination to "make the dirt fly" in the isthmus. Still, as Julie Greene reveals, Americans themselves made up only a small minority of the canal workforce and performed little of the manual labor. In 1913, for example, travel writer Harry Franck recalled that he had traveled to Panama "with the hope of shouldering a shovel and descending into the canal with other workmen" but discovered, instead, that the manual laborers came from dozens of countries and colonies, especially the British West Indies.[13]

United Fruit drew upon the same pool of laborers to undertake its own rapid expansion in Central America. Born of an 1899 merger between the Boston Fruit Company and the various enterprises owned by Minor Keith, the new company brought vertical and horizontal integration to the American banana industry, previously characterized by smaller enterprises. In the process, it built upon the labor system already established by Keith, who became the firm's vice president. This included contract farming by local residents, whose fruit was carried on company railcars and steamers, as well as carefully designed and strictly regimented corporate farms. Over the first decade of the twentieth century, UFC developed large banana enclaves in Costa Rica and Guatemala, and British West Indians composed the vast majority of its workforce.

By 1910, the firm had become the largest agriculture enterprise in the world and proudly presented itself as part of the expanding U.S. empire. It dominated Central American ports such as Puerto Barrios, Guatemala, and Puerto Limón, Costa Rica, and its "Great White Fleet" controlled much of the region's commerce.[14] Despite this success, UFC faced several threats to its authority and prestige. One subtle challenge came from the Edenic narratives of Central America that persisted in U.S. writing. Such images, once justification for imperial adventure, now clashed with UFC's need for colonial legitimization. O. Henry's *Cabbages and Kings* (1904), a collection of short stories in which he coined the term "banana republic," painted a comical picture of dissolute foreigners and lazy natives against a romantic tropical backdrop. Henry even included a political coup facilitated by the "Vesuvius Fruit Company"—possibly modeled on UFC itself.[15] A less popular but equally revealing example was Nevin Winter's 1909 travelogue, *Guatemala and Her People of Today*. Depicting Central America as "a land of perpetual summer, where fruits grow wild and a small piece of land will produce enough sustenance for a family," Winter asserted that "there is no need for a man to work hard. Earning one's bread by the sweat of his brow becomes a jest."[16]

Although echoing longstanding themes in U.S. writing, such assertions took on new meaning in the presence of a U.S. empire in Central America. Earlier embraced as a justification for expansion, these tropes now threatened to diminish U.S. achievements in the region, particularly in UFC's case. After all, if fruit grew wild and living was so easy in Central America, what was so impressive about the firm growing and exporting bananas? The firm sought to counter this image by drawing attention to its accomplishments. In the tours of its enclaves that it provided to visiting U.S. dignitaries, travelers, and writers, for example, it sought to associate its operations not only with the spirit of tropical imperial uplift, but also with the image of efficiency and innovation that marked large-scale industrialism in the United States.[17]

At the height of U.S. Progressivism, however, this emphasis carried its own perils. By the time of the 1912 presidential campaign, large corporations were falling out of favor with the American public. Both Democrat Woodrow Wilson and Theodore Roosevelt (now running as the candidate for the new Progressive Party) denounced the power of "trusts," and Wilson, in particular, criticized the Caribbean military interventions associated with President William Howard Taft's Dollar Diplomacy. Such rhetoric was cause for concern among UFC officials. Although their firm hardly competed with the likes of J. P. Morgan for public villainy, a growing number of critics denounced the company's domination of the U.S. fruit market, and some accused it of instigating coups and U.S. interventions in Central America. In late 1913, UFC and its supporters narrowly defeated a new U.S. import tariff on bananas, which Congressional proponents had argued would weaken UFC's monopoly, and in the following months, U.S. officials continued to gather information on the company. In May 1914, the U.S. consul in Puerto Limón, Costa Rica, submitted a report to the State Department entitled "The Strangulation of Competition and Elimination of Private Planters, by the United Fruit Company." Prior to the outbreak of World War I, it seemed likely the Wilson administration would file an anti-trust lawsuit against UFC.[18]

In stark contrast, the U.S. government's construction of the Panama Canal enjoyed widespread public support, especially because previous failed attempts by private companies to build the waterway convinced many Americans to accept Roosevelt's argument that the canal was too important to be left to private enterprise. Partly for this reason, few, if any, observers questioned the heroic dimensions of the canal construction, which became the great legitimizing symbol of overseas U.S. empire. Instead, by the early 1910s, a spate of publications celebrated the canal effort, though most focused on U.S. engineering and sanitation achievements. They ignored the predominantly black West Indian workforce. In American accounts of the canal construction, nonwhites in Panama primarily figured not as workers but as colonial subjects who benefited from the Canal Commission's enlightened policies. In his memoir, for example, Harry Franck declared West Indian workers "lazy negroes who, where laborers must be had, are a bit better than no labor—though not much." Also unsurprising at this high tide of Progressivism, several accounts emphasized that it was the federal government, not private capital, that was solving the greatest commercial challenge of the age.[19] At a time of growing public skepticism toward large private interests at home, the U.S. public found it easier to support the Panama Canal as a U.S. government project.

It was no coincidence that UFC began its first serious public relations offensive in this period. In particular, the company and its boosters emphasized UFC's efforts to tame Central America's tropical landscape, a feat made possible, they argued, by the firm's progressive labor system. This effort was facilitated by the American public's growing interest in the nation's overseas presence. During the 1910–14 period, as the Panama Canal neared completion, a large number of books and magazine articles surveyed the growing influence of both the U.S. government and private enterprise in the Caribbean and Pacific. One example was William J. Showalter's sweeping article "The Countries of the Caribbean," which appeared in the February 1913 issue of *National Geographic*. In it, Showalter predicted that the completion of the Panama Canal would spur the U.S. government to assume imperial supervision over Central America, resulting in an era of development and expansion "comparable to that which has taken place in Porto Rico and in Cuba." In particular, he noted that private companies had a critical role to play in spreading U.S. progress. In Guatemala, he argued, "one begins properly to appreciate the great civilizing influence of a much-maligned American corporation—the United Fruit Company." In addition to highlighting the company's success in carving orderly plantations from menacing tropical jungle, he implied that the firm's enlightened labor system would transform the lives of Guatemala workers, including the Mayan Indians, who were currently "slaves to the Guatemalan coffee planters."[20] Far from exploiting laborers, the reasoning went, U.S. companies such as UFC were bringing progress and fair labor practices to the American tropics.

Adams's *Conquest of the Tropics* was the most prominent contribution to UFC's public relations initiative. In preparing his study, Adams enjoyed extensive support and cooperation from the firm, and it seems reasonable to conclude that his account faithfully conveyed the views of UFC officials. At the time, the company perceived its most serious threat as coming not from Central American nationalists and unruly laborers but rather from anti-trust sentiment in the United States. Criticized for its virtual monopoly on the U.S. banana trade, the firm sought to prove to the American people that it was not only serving their interests as consumers but also doing the nation's work abroad. This included a concerted effort to tie the company's efforts in Central America to the imperial and progressive rhetoric surrounding the Panama Canal. It is in this context that one must read Adams's breathtaking assertions about UFC's role in the region's development. Declaring, for example, that the nations of Central America were "productive just about in proportion as American initiative, American capital, and American enterprise make them productive," Adams claimed (incorrectly) that even stable little Costa Rica had lacked a seaport and export trade before Keith and United Fruit arrived. Indeed, he argued, "[t]here has been no effective or lasting progress in all of the vast domain from the Rio Grande to Cape Horn which was not the result of Caucasian initiative and eventual supremacy."[21]

While such claims fit easily with the celebration of the Panama Canal and echoed European imperial narratives, Adams's inclusion of UFC's black laborers in his progressive discourse seemed a significant departure. To be sure, as scholars such as David Southern have shown, U.S. Progressivism often coexisted comfortably with racist convictions, and this was certainly the case with Adams.[22] Like many of the firm's chroniclers, for example, he celebrated the story of Jamaican laborers working on the Costa Rican railway for months without pay in the late 1880s for no other reason than their enduring faith in "Mistah Keith." It was a wistful (and likely apocryphal) tale of white authority and black loyalty reminiscent of the post–Civil War South. In the context of UFC's role in Central America, however, Adams's emphasis on the merits of West Indian workers contributed to a larger narrative about labor, immigration, and empire. Since the firm had begun operations in the region, Central American resentment of its employment of black migrant workers had been growing. Yet it was Central Americans' own laziness, Adams argued, that drove UFC and other enterprises to look outside the region for laborers. The "natives" loved to spend money, but "physical exertion was too high a price to pay for the comforts of the white races," he explained. "It was because of the refusal of the Indian natives to work at any price that the Jamaican and other West Indian negroes were called on, and they have responded by the tens of thousands." The results were evident. On Costa Rica's banana plantations, Adams observed, white American superintendents directed a workforce made up almost entirely of Jamaicans. Describing these laborers as "skilled and sturdy negroes" paid well for important work, he concluded that "it is to be doubted if any body of colored men anywhere in the world receive as high pay, enjoy as much comfort, freedom, and happiness as the 60,000 or more Jamaican negroes who make possible the giant activities of the United Fruit Company and competitors." Indeed, he concluded, "the lot of the average American negro is pitiful" compared to that of Jamaicans, "who can win more money and greater comfort along the coast lands of Central America." In sum, with a supply of reliable laborers, a progressive American company could transform even the desolate tropics into a workman's paradise, and perhaps avoid the racial tensions that plagued the United States in the process. Then came the crux of his argument: Central Americans, too, could prosper and progress if, like the West Indians, they consented to honest labor under company guidance. "There is every likelihood that the payment of good wages, coupled with sanitary surroundings and civilizing influences, will breed in Guatemala and in all of Central America strong, self-reliant, and progressive races of people," Adams declared, and those traits would serve as the "foundation for orderly government and national advancement."[23]

Even as Adams wrote, UFC's workforce was changing along the lines he envisioned, as more and more Spanish-speaking Central Americans entered the payroll in the mid-1910s. The main cause of this change, however, was not the benevolence of the company but rather the militancy of the very laborers it was praising. In 1909–10, racially charged strikes among West Indian workers in Guatemala and Costa Rica convinced UFC officials of the need for a racially divided workforce. Advertising the high pay and improving health conditions in its enclaves, the firm drew thousands of Central American migrants to farms in the following years. A former manager, John L. Williams, typically, welcomed this influx, but continued to regard West Indians as superior workers. In Central America, as in the United States, Williams observed, "the native population prefers to have the newly arrived immigrant do the heavy work"; as a result, nearly all of the work in the banana lands was the

"Black Man's Burden." It was an arresting inversion of a familiar phrase. Whereas Rudyard Kipling's famous 1899 poem "The White Man's Burden" had emphasized the sacrifice that the cause of empire would demand of white American men, Williams implied that it was West Indian migrants who were doing the work of empire in Central America. These black laborers had built the "banana belt," he noted, and only now, "as the jungles assume a habitable aspect," did Central Americans seek work. Like many UFC officials and U.S. diplomats in the region, Williams maintained that Central American laborers were incapable of replacing West Indians. Although they played "an important part in work with the machete and pick and shovel," they were "not strong enough to handle the fruit." "[T]he natives," he concluded, "are an anaemic race, due possibly to their continual diet of beans, rice, and corn," as well as their addiction to "native liquor." Add to these shortcomings "the numerous Saint's days on the calendar," he concluded, "and one can see how inadequate the native labor is."[24]

UFC drew upon these racialized distinctions to justify its evolving system of labor segmentation. Utilizing differential pay rates and segregated housing, the firm sought to divide West Indian and Central American workers. Over the following years, higher wages, public recognition, and company subsidies to West Indian community institutions encouraged black laborers to identify with UFC while ensuring that Central Americans would resent their black coworkers. Although this labor system stymied efforts at worker solidarity, it proved unstable. In addition to racial tension and violence among workers, the company's labor structure spurred calls among Central American workers and nationalists for the expulsion and exclusion of West Indians. The model of the progressive company as imperium was reaching its limits. As early as 1914, Central American nations implemented policies deterring black immigrants, and the wartime disruption of the banana industry prompted thousands of West Indians to leave Central America. In the short term, these developments benefited the shrinking number of West Indian employees, who increasingly held positions as foremen and supervisors over Central American work crews. Equally important, UFC officials still deemed West Indians superior workers critical to the firm's operations.[25]

Over the following years, the restriction of black immigration became a key component of rising anti-imperialist resentment in Central America. The example of the Mexican revolution, as well as growing global discussion of "self-determination," inspired Central American nationalists, even as a growing number of Americans questioned U.S. overseas interventions.[26] Often informed by the Leninist critique of capital and empire, these critics adopted a definition of "imperialism" that included not only annexation and military occupation but also financial and corporate domination. In this context, UFC became an obvious target. Following World War I, the firm's power and profits soared as it expanded its plantations, merchant fleet, and market control. But the company also came under unprecedented criticism as a "monopolistic" enterprise guilty of exploiting Central America.[27]

At the same time, UFC's strategy of labor segmentation was catalyzing resistance in Central America. By the early 1920s, Central American workers and nationalists challenged the company's labor system, especially for its demeaning treatment of Central American workers. During an anti-black strike by Spanish-speaking laborers in Puerto Barrios, Guatemala, in 1923, the Guatemala City newspaper *El Excelsior* denounced UFC for "giv[ing] preeminence to people of color, whose work is as and sometimes less efficient than that of natives."[28] Such claims swayed few American observers. U.S. Minister Arthur Geissler, for example, noted that by the time of the strike, the firm's Guatemala Division employed only about 400 West Indians, in contrast to some 4,000 Central Americans.[29] At its heart, however, the issue was not the total number of workers but rather the company's labor hierarchy. Despite protests from Central American officials and workers, UFC continued to place West Indian foremen in positions over Central American laborers. Although these policies clearly stirred local resentment, U.S. government officials supported UFC's policies and echoed its assessments of Central American workers. During a violent July 1924 uprising against West Indians in Honduras, for example, U.S. Consul Willard Beaulac expressed his sympathy for black immigrant workers, stressing that the "British negroes employed by the fruit companies are traditionally steady dependable workers, while natives can not, as a rule, be depended upon to stay at work." In fact, he warned, "an exodus of negroes would compel [the] company practically to cease operations."[30] For Central American laborers and nationalists, however, the firm's labor policies bespoke imperial arrogance.

In response, to this rising criticism in both the United States and Central America, UFC launched a new effort to remake its image. In addition to muting its more inflammatory imperial rhetoric, the company emphasized its progressive impact on the American tropics. One example of this discourse emerged from a conference on tropical medicine, which UFC hosted in July 1924 at its opulent Myrtle Bank Hotel in Kinston, Jamaica. Among the presenters was UFC's chief medical official, and former Canal Zone physician, Dr. W. E. Deeks. Like other speakers, Deeks acknowledged the role of tropical medicine in making U.S. overseas expansion possible. It was through the conquest of yellow fever and other maladies, he declared, "that Cuba was sanitated [sic]; the building of the Panama Canal became an accomplished fact; and immense areas of land in tropical countries were reclaimed from primitive jungles and placed under cultivation." But he also emphasized UFC's "welfare work" in Central America, explaining that the company had focused on improving the "health and contentment" of its workers as well as building "churches and schools to meet denominational and racial requirements."[31]

By this time, however, UFC was determined to define itself not as a responsible private branch of the U.S. empire but rather as the progressive corporate antithesis of imperialism. This effort was led by Victor M. Cutter, who assumed UFC's presidency in the fall of 1924. Newspapers across the United States hailed his rise from banana farm timekeeper to company president as proof of the firm's forward-looking character, and UFC's own newsletter welcomed him as the new leader of the "largest and most progressive agricultural company in the world." "Under Mr. Cutter's regime," it predicted, "the United Fruit Company is bound to continue in its prosperity and through the further development of its extensive industrial and agricultural interests strengthen the ties that bind the Americas." In the following years, the firm would consistently stress these themes of development and cooperation, in many ways prefiguring the U.S. government's Good Neighbor policy.[32]

The major obstacle to this effort was the growing perception, in both the United States and Latin America, that UFC reigned over Central America as a corporate imperium. As the firm's chief spokesman, Cutter sought to dispel this notion. In an October 1924 speech, he emphatically denied that his company controlled its host nations. "None of our officials or employees is allowed to mix in the politics of a foreign country," he declared. "[W]e are not exploiting any country. We use sound business methods, try to give as well as receive, and in every way to encourage the native planters and aid other natives."[33] Imperialism, in this defense, entailed political control while business remained the progressive practice of civilization.

In this public relations effort, Cutter proved more than willing to denounce U.S. government imperialism. In an August 1925 speech, for example, he criticized Washington's overbearing approach to the region. The Monroe Doctrine was a fine idea, he declared, provided it "does not carry as a corollary control or domination" and that it "be completely separated from any trace of economic imperialism." Apparently forgetting his own speech of the previous October, he even asserted the term "American" "should not apply monopolistically to citizens of the United States" and that the word "native" should not be used toward Latin Americans.[34]

To be sure, longstanding views of tropicality continued to inform the thinking of Cutter and his colleagues and often emerged in their progressive rhetoric. In a long profile feature in *Forbes* magazine in March 1926, for example, Cutter stressed the company's role in "carrying American civilization into the jungles" and noted that "many of our best tropical executives are really missionaries, in a sense."[35] Even more revealing was an article entitled "Caribbean Tropics in Commercial Transition," which Cutter published in *Economic Geography* in October 1926. Declaring United Fruit "one of the most remarkable organizations in modern American finance," he observed that in the company's Central American enclaves "vast plantations with their correlated interests—railways, docks, stores, hospitals—dominate a landscape which forty years ago was an uninhabited primeval jungle."[36] The company's admirers were even more outspoken. As one writer for *Financial Digest* declared in July 1927, when UFC first appeared in the region, Central Americans themselves "had made little progress over the conditions in which they had existed centuries ago." Claiming that the firm "has proven the principal factor in bringing prosperity to that large part of Latin America where its influence is felt," the author reminded readers that the Central America lowlands, "now given over largely to banana cultivation, were formerly pestilential swamps" where the people lived in "poverty and ignorance."[37]

Although Central American nationalists contested this imperial narrative, they rarely managed to disentangle progressivism and tropicality. Instead, they produced a kind of binary opposite: an anti-imperialist racism that mourned the passing of their own great race. Both the company and West Indians who had played a crucial role in building its enclaves became the focus of an emergent politics that denounced the corporate imperium and the demographic changes it had wrought. In Costa Rica, for example, the Economic Society of Friends of the Nation, founded by racial nationalist Marco Aurelio Zumbado, warned of the dual threat posed by United Fruit's power and its black employees. In a November 1926 petition to the Costa Rican Congress, Zumbado declared that "foreign capitalism tends to convert people into colonies wherever it goes" and that "the negro benefits only the Company [and] . . . mixes our race, which is already blackening."[38]

Against the domestic U.S. backdrop of growing fears of a "rising tide of color" and corporate ascendancy associated with Fordism, UFC mounted a complex response to these challenges.[39] In addition to muting its praise of West Indian workers, it sought to shield itself from charges of imperialism. In April 1927, for example, Cutter acknowledged Latin American fears of imperial domination and the "foreign invasion of capital" but stressed that imperialism as an economic and political policy was "valueless" and had been renounced by the people and government of the United States. He went on to condemn "narrow-minded propagandists" who equated large-scale capitalism with imperialism. Far from imperial domination, he declared, UFC and other large corporations brought stability and progress. "Undeveloped countries should welcome large developments backed by large capital, for this means responsibility and permanency," he explained. "There is nothing to be ashamed of in size, because size in any company demands just dealing, efficient management, service to customers and benefit to countries involved." In other words, corporate giants such as UFC were not the problem; they were the solution. "It must be remembered," he argued, "that all past troubles . . . have been caused by small, irresponsible companies and individuals." In contrast, large firms brought "development without exploitation."[40]

The following month, at the Pan-American Commercial Conference in Washington, D.C., Cutter again posed transnational corporations as the antithesis of imperialism. "Contrary to alleged popular impression," he maintained, "there is no exploitation today nor are there monopolistic concessions anywhere in Latin America." Therefore, there was no reason to fear large corporations. After all, he emphasized, "[s]ize means responsibility. It means that the ablest men are in charge of operations and that there will be the fullest use of modern business practice and a realization of the need for service and development."[41]

Like other industrial leaders of the Fordist era, moreover, Cutter and other company officials stressed the benefits workers enjoyed under the corporate order. In the case of UFC, these included relatively high pay, quality health care, recreational activities, and modern consumer goods available in company commissaries. As Cutter declared in an October 1927 speech, "Fifteen years ago we did a general merchandise business of $3,000,000 in the undeveloped coastal regions which surround the Caribbean. Today we are doing a business of $10,000,000." Ignoring the role of population growth in this commercial expansion, he argued the increase stemmed from "educational methods, by learning what these people wanted and giving it to them, and by . . . increasing their purchasing capacity."[42] UFC reiterated this argument in its February 1928 annual report, which highlighted the $24 million in wages paid to its workers. The following May, in a speech to the Bond Club of New York, Cutter again praised the firm's contribution to the region. In addition to its vast payroll, he noted, UFC had brought the marks of material progress to Central America: harbors, steamship service, railways, hospitals, laundries. Equally important, he noted, "manufactured goods have been made available to the laboring classes in the coast towns at lower prices than ever before, making possible an appreciable improvement in the standards of living."[43]

To a large extent, this discourse reflected the Fordist turn in the United States, and it shared the ultimate objective of a quiescent workforce. But equally important in UFC's rhetorical shift was the relationship between its changing workforce and rising Central American nationalism. No longer able to argue that Central Americans were unwilling to contribute their labor, UFC shifted its public focus from the hard work of taming the tropics to the benefits employees derived from the firm. One important vehicle for this narrative was the company's official publication, *Unifruitco*. Launched in 1925, it focused on the consumer goods and quasi-civic activities employees enjoyed in the company's enclaves. Although most articles featured white Americans, the small number of Central Americans in managerial positions sometimes appeared in its pages. In contrast to earlier accounts, however, *Unifruitco* offered few details on the conditions of the firm's wage laborers and included virtually no images of West Indians.[44] With the number of West Indian workers shrinking and anti-black sentiment growing throughout Central America in the late 1920s, the company aimed to reduce tensions with host societies at the expense of its black migrant employees.

This effort was mirrored by policy changes implemented by the U.S. government. In late 1928, President-elect Herbert Hoover undertook a goodwill tour of Latin America. Promising a policy of nonintervention, Hoover hoped to ease the resentment that had built up over the previous decades. Such efforts laid the groundwork for the Good Neighbor policy of the 1930s. UFC sought to associate itself with this diplomatic initiative. In January 1929, Cutter predicted that Hoover's tour would bring the hemisphere together "more closely than at any time in history," but he also asserted that private enterprises such as UFC had long been engaged in such efforts. After all, he noted, "the capitalist and the business man have been the real pioneers in the movement to bring about a better understanding between the United States and Latin America." Cutter again pointed to rising consumerism as evidence of corporate-driven progress in the American tropics. "In the palm-thatched huts of Costa Rica and Guatemala," he observed, "you will find victrolas and safety razors and sewing machines. These one-time luxuries, now essentials, have been bought and paid for by . . . labor in coffee and banana plantations." Like Hoover's tour, statements such as these sought to reduce regional bitterness toward U.S. imperialism and open the way to increased trade and investment.[45]

In contrast to the discourse of earlier years, the hard work of taming the tropics now seldom appeared in company accounts, and West Indian workers themselves were entirely absent. This was partly a function of demographics. By 1930, Central American racial violence and anti-black immigration restrictions had pushed most West Indians out of UFC's employment, leaving the company a predominantly Spanish-speaking workforce. In addition to demanding wage increases and better treatment, these Central American laborers joined nationalists in denouncing the company as an example of "Yankee imperialism." UFC took a number of superficial steps to defuse this tension, including forming local subsidiaries and giving banana plantations titles derived from Central American rather than U.S. place names. But the company did not revive its celebration of "frontier" work and the laborers who performed it. This was not due to any change in UFC's activities, which still included the near-constant clearing and planting of new banana lands, nor did it reflect a shift in the culture of company officials, who remained enthralled by the discourse of tropicality and progress. Rather, the key factor was that most of its laborers were now Central American rather than West Indian. Whereas earlier recognition of black immigrants had strengthened the firm's claims to authority in the region, acknowledgement of its current workforce threatened to bolster the demands of Central American laborers and nationalists.

Despite these tactical shifts, UFC's narrative of bringing progress to the tropics displayed remarkable staying power, not only among company officials but also among the West Indian migrants who had once benefited from it. One example emerged in a debate over immigration in Costa Rica. In August 1930, the national census director, José Guerrero, published an article entitled "What Do We Want Costa Rica to Be—Black or White?" In it, he warned that United Fruit's proposed expansion to Costa Rica's Pacific coast would increase West Indians' racial contamination of the nation. "The Negro is the shadow of the banana," he declared. "Although today this shadow is confined to the Atlantic Zone, it will move toward other sectors of the republic." "Those who manage black workforces in foreign lands, indifferent to the fate of other races already settled there, can dedicate themselves solely to the extraction of wealth," he noted. "[B]ut how can we Costa Ricans who live permanently on this soil be indifferent to the Negro invasion of other sections of our nation?" Echoing the widely held image of Costa Rica as Central America's only white nation, he warned that further West Indian immigration would undermine the nation's civilization and progress.[46]

Such claims clashed with the West Indian narrative of Central American development, which had much in common with that of the UFC. This became apparent when W. A. Petgrave, a West Indian resident of Costa Rica's Caribbean lowlands, published a spirited reply to Guerrero. In his letter, Petgrave denounced Guerrero's eugenic arguments, in large part by reviving a narrative of work and empire that the UFC itself no longer deployed publicly. "Were there no Minor Keith, and as a consequence no United Fruit Company, and no Negro, who was able to stand the hardships," asserted Petgrave, Costa Rica would still be languishing in poverty and indebtedness. As such, he declared, "the Negroes can with as much reason claim Costa Rica as the land of their adoption as the Spaniard can and they have every right of being proud of their achievement, of making the Atlantic [Zone] what it is."[47]

While Petgrave's response may have heartened West Indian readers, it could not reverse their declining status in Central America. By the mid-1930s, black immigrants were restricted from most of Central America and barred from employment in nearly all of UFC's enclaves. For its part, the company continued to deny its position as a corporate imperium while resisting the claims of its Central American workforce—efforts that came crashing down in the wake of Guatemala's 1944 revolution. For their part, white American "old-timers" in the banana lands continued to spin yarns over cigars and gin fizzes about the rugged "frontier" days, when rough-and-tumble Yankees braved mortal dangers to carve orderly farms from the Central American jungle. In this sense, they echoed the narrative UFC had been telling for decades. But now the contribution of West Indians was largely absent. Once featured prominently, the work of black migrants no longer held a place in the company story of bringing progress to the tropics.

NOTES

1. Frederick Upham Adams, *Conquest of the Tropics: The Story of the Creative Enterprises Conducted by the United Fruit Company* (Garden City, NJ: Doubleday, 1914), 13.
2. Ibid., 59, 138, 161–165.
3. Mary Louise Pratt, *Imperial Eyes: Travel Writing and Transculturation* (London: Routledge, 1992); Fredrick B. Pike, *The United States and Latin America: Myths and Stereotypes of Civilization and Nature* (Austin: University of Texas Press, 1992); Nancy Stepan, *Picturing Tropical Nature* (Ithaca, NY: Cornell University Press, 2001). Also on the role of tropicality in imperial perception, see David Arnold, *The Tropics and the Traveling Gaze: India, Landscape, and Science, 1800–1856* (Seattle: University of Washington Press, 2006).
4. Julia Greene, *The Canal Builders: Making America's Empire at the Panama Canal* (New York: Penguin, 2009). An excellent earlier study is Michael Conniff, *Black*

Labor on a White Canal: Panama, 1904–1981 (Pittsburgh: University of Pittsburgh Press, 1985).

5. Studies of the U.S. banana industry and West Indian immigration to Central America include Philippe I. Bourgois, *Ethnicity at Work: Divided Labor on a Central America Banana Plantation* (Baltimore: Johns Hopkins University Press, 1989); Paul J. Dosal, *Doing Business with the Dictators: A Political History of the United Fruit Company in Guatemala, 1899–1944* (Wilmington, DE: Scholarly Resources, 1993); Trevor W. Purcell, *Banana Fallout: Class, Color, and Culture among West Indians in Costa Rica* (Los Angeles: UCLA/CAAS, 1993); Aviva Chomsky, *West Indian Workers and the United Fruit Company in Costa Rica, 1870–1940* (Baton Rouge: Louisiana State University Press, 1996); Mark Moberg, *Myths of Ethnicity and Nation: Immigration, Work, and Identity in the Belize Banana Industry* (Knoxville: University of Tennessee Press, 1997); Ronald N. Harpelle, *The West Indians of Costa Rica: Race, Class, and the Integration of an Ethnic Minority* (Kingston, Jamaica: Ian Randle, 2001); Lara Putnam, *The Company They Kept: Migrants and the Politics of Gender in Caribbean Costa Rica, 1870–1960* (Chapel Hill: University of North Carolina Press, 2002); John Soluri, *Banana Cultures: Agriculture, Consumption, and Environmental Change in Honduras and the United States* (Austin: University of Texas Press, 2005); Frederick Douglass Opie, *Black Labor Migration in Caribbean Guatemala, 1882–1923* (Gainesville: University Press of Florida, 2009); Glenn A. Chambers, *Race, Nation, and West Indian Immigration, 1890–1940* (Baton Rouge: Louisiana State University Press, 2010); and Jason M. Colby, *The Business of Empire: United Fruit, Race, and U.S. Expansion in Central America* (Ithaca, NY: Cornell University Press, 2011).

6. Pratt, *Imperial Eyes*.

7. On the broader patterns of U.S. discourse on climate and labor in this period, see Daniel E. Bender, *American Abyss: Savagery and Civilization in the Age of Industry* (Ithaca, NY: Cornell University Press, 2009), chapter 2.

8. William T. Brigham, *Guatemala, Land of the Quetzal* (New York: Charles Scribner's Sons, 1887), 339, 64.

9. Richard Harding Davis, *Three Gringos in Venezuela and Central America (New York: Harper and Brothers, 1896)*, 3–5, 140–148, 270, 177–182.

10. On the Panama railroad, see Aims McGuinness, *Path of Empire: Panama and the California Gold Rush* (Ithaca, NY: Cornell University Press, 2011).

11. Watt Stewart, *Keith and Costa Rica: The Biography of Minor Cooper Keith, American Entrepreneur* (Albuquerque: University of New Mexico, 1964); Keith to Grace, 17 March 1876, box 48, notebook 130, W. R. Grace Papers, Columbia University.

12. On the Guatemalan railroad, see Opie, *Black Labor Migration*.

13. Greene, *Canal Builders*; Conniff, *Black Labor on a White Canal*; Harry A. Franck, *Zone Policeman 88: A Close Range Study of the Panama Canal and Its Workers* (New York: Century Co., 1913), 12, 29–30, 64.

14. For a solid general history of the company, see Charles Morrow Wilson, *Empire in Green and Gold: The Story of the American Banana Trade* (New York: Greenwood Press, 1968[1947]).

15. O. Henry, *Cabbages and Kings* (New York: Exeter Books, 1986[1904]).

16. Nevin O. Winter, *Guatemala and Her People of Today* (Boston: Page Company, 1909), 91.

17. On the late-nineteenth- and early-twentieth-century celebration of industrialism in the United States as the highest form of human evolution, see Bender, *American Abyss*.

18. On the tariff debate, see Marcelo Bucheli, *Bananas and Business: The United Fruit Company in Colombia, 1899–2000* (New York: New York University Press, 2005), 28–29; Chester Donaldson to Secretary of State William Jennings Bryan, 12 May 1914, M-669, reel 30, RG 59, National Archives and Record Administration, College Park, Maryland (hereafter, NARA).

19. Franck, *Zone Policeman 88*, 124. Another popular account of the canal was Frederic J. Haskin, *The Panama Canal* (New York: Doubleday, 1913).

20. William, J. Showalter, "The Countries of the Caribbean." *National Geographic Magazine* 24:2 (February 1913): 227–250.

21. Adams, *Conquest of the Tropics*, 29–36, 58–59, 138, 161–165, 267.

22. David W. Southern, *The Progressive Era and Race: Reaction and Reform, 1900–1917* (Wheeling, WV: Harlan Davidson, 2005).

23. Ibid., 162, 174–175, 183, 193, 202.

24. John L. Williams, "The Rise of the Banana Industry and Its Influence on Caribbean Countries" (master's thesis, Clark University, 1925), 20–21.

25. For a more extensive analysis of this system of labor segmentation, see Colby, *Business of Empire*.

26. David Healy, *Drive to Hegemony: The United States in the Caribbean, 1898–1917* (Madison: University of Wisconsin Press, 1988); Robert Freeman Smith, *The United States and Revolutionary Nationalism in Mexico, 1916–1932* (Chicago: University of Chicago Press, 1972), esp. 79–84; Richard V. Salisbury, *Anti-Imperialism and International Competition in Central America, 1920–1929* (Wilmington, DE: Scholarly Resources, 1989).

27. On the changing definition of "imperialism," see Emily S. Rosenberg, *Financial Missionaries to the World: The Politics and Culture of Dollar Diplomacy, 1900–1930* (Durham, NC: Duke University Press, 2003), 23, 30.

28. *El Excelsior* (Guatemala City), 5 February 1923.

29. Geissler to Orellana, 4 March 1923, M-655, reel 20, RG 59, NARA.

30. Beaulac to State Department, 14–16 July 1924, vol. 125, RG 84, NARA.

31. W. E. Deeks, "Address of Welcome" and "Activities of the Medical Department of the United Fruit Company," *Proceedings of the International Conference on Health Problems in Tropical America* (Boston: United Fruit Company, 1924), 1–5, 1006–1010.

32. "How Victor Cutter Became Head of $150,000,000 Company at 43," *Boston Sunday Post* (12 October 1924); George Kent, "Head of $150,000,000 Corporation Rose from Obscure Post in Jungle," news clipping, box 3, scrapbook 1924–26; "We Greet the New President of the United Fruit Company," *Fruit Dispatch* (November 1924), box 1, folder 8, Cutter Papers, Rauner Library, Dartmouth College.

33. News clippings, October 1924, box 3, scrapbook 1924–26, Cutter Papers.

34. V. M. Cutter, "Trade Relations with Latin America," Boston, 7 August 1925, box 2, folder 14, Cutter Papers.

35. William A. McGarry, "Building a Business Empire in Tropical Jungles," *Forbes* (15 March 1926).

36. Victor M. Cutter, "Caribbean Tropics in Commercial Transition," *Economic Geography* 2:4 (October 1926): 496.

37. "The Romance of United Fruit, a New England Corporation," *Financial Digest* (July 1927).

38. Marco A. Zumbado R., "Un aspecto del asunto: Una visión del problema," 15 November 1926, memorandum to Costa Rican Congress, Serie Congreso, no. 15400; "Sociedad Económica de Amigos del Pais: Exposicion sobre el Problema Bananero," 6 January 1927, Serie Congreso, no. 15400, Archivo Nacional de Costa Rica, San José.

39. On the rising racial anxieties in the United States, see Bender, *American Abyss*, chapters 8–9.

40. V. M. Cutter, "Relations of United States Companies with Latin America," 23 April 1927, box 2, folder 14, Cutter Papers.

41. V. M. Cutter, "Latin-American Trade Relations," 4 May 1927, box 2, folder 14, Cutter Papers.

42. V. M. Cutter, "Our Greatest Economic Problem," *Current History* (October 1927): 74–76.

43. "United Fruit Reports on Foreign Business," *New York Times* (16 February 1928); V. M. Cutter, "Destiny and Development in Latin America," 29 March 1928, box 2, folder 14, Cutter Papers.

44. *Unifruitco* (Boston: United Fruit Co., 1925–54).

45. V. M. Cutter, "What Hoover Has Accomplished in Latin America," *Financial Digest* (January 1929).

46. José Guerrero, "Como se quiere que sea Costa Rica, blanca, o negra?" 13 August 1930, *La Tribuna*. For an excellent analysis of his article, see Putnam, *Company They Kept*, 73.

47. W. A. Petgrave, "A Reply to Audacity," 20 August 1930, *The Searchlight*, copy enclosed in Charles C. Eberdhardt to State Department, 23 August 1930, box 5581, folder 1, RG 59, USNA.

12

What Is Imperial about Coffee?

Rethinking "Informal Empire"

AUGUSTINE SEDGEWICK

What is imperial about coffee? On the one hand, imperialism in the specific sense of territorial conquest and political control has been a salient factor in coffee's long global history. Empires have produced coffee colonially in South and Southeast Asia, in the Americas and the Caribbean, and in Africa. But on the other hand, and in contrast to the tropical commodities with which it is often lumped—especially sugar and tea—coffee became a mass-consumer commodity only after newly independent Latin American countries turned to export-led development in the nineteenth century.[1] Moreover, unlike commodity forms of enclave colonialism—especially bananas, rubber, and more or less anything mined from the earth—the firms that have sold coffee as a consumer product have not usually owned the land on which it is cultivated. And finally, because the technical requirements of its production are flexible, and yields and margins are not necessarily improved by scaling up—in contrast to most manufactured consumer goods, and especially branded goods—small producers and family farmers have survived even among the largest, richest growers.[2] For all these reasons, when historians list the ways coffee has linked people and places over five centuries, they cite "trade, investment, immigration, conquest, and cultural and religious diffusion."[3] In other words, in the aggregate, trade and investment preponderate, exchange trumps extraction, and coffee contains more of the liberal than the imperial.[4]

This is the lens through which scholars have most often viewed the coffee history of the United States.[5] In this view, coffee appears as the potable form of the Monroe Doctrine, surpassing tea as the staple stimulant in the American diet exactly because it was produced abundantly in countries that had liberated themselves from European colonial control. The repeal of U.S. import duties in 1832, when decolonization was still an uncertain outcome of the American revolutions, kept prices low, promoting consumption and, in direct proportion, the growth of hemispheric commerce and formally liberal inter-American relations.[6]

Coffee's importance as a medium of hemispheric influence helps to explain why the U.S. has proven uninterested in producing coffee in its own colonial possessions, despite ample opportunities to do so. After the United States toppled Spain's American empire in 1898 and claimed the coffee-rich spoils for itself, none of its new island territories was put to work providing the domestic market with coffee. To the contrary, the tariff structure imposed on Puerto Rico and Cuba discouraged coffee production in favor of sugar. The story was much the same in Hawai'i. Meanwhile, in the Philippines, once among the world's leading coffee producers, pests had sent the industry into decline in the early 1890s, and no comprehensive effort was made to reverse that trend after 1898.[7] Instead, as per capita consumption rose along with immigration and industrialization, the U.S. outsourced its new "domestic" coffee industry to Latin America.

In this sense, to ask what is imperial about coffee is also to ask what is imperial about the United States—the "anti-colonial empire" nonpareil and, by no coincidence, the world's leading coffee consuming nation for more than a century—and especially its relations with Latin America.[8] If one academic view contends that there is comparatively little that is imperial about coffee, a dissenting and perhaps minority view insists that imperialism and free trade are not exclusive categories. Many historians have argued that the subjugation of one society to another can proceed in the absence of formal political and territorial control—through what is most often called "informal empire."[9] It is in exactly this "informal-imperial" sense that historians have described the rise of coffee and other export commodities after independence as a "second conquest of Latin America." Yet "conquest" here is merely a metaphor for the difference between the colonial and postcolonial periods, imperial extraction and liberal trade.[10] By this argument, whatever is imperial about coffee inheres in the market for it, in the terms of its exchange. As the price of coffee, a commodity produced on a competitive basis around the globe, has deteriorated over time against the price of the value-added manufactured goods produced in coffee-consuming countries, and against the price of capital itself, formal market equality has secured and generated substantive inequality and a de facto loss of sovereignty.[11]

This informal-imperial framework exposes power concealed in market relations that aspire to pass as equal or neutral, but it is limited in other significant ways. As Paul Kramer has argued, the concept of informal empire, developed as a critique of a liberal view of capitalism, tends to abstract "the relationship between capitalist social relations and state power." In consequence, Kramer writes, it obscures "the very political, social, economic, and cultural production and reproduction— and contestation—of capitalist relations on informal empire's varied grounds."[12] That is, the concept of informal empire tells us nothing about how coffee is produced, or about how its movement through space into consumption is produced. It assumes the existence of coffee in its exchangeable, consumable commodity form—ultimately a mystified, consumer's view, setting out for the supermarket or the café without a doubt that coffee will be there for the buying. More troubling, to accept the legitimacy of the category "informal empire," even as a mode of critique, is to implicitly assent to a limited definition of "empire" pure and simple that has itself worked as an instrument of imperial power, enabling, for example, the United States to describe its relations to coffee-producing countries in terms of freedom because it trades with them. That definition is not unanimous.

Two Alternative Views

How would "informal empire" look if capitalist social relations were restored to the picture? There are at least two alternative ways of thinking about what is imperial about coffee, and these are less about the criteria according to which historians might classify a particular relationship as imperial than the conditions under which people in specific historical situations have experienced and described them as imperial. These ways of thinking diverge from the conventional academic/consumer analysis on several key points. Most importantly, they reverse the lens and focus on production rather than exchange. This has several consequences, one of which is to expand the meaning of "coffee" itself. From the perspective of a producer, whether employer or employee, grower or worker, "coffee" is not merely a bean and a drink, already an internationally tradable and consumable commodity, but a plant, an industry dedicated to the cultivation and processing of that plant into its commodity form, and a social relation of production in that industry: coffee. Seeing coffee this way, as a hybrid, living eco- and social system, shifts the ground under the title question, undercutting the residual liberal assumptions concealed in an exchange-based concept of "informal empire," and bringing to the foreground its "formal" properties.

This distinction is not merely academic. The question of who decides what is and what is not imperial has often been inseparable from questions of what working people are up against and what they can possibly do about it. Certainly the people who deployed the concept of the imperialism of coffee in El Salvador in the late 1920s and early 1930s were concerned not with matters of definitional or conceptual purity, but with material processes in which they were embedded, in which, in fact, their lives were at stake. They used a language of imperialism to make sense of those processes and their consequences, to communicate their ideas with each other, and to try, in different ways, to get a working handle on transformational possibilities and opportunities.

The first of these alternative ways of thinking about the imperialism of coffee can perhaps be described as "nationalist." Here is what the Salvadoran journalist and social critic Alberto Masferrer saw in the late 1920s, at the height of the global "export boom" that exploded old social patterns and ways of life and enthroned coffee, the tree, the industry, and the social relation, in El Salvador, transforming the country into one of the world's leading producers and exporters of coffee: "The conquest of territory by the coffee industry is alarming. It has already occupied all the high ground and is now descending to the valleys, displacing maize, rice, and beans. It goes in the manner of the conquistador, spreading hunger, and misery."[13] In effect, Masferrer argued that conquest was not past, not a settled fact that lived on in an unequal exchange relation, but an open file.

Masferrer deployed this view of coffee as an ongoing imperial project to contest a narrower definition of imperialism held by the Salvadoran elites who made up the majority of the audience for his newspaper, *La Patria*, and he did so with a specifically nationalist political agenda in mind. Across Latin America, "liberal" elites who aimed to secure national sovereignty in the postcolonial period through export-led development equated independence with free participation in the world market. Masferrer disagreed. He was not concerned to judge independence along a spectrum of terms of trade, but instead by social and material terms of production. And if the terms of exchange had changed with decolonization, the terms of production had not.

Yet Masferrer's critique did not extend to the liberal nation-state itself. He argued that the problem of coffee's conquest could be resolved by a change in national politics, by implementing particular reforms, particularly those he identified as key tenants of "the vital minimum," the basic, universal rights that it fell to the nation to secure for its citizens: food, clothing, shelter, water, work, education, health care, rest and recreation, and recourse to a just legal system. As one historian of Masferrer's thought has observed, in his programmatic nationalism "the strength of the state and the health of its citizens were directly proportionate."[14] The imperialism of coffee had corrupted the national project in El Salvador in these two ways at once.

Masferrer's nationalist-reformist politics achieved a moment of ascendance in the late twenties and early thirties, in the first stages of the global depression, when the price of coffee fell by as much as two-thirds. Masferrer had the ear of Arturo Araujo, a president who had been born into the coffee elite but fashioned himself a social-democratic reformer. Yet the reformist program they developed was not as strong as the forces between which it was designed to mediate. The most glaring aspect of its weakness was that Masferrer's nationalist notion of the imperialism of coffee relinquished a broader perspective on the embeddedness of the national coffee industry, and the social relations and processes of production in that industry, in a global system of production and exchange. This artificial emphasis on the nation as a comprehensible historical protagonist made change appear as if it were at hand, as if it were more possible than it was—as if coffee growers who had pushed the coffee industry through space and time in the manner of conquistadors could be convinced to participate in the true national project by a simple reminder of the possibilities of that project, or by simple political means.

That was not how everyone saw it. While Masferrer was calling for reform, other groups rejected the idea that the "minimum" was enough and called for something more thoroughgoing. Their program was shaped by their own perception of the imperialism of coffee.

Jeffery Gould and Aldo Lauria-Santiago have documented the long history of organized opposition to both coffee capitalism and Yankee imperialism from the Salvadoran left. This opposition intensified in the interwar period in response to U.S. military intervention on the Central American isthmus, a 1923 loan on unfavorable terms from private American banks but secured by U.S. control of Salvadoran customs revenue, and the intensification of coffee production. When, in the global crisis of the twenties and thirties, the conditions on El Salvador's coffee farms deteriorated beyond their usual low standards, when wages evaporated and rations shrank to starvation levels, these two strands of opposition, anti-imperial and anti-capitalist, came together in new ways. The increasingly unified workers' movement, led after 1930 by Farabundo Martí, who had fought the American occupation of Nicaragua with Sandino, mobilized unprecedented numbers of coffee workers in the western coffee districts, the heart of the export economy. As the workers' groups gained strength, they also attracted suppressive attention not only from the Salvadoran government but also from the United States, which pushed Salvadoran officials to crack down on "Bolshevist" activity.[15]

In response, the Salvadoran leftists pushed back from a radicalized position. The making of common cause among urban and rural workers was the critical step in the growth of the left in El Salvador into a major social and political force. The nexus of workers' groups grew because organizers "opened new spaces of sociability that permitted communication of . . . revolutionary ideas" in the coffee districts.[16] The challenge for these organizers was not to convince people that there was a problem. The problem hungry coffee workers knew as intimately and unmistakably as they knew their own bodies. But the solution was harder to articulate—the idea that joining a union, joining other workers in a concerted campaign, would make a positive difference. To help make their case, union organizers carried pictures with them on the walking circuits they made in the countryside, graphic media through which they communicated their ideas and plans to diverse but largely illiterate audiences of working people.[17]

These drawn images hit all the touchstones of what scholars would describe as informal empire: "Nacional City Bank," "Yunay Frute," the "Internacional Rail-way." Their cartographic symbols included the American flag, the U.S. dollar, the Union Jack, heavy artillery, and warships. The most dramatic of the drawings depicted lines of power emanating from the United States, crossing the oceans, and penning in Latin America. These lines traced the trajectories of the telegraph cables across which price quotations and payments traveled from the United States; they traced the wakes of gunboats; they traced the paths of coffee from plantations in Latin America into the United States and Europe.

But they were also strikingly imprecise. In fact, on the drawing that depicts these lines of imperial power, no line actually connects the United States and El Salvador. Partly in consideration of this imprecision, Gould and Lauria-Santiago have argued that these graphic representations express a stock, even reductionist, Marxist-Leninist concept of capitalist imperialism. Perhaps so. Yet there is a way in which the imprecision of these drawings and their stock characterizations makes their use in Salvadoran labor organizing in the context of the world depression all the more interesting. Consider this: When leftist organizers went to make their case to people who worked coffee on specific coffee farms for specific coffee growers, they did not begin by caricaturing or villainizing individual plantation owners. Instead of personalizing and particularizing the problem and their proposal, they put it in the largest possible frame. They made reference to imperialism as "la ultima forma del capitalismo." They described the displacement of British imperialism by Yankee imperialism. Why? How did these ideas of imperialism help to clarify the experiences of the workers— primarily coffee workers—the organizers were asking to join the union and campaign?

The images were didactic tools, pictures of a problem that implied a solution. In effect, the drawn graphics argued that imperialism was the ultimate form of capitalism not simply in that capitalism had moved through stages until it became, eventually, imperial, but also because coffee capitalism had taken ultimate form on the ground in El Salvador as an imperial relation. Going well beyond Masferrer's reformism, the graphics argued that no matter who the plantation owners were, no matter which politicians happened to be in power, no matter what the wages were on a given day or in a given year, coffee was an imperial system of spatial and social control that demanded a systemic response at the same transnational scale.

And after making this case with images of the transnational ligatures of imperial power, the organizers then made the step that historians often don't make. They made the step from "imperialismo yanqui" to the conditions on particular plantations, from gunboats and loans and banks to everyday social and material life. After they had discussed their diagrams of the problem, the organizers asked about conditions on particular plantations.[18]

If any of the people present at these meetings had worked on or around James Hill's coffee plantations, this is what they might have seen unfold in the first decades of the twentieth century, this is what they might have thought when they heard that question, and this is an outline of the answer they might have given.

"In the Manner of a Conquistador"

James Hill was a son of Manchester who set out from England in 1888, when he was still a teenager, to make a go of business in El Salvador. Soon after he arrived, he put his capital, credit, and connections to work exporting coffee back to Europe. Before long, Hill moved into production, too, where there were ready opportunities, for his arrival coincided with the rise of new markets in land and labor, the crux of a transition that would remake El Salvador.[19]

In certain ways, Hill was precisely representative of a generation of European and North American immigrants to Latin America who came armed with investment capital, good credit, and promising connections to the world economy. Especially in the half century before 1929, this immigrant elite contributed money and knowledge alike to the reconfiguration of Latin American economies in the service of global industrial capitalism, and just as its center of gravity was shifting from Europe to the United States. In a sense, they helped to fund this shift and carry it through. It was manifest in El Salvador at several levels.

When El Salvador won its independence from Spain in 1821 there was not a single coffee tree within its borders. A little more than a century later, one of the world's smallest countries became its third-largest producer of coffee by volume, behind only—though well behind—Brazil and Colombia. If El Salvador would never match Brazil and Colombia in terms of volume, it surpassed them by other metrics. It was the world's most intensive coffee producer, squeezing out the highest yields per acre, and it was especially dependent on coffee. Coffee accounted for 93 percent of El Salvador's export earnings in 1929 and close to 50 percent of its domestic product.[20] El Salvador was a coffee economy of unmatched intensity, and this singular dedication to coffee meant that the fluctuations of the world market were felt more strongly in El Salvador than elsewhere.

In other respects El Salvador was typical. It achieved its position in the world coffee economy through a process absolutely characteristic of its time and place. As was the case across Latin America, coffee capitalists in El Salvador, "native" criollo elite and immigrant elite alike, amassed the pool of start-up resources they required through theft and violence cloaked in law and passing as liberalism. Their liberalization program took shape in the second half of the nineteenth century around a modernizing project—privatization of traditional communal lands—that made the basic factors of production, land and labor, available for purchase simultaneously.[21]

In El Salvador specifically, the best land for coffee growing ran up the slopes of the volcanic highlands, where the temperature was mild and the topsoil was thick. For the same reasons, these areas were densely settled by subsistence-farming peasant communities. When the market-oriented liberal regime took land from these "unproductive" communities and put it up for private sale in the 1880s, the uprooted people were consolidated into a workforce for the coffee farms by vagrancy laws enforced by a new arm of the national police.[22] Where coffee plantations did not replace cultivated communal lands, they swallowed woodlands that had been an important factor in subsistence economies: the source of game, fruit, fuel, and medicine.[23] It was not simply the case that privatization victimized Indian and ladino peasant communities. Rather, land privatization began once it had become possible to victimize peasant communities, once the central state had become strong enough to manage the consequences.[24] Afterward, the coffee economy's repressive apparatus, in part private, in part public, grew in proportion to coffee's share of El Salvador's exports.[25]

If there were sections of the peasantry that emerged from privatization with small plots of their own, the situation undoubtedly favored the capitalist elite, especially over time, as the shape and nature of the Salvadoran coffee industry and the world economy more generally changed.[26] Before 1914, Europe was unquestionably the best market for Salvadoran coffee. European consumers much preferred "mild" coffee from Central America and Colombia to the Brazilian coffee, thin, bitter, cheaper, that dominated the U.S. market. Importers in Europe, and in Germany especially, paid a premium for Salvadoran coffees.

Then world war changed commercial patterns by force. With European capital frozen and the European market closed to Latin American exports, U.S. bankers picked up Salvadoran accounts and U.S. ports, especially San Francisco, took more of the country's coffee. In connection with these changes in the world market, the gap between large and small landholders in El Salvador began to increase. Concentration of coffee-producing land in elite hands took off after 1914.[27] The reasons are multiple: the erosion over time of the fertility of land planted in coffee, which especially hurt smallholders, whose plots were often marginal to begin with and who lacked capital to invest in new land or in chemical fertilizers to restore the old; the increasing world market preference for coffee beans that had been washed during processing, which shifted profits toward the owners of processing plants; the cumulative effects of the comparative advantage of large producers, especially access to credit, which increased the more tightly El Salvador's coffee industry was integrated into systems of international finance; and the related fact of price volatility, which hurt most those who could least afford to ride out the troughs.

The first three decades of the twentieth century delivered to El Salvador "three intense cycles of rapid economic growth, each based on a doubling or tripling of the price of coffee followed by a period of decline."[28] Coffee producers with cash reserves or access to credit capitalized on the volatility. One family whose interests had been primarily in banking moved into coffee aggressively; they had three farms in 1914 and twenty by 1929.[29] James Hill expanded his holdings from five to eleven plantations between 1917 and 1919, through the trough of the wartime downturn, and acquired three more during the postwar boom.[30] Because the country's private banks didn't serve small borrowers, they had to borrow from rich neighbors, who were known to "lend at exorbitant rates on short terms" and always with an eye toward acquiring more land.[31] By increments, the concentration of land and productive capacity in elite hands accomplished what legal privatization had initiated, liquidating the social institutions and networks that had insulated peasants, Indians, and smallholders against the demands of the export economy for their land and labor. Increasing numbers went to work for growers such as James Hill.

Sweetness and Hunger

Like Colombian coffee and coffee from other regions of Central America, Salvadoran coffee is what traders at the time called "mild" coffee. "Mild" was an expression of quality codified by importers and roasters in San Francisco at the turn of the twentieth century to distinguish the coffees available via the steamship routes linking California to the Pacific coast of Latin America from Brazilian coffees, and to thereby boost their value. Mild coffees could not compete with Brazilian on price. If all coffee tasted the same, Brazil could and probably would have monopolized the world market. But mild coffees were "sweet" in the cup, while Brazilian coffees were comparatively thin and sour. The viability of the coffee industry in El Salvador and other mild-coffee countries depended on the ability and willingness of consumers to pay a premium for this sweetness, and on the ability of producers to compress this price difference into a premium that seemed the natural expression of the quality difference.

The sweetness that made mild coffee seem worth paying for resulted from the sugars and fats that developed in the seed of each coffee cherry as it matured. So the production of sweetness reduced to two steps: the cultivation of the photosynthetic process that led to the sexual maturity of the plant, and abrupt intervention into that process to capture ripeness in fungible form. The second and climactic step, capturing ripeness by harvesting coffee, required, first of all, abundant labor. Each 100-pound, export-ready sack of coffee beans represented about a week's work for a single picker during a limited window of roughly six weeks variably between November and February. By the mid-1930s, Hill employed more than 4,000 people during the harvest.[32]

Producing mild coffee successfully also required quality labor. Coffee cherries, which look and feel in the hand like oblong cranberries, grow on tough stems in thick clusters that snake around slender branches. A worker picking coffee in Brazil on the high-volume, low-price model might encircle a branch in her palm or between his first finger and thumb and strip it clean with a single pass, shedding leaves, twigs, and cherries all at once into a screen or onto the ground. Stripping branches would produce a harvest of uneven ripeness and spoil future harvests by damaging the tree. It was not that the quality of the crop was of no concern in Brazil, but that Brazilian coffee had a comparatively low quality ceiling.[33]

In contrast, where quality was at a premium, harvesting required an abundance of care. It proceeded not by stripping branch after branch, but in multiple waves of picking done selectively and delicately, by rapid contraction of the thumb and the first two or three fingers around one or two cherries at a time, each contraction augmented and completed by a quick quarter turn of the wrist. James Hill expected his harvest workers to collect 20,000 cherries a day in exactly this way.[34]

The demands of quality production shaped patterns and practices of labor discipline. First and foremost, they confounded the idea of supervision. Getting thousands of people to work with the requisite level of care and detail, across the vast archipelago of Hill's plantation complex, amid thickets of coffee trees that met in tangles of branches and riots of leaves, required something more. Hill and his coffee-growing peers required the cooperation—though that word gives the wrong sense of the requirement—of the people they employed. Hill won their compliance through food. The prerequisite for this approach to labor management was hunger.

The importance of hunger was axiomatic among coffee growers. They saw it as the only firm terrain on which their interests could be reconciled with those of their employees. By convention and convenience, and in unison with planters across the global tropics who lamented the "natural" connections between soil fertility and native laziness, Salvadoran coffee planters explained the fundamental conflict of interest between employer and employee as a matter of biology, of race in place. Hill told a traveling journalist that his workers could do twice as much as they did, but they were "born lazy, and once they've got enough to eat, don't care." Another planter echoed Hill's comment: His workers' "wants were so easily satisfied that when they had earned enough to exist they stopped."[35] Facing this impasse, coffee growers sharpened the trope into a prod. One grower described how, when a worker didn't keep pace, "the man's food is withheld, and this quickly puts activity into his unwilling limbs."[36] Coffee growers turned the metabolic process on its head: Hunger gave energy for labor, eating produced idleness.

In theory, legal dispossession cut off coffee workers from the means of subsistence, but in practice calories overspilled property lines. Energy was available to people who weren't its deeded owners as fruit that grew on the trees used to shade the coffee trees, as beans that were used as groundcover to enrich the soil, and as game that lived among the coffee and fed on the immanent richness of its ecosystem. The foraging of these food sources constituted a subeconomy through which landless coffee workers could pursue some basic caloric independence. From a grower's perspective, this was inefficiency. Instilling hunger that could be reliably mobilized as labor required that growers extend their monopolistic control from land titles to the land's actual and potential energy.

Some coffee growers went about this as they had achieved and preserved land monopolization—by force and terror. For example, one of Hill's neighbors kept orange trees—most likely to shade his coffee and produce a small crop for local markets. When he caught his workers picking oranges instead of coffee, he put a stop to it by putting a bullet through a worker's forehead.[37] An overseer on another nearby farm was said to have beaten a ten-year-old to death for eating a mango from one of the plantation's trees.[38] But violence also had its costs. Coffee workers could choose, within limits, where to work for the harvest season. Salvadoran growers in particular depended for harvest labor on the annual arrival of migrant workers from around the country and from Honduras. Surely stories, advice, and warnings moved along these routes too.

Violence suffused the social context of coffee production, but within that context James Hill seems to have eschewed direct violence as a tool of everyday management and administration. Instead, he approached the problem of labor mobilization and control through the control of space and energy. He imposed a strict structural order on his plantations to route the sun's energy to his trees through the earth with the least possible loss, the fewest nutrients turned into something other than something that would become coffee. He aimed to establish an energy monopoly that produced coffee and hunger in corresponding amounts.

For example, Hill seeded the ground of coffee groves thickly with beans that replenished the soil with nitrogen that coffee trees sucked up and turned into new cells, new branches, new harvests. Hill planted several classes of beans on his plantations, and each had unique properties that shaped its specialized usages. Near new trees, Hill planted cowpea, or black-eyed pea, since it provided the most enrichment; in sloped areas, he planted cowpea or jackbean, because their root systems penetrated deep into the soil and prevented runoff and erosion; near all roads, he planted velvet bean.[39] The United Fruit Company had introduced the velvet bean to Central America in the early twentieth century on its Atlantic Coast banana plantations. Hill was an early adopter. Not only was velvet bean a fast-growing annual that left a thick layer of humus on top of the soil, and not only did it double as a good source of animal feed, it was also particularly well suited for labor-intensive plantation agriculture because it was poorly suited for human consumption. Unless it was prepared carefully, boiled and reboiled, and sometimes even then, toxins in velvet bean caused whoever ate it vomiting and cramping intestinal pain at best and psychosis at worst.[40] Planting velvet bean where public roads intersected his private property, Hill defended his energy monopoly against pillage from outside.

Coffee growers in El Salvador also interplanted coffee with shade trees to facilitate even ripening and decrease labor costs. In the early years of El Salvador's coffee industry, hardy, common fruit trees—mango, papaya, avocado, and others—were most often used as shade. Workers quickly learned to look for a coffee farm liberally dotted with fruit trees, which they treated as "a common resource," eating as they worked to supplement their daily rations of tortillas and beans.[41] But after World War I, Hill extended the system of private property to the fruit trees on his plantations by exercising his right to cut them down. Other growers apparently did the same. By the late twenties, fruit trees had all but disappeared from the coffee regions.[42]

In these ways, Hill engineered his plantations to feed his trees and starve his workers. The idea was to make eating a condition of working. Hill used his control over hunger and food to structure the workday. When there was work that urgently needed to be done, including the work of the harvest, he used food to attract workers to it. That meant adding a third meal, always breakfast, to workers' daily compensation, one more thick corn or flour tortilla and one more cupful of beans cooked in salt water. Breakfast was invariably the extra meal because it was a way of obligating people to show up on time. So breakfast was before six or not at all; lunch was at noon and never before; and dinner was at five promptly—just as important as an early breakfast, to prevent thefts after dark.[43] Those who wanted to eat arrived to work on time, left on time, and in the interim worked as directed.[44]

The War for Coffee

That was the vision. That was Hill's dream of so controlling space that he could contain the pathways of energy and nutrients within property lines, creating from this regime of spatial control a regime of labor control that reduced people to perfectly efficient instruments of his will, simple mechanisms in a photosynthetic-metabolic circuit of energy transmission from sun to soil to trees to coffee cherries to beans to sweetness in the cup. Free of friction, free of noise, free of static, infinitely profitable.

That vision was immensely powerful and profitable, but it was never fully realized. Hill's workers did everything they could to contest and confound his campaign to transform them into mechanisms that took in and expended standardized quantities of energy in the course of routinized operations. Their struggles focused on the most basic necessities and the largest possible goals. They proceeded haltingly and unevenly, working at spontaneous flashpoints of individual opportunity and along thick, strategic social networks of kinship, friendship, love, and lust. They sought out the weakest seams of Hill's system of spatial and social control and ripped holes in it when they could—sometimes literally. Hill explained to a U.S. journalist in the twenties that if a planter had good fruit trees, he might just go ahead and "cut a hole in the fence in a convenient spot as he knew the peasants would cut one anyway."[45] This was the problem to which deforestation was the only answer.

Hungry workers also opened space in time by taking advantage of Hill's inability to control all of his land simultaneously and perpetually. Calories leaked into these spaces in time. For example, unlike velvet bean, cowpea and jackbean were excellent food crops. As soon as they were mature enough to harvest, a scramble to do so started. Hill put workers on the job to do it as quickly as possible. He knew that until the task was done other workers would be harvesting the beans for themselves. Hill wasn't planning to eat them, or to serve them, for that matter. Instead he wanted to harvest the seeds to replant on his own plantations and to sell to neighboring growers, a sideline in the byproducts of spatial control.[46]

Darkness—the dark of night and dark pockets of space within the coffee groves—was a key ally of coffee workers. Night was not only a time when no work took place; it also concealed the ways people used their time away from work. This time could be especially valuable during the harvest season. Workers might leave a sack of picked coffee hidden among the trees or buried in the ground and return at night to carry it away, taking it to the market for their own account. Or they might secrete a handful of cherries every now and again in a bag hidden under their clothes. Or they might continue to pick for themselves after most of the workers had gathered to weigh their daily harvest and collect their pay.[47] Such tactics were most common after four in the afternoon, when picking stopped and weighing started, and after six in the evening, when the sun went down. To prevent this leakage, Hill ordered his managers never to leave the coffee groves without making sure that all the workers had left as well.[48]

Yet the human systems Hill relied on to turn his vision of spatial control into social control were also full of holes. Managers and supervisors were tightly linked into the social networks within which coffee production took place. Hill did everything he could to sever these links. He avoided employing managers on plantations near where they had been raised. He shifted managers from plantation to plantation. He tried to prevent fraternizing. He ordered one manager: "To manage these people you need to separate yourself from all friendly contact with them. It's impossible to control them in the day and to make them obey you if you're socializing with them at night."[49]

Yet Hill was perpetually, infuriatingly, and perhaps predictably unable to get his managers and supervisors to adopt his standards. There were many reasons for this. Managers were probably scraping by themselves—a small bribe could make a difference. Managers were also always subject to demotion back to the general workforce, in which case a repu-

tation for kindness might soften the landing. In light of such considerations, some managers inflated the work totals of favored workers, who
were able to earn increased rations and wages as a result. Some managers
brought their families, their friends, or their mistresses to live with them,
and nourished them with Hill's proprietary food and shelter. Others
simply seem to have been more empathetic than Hill would have liked.
"Who is giving the breakfast rations left-over from the morning to people
in the afternoon?" Hill demanded of one of his managers. "Anyone who
does this is a complete idiot, because it takes out of your hands one of the
few means that you have of requiring people to show up for work early."[50]

More or less immediate and opportunistic strategies of resistance to
and survival within the regime of coffee productivity were interwoven
with and plugged into other organized, institutional, collective efforts.
Even before the concerted push by urban activists and leftist workers'
groups to organize coffee plantations, coffee workers met among themselves to contest the reigning system of coffee production. Hill knew as
much, and he was happy to discuss it with a U.S. journalist who asked.

> "Bolshevism? Oh, yes," said Mr. Hill cheerily. "It's drifting in. The work-
> people hold meetings on Sundays and get very excited. They say: 'We
> dig the holes for the trees! We clean off the weeds! We prune the trees!
> We pick the coffee! Who earns the coffee, then? . . . We do!' . . . Why,
> they've even picked out parcels that please them most, because they like
> the climate or think that the trees are in better condition and will produce
> more. Yes, there'll be trouble one of these days."[51]

Hill knew that his workers saw the future in terms of a radical reor-
ganization of productive space, an inversion of the social relations of
production based on the ownership and control of land, and he prepared
for the eventuality of trouble as a matter of course.

When they were mobilizing coffee workers in the Salvadoran countryside, leftist organizers not only drew pictures of the problem but also
of the world they believed they could bring into being—"La Dictadura
del Proletariado." This dictatorship of the workers was not necessarily
a standard image of liberation by technology cribbed from doctrinal
tracts. It was a picture of a paradise of food that derived from the control of space and control of the distribution of resources through space.

At the top were the people. Just below them was the source of all common wealth and welfare: food production, cornfields, and livestock. Everything else followed from grain and meat. First the general economic council, the door through which all food moved into distribution. Then, immediately under the economic council, so close to it as to be inseparable, so tightly knit to the will of the people as to be inextricable from their control, was the infrastructural system of food distribution. All other forms of power, industrial power, military power, electric power, branched out from the power of the people to feed themselves. In effect, it was a picture of the world they lived in turned on its head, "imperialism yanqui" overthrown.

Was it also an image that set people into motion? In January 1932, as coffee prices fell and wages followed, and in the wake of a stolen election, bands of working people linked to the International Communist Party through the nexus of local leftist groups refused to continue to work "only for the tortillas," and joined together to "make the workers the owners." The state responded to their uprising by slaughtering tens of thousands of "communists," including many who had not in fact participated in the rebellion. The big coffee growers threw their material and political support behind the upstart president, Maximiliano Hernández Martínez, who oversaw the killing.[52]

At the same time, in the global frame, the world crisis of capitalism hastened shifts that were already under way and pushed the coffee countries of Latin America especially into still closer relations with the United States. The leading coffee consuming countries in Europe moved to protect their economies behind tariff walls and other obstacles to international exchange. In contrast, the United States kept its coffee market open as a point of grand strategy. What had been a competitive, multipolar global trade came to be in effect unipolar, dominated by the United States, which became the destination for virtually all of James Hill's coffee and the vast majority of Salvadoran and Latin American coffee more generally.

With the effective colonization of the world market by the United States, coffee prices hit new lows. For Hill—as undoubtedly for others— what this shift required was a tightening of the screws and a containment of the consequences. Yet the sweetness he achieved by instrumentalizing hunger, an approach secured by state violence and subsumed into the sphere of legitimate liberal commerce through ongoing commercial relations with the United States, allowed him to win viable prices and large orders from importers in San Francisco and New York. Between 1929 and 1941, Hill nearly doubled the area of land he had under cultivation and elevated his annual yields to a new plane, making a harvest of a crisis that swamped many of El Salvador's most prominent families and besieged its working people.

In the United States, Hill's coffee appeared as the negative image of its production—as a source of energy and pleasure. Coffee contains very few calories, but of course it does have energy value as a stimulant, a spur to brain and muscle work that recruits stored calories for immediate metabolism. To make people work at producing coffee, Hill starved them of energy by controlling the space they inhabited; from their hunger he crystallized a source of energy that was abundantly available to people who drank it because they needed a pick-me-up, because they wanted to keep going, because they wanted to do more work.

The Dictatorship of the Consumer

If we see the imperialism of coffee as not merely an "informal" relation, not merely a market or an exchange relation, but rather a social relation that ultimately inheres in the control of space, this might also change how we see coffee the exchangeable and consumable commodity. "Fair trade" and "equal exchange" certifications advance a promotional argument about the unfair structure of the coffee market, but where are the coffees that cut against the conquest and control of space, against instrumentalized hunger—against the conditions on which market relations are founded, on which market relations have depended, and which market relations obscure? Recent scholarly research suggests that the most common certified coffees are of limited value for this purpose.[53] As a result of the failure of these certifications to make a substantive difference in this regard, activist entrepreneurs and organizations are increasingly targeting hunger and access to productive resources, rather than low prices or poverty in general, as the most pressing social problems in the global coffee industry.[54]

The leading programs that do so aim for "food sovereignty" for coffee workers. The concept of food sovereignty goes beyond the related idea of "food security" by promoting not only a sufficiency of food but also local control of the productive space and resources that generate a sufficiency.[55] This form of sovereignty has been increasingly articulated as a human right, and it does seem basic to the viability of the Western concept of the human being as a choice-making entity. As Hill and his colleagues knew well, without food sovereignty there could be no choice, only a question of what must be done next in order to eat. But if—in precise opposition to a main current of its long global history—coffee production were to take place within a context of food sovereignty, a context in which hunger is not an instrument of labor discipline, perhaps it could be described as entrepreneurial rather than imperial.

I do not intend this as an unreserved endorsement. After all, Joseph Conrad put the words on paper by Kurtz's hand: "By the simple exercise of our will we can exert a power for good practically unbounded." That is also the quotation Joan Didion used for the epigraph to *Salvador*, her document of coffee's long war of conquest in El Salvador, and of the murderous role the United States played in suppressing the return of the 1930s workers' campaign in the 1970s and 1980s. Indeed, the increasing availability of "food sovereignty" coffees vests people who buy coffee with a power over people who work coffee that is yet more like the imperial power of a self-fashioned savior, more like a dictatorship of the consumer. That is the power to grant to other people the power and the freedom to determine the terms on which they eat and work and live—and it is also the power to refuse to do so, to deny them that power and that freedom.

NOTES

1. William Roseberry, "Introduction," in Roseberry et al., eds., *Coffee, Society, and Power in Latin America* (Baltimore: Johns Hopkins, 1995) p. 2.
2. Roseberry, "Introduction"; William G. Clarence-Smith and Steven C. Topik, "Introduction: Coffee and Global Development," and Topik, "The Integration of the World Coffee Market," in Clarence-Smith and Topik, eds., *The Global Coffee Economy in Africa, Asia, and Latin America, 1500–1989* (New York: Cambridge University Press, 2003).
3. Clarence-Smith and Topik, "Introduction," 1.
4. Topik, "Integration," 29–30.
5. Michael F. Jiménez, "'From Plantation to Cup': Coffee and Capitalism in the United States, 1830–1930," in Roseberry et al., eds., *Coffee, Society, and Power*, 38–64.
6. Topik, "Integration," 37–39.

7. William G. Clarence-Smith, "Coffee Crisis in Asia, Africa, and the Pacific, 1870–1914," in Clarence-Smith and Topik, eds., *Global Coffee Economy*.

8. On the U.S. as the paradigmatic free-trade empire, see Thomas McCormick, "From Old Empire to New: The Changing Dynamics and Tactics of American Empire," in Alfred W. McCoy and Francisco A. Scarano, eds., *Colonial Crucible* (Madison: University of Wisconsin, 2009) pp. 75–79.

9. Two prominent examples: John Gallagher and Ronald Robinson, "The Imperialism of Free Trade," *Economic History Review*, new series 6:1 (1953) pp. 1–15; and William Appleman Williams, *The Tragedy of American Diplomacy* (1959; 50th anniv. ed., New York: W.W. Norton, 2009) pp. 18–57.

10. Stephen C. Topik, "Coffee," in Topik and Allen Wells, eds., *The Second Conquest of Latin America: Coffee, Henequen, and Oil during the Export Boom, 1850–1930* (Austin: University of Texas Press, 1997).

11. John M. Talbot, *Grounds for Agreement: The Political Economy of the Coffee Commodity Chain* (Lanham, MD: Rowman & Littlefield, 2004).

12. Paul A. Kramer, "Power and Connection: Imperial Histories of the United States in the World," *American Historical Review* 136 (December 2011) pp. 1374–1376.

13. Masferrer quoted in Everett Alan Wilson, "The Crisis of National Integration in El Salvador, 1919–1935" (Ph.D. diss., Stanford University, 1970) p. 122.

14. See Karen Racine, "Alberto Masferrer and the Vital Minimum: The Life and Thought of a Salvadoran Journalist, 1868–1932," *The Americas* 54:2 (October 1997) pp. 209–237; quotation 211.

15. Jeffery Gould and Aldo Lauria-Santiago, *To Rise in Darkness: Revolution, Repression, and Memory in El Salvador, 1920–1932* (Durham, NC: Duke University Press, 2008) pp. 1–169. See also Aldo Lauria-Santiago, *An Agrarian Republic: Commercial Agriculture and the Politics of Peasant Communities in El Salvador* (Pittsburgh: University of Pittsburgh Press, 1999). For the loan specifically, see Emily S. Rosenberg, *Financial Missionaries to the World: The Politics and Culture of Dollar Diplomacy* (Durham, NC: Duke University Press, 2004) pp. 108–112.

16. Gould and Lauria-Santiago, *To Rise in Darkness*, 64.

17. These are collected as an appendix to Jorge Schlesinger, *Revolucíon comunista: Guatemala en peligro?* (Guatemala City: Castañeda, 1946); two are reproduced and discussed in Gould and Lauria-Santiago, *To Rise in Darkness*, 65–69.

18. Gould and Lauria-Santiago, *To Rise in Darkness*, 68.

19. See Lauria-Santiago, *An Agrarian Republic*. On the formation of the coffee elite in El Salvador and Central America more generally, see Jeffery M. Paige, *Coffee and Power: Revolution and the Rise of Democracy in Central America* (Cambridge, MA: Harvard University Press, 1997) pp. 13–95; and for Hill specifically, see p. 19.

20. Alejandro D. Marroquín, "Estudio Sobre la Crisis de los Años Treinta en El Salvador," *Anuario de Estudios Centroaméricanos* 3 (1977) p. 118.

21. For a synthetic comparative look at this process across national contexts, see Robert G. Williams, *States and Social Evolution: Coffee and the Rise of National Governments in Central America* (Chapel Hill: University of North Carolina, 1994).

22. See C.F.S. Cardoso, "Historia Economica del Café en Centroamérica (Siglo XIX)," *Estudios Sociales Centroaméricanos* 4 (January 1975); David Browning, *El Salvador: Landscape and Society* (New York: Clarendon Press, 1971) pp. 216–218; Rafael Menjívar, *Acumulación Originaria y el Desarrollo del Capitalismo en El Salvador* (San José, Costa Rica: EDUCA, 1980).

23. Wilson, "Crisis," 29.

24. Hector Lindo Fuentes, *Weak Foundations: The Economy of El Salvador in the 19th Century* (Berkeley: University of California Press, 1991) pp. 131–136.

25. Ana Patricia Alvarenga, "Reshaping the Ethics of Power: A History of Violence in Western Rural El Salvador, 1880–1932" (Ph.D. diss., University of Michigan, Ann Arbor, 1994).

26. Aldo Lauria-Santiago emphasizes the unevenness and incompleteness of this process, the survival of smallholders and Indian land claims. See *Agrarian Republic*. On the capital intensity of coffee production over time, see Browning, *El Salvador: Landscape and Society*, 168–169.

27. Lauria-Santiago argues that the twenties boom was the context of this process, but I suspect, based on Hill's experience, that the wartime slump was just as important if not more so. See *Agrarian Republic*, 157 and 234.

28. Gould and Lauria-Santiago, *To Rise in Darkness*, 2–3.

29. Gould and Lauria-Santiago, *To Rise in Darkness*, 7. The Guirola family owned a plurality interest in the Banco Salvadoreño, a competitor of the Banco Occidental.

30. Figures from "Cosechas de café de fincas propias, 1917–1947," in the uncollected papers of J. Hill y Cia., Las Tres Puertas, Santa Ana, El Salvador (hereafter JHP). Copies in author's possession.

31. Belarmino Suarez quoted in Wilson, "Crisis," 45.

32. J. Hill, "Raising Coffee in Salvador," *Tea and Coffee Trade Journal* (December 1936) p. 424.

33. For the "carelessness" of Brazilian production, see Warren Dean, *Rio Claro: A Brazilian Plantation System, 1820–1920* (Stanford, CA: Stanford University Press, 1976) pp. 36–38.

34. Hill, "Raising Coffee."

35. Quotations in Arthur Ruhl, *The Central Americans: Adventures and Impressions Between Mexico and Panama (New York: Charles Scribner's Sons, 1928)*, 203 and 199, respectively.

36. Rodolfo Duke quoted in Alvarenga, "Ethics of Power," 80–81.

37. Criminal contra Enecon Godoy por homicidio en Eulalio Ventura, Fondo Judicial, Departamento de Santa Ana, 1930, Box 101, Archivo General Nacional, San Salvador, El Salvador.

38. Gould and Lauria-Santiago, *To Rise in Darkness*, 200.

39. Libro de órdenes para trabajo en las fincas, ca. 1919–21, JHP.

40. Daniel Buckles, Bernard Triomphe, and Gustavo Sain, *Cover Crops in Hillside Agriculture: Farmer Innovation with Mucuna* (Ottawa: International Development Resource Centre, 1998).

41. Wilson, "Crisis," 122.
42. Wilson, "Crisis," 122–125; quotation 122.
43. Libro de órdenes para trabajo en las fincas, ca. 1919–21, JHP.
44. Hill quoted in Ruhl, *Central Americans*, 203.
45. Ruhl, *Central Americans*, 204.
46. Libro de órdenes para trabajo, ca. 1919–21, JHP.
47. Alvarenga, "Ethics of Power," 96–97 and 176.
48. Libro de órdenes para trabajo, ca. 1919–21, JHP.
49. Ibid.
50. Ibid.
51. Ruhl, *Central Americans*, 204.
52. See especially Gould and Lauria-Santiago, *To Rise in Darkness*; and Jeffrey L. Gould, "On the Road to 'El Porvenir,'" in Greg Grandin and Gilbert M. Joseph, eds., *A Century of Revolution: Insurgent and Counter-insurgent Violence during Latin America's Long Cold* War (Durham, NC: Duke University Press, 2010).
53. For example, Daniel Jaffee, *Brewing Justice: Fair Trade Coffee, Sustainability, and Survival* (Berkeley: University of California Press, 2007) pp. 165–198; V. Ernesto Mendez et al., "Effects of Fair Trade and Organic Certifications on Small-scale Coffee Farmer Households in Central America and Mexico," *Renewable Agriculture and Food Systems* 25:3 (2010) pp. 236–251.
54. For example: the programs sponsored by Coffee Kids, a charity founded by a Rhode Island coffee roaster (www.coffeekids.org); and the coffee produced by the California-based NGO Community Agroecology Network (store.communityagroecology.net/ProductDetails.asp?ProductCode=AE_NICA).
55. See Hannah Wittman, Annette Aurelie Desmarais, and Nettie Wiebe, eds., *Food Sovereignty: Reconnecting Food, Nature, and Community* (Halifax, NS: Fernwood Publishing, 2010).

13

Home Land (In)security

The Labor of U.S. Cold War Military Empire in the
Marshall Islands

LAUREN HIRSHBERG

Cold War Insecurity in the Marshall Islands

During the Cuban Missile Crisis, Americans came the closest to the Cold War's unthinkable hot consequences, as the prospect of mutually assured destruction moved from distant hypothetical to proximate reality. As President Kennedy worked to negotiate a resolution to the crisis, the repercussions of the nuclear arms race threatened to penetrate the security of American domestic life, both within the interior of the nation and the intimate spaces of the American home.

While Americans imagined these horrific possibilities, thousands of miles away Marshallese colonial subjects within the U.S. empire were already coping with the Cold War arms race in their homes. Since 1946, when the United States began nuclear testing in the Northern Marshall Islands, hundreds of Marshallese had lived with the hot consequences of the U.S Cold War national security mission. This postwar project justified imperial expansion into and the destruction and contamination of the Marshall Islands. After concluding the U.S. nuclear testing campaign in 1958, the military shifted its sights to intercontinental ballistic missile (ICBM) testing and identified Kwajalein Atoll as the ideal location. The world's largest coral atoll was quickly transformed into a U.S. "catcher's mitt" in the Pacific.[1]

Since the early 1960s, U.S. scientists and engineers have migrated to Kwajalein to analyze data on missiles launched more than 5,000 miles away from California's Vandenberg Air Force Base. They have relocated their families to this Marshallese island in the Central Pacific, which came to house highly sophisticated radars and missile launch pads alongside suburban amenities aimed at supporting American family life. Suburbia on Kwajalein has offered a home away from home for the families of these scientists and engineers working to advance America's growing military arsenal.

In contrast to their American counterparts, Marshallese workers are commuters, excluded from residency on Kwajalein in 1951, when the island was under naval governance. Since then Marshallese men and women have ferried daily from the nearby island of Ebeye to help maintain American domestic life on Kwajalein. These workers do not live in Kwajalein's suburban landscape, but rather amid Ebeye's crumbling infrastructure left in the wake of U.S. colonial neglect. Separated by three miles of reef, Kwajalein and Ebeye reside within the western chain of the Marshall Islands, located approximately 2,100 miles southwest of Hawai'i. In any given year, since the 1960s, the suburban setting atop the coral foundations of Kwajalein Island has been home to approximately 20 military personnel and between 1,200 and 5,500 civilian personnel. Marshallese labor has typically accounted for about one quarter of the workforce on Kwajalein.

In recent decades, sunbelt studies scholars have revealed the essential role knowledge workers played in the rise of the military industrial complex following World War II.[2] Largely absent from this analysis has been a focus on the equally essential role of construction and service labor supporting the residential and work environments for these white-collar workers, and the spatial transformations that took place to house these workforces. Literature on knowledge work during the Cold War has also focused heavily on labor within a national framework and less on those moving through the space of a growing military imperial industrial complex. Thus, the challenges facing military workers in managing and disciplining civilian labor in these emerging hybrid workspaces have also been underanalyzed. This chapter aims to interrogate the diverse history of labor on Kwajalein, a history in which the lines of the nation and the empire became blurred. Within its expanding postwar base empire, U.S. military labor took on national and imperial dimensions that converged on Kwajalein, where the national security mission entailed the work of displacing and disciplining the region's colonized subjects.

This chapter analyzes the entangled labor histories of U.S. and Marshallese workers who have contributed to the U.S. Cold War mission. In doing so, I explore the production of a new Marshallese home on Ebeye, which evolved to become the most densely populated space in the Pacific. As Kwajalein's row housing, ballparks, and swimming pools offered U.S. workers and their families a portrait of security amid a broader context of Cold War risks, residential life for Marshallese workers on Ebeye proved increasingly insecure. This chapter reveals how local manifestations of the U.S. Cold War national security project spurred new spaces of insecurity for Marshallese colonial subjects and workers.

What might be most notable was that Kwajalein was not exceptional during the Cold War, but the enforcement of segregation and surveillance seemed to be on steroids in the Pacific. Indeed, the tensions underlying a desire for cheap labor amid the need to contain racialized service workers in spaces of American suburbia spanned the continental landscape in the postwar era. Just as the distances created by residential segregation within the continent made it easier for those whose privileged domestic lifestyles were built upon segregated service labor to unsee these residential disparities, so too was this the case in the Marshalls. But on Kwajalein, the spatial isolation of the island, bounded by lagoon and reef, combined with a military colonial regime to make the seeming separation and containment of such disparate worlds even more stark. Just as Americans living amid the presumed security of increasingly gated suburban communities have had the privilege to ignore the insecure and invisible spaces to which their commuting service employees often return home, they have also enjoyed the luxury of remaining blind to those shared conditions facing the army of colonized workers overseas whose labor in the expanding U.S. base imperium enabled their sense of national security.

On Kwajalein, the export of segregation policies to discipline labor throughout spaces of U.S. empire also transcended the geographic and temporal boundaries of the island's story. As scholars of empire have revealed, such structures have deep roots outside the U.S. imperial Pacific, including in the Panama Canal Zone, the Amazon, and Saudi Arabia.[3] But Kwajalein and Ebeye's histories reveal distinct ways that military, civilian, settler, and colonized labor converged to both buttress and challenge an expanding U.S. empire during the Cold War. Furthermore, the story of both islands illuminates how U.S. national security on a global and local level—securing the American way of life at home and overseas—remained tied to the increasing insecurity of colonized subjects under U.S. empire.

The Rise of a U.S. Military *Imperial* Industrial Complex in Micronesia

The U.S. Army constructed Kwajalein as a segregated suburban missile range alongside a broader project of U.S. imperial expansion throughout Micronesia. Following Japan's defeat in World War II, the United States signed a trusteeship agreement with the United Nations in 1947 that gave the United States strategic control over Japan's former Micronesian colonies.[4] The agreement entailed a contradictory mission for the United States: helping the region's inhabitants achieve self-determination, while simultaneously using the islands for defense. A newly created U.S. colonial bureaucracy called the Trust Territory Government would be charged with the former task, while the U.S. military would take up the latter. Never soliciting input from Micronesians, the trusteeship agreement promoted a U.S. quest to take whatever means necessary— including any land desired—within the Trust Territory to carry out an indeterminate mission to promote national security. As a new U.S. colony, the Marshall Islands became the primary location where the U.S. would test an increasingly destructive range of nuclear and missile weaponry.[5]

By sanctioning U.S. imperial control over Micronesian lands to support U.S. defense, the U.N. trusteeship agreement helped hasten the rise of a U.S. military imperial industrial complex during the Cold War.[6] In his 1961 farewell speech, President Eisenhower warned Americans of the potential consequences that would emerge from the disproportionate influence of the "military industrial complex" on American society. He did not however identify the simultaneous consequences awaiting colonial subjects around the world whose homelands would become the testing grounds for this military buildup. The Marshallese first became intimately aware of their vulnerability during the U.S. nuclear testing campaign in their islands.[7] The U.S. Navy used Kwajalein as a support base during this 12-year campaign, which included 67 atmospheric nuclear tests in the Northern Marshall Islands, including the 1954 hydrogen bomb detonation at Bikini Atoll. After this nuclear assault, the United States then designated Kwajalein as the primary site for ICBM testing in 1959.[8]

Knowledge Work on Kwajalein

American engineers and scientists became the island's workforce most directly connected to the task of securing the nation. The highest paid of Kwajalein's civilian contractors, these knowledge workers migrated to the island in the early 1960s to research the impact of ICBMs launched from Vandenberg Air Force Base. They conducted and analyzed missile interception operations between the two spaces, making history in July 1962 with the first successful interception. Following this historic feat, the Department of Defense expanded Kwajalein's missile technology to include advanced radars and satellites capable of tracking and targeting ICBMs launched from within and outside the atmosphere.

Kwajalein's scientists and engineers entered their new work environment with Cold War threats looming. A 1960 tour pamphlet delineating Kwajalein's facilities informed new employees that "whether or not we have our defense ready in time will depend to a significant extent on the quality and timeliness of the construction, installation and testing done here at Kwajalein." Organized by the U.S. Army Corps of Engineers, their tour detailed Kwajalein's capability to intercept incoming missiles traveling at 15,000 miles per hour and warned visitors of the all-encompassing threat of attack. This threat could arise from any side of the planet, from offshore submarines, earth satellites, or lunar bases. The tour pamphlet reinforced the urgency of the work on Kwajalein, concluding: "in this game, time is precious, precision is essential."[9]

Kwajalein's knowledge workers labored in a setting marked by security fencing around radar transmitters with special tunnels built to secure personnel walking through the facilities. Some buildings were covered in metal to protect them from the impact of missile radars.[10] In addition to the presumed risks involved in operating such technologies was the reality of why the military chose to test these weapons in the middle of the Pacific. The key rationale was the region's distance from large population centers in the United States. A 1994 military report reflected upon the decision to select Kwajalein, noting that the island's "remote location with extremely sparse population [provided] a safe and secure environment for test operations."[11] Moving the threats of missile testing errors and potential Soviet retaliation to the middle of the Pacific, the U.S. military placed both Marshallese and Americans residing within the atoll at greater risk to the real dangers of the "Cold" War.

While military and civilian contractors' manuals narrated Kwajalein as a safe suburban island, ideal for raising a family, in effect incoming employees and their dependents were sitting ducks. Americans settled into an environment only as safe and secure as the accuracy of those operating the missile tests on Kwajalein and Vandenberg. Those whose labor remained most intimately tied to missile testing likely worked with the greatest awareness of the risks involved in living among this "sparse population." Military rules and regulations reminded all on the island of Kwajalein's precarious position. One welcome guide detailing such rules indicated that during certain "technical operations on the island" all individuals, except authorized personnel, must "take cover." Residents were also instructed to keep "lights out" and consult the island newspaper for safe areas during various operations.[12]

Kwajalein's risks also came with opportunities for scientists and engineers, who became an elite cohort. Kwajalein's knowledge workers had the unique experience of witnessing and surviving deployments and interceptions in close proximity. As noted in a Bell Laboratories retrospective report commemorating Kwajalein's employees, "by any conceivable standard, the Kwajalein experience was an extraordinary one."[13] The report continued, noting that "in a defense program broadly concerned with what is referred to as the 'unthinkable,' many people worked exclusively with hypothesis and prediction—except at Kwajalein . . . [where] the countdowns were real, the engagements were live, and the results— far from being theoretical—were concrete and clear."[14] Such concrete exercises would have placed unimaginable pressure on knowledge workers whose families resided within eyeshot of any missile testing errors. Kwajalein's landscape of futuristic technology remained just a short bike ride away from the presumed security and serenity of the island's suburban family setting.

Producing and Maintaining the American Way of Life in the Marshall Islands

To help recruit the nation's top scientists and engineers to move their families to the Central Pacific and secure the American way of life, the Army constructed a setting marked by a variety of familiar small town suburban luxuries. Those families were cared for and those luxuries were maintained by another labor force on Kwajalein: Marshallese service workers.

As Kwajalein's knowledge workers gained elite status, another set of workers labored to produce an atmosphere of security and abundance for these knowledge workers' families. To construct Kwajalein's dual landscape of Cold War insecurity and security—with missile facilities within eyeshot of a quaint suburban community—the military recruited an additional workforce comprising both U.S. and Marshallese laborers.

A construction boom followed Kwajalein's 1959 designation as the military's newest missile range, with several Hawai'i-based firms winning lucrative contracts. These firms sent a substantial number of construction workers to Kwajalein during the early 1960s, including a large contingent of Japanese American and Native Hawaiian laborers. These male workers arrived unaccompanied and lived in the island's bachelor housing. Kwajalein's longest-tenured resident, Jimmy Matsunaga, estimated at least 2,000 of the 5,500 workers at the height of Kwajalein's construction boom came from Hawai'i.[15] Matsunaga also came to Kwajalein from Hawai'i in 1966, but worked in shipping services, one of the many employment opportunities in island maintenance that emerged alongside construction.

Through the 1960s and 1970s, Kwajalein's transformation into a world-class missile instillation built upon a wide range of labor. Nate Jackson Jr. came to Kwajalein 1970 to work as the island photographer, and later took a position as boat captain ferrying Marshallese workers between Ebeye and Kwajalein. In a recent interview, Jackson fondly recalled the American kids whom he got to know by taking their pictures for the island yearbook. He described a familial intimacy on Kwajalein, explaining how he considered all the "Kwaj kids" his own children.[16]

Jackson's employment history illuminates the military imperative of capturing a portrait of American family life on Kwajalein while ensuring that portrait remained separate from Marshallese family life (as marked by the daily ferry ride). The former also drew upon the labor of other American professionals including doctors, nurses, teachers, and faith leaders.

In addition to paid labor, several wives worked in Kwajalein's unpaid domestic economy through homemaking and volunteer work, supporting school programs and other activities on the island. This combination of paid and unpaid labor contributed to the production of a thriving American community in the Marshall Islands. In the mid-1960s, one military official reflected on the island's miraculous transformation, stating, "from the scarred battleground of 1944, Kwajalein [became] a clean, modern, attractive, self-contained community closely resembling most small modern American cities."[17]

Benefits for Americans working and residing in this emerging community proved substantial over time. For each American labor sector Kwajalein offered a path toward upward mobility. While salaries for scientists and engineers may not have always competed with their stateside earnings, Kwajalein's subsidized lifestyle offered all who worked and lived there a unique opportunity to save. A 1975 finance column in the employee newsletter put out by Kentron, the island's telephone and communications contractor, explained how employees working for 18 months or longer on Kwajalein could expect to save nearly 50 percent of their gross earnings. This compared with a U.S. average of about 8 to 10 percent at the time.[18]

With subsidized housing, tax-free shopping, and no automobile expenses (cars were banned), U.S. workers could live a comfortable lifestyle while investing their savings in property elsewhere. These workers gained wealth on Kwajalein at the expense of Marshallese who were displaced throughout the atoll to enable U.S. missile testing. From the 1960s through today, hundreds of thousands of Americans have taken advantage of Kwajalein's subsidies and its seemingly idyllic setting to raise their families. Some recall their "Kwaj" experience as utopian; a popular slogan adorning island memorabilia reads "Almost Heaven."

Supporting this heavenly experience was the labor of Marshallese workers commuting from Ebeye to serve the U.S. national security mission on Kwajalein. Comprising Kwajalein's lowest-paid employees, they worked in landscaping, facility maintenance, food services, and other wage labor. While many Marshallese men took up gendered work land-scaping outside American homes, Marshallese women supported American family life from the interior as domestic servants. Having access to these inexpensive servants constituted a luxury that for many Americans further signified their social mobility on Kwajalein.

The roots of Marshallese domestic labor on Kwajalein date back to the postwar era when Marshallese women provided services to the Navy that included housecleaning, laundry, and ironing.[19] Marshallese domestics continued to serve Americans on Kwajalein through the island's transition to a missile installation. Descriptions of Marshallese domestic work began appearing in 1960s military and civilian contractors' welcome manuals for American employees. The manuals cited military rules regulating this service, while narrating the role of Marshallese domestic work in a way that naturalized American entitlement to Kwajalein. These introductions to the region's indigenous population positioned Marshallese as foreign to and subservient within an American domestic space.[20] For example, a 1961 Bell Laboratories guide for incoming employees detailed the availability and cost of Marshallese domestic help ($1.50 to $1.80 per day, depending on family size), noting, "They are transported to Kwajalein in the morning and returned to *their* island (Ebeye) at the end of the day."[21] The Bell guide regretted that there were not enough women to provide a "domestic servant" for each and every family.[22]

A few years later, the Transport Company of Texas welcome guide emphasized rules against Marshallese domestics staying on the island past work hours. The guide noted the women needed to return to Ebeye by 4:45 p.m. daily, adding, "None are allowed to remain overnight or into the evening."[23] Company officials also reassured Americans they had already considered the risks involved with bringing Marshallese servants into their homes. The guide added, "maids are also given physical examinations at the hospital before being employed."[24] These physical examinations signified a common colonial predicament centered on the desire to employ colonial subjects in the most intimate spaces while also addressing fears of potential diseases contaminating this realm of intimacy.[25]

In addition to enumerating rules governing Marshallese labor on Kwajalein, one welcome guide also included descriptions of Micronesian racial features alongside a caricatured illustration of a young Micronesian woman. In a section entitled "Basic Micronesian Racial Stock," the 1961 Bell guide contextualized Marshallese racial characteristics, attempting to account for variations in physical appearance among Pacific Islanders. The manual identified "the full-blooded Micronesian islanders . . . [as having] complicated *breed* lines."[26] Suggesting an almost species-like differentiation—a narrative connected to deeper colonial discourse depicting natives as savages—such descriptions situated alongside regulations on Marshallese labor positioned these workers as a racially foreign presence on Kwajalein. Marshallese were commuters who entered America each morning and returned to Micronesia at the end of the day.[27]

Military Labor on Kwajalein

As the governing power on Kwajalein, the labor of U.S. military leaders prominently illuminates the entanglements between national defense and imperial administration in the Marshall Islands. Working under a trusteeship agreement that framed their labor as a national security imperative, military leaders carried out their mission with a sense of national entitlement to Marshallese land and labor, and distanced from the colonial "development" project relegated to the Trust Territory Government. For military leaders, the defense task of protecting the distant American home entailed the work of securing privileges for Americans laboring and residing on this local replica.

Because the underfunded and poorly administered Trust Territory Government failed to spur economic growth and opportunity across Micronesia, Marshallese migrating to work on Kwajalein did so within a limited range of options.[28] Jobs on Kwajalein proved the best option for many Marshallese workers as wages, while much lower than those paid to Americans, were higher than in other parts of the Marshalls. Thus the Army could ignore the increasingly dire conditions on Ebeye, knowing it would continue to have a steady supply of Marshallese workers on Kwajalein.

In 1968, the U.S. Army established new regulations that solidified Americans' residential and consumer privileges on Kwajalein. The Army's new rules prohibited Micronesians from shopping at the island's stores and freely patronizing other island facilities, such as restaurants and laundry services. In an open letter to American residents in the Kwajalein newspaper, Colonel Frank C. Healy explained how the new policies aimed to prevent unfair competition with Trust Territory merchants on Ebeye, who could not offer tax-free items like Kwajalein's stores. He also detailed how Micronesians shopping on Kwajalein interfered with the sales tax revenue on Ebeye, and made stock maintenance extremely difficult on Kwajalein. Healy noted that Kwajalein's store managers struggled to adapt to "the less predictable desires of some 4,000 Micronesians residing on Ebeye," causing American shoppers to suffer.[29]

The Army's lengthy list of regulations governing purchasing rights, access privileges, and free exchange included rules for Americans residents and Marshallese workers. Concerned that Americans might buy goods for Marshallese, the regulations instructed that, almost without exception, all purchases by Kwajalein residents had to be for personal use or gifts to immediate family members. Gifts purchased for those on other islands had to be valued at fifteen dollars or less, could be given only during Christmas, and could not include alcohol. Army rules also limited the hours within which Marshallese workers could eat at Kwajalein's eateries.[30] The late 1960s saw an influx of American workers on Kwajalein, and Army policies would ensure no Americans had to wait for their meals on account of Marshallese workers.

The Army's new policies and surveillance practices monitoring Marshallese compliance further marked this indigenous workforce as not only foreigners in their homelands but also criminals.[31] The regulations noted that a system to record items given to Micronesians would be maintained, and all items removed without proper authorization would be confiscated. Any violations would be reported to the "police blotter" and those abusing purchasing privileges would undergo investigation. Consequences for violations included the impoundment of goods and 14 days suspension of entry authorization for Micronesians in violation, which could seriously jeopardize employment status.[32] Over time the Army would erect a security checkpoint at the ferry dock to Ebeye where guards could inspect all items leaving Kwajalein daily, a structure that remains in place today.[33]

The military's dehumanizing methods for increasing surveillance over Marshallese workers came through in a 1968 photograph in the

Trust Territory's *Micronesian Reporter*. The image, appearing in P. F. Kluge's article, "Micronesia's Unloved Islands: Ebeye," shows the panoptic figure of a white American guard watching over Marshallese domestics en route to Kwajalein on the Tarlang ferry.[34] Suggesting how Marshallese workers were criminalized, the caption reads: "The guard is tired. He works the night shift and the morning boat is the end of his day. But for the hundreds of Marshallese who jam the decks of the Tarlang, the day is just beginning. And other guards will scan their comings and goings on Kwajalein."[35]

The Army regulations generated a backlash among both Marshallese and Americans in various positions, all decrying their discriminatory nature. Following their implementation, the Marshallese Nitijela (legislature) sent a resolution to the United Nations, petitioning the Security Council to review the entire basis for the U.S. presence in the region. Resolution co-author, Marshallese *iroij* (chief), and future president Amata Kabua wrote that the resolution constituted "one of the first attempts by the peoples of Micronesia to cry out to the world for help in righting the unjust neocolonial situation under which we now exist."[36] Citing various grievances concerning U.S. colonialism in the Marshall Islands, the resolution specifically noted that "the most rigid form of segregation [existed on Kwajalein] . . . in which Micronesians are not permitted to live on the same islands as the Americans, to shop in . . . the stores, or even take home with them anything of value which Americans might freely give them."[37]

For the Americans charged with administering the colonial structure of the Trust Territory, the regulations were seen as an affront to the U.S. mission in the Pacific. Working as the Trust Territory district administrator representative on Ebeye, Dr. William Vitarelli was outraged by the military's indifference to its Marshallese workers. In the 1968 *Micronesian Reporter* article cited above, Vitarelli said he "hoped that the Army would realize its responsibility to the people who sweep its floors and cook its meals. . . . But the responsibility goes as far as paying money. After that, it's get the hell out and don't take anything with you."[38] Territory high commissioner W. R. Norwood also challenged the Army to repeal its regulations. In a letter to Colonel Healy, Norwood explained that Marshallese on Ebeye found the new policies and their tone demeaning. He said he viewed the new restrictions as "offensive to the Trust Territory Administration and as seriously encumbering our ability to deal effectively with the already difficult Ebeye problems which are almost entirely the result of the KTS [Kwajalein Test Site] programs."[39]

Norwood's letter alluded to deeper cleavages developing between the military and the Trust Territory Government over the relationship between Kwajalein and Ebeye. By 1968, Ebeye was nearing a state of crisis due to a lack of resources and adequate planning to support a population that had been growing at an unsustainable rate due, in part, to Army displacements of Marshallese for missile testing. Adding to this density, nuclear refugees displaced from the contaminated Northern Marshall Islands had migrated to Ebeye.[40] By 1978, the population of the 78-acre island had reached 8,000, making Ebeye the most densely populated space in the Pacific. (Kwajalein's population peaked at around 5,500, living on 900 acres.) American attorney Mary M. Kearney, who had been working on behalf of Kwajalein landowners to help secure compensation for their land, offered a portrait of Ebeye's density at the time: she explained that if the entire population of the United States (then 224 million) were placed into the state of Connecticut, the resulting density "would be considerably less than that of Ebeye."[41]

As a crisis of poverty erupted on Ebeye, Kwajalein's service workers were still excluded from living where they worked. The structure of these workers' segregation enabled the Army to argue that the Trust Territory was responsible for those living on Ebeye. While the trusteeship agreement mandated the U.S. support Micronesians toward self-determination—including economic support—Ebeye offered a unique challenge for Trust Territory administrators and Army officials. Because Ebeye's density grew in direct relation to military operations on Kwajalein, Trust Territory administrators demanded the heavily resourced Army invest in the island's infrastructure. They argued that the Army was responsible for Ebeye since the island housed Kwajalein's service sector and those the Army displaced for missile testing. The Army claimed its responsibility lay solely with those residing on Kwajalein, downplaying its reliance on Marshallese service labor and ignoring the continued crisis on Ebeye. The contradictory missions of the trusteeship agreement led these two arms of the same imperial body to point the finger of responsibility for Ebeye at each other through the 1970s. All the while, Ebeye's colonized workers faced increasingly dire circumstances.

Airing the Army's Dirty Laundry

Since the 1960s, water shortages on Ebeye have further emphasized the Marshallese workers' colonial status and substandard living conditions. In particular, water became a key contested resource between Marshallese workers and Kwajalein, revealing how, to the island's most privileged American knowledge workers, the Marshallese service workers remained invisible; it was Marshallese labor that enabled their luxurious domestic refuge on Kwajalein, while displaced Marshallese lacked adequate water for drinking and sanitation on Ebeye. When the Army announced in 1968 that Marshallese domestics would be prohibited from using Kwajalein's laundry facilities, it defended the policy as necessary due to a strain on these facilities after an influx of American employees, adding that it also prevented Marshallese women from carrying bundles off Kwajalein that could hide illegally obtained goods.[42]

On Ebeye, which lacked laundry facilities as well as sufficient clean water, the Army's policy evoked an immediate outcry. Within a day of its announcement, a collective of 20 Marshallese representatives including workers and political leaders wrote to Colonel Healy stressing the importance of Kwajalein's laundry facilities. They stated, "Most of our people leave our homes every morning at 6 a.m. to go to Kwajalein to participate with your important mission."[43] Asserting their contribution to Kwajalein's national defense mission, the authors described the importance of wearing clean, ironed clothing when working alongside Americans. They noted that without access to Kwajalein's facilities they would be limited to hand washing on Ebeye, where there was not enough water for drinking and washing. The letter concluded, "We feel strongly that this rule will bring great hardship for our people who participate with your important mission."[44] Highlighting the essential role of Marshallese workers in the Army's national security project on Kwajalein, the collective challenged the military's tendency to ignore this dependency, a tendency that allowed the Army to distance itself from any responsibility for Ebeye.

A collective of Marshallese women sent a letter to Healy also challenging the laundry policy and alluding to potential consequences if it remained in place. Signed only by "Marshallese Maids" (suggesting job security concerns), the letter detailed the hardships brought on by the new rules. Describing how their 12-hour workday on Kwajalein left little time to care for their own families on Ebeye, the maids questioned why they could not use laundry facilities in the houses where they worked.[45] Stating they understood why Kwajalein's growing population meant they could no longer use the public facilities, they added that American families had communicated a willingness to let them use their machines. They asserted that they would hate to quit their jobs, but conditions had become very difficult and they wanted an explanation for the new policy.[46]

Healy's response to the maids reveals the degree to which the Army's labor entailed the task of policing both the physical and narrative boundaries of Kwajalein as a space of exclusive American domestic and consumer privileges. Healy explained that if American women chose to work, they did not do personal chores while on the clock. He wrote, "This is true on Kwajalein as well as back in the United States. . . . If the Marshallese Maids are striving to meet American standards of living, then they must accept the fact that to earn a day's pay a day's work must be done in return."[47] Mythologizing both American and Marshallese women's options, Healy obscured the imperial history structuring the experiences of American workers on Kwajalein and Marshallese workers on Ebeye.

Further disavowing the existence of a U.S. empire, Healy concluded his letter emphasizing that Army regulations had not intended to be arbitrary or unduly restrictive, but rather aimed to benefit Marshallese and Americans. He stated, "it is hoped that they [the Marshallese] will be encouraged by it to build up private enterprise of their own on Ebeye, and concentrate more fully on improving their situation by hard work and initiative as have these Americans whose ways they are striving to emulate, rather than by taking advantage of the easiest solution to every problem."[48] Positioning Marshallese within the familiar "bootstraps" narrative, Healy further naturalized Kwajalein as an American space, outside the realm of empire. In his portrait, Americans on Kwajalein enjoyed privileges because of hard work, not because they arrived to this imperial space where their housing, shopping, and even laundry were subsidized. Suggesting that Marshallese on Ebeye could attain the degree of economic stability characterizing the American way of life on Kwajalein, he ignored the colonial structure under which its Marshallese workforce lived and the essential role of military operations on Kwajalein in determining that structure.

Healy's exceptionalist narrative and the Army's broader efforts to obscure the imperial nature of the U.S. presence on Kwajalein would continue to be challenged by Marshallese workers, political leaders, and American residents on Kwajalein. In addition to voicing their concerns, some Americans and Marshallese simply ignored the Army regulations. Interviews with several former Marshallese domestics indicated that American families allowed them to do laundry in their homes after the implementation of the new rules.[49] These laundry-inspired subversive acts revealed the instability of Army control on Kwajalein, and the fault lines would continue to grow through the 1970s and 1980s.[50] During this period, the Army came under intense media scrutiny for its discriminatory treatment of Marshallese workers and continued neglect of Ebeye. The resulting news stories combined with U.S. Senate hearings on the status of Ebeye in 1976 to provide a platform for Marshallese workers to air their grievances about life on Ebeye and labor on Kwajalein.

By 1982, Ebeye not only housed the Army's essential (though devalued) service sector, it also became a launchpad for the most consequential Marshallese protest against U.S. colonialism in the region. In June 1982, 1,000 Marshallese men, women, and children sailed from Ebeye to reclaim their home islands throughout Kwajalein Atoll in a movement they called Operation Homecoming. The unarmed protestors—comprising landowning families, many of whom had been displaced to Ebeye for missile testing purposes—challenged the Army's unjust compensation for their islands and the economic neglect of Ebeye. By reclaiming their islands, protestors also reclaimed the narrative of home and belonging in the region, unsettling the portrait of American entitlement on Kwajalein.

Erupting amid the broader global context of decolonization, Operation Homecoming temporarily penetrated the military's structure of segregation, and delayed missile-testing operations. The Army responded with disproportionate violence against the protestors, but by the end of the four-month occupation agreed to increase lease payments and offer some funding for Ebeye improvement projects. Four years after the protest, Kwajalein and Ebeye would come under the governance of the newly decolonized Republic of the Marshall Islands, which leased Kwajalein to the Army under a compact of free association with the United States.[51] Kwajalein's missile operations continue today with the support of both American and Marshallese labor, as does the structure of segregation that divides these workers between Kwajalein and Ebeye.

Conclusion

With formal colonialism ending for the Marshall Islands in 1986, the trusteeship agreement became a relic of the past. But its 1947 signing had heralded the commencement of the Cold War and foreshadowed the transformation of the U.S. role in the world thereafter. Marrying the postwar mission of U.S. national security to that of the world, the agreement marked the expansion of a U.S. military empire that would continue to grow beyond the Cold War, culminating today in U.S. possession of some 1,000 military bases outside the 50 states and Washington, D.C., with troops positioned in 150 foreign nations.[52]

Kwajalein's history reveals the tensions embedded in the U.S. postwar quest for security as they played out on the ground between U.S. civilian and military workers and Marshallese workers, all of whose labor proved essential to fueling this imperial expansion. Military labor aimed to transform and govern the island as a space projecting security outward to the national home and inward towards its local replica. Kwajalein's knowledge workers labored in close proximity to the island's idyllic small town setting that housed their families in a portrait of domestic security. This portrait remained in constant contradiction with the risks imposed by the knowledge work, risks signaled by frequent light shows above Kwajalein's lagoon as reentry missiles streaked the sky like lightning bolts before hitting the water. Missile touchdowns marked the success of communication across 5,000 miles of the Pacific to Vandenberg, illuminating the interdependency of the expanding network of the nation's knowledge labor stateside and into the stretches of U.S. empire overseas.

While attention to the nature of U.S. empire in structuring the conditions of Marshallese service labor remained off the Army's agenda, such neglect proved unsustainable as Operation Homecoming revealed. The protest made increasingly visible that which the military's segregation policies had attempted to make invisible: the Army's dependency upon a colonized service force whose presence on Kwajalein underscored that this space of American domesticity indeed resided within the Marshall Islands. No suburban housing, golf course, or baseball diamond could erase that which remained viscerally evident: that Americans were not at home, but rather temporary settlers foreign to this Marshallese island. As the United States has retained (even as it disavows) its growing military empire from the Cold War through the War on Terror, an expanding array of workers have labored to create such illusions of U.S. domesticity and national security at distances far beyond most Americans' imagination.[53]

"The wheels of militarization," Cynthia Enloe has argued, "are greased by ... popular inattention."[54] While referring to Iraq, Afghanistan, South Korea, the Philippines, and Japan, Enloe's caution is no less relevant to Kwajalein. American inattention to these histories has few consequences for Americans; they suffer little from the repercussions of imperial expansion, but continue to benefit from it enormously, even if to inattentive eyes, invisibly. As Americans ignore this history, they also ignore the localized and global repercussions of the impact of their expanding empire and the histories of the labor essential to it. The Marshall Islands continue to feel the impact of U.S. empire today as Marshallese suffer the long-term consequences of displacement, radiation-related illnesses, and broader national economic dependency upon the United States. Meanwhile, Kwajalein remains an indispensable location—a laboratory of strategic defense—and an island layered with a richly contested labor history.

NOTES

1. This essay draws on material in Lauren Hirshberg, "Nuclear Families: (Re)producing 1950s Suburban America in the Marshall Islands," *OAH Magazine of History*, vol. 26, no. 4 (October 2012).

2. Margaret Pugh O'Mara, *Cities of Knowledge: Cold War Science and the Search for the Next Silicon Valley* (Princeton, NJ: Princeton University Press, 2005), and Richard M. Bernard and Bradley R. Rice (eds.) *Sunbelt Cities: Politics and Growth since World War II* (Austin: University of Texas Press, 1983). Also see Anita Malini Seth, "Cold War Communities: Militarization in Los Angeles and Novosibirsk, 1941–1953" (Ph.D. dissertation, Yale University, 2012).

3. Julie Greene, *The Canal Builders: Making America's Empire at the Panama Canal* (New York: Penguin Press, 2009); Greg Grandin, *Fordlandia: The Rise and Fall of Henry Ford's Forgotten Jungle City* (New York: Henry Holt Books, 2009); and

Robert Vitalis, *American Kingdom: Mythmaking on the Saudi Oil Frontier* (London: Verso, 2009).

4. Greg Dvorak, "Seeds from Afar, Flowers from the Reef: Re-Membering the Coral and Concrete of Kwajalein Atoll" (Ph.D. dissertation, Australia National University, Canberra, 2007).

5. Hirshberg, "Nuclear Families." The Marshall Islands (today, the Republic of the Marshall Islands) constitute one island nation on the eastern edge of Micronesia, a subregion of Oceania. In addition to the Republic of the Marshall Islands, Micronesia also includes the Commonwealth of the Northern Marianas Islands, the Federated States of Micronesia, Guam, Kiribati, and the Republic of Palau. In several military and Trust Territory documents the terms "Micronesian" and "Marshallese" are used interchangeably. I have followed that usage throughout this chapter to reflect those documents, not to suggest a conflation between the two terms, as while "Micronesian" encompasses the category "Marshallese," the reverse is not true. Additionally, not all Marshallese or others within the territory designated Micronesia use this term for regional self-identification.

6. A number of works on U.S. base histories have contributed to this analysis: Cynthia Enloe, *Banana's Beaches and Bases: Making Feminist Sense of International Politics* (Berkeley: University of California Press, 1989); Mark L. Gillem, *America Town: Building the Outposts of Empire* (Minneapolis: University of Minnesota Press, 2007); Jana Lipman, *Guantanamo: A Working Class History between Empire and Revolution* (Berkeley: University of California Press, 2009); David Vine, *Island of Shame: The Secret History of the U.S. Military Base on Diego Garcia* (Princeton, NJ: Princeton University Press, 2009).

7. Holly M. Barker, *Bravo for the Marshallese: Regaining Control in a Post-Nuclear, Post-Colonial World* (Belmont, CA: Wadsworth, 2004).

8. Hirshberg, "Nuclear Families."

9. Open House Nike Zeus Facilities, Army Rocket and Guided Missile Agency, U.S. Army Corps of Engineers, November 20, 1960. Pacific Collection, University of Hawai'i at Māanoa (hereafter UH Mānoa).

10. Ibid. While I have not uncovered any official studies on the impact of radiation on Kwajalein, Dvorak discusses this in relation to his father who worked as an engineer on Kwajalein and developed cancer following his time on the island. See Greg Dvorak, "Remapping Home: Touring the Betweenness of Kwajalein" (master's thesis, Center for Pacific Islands Studies, University of Hawai'i at Mānoa, 2004).

11. "United States Army Kwajalein Atoll," published by U.S. Army Space and Strategic Defense Command, 1994. Located at Gov. Docs., UH Mānoa. The identification of the Marshall Islands as militarily strategic due to its "sparse population" earlier informed the 1946 selection of Bikini Atoll as the target of U.S. nuclear testing.

12. "A Guide to Kwajalein," prepared by the Kwajalein Office of the Defense Information Office, Bell Telephone Laboratories, September 1, 1966, Trust Territory Archives (TTA), reel no. 993. Located at Hamilton Library, UH Mānoa.

13. A 104-page report/narrative on the experience at Kwajalein for Bell Laboratories employees between 1960 and 1975. Published circa 1975. Report is prefaced by C. A. Warren, executive director of SAFEGUARD Division of Bell Laboratories, and was obtained at the Archive Repository National Register, National Historic Landmarks, Washington, D.C., in a folder labeled "Kwajalein Island Battlefield." Quoted from p. 1.

14. Ibid.

15. *Kwajalein Hourglass*, vol. 46, no. 61 (August 5, 2006). I did not locate any documents in my research on the demographics of the island during this period, but oral history interviews suggested there were a sizeable number of workers from Hawai'i during the 1960s and 1970s. Elsewhere I've written about how Kwajalein's diverse labor force/residential community distinguished the suburban character of the island from its continental counterparts', which were marked by racial homogeneity during this period. See Hirshberg, "Nuclear Families."

16. Oral history interview by author with Nathaniel Jackson Jr. on October 17, 2010. Hawai'i (Big Island), HI.

17. "A Small Pamphlet on the Nike-X Project on Kwajalein Island, Marshalls," October 10, 1964, Trust Territory of the Pacific Islands Archives (hereafter TTA), reel no. 993.13, UH Mānoa. The battle reference is to America's defeat of Japan on Kwajalein in 1944, when Americans took control of the island.

18. *Pacific Echo*, Kwajalein Missile Range, a ten-page employee newsletter for Kentron Hawai'i Ltd., October 1975, financial column written by Bill Patton, TTA, reel no. 095, UH Mānoa.

19. Memorandum No. 23–52 by Commanding Officer E. M. Arnold of U.S. Naval Station, Navy 824, Subject: Employment of Marshallese as Domestic Servants, June 21, 1952. Located in RG 313, Box: Naval Station Kwajalein, Pacific Archives, San Bruno. Pp. 1–3.

20. Hirshberg, "Nuclear Families."

21. "A Guide to Kwajalein Pacific Missile Range Facility," Bell Telephone Laboratories Incorporated, January 1961. Pacific Collection, UH Mānoa. (emphasis added).

22. Ibid.

23. "Welcome to Kwajalein," Transport Company of Texas, published circa 1963–64. Pacific Collection, UH Mānoa.

24. Ibid.

25. For more on disciplining intimacy in colonial spaces, see Ann Laura Stoler, *Carnal Knowledge and Imperial Power: Race and the Intimate in Colonial Rule* (Berkeley: University of California Press, 2002); Ann Laura Stoler, *Haunted by Empire: Geographies of Intimacy in North American History* (Durham, NC: Duke University Press, 2006); Anne Perez Hattori, *Colonial Dis-Ease: U.S. Navy Health Policies and the Chamorros of Guam, 1898–1941* (Honolulu: University of Hawai'i Press, 2004).

26. "A Guide to Kwajalein Pacific Missile Range Facility," Bell Telephone Laboratories Incorporated, January 1961. Pacific Collection, UH Mānoa (emphasis added).

27. Hirshberg, "Nuclear Families."
28. Donald F. McHenry, *Micronesia: Trust Betrayed, Altruism vs. Self Interest in American Foreign Policy* (New York: Carnegie Endowment for International Peace, 1975); David Hanlon, *Remaking Micronesia: Discourse over Development in a Pacific Territory, 1944–1982* (Honolulu: University of Hawai'i Press, 1998).
29. "Purchase and Removal of Goods—KTS," Global Associates Procedure 4520-1, December 1967 and January 1968. TTA, reel, no. 987, UH Mānoa.
30. Ibid.
31. Hirshberg, "Nuclear Families."
32. "Purchase and Removal of Goods—KTS," Global Associates Procedure 4520-1, December 1967 and January 1968. TTA, reel, no. 987, UH Mānoa.
33. Hirshberg, "Nuclear Families."
34. Ibid.
35. See P. F. Kluge, "Micronesia's Unloved Islands: Ebeye," *Micronesian Reporter*, vol. XVI, no. 3 (Third Quarter, 1968).
36. Kabua, Amata, "Petition from Marshall Islands Nitijela Concerning the Trust Territory of the Pacific Islands," presented to the United Nations Trusteeship Council, October 22, 1968. This seven-page petition is located in T/Pet.10/46 at the Library of Congress, Washington, D.C.
37. Ibid.
38. Kluge, "Micronesia's Unloved Islands: Ebeye."
39. Letter from High Commissioner W. R. Norwood to Colonel Frank C. Healy, Commanding Officer, Kwajalein Test Site, written on February 3, 1968. Located in RG 126, Records of the Office of Territories: Land, Ebeye at NARA, College Park.
40. Such nuclear refugee migrations took place at different times during the nuclear testing campaign. During the 1970s, Marshallese refugees were temporarily returned to their home islands only to absorb greater amounts of radiation through contaminated food sources, and thus underwent a second wave of displacements throughout the Marshall Islands. Ebeye was one of the main urban areas to which nuclear refugees migrated throughout this period.
41. David Hanlon, *Remaking Micronesia: Discourse over Development in a Pacific Territory, 1944–1982* (Honolulu: University of Hawai'i Press, 1998), 196–197.
42. "Purchase and Removal of Goods—KTS," Global Associates Procedure 4520-1, December 19, 1967. TTA, reel no. 987, UH Mānoa.
43. Letter to Colonel Healy from representatives of the Kwajalein workforce, Kwajalein Atoll Congress, Council Members, Medical Officers and Distad Representatives on January 19, 1968. TTA, reel no. 987, UH Mānoa.
44. Ibid.
45. Letter to Colonel Healy from "Marshallese Maids," written on January 19, 1968. TTA, reel no. 987, UH Mānoa.
46. Ibid.
47. Letter from Colonel Frank C. Healy to Mr. Ataji Balos, Acting Assistant DISTAD Representative written on January 25, 1968. TTA, reel no. 987, UH Mānoa.

48. Ibid.
49. Oral history interviews by author interpreted by Rachel Miller with Neilat Zackhrias (May 14, 2010), Getruth Clarence (May 18, 2010), Cinderella Silk (May 15, 2010), Kenye Kobar (May 2010), and Madeline Balos (May 20, 2010) on Ebeye, Marshall Islands.
50. Cynthia Enloe, *Maneuvers: The International Politics of Militarizing Women's Lives* (Berkeley: University of California Press, 2000). On these specific themes, see chapter 2, "The Laundress, the Soldier and the State."
51. The 1986 compact structured a continued relationship between the United States and the Republic of the Marshall Islands that included financial support, access to certain U.S. domestic programs, residency, and jobs in exchange for continued exclusive U.S. military access in the region.
52. Vine, *Island of Shame.*
53. Sarah Stillman, "The Invisible Army: For Foreign Workers on U.S. Bases in Iraq and Afghanistan, War Can Be Hell," *New Yorker* (June 6, 2011).
54. Setsu Shigematsu and Keith L. Camacho (eds.), *Militarized Currents: Toward a Decolonized Future in Asia and the Pacific* (Minneapolis: University of Minnesota Press, 2010), vii.

ABOUT THE CONTRIBUTORS

DANIEL E. BENDER is Canada Research Chair in Global Culture and Professor of History at the University of Toronto. He is the author of *Sweated Work, Weak Bodies: Anti-Sweatshop Campaigns and Languages of Labor* and *American Abyss: Savagery and Civilization in the Age of Industry*. *Animal Empire: Zoos and the American Exotic* is forthcoming, and he is currently working on a book project about imperial hotels, food, and labor from Singapore to Havana.

CHRISTOPHER CAPOZZOLA is Associate Professor of History at the Massachusetts Institute of Technology. He is the author of *Uncle Sam Wants You: World War I and the Making of the Modern American Citizen*, and is at work on *Brothers of the Pacific*, a transnational history of Filipinos in the U.S. armed forces in the twentieth century.

JASON M. COLBY is Associate Professor of History at the University of Victoria. He is the author of *The Business of Empire: United Fruit, Race, and U.S. Expansion in Central America*. He is currently working on a book project entitled *Days of the Killer Whale: Business, Orcas, and the New Pacific Northwest*.

KEVIN COLEMAN is Assistant Professor of History at the University of Toronto. His first book, *A Camera in the Garden of Eden: The Self-Forging of the Banana Republic*, is forthcoming.

DOROTHY B. FUJITA-RONY is Associate Professor of Asian American Studies at the University of California, Irvine. She is the author of *American Workers, Colonial Power: Philippine Seattle and the Transpacific West*.

VERNADETTE VICUÑA GONZALEZ is Associate Professor of American Studies at the University of Hawaiʻi at Mānoa and Director of the Honors Program. She is the author of *Securing Paradise: Tourism and Militarism in Hawaiʻi and the Philippines*. Her latest projects are a genealogy of imperial intimacies and a material culture study of the gendered labor of hospitality.

JULIE GREENE is Professor of History at the University of Maryland at College Park. She is the author most recently of *The Canal Builders: Making America's Empire at the Panama Canal*, which was awarded the James A. Rawley Prize for the best book on the history of race relations by the Organization of American Historians. Greene is currently writing a book titled *Movable Empire: Migration, Labor, and Race in the Making of U.S. Global Power, 1865 to 1917*. With Ira Berlin, Greene is also Co-Director of UMD's Center for the History of the New America.

CINDY HAHAMOVITCH is the Class of '38 Professor of History at the College of William & Mary. She is the author, most recently, of *No Man's Land: Jamaican Guestworkers in America and the Global History of Deportable Labor* and is currently working on a global history of international labor migration since the banning of the slave trade.

LAUREN HIRSHBERG teaches U.S. and Pacific History at UCLA. She earned her Ph.D. from the University of Michigan in 2011 and held an ACLS New Faculty Fellows Postdoctoral Fellowship at UCLA from 2012 to 2014. She is completing a book entitled *Suburban Empire: Cold War Militarization in the U.S. Pacific*.

MOON-HO JUNG is Associate Professor and Walker Family Endowed Professor of History at the University of Washington. He is the author of *Coolies and Cane: Race, Labor, and Sugar in the Age of Emancipation* and the editor of *The Rising Tide of Color: Race, State Violence, and Radical Movements across the Pacific*. He is writing a new book entitled *The Unruly Pacific: Race and the Politics of Empire and Revolution, 1898–1941*.

JANA K. LIPMAN is Associate Professor of History at Tulane University. She is the author of *Guantanamo: A Working-Class History between Empire and Revolution*. She is currently working on a book on Vietnamese refugee camps in Southeast Asia at the end of the Cold War.

SEUNGSOOK MOON is Professor of Sociology at Vassar College, where she served as Chair of the department and Director of the Asian Studies Program. She is the author of *Militarized Modernity and Gendered Citizenship in South Korea* and co-editor of and a contributor to *Over There: Living with the U.S. Military Empire from World War II to the Present*.

AUGUSTINE SEDGEWICK has published essays on capitalism, imperialism, and commodities in *History of the Present* and *International Labor and Working-Class History*. His forthcoming book asks how coffee became the beverage of American capitalism and why it matters. He earned his Ph.D. in the History of American Civilization from Harvard University.

ANDREW T. URBAN is an Assistant Professor in the American Studies and History departments at Rutgers University, New Brunswick. His forthcoming book, *The Empire of the Home: Race, Domestic Labor, and the Political Economy of Servitude in the United States, 1850–1920*, explores the production of American domesticity and its intersection with immigration and empire.

ANDREW ZIMMERMAN is Professor of History at the George Washington University in Washington, D.C. He is the author of *Anthropology and Antihumanism in Imperial Germany* and *Alabama in Africa: Booker T. Washington, the German Empire, and the Globalization of the New South*. He is also the editor of *Marx, Engels, and the United States Civil War*. Currently he is working on a book analyzing the American Civil War as a confluence of transnational revolutionary movements against slavery and against wage labor.

INDEX

Foreign relations, U.S., 5–6
"Formal" empire, 4, 25n4
Fort McKinley, 85
Foucault, Michel, 60, 108
France, U.S. military in, 142–43, 154
Franck, Harry, 294, 296–97
Free traders' 1854 equalization bill, 236
French Empire, 140
Fuentes, Salvador, 120
Fuentes Jiménez, Victor Manuel, 115–16

Gandhi, Mohandas, 241
Garavito, Julio, 117
García Márquez, Gabriel, 117; *One Hundred Years of Solitude*, 118
Gardner, Martha Mabie, 192
Gbe societies, 271–72
Geissler, Arthur, 301
George, Henry, 189
Germany: colonialism, 271–74; sexual labor in, 146, 150–51; Togo and, 267–68; Tove and, 274–77, 286n32; U.S. occupation of, 146, 154
Gibson, Otis, 185–87
Girón, Álavo, 120
Gladstone, John, 233, 234–35
Global trade, Chinese domestic labor and, 188–91
Gordon, Linda, 8
Gorgas, William, 52
Gould, Jeffery, 317, 318
Great Britain: indentured servitude in, 229; wartime U.S. military presence in, 144–45. *See also* British Empire
Greene, Julie, 15, 291, 294
Grimm, Henry, 192
Gruner, Hans, 276, 277, 279, 286n32
Guam, 62
Guatemala, Land of the Quetzal (Brigham), 292–93
Guerrero, Bernardino, *104, 105, 126*
Guerrero, José, 307

Guestworker programs: agricultural, 243–44; Caribbean, 244–48, 252–53; consent and, 229–30; coolie trade and, 241–42; global spread of, 256; indentured labor and, 230, 255; Mexican, 248, 262n70; privatization of, 252–53, 262n69; slavery and, 228; during World War II, 243
Guestworkers: contracts, 253; deportation of, 231, 251–52; indentured labor and, 228; Jamaican, 247–51; protection of, 255; slavery and, 228; term, 256n3; wages, 248
Guevara, Pedro, 212

H-2A program, 230
Hahn, Steve, 269
Hall, Stuart, 36
Harding, Warren G., 87
Harris, Shepherd Lincoln, 270
Harrison, Hubert, 59, 81
Hastings, Robert, 214
Haunted by Empire (Stoler), 13
Hawai'i: hospitality in, 162–63, 165; Japanese in, 77–78; kama'aina claims to, 167–68; labor force, 62; labor history in, 165; labor violence in, 167; militarization of, 173–74; Native Hawaiian labor, 18, 62; plantation economy, 166; sugar industry in, 61–63, 67; tourism in, 161–62; U.S. annexation of, 62, 162–63
"Hawaiiana," 177
Hawaiian labor strike, 59–71; end of, 71; eviction of striking workers from plantations, 70–71; Filipino workers in, 64–65; Hawaii Laborers' Association, 71; HSPA and, 69; HSPA's campaign to delegitimize, 72; Japanese workers in, 60, 64–65; Palmer Plan and, 68–69; planters' responses to, 66–67; race and, 66, 68–69, 78–79; racialization of workers and, 72; U.S. response to, 65–66; wages and, 63–64

Pregnancy and childbirth in sexual labor, 139, 147, 152–53

Progressivism, 22, 51; corporations and, 296; racism and, 298

Prostitution: British Empire and, 157n19, 158n39; camptown, 148–49; concubinage and, 140; licensed, 141–42, 146; medically supervised, 138–41, 151, 156n14; in Philippines, 141–42; race and, 144, 157n19; in South Korea, 145; unregulated, 143; U.S. military and, 137, 143, 146–47, 152

Protectors of Immigrants, 229, 231

PSR. See Partido Socialista Revolucionario

Public health, medically supervised prostitution and, 141

Puerto Rico, U.S. and, 62

Pullman boycott, 44

P'yŏngt'aek, South Korea, 137–38

Quintero, José María, 120

RAA. See Recreation and Amusement Association

Race, 9, 36, 48–50; British Empire and, 140, 157n19, 232, 253, 290, 294; California agriculture and, 211; class and, 53–54; domestic labor and, 185–86; Hawaiian labor strike and, 66, 68–69, 72–79; indentured labor and, 237; interracial solidarities, 59–84; Jamaican guestworkers and, 251; labor and, 53; Marshallese and, 343–44; migrant farmworkers and, 244–45; Panama Canal Zone and, 52–53; prostitution and, 144, 157n19; sexual labor and, 140–42, 147; solidarity and, 15; state and, 72–79; transient workers and, 18–19; tropicality and, 289–311; U.S. empire conquests and, 48–49

Racialized labor systems, 22

Racism, 39, 44; anti-Japanese, 75; capitalism and, 39; Hawai'i tourism and, 166; military and, 49; New Deal and, 12; Progressivism and, 298; Tuskegee and, 270, 278; violence and, 44; West Indian labor force and, 304

Railroads, 199; in Central America, 293–94

Rancière, Jacques, 123

Read, George W., 96

Reconstruction, 39, 268–69, 283

Recreation and Amusement Association (RAA), 146

Renda, Mary, 45

Republic of Hawai'i, 163, 165

Republic of Marshall Islands, 350; U.S. and, 356n51

Ricarte, Artemio, 73

Riley, Bennett, 193

Riveral, Tomas, 97

Robinson, John Winfrey, 269–70, 280–81

Rohrbach, Paul, 279

Roosevelt, Franklin Delano, 222, 246

Roosevelt, Theodore, 40, 296; Panama Canal and, 110, 294

Roper, Edward, 196

Rural space, 208–9

Russo-Japanese War, 72–73

San Francisco, California, 46, 185–86, 191, 321–22; Chinese servants in, 185, 194, 202n1; militarization of, 210–11, 216; *Yick Wo v. Hopkins*, 197

Sargent, Aaron, 185–87

Scarano, Francisco, 3

Scoble, John, 235

Scott, James C., 72

Scott, Rebecca, 10

Secret Soldiers' Union, 85, 87, 88, 97; "Declaration of Independence," 93–94

Security apparatus, modern U.S., 73

Serrano, Nicanor, *104*, 105, 114

Service economy, 2

CPSIA information can be obtained
at www.ICGtesting.com
Printed in the USA
LVHW110233260922
729268LV00003B/139